GOD FORBID

Recent titles in

RELIGION IN AMERICA SERIES
Harry S. Stout, General Editor

The Soul of Development
Biblical Christianity and Economic
  Transformation in Guatemala
Amy L. Sherman

The Viper on the Hearth
Mormons, Myths, and the
  Construction of Heresy
Terryl L. Givens

Sacred Companies
Organizational Aspects of Religion and
  Religious Aspects of Organizations
Edited by N. J. Demerath III, Peter Dobkin
  Hall, Terry Schmitt, and Rhys H. Williams

Mary Lyon and the Mount Holyoke
  Missionaries
Amanda Porterfield

Being There
Culture and Formation in Two
  Theological Schools
Jackson W. Carroll, Barbara G.
  Wheeler, Daniel O. Aleshire, and
  Penny Long Marler

The Character of God
Recovering the Lost Literary Power of
  American Protestantism
Thomas E. Jenkins

The Revival of 1857–58
Interpreting an American
  Religious Awakening
Katheryn Teresa Long

American Madonna
Images of the Divine Woman in
  Literary Culture
John Gatta

Our Lady of the Exile
Diasporic Religion at a Cuban Catholic
  Shrine in Miami
Thomas A. Tweed

Taking Heaven by Storm
Methodism and the Rise of Popular
  Christianity in America
John H. Wigger

Encounters With God
An Approach to the Theology of
  Jonathan Edwards
Michael J. McClymond

Evangelicals and Science in
  Historical Perspective
Edited by David N. Livingstone, D. G. Hart
  and Mark A. Noll

Methodism and the Southern Mind,
  1770–1810
Cynthia Lynn Lyerly

Princeton in the Nation's Service
Religious Ideals and Educational
  Practice, 1868–1928
P. C. Kemeny

Church People in the Struggle
The National Council of Churches and the
  Black Freedom Movement, 1950–1970
James F. Findlay, Jr.

Tenacious of Their Liberties
The Congregationalists in
  Colonial Massachusetts
James F. Cooper, Jr.

Black Zion
African American Religious Encounters
  with Judaism
Yvonne Chireau and Nathaniel Deutsch

God Forbid
Religion and Sex in American Public Life
Kathleen M. Sands

GOD FORBID

Religion and Sex in American Public Life

Edited by
Kathleen M. Sands

OXFORD

UNIVERSITY PRESS

2000

OXFORD
UNIVERSITY PRESS

Oxford   New York

Athens   Auckland   Bangkok   Bogotá   Bombay   Buenos Aires
Calcutta   Cape Town   Dar es Salaam   Delhi   Florence   Hong Kong
Istanbul   Karachi   Kuala Lumpur   Madras   Madrid   Melbourne
Mexico City   Nairobi   Paris   Singapore   Taipei   Tokyo   Toronto

And associated companies in
Berlin   Ibadan

Copyright (©) 2000 by Oxford University Press

Published by Oxford University Press, Inc.,
198 Madison Avenue, New York, New York 10016

Oxford is a registered trademark of Oxford University Press

Library of Congress Cataloging-in-Publication Data
God forbid: religion and sex in American public life / edited by Kathleen M. Sands.
p. cm. — (Religion in America series)
Includes bibliographical references and index.
ISBN 0-19-512162-7
1. Sexual ethics—United States.
2. Sex—United States—Religious aspects.
3. Sex and law—United States.
I. Sands, Kathleen M., 1954–
II. Religion in America series (Oxford University Press)

HQ18.U5 R45   2000
291.1'78357'0973—dc21   99-046265

1 3 5 7 9 8 6 4 2
Printed in the United States of America
on acid-free paper

Acknowledgments

Research for this volume was done during a fellowship at Harvard University's Center for the Study of Values in Public Life. I am very grateful to the center for affording me the time to retreat from the world long enough to think about it, and to the University of Massachusetts for a leave. I would like to thank Brent Coffin for his collegial support during that fellowship. I am thankful to Ronald Thiemann and all of the members of Harvard's Democracy Seminar in the fall of 1997; I benefited greatly from the papers and conversations that were shared there. My sincere appreciation also goes to the Women's Studies Department at Smith College, whose faculty colloquium I was pleased to help facilitate in January 1997. Many of my own ideas on the theme of this volume were planted in those few days. Thanks to Mary Shanley, who joined us at Smith and from whom I learned much about translating ethics into politics and law. I am very grateful to Martha Ackelsberg and Judith Plaskow for extending that invitation to me, and for their generous hospitality. My thanks to Meredith Ramsey for encouraging my work in the area of religion and public policy. And to my good colleagues, the contributors to this volume, who joined me in creating this new kind of conversation, my heartfelt thanks. May the conversation grow.

January 2000   K. M. S.
Boston, Massachusetts

Contents

Contributors   ix

Introduction   3
    Kathleen M. Sands

Part I   Foundations: Progressive Religion and Sexual Ethics

1   Decentering Sex: Rethinking Jewish Sexual Ethics   23
    Judith Plaskow

2   The Social Construction of Sexuality: Implications for the Churches   42
    Christine E. Gudorf

3   Public, Pubic, and Private: Religion in Political Discourse   60
    Kathleen M. Sands

Part II   Families and Family Values: Historical, Ideological, and Religious Analyses

4   Church, Feminism, and Family   93
    Rosemary Radford Ruether

5   Why Sexual Regulation?: Family Values and Social Movements   104
    Janet R. Jakobsen

6   Religious Liberty, Same-Sex Marriage, and the Case of Reconstructionist
    Judaism   124
        Rebecca T. Alpert

Part III   Sticks and Stones: The Language of Public Debate

7   The Policing of Poor Black Women's Sexual Reproduction   135
        Traci C. West

8   Too Sexy for Words: The Changing Vocabulary of Religious Ethics   155
        Mary E. Hunt

9   The Bible, Heterosexism, and the American Public Discussion of Sexual
    Orientation   167
        L. William Countryman

Part IV   Contested Issues in Law and Public Policy

10   Religion and Reproductive Policy   185
        Daniel C. Maguire

11   Reproductive Technologies: Ethical and Religious Issues   203
        Thomas A. Shannon

12   "To Make Martyrs of Their Children": "Female Genital Mutilation,"
     Religious Legitimation, and the Constitution   219
        James McBride

13   Politicians, Pastors, and Pimps: Christianity and Prostitution Policies   245
        Rita Nakashima Brock

     Index   263

Contributors

REBECCA ALPERT is Assistant Professor of Religion and Co-Director of the Women's Studies Program at Temple University. She is author of *Like Bread on the Seder Plate: Jewish Lesbians and the Transformation of Tradition* (Columbia University Press, 1997) and editor of *Contemporary Voices of the Religious Left: A Sourcebook* (Temple University Press, 2000)

RITA NAKASHIMA BROCK, Ph.D., is Director of the Bunting Fellowship Program at the Radcliffe Institute for Advanced Study, Harvard University. She is the author of *Journeys by Heart: A Christology of Erotic Power* (Crossroad Publishing Company, 1991) and co-author of *Casting Stones: Prostitution and Liberation in Asia and the United States* (Fortress, 1996). She is currently co-authoring a book about feminist theological reflections on the death of Jesus.

L. WILLIAM COUNTRYMAN is Professor of New Testament at the Church Divinity School of the Pacific in Berkeley, California, and a member of the Interdisciplinary Studies Committee of the Graduate Theological Union. His most recent books are *Living on the Border of the Holy: Renewing the Priesthood of All* (Morehouse Publishing Company, 1999) and *The Poetic Imagination: An Anglican Spirituality*.

CHRISTINE E. GUDORF is Professor of Religious Studies at Florida International University in Miami. Her chief research interests have been sexuality and health, especially in the developing world. Her most recent book, with Regina Wolfe, is *Ethics in World Religions: Cross Cultural Case Studies* (Orbis Press, 1999).

MARY E. HUNT is the Co-Director of the Women's Alliance for Theology, Ethics, and Ritual (WATER) in Silver Spring, Maryland. She is an adjunct professor in the Women's Studies Program at Georgetown University. She is currently working on feminist ethical method.

JANET R. JAKOBSEN is Associate Professor of Women's Studies and Religious Studies and Co-Coordinator of the Committee for Lesbian, Gay, and Bisexual Studies at the University of Arizona. She is the author of *Working Alliances and the Politics of Difference: Diversity and Feminist Ethics* (Indiana University Press, 1998). She has also worked as a lobbyist and political analyst in Washington, D.C.

DANIEL MAGUIRE is Professor of Ethics at Marquette University and President of the Religious Consultation on Population, Reproductive Health, and Ethics, an international feminist collegium of scholars from the world's religions. His last two books are *Ethics for a Small Planet* (SUNY Press, 1998) with Larry Rasmussen, and *The Moral Core of Judaism and Christianity: Reclaiming the Revolution* (Augsburg/Fortress Press, 1993).

JAMES MCBRIDE is currently on leave from Fordham University, practicing law as an associate at Schutte, Roth, and Zabel, LLP, in New York City.

JUDITH PLASKOW is Professor of Religious Studies at Manhattan College. Author of *Standing Again at Sinai: Judaism from a Feminist Perspective* (Harper, San Francisco, 1991) she is currently at work on a sexual ethic and theology entitled *De-Centering Sex*.

ROSEMARY RADFORD RUETHER is Georgia Harkness Professor of Applied Theology at Garret-Evangelical Theological Seminary. Her most recent books are *Women and Redemption: A Theological History* (Fortress Press, 1998) and *Reimagining Families* (Beacon Press, 2000).

KATHLEEN M. SANDS is Associate Professor of Religious Studies at the University of Massachusetts, Boston, and author of *Escape from Paradise: Evil and Tragedy in Feminist Theology* (Fortress Press, 1994).

THOMAS A. SHANNON is Professor of Religion and Social Ethics in the Department of Humanities and Arts at Worcester Polytechnical Institute. He is the editor and author of several books on ethics and bioethics, including *An Introduction to Bioethics* (Paulist Press, 1997) and *Made in Whose Image?: Genetic Engineering and Christian Ethics* (Prometheus Books, 1999).

TRACI C. WEST is Assistant Professor of Ethics and African American Studies at Drew University. She is author of *Wounds of the Spirit: Black Women, Violence, and Resistance Ethics* (New York University Press, 1999).

GOD FORBID

KATHLEEN M. SANDS

Introduction

We Americans have subjected ourselves to many a public conjunction of religion and sex. First came the Moral Majority in 1979, the rise of the Religious Right, and the minting of family values as the new currency of politics. Religious and moral values were invoked by Supreme Court justices in 1986 when they decided that homosexual sodomy was not entitled to constitutional privacy. Since the Defense of Marriage Act became federal law in 1996, religious authority has been called upon by social conservatives as they attempt, state by state, to legislate an exclusively heterosexual definition of marriage. Opposition to sex education in public schools has become a key organizational point for the Religious Right, which often establishes school boards as its local base. Abortion and gay rights remain the social issues in regard to which religious groups are most politically visible and have become ideologically (if not logically) linked with the whole agenda of religious conservatism, from school prayer to reduced taxation and diminished government. In the 1990s teen pregnancy and single motherhood in general have been invested with tremendous social significance and, particularly with the Personal Responsibility Act of 1996, remanded to the special care of "faith-based" organizations.

We could list many more conjunctions of this type, but the culmination (let's hope) was the unprecedented spectacle of a president forced to confess a sexual affair on television. Although Bill Clinton's initial response was to insist that the matter was private,[1] he was quickly given to understand that nothing less than an altar call would be politically demanded of him. And that he performed at the prayer breakfast of September 21, 1998, in the language of "a broken and contrite heart," which he cited from his personal Bible, followed by well-publicized sessions with a team of spiritual counselors. For a short season, clergy and theologians of every sort enjoyed an unusual opportunity to issue judgments from the highest of mountain-tops, something even progressive religionists found hard to resist. Nor was this out-pouring of religious language confined to religious leaders. In every quarter, the public discourse surrounding the Lewinsky scandal was as much dominated by the language of forgiveness and repentance as by that of crime and punishment, as if Clinton had cheated on his constituency rather than on his wife. Triple-bound by the public conflation of sexual propriety, religious rectitude, and political legiti-macy, Clinton within another couple of months was being accused of misusing the language of repentance for political purposes.[2] However, *why* he should have been using the language of repentance in the first place, what bearing this sexual fling bore on his obligations as president or as a citizen, what judicial machinations had to be deployed to drum these furtive genital acts into a constitutional crisis—these questions disappeared whenever religion descended into the discussion.

Although the polls told us that most Americans were sick unto death of this af-fair well before its end, it was also clear that we did not have a robust ethical lan-guage in which to express this dismay. The best that Clinton's religious allies could do was lament his sins as a mirror of America's own moral decay, or humbly confess that there but for the grace of God go we all.[3] Most public objections to this inqui-sition, however, were plainly cynical: disgust for Clinton's character was more or less counterbalanced by disgust for the prurient moralism of his political oppo-nents. History may well include some such judgments in its memory of this presi-dent. But it is the freedom of Americans and the maturation of our political ethics that are important about the Lewinsky scandal, not the personal legacy of a presi-dent. For sexual privacy is a vital social good that few of us are willing to do without, and that is not because sexual behavior is trivial. Quite the contrary, it is because our choices about sexuality are so vital to our life projects. For that reason, a society that does not allow the widest possible latitude for those choices cannot, for most Americans, be a good enough society. Plainly, that latitude is empty unless it in-cludes the freedom to make choices that are unconventional, that prove misguided, or that violate personal promises. This does not mean that people should not try to influence each other's sexual ethics by ordinary social means, just not by coer-cion, intimidation, or force. Who among us would really want to live with the alternative?

In these and countless other instances, public discourse in the United States is making ever more rapid and unreflective equations among politics, conservative re-ligion, and conventional sexual mores. In the process, a host of obvious questions go unasked. How do the sexual acts of individuals—say, acts of a particular physical structure, or that betray a relationship, or that touch a partner of the same gender—bear on the *public* good? Or do they? And why are particular, widely contested sexual mores now being made politically requisite? Why, for example, is the father-dependent, heterosexual, nuclear family being made the basis of law and public policy, exactly when this model of family is less and less reflective of American re-ality or of a moral consensus?

Parallel questions can be posed about religion. How can the weight of religion be placed against abortion rights, or same-sex marriage, or sex-positive public school curricula, when religious groups are profoundly divided, within themselves and among each other, on these very questions? Why is it that religionists with progressive views on sexuality—and there are many, as these chapters document— cannot garner anything like the public authority that is granted to conservative views under the auspices of "religion"? Even if Christians agreed amongst themselves (and they do not) or if Jews agreed amongst themselves (and they do not) about marriage, or reproductive ethics, or homoeroticism—why would the Bible or the "Judeo-Christian tradition"[4] have political authority in our presumably secular society? Why are religious freedom and sexual freedom construed as if they belong to different camps, as if the ground gained by one were always lost by the other? Is not every citizen entitled to both, and do they not both attach to the First Amendment?

Finally, there are questions to ask about sex. Why are sex and reproduction now taken as the central concerns of religion, such that "family values" covers the entire political agenda of religious conservatives, while the social concerns of religious progressives get almost no public hearing? Why has "the family," with all that encodes, become a point of doctrine across the political spectrum, so that hardly anyone dares attempt public office without pledging fealty to this term? When did Americans agree to relinquish the freedom to work out our sexual and reproductive lives according to our individual consciences and dreams? Or did we ever really have this freedom?

Worst of all, the invocation of religion only makes it harder to answer or even ask these questions, as if "religion" were not only a conversation-stopper but a thought-stopper as well. This sclerosis of dialogue and rationality is among the most unfortunate aspects of what has been called the de-privatization of religion. Whether this de-privatization represents a reentry of religion into the public sphere or simply a new degree of visibility, whether it promises to fulfill the best of modernity's promises or threatens a regression to authoritarian domination—all of this can be disputed.[5] In any case, it would be too simple to trace its origins to the rise of the Religious Right in the 1980s. The involvement of religion in the civil rights movement is the most common counterexample, but it is certainly not the only one. The longer the historical view, the less clear it is that religion in the United States ever has been or could be simply "private."

The question, then, is not when and why religion in the United States went public, but in what forms has religion enacted itself publicly and to what ends has it done so. Putting the question this way, we could notice three distinct developments in the past two decades. First, there has been a dramatic shift from left to right in the political force exerted by religion in America. Secondly, under the authority of "religion," the feminist critique of sexual arrangements has been suppressed and individual compliance with "traditional" sexual morality has taken on explicit and incomparable public significance. Thirdly, the de-privatization of religion in America is now correlated with the *privatization* of government, and sexuality is the vehicle for this exchange of public functions.

The inefficacy of religious progressivism is part and parcel of the inefficacy of the U.S. Left in general, but it also has dimensions specific to the representation and misrepresentation of religion. For although our popular media do not evince much interest in the social concerns of the Left, they are ever more interested in "religion." In television and film, the current religious impulse is entirely sentimental and nostalgic, absorbed with angels and heaven rather than with the ambiguities of mere earthly existence. As Mark Silk has shown, the news media are driven by their own religious apologetic; their stories of religion exemplify a handful of simple morals, all based on the premise that religion is a good thing.[6] Judging from the stories we tell ourselves nowadays, Americans by and large expect religion to be a source of comfort and conventionality, and to have the family, not society or politics, as its locus. Contrast, for example, the attention slathered on the conservative statements of the U.S. Catholic hierarchy concerning homosexuality with the relative inattention to their far more progressive statements on the economy, war, and peace.

The result is an astonishingly distorted public profile of religion. How many Americans are aware, for example, of the gay and lesbian groups that exist within virtually every religious denomination in the United States? Or of the Religious Coalition for Reproductive Choice, which has more than forty affiliates? Or the feminist organizations within dozens of religious groups, and their various alliances, such as the WomenChurch Convergence? When such groups draw the ire of religious conservatives, as was the case with the "Re-Imagining Conference" of 1993, then, evidently, they become newsworthy.[7] Yet their continuation and growth over decades, although profoundly altering the face of religion in the United States, have registered barely a blink of the public eye.

Certainly, the most important reason for the relative invisibility of progressive religion is the political and economic power that has now rallied behind conservative religion. However, there are also several reasons pertaining to progressive religion itself. One is that religious progressives and liberals, informed by the social sciences, understand that the lines of causality run as much or more from social and economic structures to individual lives as in the opposite direction. So it is those structures upon which their public statements most often focus. Moreover, when it comes to sexuality and reproduction, progressives tend to express their views in secularist terms, such as the separation of church and state. For progressives, this is very much to the point, for they do not believe that religious and political ethics are precisely conterminous. However, having made this distinction, over which the Religious Right rarely pauses, religious progressives are faced with the problem of reformulating exactly how these ethical dimensions *are* to be related. Like libertarians across the political spectrum, religious progressives are reticent about public regulation of sexuality, whether or not they regard the behavior in question as moral. But how does this political orientation—or does it—reverberate on sexual ethics as part of religious ethics? How does a commitment to gay civil rights, for instance, affect the traditional religious privileging of heterosexuality? How does the social commitment of religious progressives to gender equality challenge their religious models of the family? If a denomination were to support the decriminalization of prostitution, what would that imply about their moral estimation of sex work? Or would it imply anything? Progressive religious groups often lack clarity about the morality of these controverted acts, about the public goods (if any) that are at stake in them, about the role and limits of their own religious traditions and authorities in the determination of law and policy around these issues. That is often due to a lack of internal consensus on the substantive religious issues. Unfortunately, it can weaken their libertarian impulse, for few groups (other than the American Civil Liberties Union) can demonstrate hardy support for civil rights, the actual exercise of which they are unable to confidently condone.[8]

The particular inaudibility of progressive religion on issues of sexuality and reproduction has a tremendous cost now, when these have become at once the site of religion's greatest authority and the ideological centerpiece of politics. The bearing of children within or outside marriage, one's patterns of childrearing, the gender(s) of one's sexual partner(s), the choice to continue or to terminate a pregnancy, the sexual exclusiveness or non-exclusiveness of marriage partners, the chastity of youth, even the aesthetic style of one's sexual acts—these and other intimate decisions have become the matters of the greatest public moment. Everywhere, "family" is the icon of goodness and the standard of value. Even my YMCA is filled with self-advertisements boasting its success in "Building Stronger Families." Neither "building stronger people" nor "building stronger communities" will do, evidently; only this singular manner of molding American bodies into American society.

Contrast with the 1960s is instructive here, as it is in regard to the political location of religious activism. One blanches to contemplate what a multimillion dollar investigation would have turned up about the sexual adventures of a John F. Kennedy or even a Martin Luther King, Jr., or how any leader of their time might have responded if entrapped into choosing between perjury and revealing his intimate improprieties to the world. In their time, though, these sorts of confessions and penances had not yet been appended to the job description of president or social prophet. This is not to deny that the heterosexual, married lifestyle was the requisite public image then as much as now, nor to propose the 1960s as a golden age. The salient difference is that then it was possible for routine, practical contradictions of public sexual mores to flourish in the shadows—at least for those (usually men) who benefited from the moral compliance of others (usually women). The room for contradictions, in fact, was what made the ideal appear to work. This old bargain does not work so well, however, when the ideals themselves are openly contested rather than secretly compromised. That is just what has occurred in the interim, through feminist critique of the double standard and the father-headed family, through the social decline of the nuclear family, and through the emergence of new sexual and reproductive patterns. In order to suppress those critiques and alternatives, something new and extraordinary is occurring: actual compliance with the old ideals is beginning to be enforced on everyone, from welfare mothers to the president.

From one angle, this reimposition of conservative sexual mores amounts to the *de-privatization* of religion, which, as the supposed guarantor of family values and personal responsibility, becomes a new keystone for public life. From another angle, it is the *privatization* of government. For example, what were previously public obligations, requiring public funds, become the voluntary activities and charitable expenditures of civic institutions and private business. The effect of shifting public attention to the private and civic spheres is to dismantle the commitment to social analysis upon which the Great Society and the New Deal before it were based. In this way, an important piece of ideological work is accomplished for the political economy, which is shielded from scrutiny as to its structural inequities. Practically, too, the "downsizing" of government (the term itself a testimony to the triumph of market values) removes the chief obstacles to the expansion and consolidation of capital and repositions government as the facilitator of these economic trends, nationally and globally. These economic and political shifts certainly do not serve families very well, even "traditional" ones, as the chapter by Rosemary Ruether in this volume shows. Nor are the interests of social conservatives, among whom the Religious Right belongs, exactly the same as those of the economic conservatives now championing an ever–less-regulated global market. The rhetoric of family values elides those contradictions, thus sanctifying and safeguarding the uneasy marriage of social and economic conservativism, as Janet Jakobsen astutely argues in chapter five.

Social provision is a vivid example of this current exchange of public and private functions through the medium of sexual mores. Attributing poverty to moral turpitude in the form of "illegitimate" childbearing, the Personal Responsibility Act proposes that the answers to poverty are marriage and wage work. Because the answers are situated at the level of individual morality, especially sexual morality, religion is thought particularly suited to execute this program; under the Charitable Choice Provision, it is given vastly expanded opportunities and incentives to do so. The program, of course, hinges on the assumption that the childrearing of one parent (guess which) can be adequately subsidized by the paid labor of the other, thus presuming as normative the marginalization of childbearing women from public life. The economic impossibility of this arrangement for those at the bottom of the economic ladder is explained by the bite of taxes into paychecks, while liberal Democrats call ever more weakly for a higher minimum wage, a more equitable health care system, and affordable child care. Needless to say, the reduction of taxes happens also to hasten the diminishment of government and its reduction to an agent of corporate capital.

It is tempting to try to resolve these controversies by appealing to familiar distinctions between the public and the private, or the religious and the secular. Against the Religious Right's attacks on sex education in public schools, liberal secularists typically argue that religion as such has no place in public schools. Against attempts to restrict abortion or deny civil rights to gays, they claim that sexual behavior as such is private and must not be subject to public scrutiny. Conservative religionists, interestingly, also use metaphors of intrusion. They contend that the state oversteps religious freedom when public school curricula offend the religious sensibilities of parents, or when law permits or policy condones sexual behavior that dominant traditions presumably condemn. However, the twin dichotomies of private and public, religious and secular are part of the problem because these terms, most often, are highly ideological. That is, they proclaim positions but do not explain how anyone else might reasonably arrive there. Ideology of its nature is protean; it adjusts itself to cover social critiques or to preserve power relations under changed social circumstances. So it is the powerful who are least interested in rendering ideology transparent. And there are powerful interests on both sides of these dichotomies. They conspire to support the boundaries between private and public, religious and secular, even if they fight over just where those boundaries should be placed.

The language of sexual privacy is a good illustration. Depending on whether or not one enjoys a position of privilege, privacy can mean that one is *not compelled* to expose something to the public eye, or that one is *not allowed* to expose something publicly. Heterosexuals are free to think of sexuality in the former way, an assumption that was judicially confirmed in the *Griswold* decision (1965), which conferred the penumbra of privacy upon contraception, and in the much disputed *Roe* decision (1973), which did the same for first-trimester abortions. Socially and culturally, however, heterosexuality is hardly "private," since it is on ubiquitous public display. Paradoxically, it is the very ubiquity of heterosexual display—its *pervasive publicity*—that renders it invisible to straight people, who may actually believe that they are quite "private" about their sexuality. In contrast, gay and lesbian people cannot afford to overlook the fact that heterosexuality is publicly normative. If they display even the mildest of sexual expressions (say, holding hands with a lover while strolling down Main Street), it will be complained that they are flaunting their sexuality in public. If they are punished for this with social ostracism and discrimination, they will in most states have no legal recourse.[9] The coup de grâce is that, in addition to lacking a social right to public existence, homosexuals also are denied (since the *Bowers* decision) a constitutional right to sexual privacy. The lesson is not hard to discern: those with power own both the public and the private, while those without have neither.

The religious/secular dichotomy is subject to similar incoherences, which nonetheless do not weaken the dichotomy itself. For example, as constitutional scholar Stephen Carter has argued, religious beliefs, symbols, authorities, or institutions are often excluded from or marginalized within public life, simply by virtue of being "religious." Why is it, Carter asked, that a group representing a particular ethnicity can demand representation within a public school curriculum, while a religious group, simply because it *is* religious, cannot? Why would belief in "a woman's right to choose" be acceptable within public discourse, while belief in "the sanctity of [fetal] life" not be?[10] And why, religious conservatives ask, has America's political commitment to secularism been applied with particular rigor against Christianity? Why has disestablishment, in their view meant largely to enable religious freedom, come to be applied in ways that perversely abridge the religious expression of what is still the majority of Americans?

However, while religionists rely upon the special privileges conferred by the religious freedom clause of the First Amendment, they often want to evade the special exclusions that are linked with those privileges and that are inscribed in the no establishment clause. This is so for religious groups across the political spectrum. The most remarkable illustration in recent history is the wildly diverse coalition that allied in support of the Religious Freedom Restoration Act of 1993 (RFRA), in the wake of a Supreme Court decision (the "peyote case") limiting religious freedom. RFRA, which the Supreme Court struck down in *Boerne* (1997), claimed extraordinary latitude for religiously motivated action, even in violation of facially neutral law.[11] Its supporters included the Christian Coalition, the

Native American Church, the Baptist Joint Committee, the National Council of Churches, the Union of American Hebrew Congregations, the Unification Church, and the U.S. Catholic Conference. Just as notably, the RFRA alliance was joined by two of the most devoutly *secularist* organizations in the United States — People for the American Way and the American Civil Liberties Union. It mattered not for these odd and temporary allies whether one's institutional tent was pitched on the secular or the religious side of the border, whether one was more interested in protecting state from church or church from state. The RFRA coalition demonstrated that even those who fiercely disagree about where the wall between church and state should be placed can nonetheless join forces in raising that wall as high as the heavens.

Despite very different investments in "the religious" and the "secular," then, there are shared interests among secularists, religious conservatives, and religious progressives in making much of this dubious distinction. Religious progressives, for example, may at times experience church-state separation as a limitation upon themselves, but more often they experience it as a way to curtail the influence of their religious opponents on those "secular" spheres wherein religious progressives feel at home. In this, they have something in common with secularists, most of whom work on principles that snugly complement those of religious conservatism. Instead of demanding the privileges of religion without the exclusions, secularists often want religion to be specially excluded but deprived of its special privileges. An illustration is the study of religion in public schools, an obvious way (one would think) to promote better public discourse around the issues discussed in this book, as well as many other public issues. Strangely enough, while disagreeing strongly on the *practice* of religion (i.e., prayer) in public schools, secularists and religious conservatives share a mistrust, sometimes disdain, for the academic *study* of religion. The reasons are different, but they fit as tightly as puzzle pieces: conservative believers often fear that religious faith will be harmed or demeaned by scholarly dispassion, while many secular academics suspect the study of religion will impugn the objectivity of the academy as a whole.

Herein also lies one reason why secular progressive groups — especially those dealing with sexual and reproductive issues — have been so slow to make alliances with religious progressives. In the 1990s this has changed somewhat. The Human Rights Campaign honors gay and lesbian religious leaders; the National Abortion Rights Action League's website links with the Religious Coalition for Reproductive Rights, and so forth. Still, the many years of simplistic caricatures and uninformed hostility about religion within the gay rights, reproductive rights, and feminist movements released a long-acting toxin that can still be tasted in colloquial discourse. There are many reasons, some very good, for the tension between these movements and "religion" as they have known it. But there is also a bad reason: the deeply rooted tendency of liberal thought to authorize itself precisely as secular, that is, as "not religion." Popular liberal rhetoric thereby avoided articulating a social ethic of its own. This avoidance has been most marked in areas of sexuality, where liberalism retreated to the fortress of "privacy," insisted on its own moral neutrality, and rained constant accusations of intolerance on the heads of its opponents. No wonder, then, that conservatives can win so many political battles simply by framing the issues as moral or ethical. Once those rhetorical guns roll out, secularists are forced from the field.

The historical roots of the secularist antipathy to religion go deep. Modernity is, in so many ways, a freedom from religion—the freedom of government from ecclesiastical authority, of inquiry from the ecclesiastical magisterium, of the market from the consolidated wealth of church and crown (and, we might add, from religious constraints against usury or religious demands on behalf of the poor). Modernity thus recreated "religion" as a new thing under the sun—new not only because qualitatively different cultural formations (e.g., Hinduism, Islam, and Christianity) were to become, as "religion," the same thing, but also because this monolith called "religion" was now constructed as modernity's inner contradiction. Religion, in this particular sense, really cannot be "modern." Rather than providing direct legitimation for the social order, as did Christianity in the Middle Ages, religion in the modern era came to provide a sort of negative legitimation, validating modern secularity as "not religious." It is in precisely this negative form that religion has remained ideologically necessary for modern American society.

This is also how the double wedding of these ideological pairs was effected, so that the dichotomy of private and public came to supplement that of religion and secularity. While religion offered negative legitimation to modernity, the private filled in the positive legitimation. Like "the religious," the "private" became an ideological absolute, set beyond the bounds of inquiry, the reach of history, or the vicissitudes of society. As the religious relies on the law of God, so the private relies on law of nature and purports to supply sure foundations for social order. Certain human traits, posited as universal, became the basis of equality claims; certain human differences, also posited as universal, became the basis of social roles. Among the differences, gender was particularly salient, for the division between public and private was simultaneously a division of gender, consigning women to the domestic sphere—on the authority, if not of God, at least of nature.

It is commonly noted that modernity is in crisis. In the United States, one manifestation of that crisis has been the realigning of the private and the public, the religious and the secular, around the theme of family. That realignment has been provoked through deep, sustained critiques and alterations of the private. Just as the modern era was initiated when the authority of religion was disrupted, so the postmodern moment begins with threats to the private, particularly in the forms of capital and "traditional" sexual arrangements. Under these circumstances, religion returns as a direct, positive legitimation of the social order, an ideological reinforcement of privacy.

The critique of private capital and the free market exposes the undue influence of private capital in the public arena. The public, then, is in danger of being exposed as not really public at all. At the same time, the purported freedom of the market is called into question when capital accumulates and consolidates, and the economic freedom of some parties visibly inhibits or crushes that of others. These critiques are certainly not new, but the unprecedented expansion of the global market affords many new points of rupture at which they might break through. Family values, by shifting the focus from government and business to the moral character of individuals, plugs these ideological leaks. Moreover, through its alliance with religion, family values discourse effectively equates the critique of private capital with the Marxist rejection of religion. It thereby erases religious critiques of the maldistribution of wealth, which predate Marx by millennia, not to mention the religious adaptations of socialism that remain live political options in other parts of the world, for example the Christian socialist parties of Europe.

Whereas the critique of private capital shows that not everyone is entitled to economic "privates," the critique of gender shows that women lack access to the public. It was feminism, in both its nineteenth- and twentieth-century forms, that brought this critique home, so to speak. Second-wave feminists went further in their critique of "natural law" and their analysis of sexual and social life according to the maxim that "the personal is political." The "private," they showed, had been socially and historically made up in the service of a male supremacist political agenda; it could therefore be remade or unmade in service of an egalitarian social vision. Here again, the relationship with religion was decisive, for in sharp contrast to most of its nineteenth-century forebears, second-wave feminism established itself as resolutely secularist, even actively hostile, to religion.

Certainly, there were the most serious reasons for feminists to break the heavy links that in the nineteenth century came to specially bind women with religion, just as there were the most serious of reasons for breaking the identification of women with sexual and reproductive functions. There also were and are the most profound reasons for a feminist critique of religion. However, this very critique has been produced in great detail by religious feminism in these same decades, along with a whole set of religious revisions that continue to have tremendous impact on religion in the United States. Few strong alliances have been forged between secular and religious feminism, and this has been costly for both. It has inhibited feminism's appeal to women for whom religion is a crucial part of their identity, and this includes many women who are poor and nonwhite. It also deprived secular feminism of a rich source of social visions, because religions, notwithstanding their presumptive patriarchalism, also mandate some version of justice, compassion, and the more equitable distribution of wealth. Because of their comprehensiveness, religious visions of society can model various ways in which the critique of patriarchalism can be connected with other sorts of social critique. Absent those connections, second-wave feminism is often perceived, and has often been, largely a means through which white middle class women reach out for a larger and more immediate share of the economic pie.

The two critiques of the private, as capital and as gender, both placed in opposition to religion, produced the climate in which family values ideology has been able to flourish. In family values, we have a new marriage of the religious and secular with the private and public, the purported law of God with the purported laws of nature. Family values is advanced as if it were not religion, but that can occur only because it functions very much like the cultural phenomena that Robert Bellah, following Rousseau, called "civil religion."[12] For its adherents, and for the sociologists against whom Bellah was arguing, what Bellah called "civil religion" appeared only as a lowest common denominator. In this sense, like all effective norms, it did not appear at all. The notion of secularism gives this process an added boost. For it belongs to the notion of secularity to obscure the religious specificity of the public sphere, just as it belongs to the notion of sexual "normality" to melt heterosexuality into the public landscape.

Like civil religion as described by Bellah, family values cannot but draw upon a specific religious context and history—in this case, versions of the "Judeo-Christian tradition" for which conventional sexual arrangements are central religious commitments. Specificity as such does not count against the validity of "family values" or any other public ethos. Nor, given the ideological relationship between the religious and the secular, is family values discredited simply because of its association with religion. Rather, the question is whether the ideals sacralized by family values are sufficiently critical to advance American culture toward its best ideals. It is worth recalling that part of what commended civil religion to Bellah was that, in addition to sacralizing certain values, it could also deploy those ideals for social self-critique. This implies that an adequate civic ethos would have to be sufficiently capacious to reflect the range of American culture. It also requires a certain dialectic between these criteria. People have to recognize an ideal or value as their own in order to be criticized by it, yet an indiscriminately capacious social ethos would have no critical edge.

On those criteria, family values must be judged utterly inadequate as a civic ethos for the United States. One inadequacy is its religious scope. For it is just while—and just because—the United States is becoming less and less exclusively Christian that Christianity or the Judeo-Christian tradition is openly anointed as what William Countryman calls "chaplain to the status quo." Family values discourse not only is confined largely to the "Judeo-Christian tradition," but it also defines that tradition so narrowly as to radically truncate even the range of views that are internal to Judaism and Christianity. That is only the surface of the problem, however, because in recent decades America has become more and more of a religious "mosaic," to borrow an image from scholar of religion Diana Eck.[13] Islam, the fastest growing religion in the United States and destined soon to become our largest minority religion, is the preeminent example. But today all the religions of the world are American religions, as Eck's pluralism project has abundantly documented. And then there are the many Americans whose religious affiliations are little more than nominal, whose religious identities are shifting and syncretistic, or who profess no religious belief of any kind. The "traditional" family is being canonized under circumstances that are exactly parallel—that is, at precisely the moment when that model faces an unprecedented array of challenges and alternatives. These alternatives are every bit as valid as are the multitudes of religions that now claim standing as "American." In many cases, they *are* religious alternatives, as the chapters in this volume demonstrate. Even when they are not, however, these alternative forms of sexual life concern personal belief, interpersonal association, and free expression in the most serious ways. On what grounds can those freedoms be abridged when they are not specifically "religious"?

For now, the "personal is political" is back. And it is back with, quite literally, a vengeance—against feminism and on behalf of free market capitalism. Reformulated as family values, that principle now endangers the freedoms for which feminists and sexual dissidents have fought. In standing for those freedoms, it is vital to remember that they are linked with other social goods, just as their abridgment is bound to other social ills. Authentic sexual and reproductive freedom, although good in and of itself, requires much more and produces much more than an expanded menu of personal lifestyle options. To have a society in which women have both the right and the means to control their reproductivity, in which the bearing of children does not exclude parents from full participation in public life, in which heterosexuality is no longer requisite, in which gender is improvised rather than assigned, in which people can work out their sexual life plans in peace and affirm their intimate associations publicly—to have all of this would be to inhabit a world much revised, not only in its sexual arrangements, but in its political economy and social structures as well.

There are many ways to tell the story of religion and sex in American public life, many vantage points from which to tell it, and a variety of ways the moral of that story might be explained. It will be helpful, then, to clarify what these chapters do and do not have in common, and what terrain they cover.

The chapters cluster into four areas. The first concerns basic theoretical issues that determine our views of how religion and sex ought to and ought not to meet in public life. Judith Plaskow, in the context of progressive Judaism, addresses a paradox that faces all progressive religionists. As she observes, progressive scholars of religion must address the sexual issues that so predominate the public sphere and that worry and disturb religious practitioners. The quandary is how this can be done without according sex the undue significance heaped upon it by conservatives. Plaskow's own solution is to "de-center sex," while "re-centering sexuality" in the sense of studying the social and ideological structures that shape our sexual lives. Christine Gudorf addresses an equally fundamental issue: how to integrate the critique of "essentialism" and the shift to "constructivism" that are now widely accepted within the academy. For all ethicists, this forces a clarification of the sources of moral norms; for religious ethicists, it also entails a need to find some rapprochement between constructivism and the authoritative sources of their own tradition. Gudorf's essay is a programmatic sketch of how this might be done on the cutting edge of a religious tradition, in her case Roman Catholicism. My own chapter probes the category of "religion" itself. Taking gay rights and social provision as case studies, I try to tear the ideological veil that makes religion such a unique and inscrutable category in American life. This not-so-modest proposal, I think, promises benefits and challenges on both sides of the division between the religious and the secular.

The second section examines the family from historical, ideological, and religious points of view, illuminating a category that now dims public discourse. Rosemary Ruether shows that Christianity historically has had a far more complex—and, for most of its two millennia, a far more negative—view of family than is commonly acknowledged. Her chapter stands as a corrective to both the conservative misappropriation of Christian sexual ethics and to secular feminism's often simplistic rejection of Christianity. Janet Jakobsen's contribution offers both an analysis of the infamous feminist "sex wars" and an intertextual exegesis between the Christian Coalition's "Contract with the American Family" and the Republican "Contract with America." Like other authors in this volume, Jakobsen understands the global economy as the context in which family ideology must be understood, and she traces the ways in which sexual regulation, by circuitous and often contradictory means, is made to facilitate socioeconomic domination. Rebecca Alpert, writing from a Reconstructionist Jewish perspective, argues for same-sex marriage on the grounds that it promotes the familial and marital values of progressive Judaism. And, since religious weddings also can have civil standing, same-sex weddings might also provide opportunities for religious witness and authority to be exercised on behalf of justice for gay and lesbian people.

What makes our national debates about sexuality so intractable is not only the content of the positions, but also the language and the symbols in which they are cast. The chapters comprising the third section of this volume make transparent the ideologically charged terms of some key debates. Traci West articulates plainly the demeaning references to black women's sexuality that have been explicit or implicit throughout the welfare debate and that have a history with roots in slavery. This rhetorical assault, she argues, has facilitated the material assault on the lives of poor black women that is now taking place through public policy. Mary Hunt examines the misrepresentation of gays by the Religious Right, and of the feminist Re-Imagining Conference by the news media. Hunt places these cultural skirmishes within their broadest context, which includes globalization, religious pluralism, changing sexual mores, and shifting moral vocabularies. William Countryman offers a scholarly reading of the Genesis creation accounts, which have been accorded incomparable significance in relation to gender roles and sexual preference. He argues that if, for many Christians, those accounts seem to clearly oppose homosexuality, that is only because they are being read through the dark glass of what "we" already presume to know. Together, these essays point the way to public discussions that are far more respectful of differences and disagreements, far more direct and honest, than have been our reigning public rhetorics. As Countryman's essay suggests, they also open the way for a more genuine encounter of religious people with their own authoritative sources, such as the Bible. For only when the ideological baggage of these sources is unpacked can they be expected to say something new.

The final section takes up areas of law and policy where detailed analysis is needed and where religion, for better and for worse, already has been involved. Two of these essays are concerned with reproductive ethics in social and political perspective. Daniel Maguire looks at contraception and abortion in an interreligious and international context. Religion and sex, he argues, are linked as power, and this opens up the possibility of religious tyranny, especially in the form of "pelvic orthodoxy." To break that tyranny, we need among other things a fuller understanding of religious history. Maguire provides that by lifting up a distinct pro-choice position that has always existed within Christianity itself. Thomas Shannon, writing about assisted reproduction, is working within Catholic ethics, where he draws surprising implications from traditional teachings. Ultimately, he concludes, Catholic sexual ethics are limited because of their continued reliance on a biologistic understanding of natural law. Catholic social ethics, he argues, have more to contribute to the public discussion of assisted reproduction, which is sorely lacking in attention to the questions of economic justice that AR entails.

The last two essays concern the much controverted issues of female genital mutilation (also called female circumcision) and prostitution. James McBride's concern is with possible constitutional challenges, based on the principles of equal protection and free exercise of religion, to laws that now prohibit FGM. Arguing meticulously from both constitutional law and feminist ethics, he concludes that neither constitutional principles nor cultural pluralism can be appropriately used to justify practices that, in his view, inflict serious and irreversible bodily harm upon girls. Rita Nakashima Brock deals with an issue wherein religion, law, and policy have all played their parts, often in concert, to exploit and demean women. Her analysis of prostitution vividly illustrates how laws and moral norms can produce whole classes of persons who are socially destined to break them and to be cruelly punished for doing so. It is a painful, pointed lesson, applicable not only to prostitution but to many other ethical and political questions this volume engages.

Although these essays accomplish a great deal, there are some things they do not accomplish. First, they do not provide a demographic representation of the range of religion in the United States. One reason is that scholarship in religion need not identify itself with a particular religious tradition; several of the essays herein do not. It is also due to the gap between the pace of demographic change and the pace at which intellectuals from emerging groups enter the public sphere. To be sure, scholars are writing about or from Islamic, Buddhist, Hindu, or other non-Jewish or Christian perspectives on issues with which this volume is concerned. For now, however, their work mostly approaches these issues from different angles than those this volume tries to capture. When they consider issues such as population and development, they are usually doing so in an international context.[14] Similarly, when they debate issues such as abortion and homosexuality, their concern is usually to clarify and develop the ethics of their own religious tradition, for example, the implications of Buddhist rituals for mourning aborted fetuses.[15] And when they address the United States, it is still most often from an external perspective, for example, the tension between Islamic versus Western perspectives on questions such as women's rights and secular government.[16] Within a decade or two, there will probably be a wealth of scholarship in which these religious traditions, *as part of the American mosaic*, engage directly in public discourse and law and policy debates about these issues. But that day has not yet arrived. In the meanwhile, these contributions open wide the door to pluralism, through their reflections on globalization and religious diversity, and by exposing the *intra*-religious complexity within the religious traditions that are now dominant in the United States.

These essays also are not to be read as "the" progressive religious view on any of the particular issues they address. Not all religious progressives would agree that prostitution should be decriminalized, or that laws against FGM do not violate religious freedom, or that the Defense of Marriage Act does—although each of these positions is soundly argued herein. Nor do the contributors all agree with each other. Shannon's Roman Catholic ethic, for example, which sifts carefully through the traditional sexual norms of love and procreation, is quite different than Gudorf's, which flatly rejects procreationism and makes mutuality in pleasure normative. The essays that operate within religious traditions are also distinguished by the fact that each of those traditions has its own authoritative sources, its own history of interpretation and debate. Jewish scholars must be concerned with halachah and Torah, Protestants with the centrality of the Bible, Roman Catholics with natural law and the hierarchical magisterium. This, too, is relevant to public discourse because to enter that discourse with different traditions and sources is the common situation of Americans. Watching how these scholars position themselves within complex religious traditions and then discern how their traditions do or do not bear on public debate, one can learn much about what it means to live well in the multiple, complex communities that most of us must navigate daily.

In demonstrating the heterogeneity across and within religious traditions, these essays entrain an understanding of religion itself that can be of great benefit to public discourse. We begin, as scholars of religion, with the simple premise that it is possible and salutary to *think* about religion. Often, those who speak most loudly for "religion" in public display very little actual knowledge of their own (Christian) history or scriptures, not to mention of traditions and scriptures that are not their own. Alas, it is easy to believe in a religion, like in a new love, without actually knowing anything about the object of your devotion. Certain styles of faith, romantic or religious, are best sustained in the absence of knowledge, but you won't get far with them when the honeymoon ends and conflicts begin. Thinking about religion entails connecting religious experience with other modes of human knowledge, such as history, political science, critical theory, psychology, biology, and literary criticism. All of those disciplines and others inform these essays, and through them religious positions on sexuality become more publicly intelligible, communicable, and even negotiable.

In addition to returning religion to the realm of the intelligible, this volume also returns public discussion of religion to the realm of history. Again, this is meant to unsettle the popular discourse in which religious appeals are, *ipso facto*, appeals to eternal truth. Approaching religion historically allows us to crack popular chestnuts like the "traditional" Christian family. And, in lifting up conflicting strains of the same religious tradition, it allows us to rub those conflicting strains together to spark new insights. Historically, in fact, this is how traditions have always gone on, and this is how they can find their way forward today.

Like other historical traditions, religions must struggle in the tension between majorities and minorities, structure and change, authority and interpretation, self-idealization and self-critique. These chapters enact those struggles, and in enacting them show that the problematics of religious discourse in public are not qualitatively different from those of political discourse as such. Certainly, this implies that there are no grounds for excluding religion from public discourse; at the same time, it means that religionists must commit themselves to making sense to citizens who are not religious at all, or who are not religious in the same way.

The concept of religion at work in these pages, then, is sharply distinct from the social conservativism that posits a particular type of religion as the blueprint for society. It is also distinct from the secular liberalism for which religion is a sheerly private matter. For these essays, religions are social visions, ideas about how human beings ought to structure their common lives. However, we live in a culture with many such visions, many such worlds, and to foster the coexistence of those worlds is a commitment of any religious sensibility that could be called progressive. When these essays commend religious principles to their fellow citizens, they do so with a integral respect for democratic processes and institutions. And when they criticize religious activities in the public sphere, the failure of religious groups to promote democracy is a common basis for that critique.

This focus on social vision is perhaps the most salient common feature of these chapters; everything they have to say about sexuality and reproduction is placed firmly in the context of their social ethics. In this, they differ markedly from most public religious discourse on these issues, which instead focuses directly and exclusively on sexual norms. For progressive scholars of religion, the ethical weight and meaning of sexual acts stem from how they affect and are affected by the quality of social and interpersonal relations, not only (and sometimes hardly at all) from the conditions or structures of discrete acts.

This less regulative attitude toward sexuality is also linked with a commitment to feminism—that is, to the correction of all structures, whether religious or familial, economic or social or political, that systematically establish male supremacy and female inequality. A basic feminist insight is that in patriarchal contexts, norms about sexuality are at the same time norms about women, and the control of sexuality is at the same time the control of women. Patriarchal sexual norms weld women and sexuality and cast them, together, as a degraded, dangerous, or inferior aspect of existence. These chapters, as part of a quite developed contemporary trend in religious ethics, entail a revaluation of sexuality in which that stain is removed. Human beings, all of us, are affirmed as integral body-selves, and sexual pleasure is affirmed as an intrinsic good. The burden of proof, as it were, shifts. Rather than presumed guilty until proven innocent, sexuality is presumed, if not innocent, at least not intrinsically harmful.

However, it is not simply that progressives want less sexual regulation; they also want different norms and attitudes toward sexuality. Those different norms, of course, are far wider and far more welcoming of sexual and cultural diversity than are conservative sexual ethics. But that is not because progressives believe that there is no connection between sexual behavior and the social good. On the contrary, it is because progressives have a *different* social vision than do conservatives that they also envision the quite different sexual mores that would promote and be promoted by such a vision.

For these reasons, these authors and other progressive thinkers find themselves disputing the very terms in which many of these public debates have been cast. West disputes the casting of welfare as an issue of sexual behavior, when it should be an issue of poverty and racism. Brock disputes the casting of prostitution as a matter of individual sexual morality, when it should be an issue of social injustice against women. I dispute the casting of gay rights as a question about the fixity of homosexual orientation, when it should be a question of why heterosexuality has been made normative.

In all of these chapters, to change the terms of the debates means to reactivate the socially critical themes within religious traditions, refusing the assignment of religion to personal character and family relations alone. These social themes include the mandate to end poverty and exploitation, to welcome back those who have been marginalized, to delight in the goodness of creation, and to exercise compassion for the suffering. These are themes that appear, in one way or another, in all religious traditions. They are also the points at which religious ethics can come into dialogue with the narrower but still ethical principles that constitute American society, such as the dignity and equality of persons and the right of all citizens to democratic participation, due process under the law, and equitable access to basic social goods.

We expect that this volume will temper these highly polemical public arguments with the broader knowledge, the more patient inquiry, and the more precise conceptualizations that are the product of hard scholarly work. We may also hope that, in restoring the critical dynamic of religion to public discourse, these essays demonstrate that public debates can be exercises in social self-critique, not just power struggles among conflicting interests. That debates around religion and sex in America have been the latter, there can be no doubt. To believe they can be something more is indeed an act of faith.

Notes

1. Televised statement, 17 August 1998.
2. A "Declaration Concerning Religion, Ethics and the Crisis in the Clinton Presidency" was issued in Chicago on 11 November 1998 and signed by more than eighty scholars of religion and public life. Their chief argument, lest Clinton's public repentance were to lessen the momentum behind impeachment, was that religious language should not be used to forestall appropriate political and judicial processes.
3. See for example, "Clergy respond to Clinton Affair," *Christian Century,* 7 October 1998, 894; James Wall, "There but for the Grace of God" (editorial), *Christian Century,* 14 October 1998, 922; Zalman Schachter-Shalomi, "We Need a Ba'al Teshuvah President," *Tikkun* 13, no, 6 (November–December 1998): 10.
4. I place cautionary quotation marks around the term "Judeo-Christian tradition," which is religiously biased inasmuch as it is only from a supercessionist Christian viewpoint that these two traditions can be seen as "one." My repetition of this term, which is frequently used by Christian conservatives and even by ostensible secularists, should not be taken as an endorsement of the theology it implies.
5. Cf. Jose Casanova, *Public Religions in the Modern World* (Chicago: University of Chicago Press, 1994). Casanova's perspective on the de-privatization of religion is more sanguine than mine. He is also concerned with de-privatization as a global, rather than simply a U.S., phenomenon.
6. Mark Silk, *Unsecular Media: Making News of Religion in America* (Urbana: University of Illinois Press, 1995).
7. See the chapter by Mary Hunt in this volume.
8. On this tendency in progressive Judaism, see Rebecca Alpert's chapter in this volume.
9. As of this writing, ten states have gay civil rights laws: Wisconsin (1982); Massachusetts (1989); New Jersey, Vermont, and California (1992); Minnesota (1993); Hawaii and Connecticut (1994); Rhode Island (1995); and New Hampshire (1997).
10. Stephen Carter, The Culture of Disbelief: How American Law and Politics Trivialize Religious Devotion (New York: Anchor, 1993).
11. No. 95–2074. Although criticizing in detail this interpretation of religious freedom, the Court's primary reasons were narrower: RFRA, in attempting to legislatively overstep a

previous Supreme Court ruling (*Oregon v. Smith*, 1990), had violated the separation of powers.

12. Robert Bellah, "Civil Religion in America," repr. in *Beyond Belief: Essays on Religion in a Post-Traditional World* (New York: Harper and Row, 1970), 168–89.

13. Diana Eck/Pluralism Project, Harvard University, *On Common Ground: World Religions in America* (CD Rom) (New York: Columbia University Press, 1997); Eck, *Encountering God: A Spiritual Journey from Bozeman to Banaras* (Boston: Beacon Press, 1993); Eck, "Challenge to Pluralism: God in the Newsroom," *Nieman Reports* 47, no. 2 (Summer 1993): 9.

14. See Daniel Maguire's chapter in this volume for discussion of religious influence on these discussions at the Cairo Conference on Population and Development of 1994.

15. See the debate among feminist scholars of religion on this question in Elizabeth Harrison, "Women's Responses to Child Loss in Japan: The Case of Mizuko Kuyō" and Jgeta Midori, "A Response," *Journal of Feminist Studies in Religion* 11, no. 2 (Fall 1995):67–94, 95–100.

The Dalai Lama's responses to homosexuality are an interesting example of a minority tradition struggling to respond to American culture. After a meeting with gay and lesbian scholars, in which he frankly admitted not knowing the source of Buddhist prohibitions of homoeroticism, he issued a press release opposing "violence and discrimination based on sexual orientation" and urging "full recognition of human rights for all" (see Steve Peskind, "Buddha's Way," *The Advocate*, 22 July 1997, 11). It may be significant that the Dalai Lama chose the language of "human" rather than "civil" rights, however; in the United States this is often the terminology preferred by religious leaders, such as Catholic bishops, who oppose gay civil rights laws.

16. See for example Ali A. Mazrui, "Islamic and Western Values," *Foreign Affairs* 76, no.5 (September–October 1997):118.

Foundations

Progressive Religion and Sexual Ethics

JUDITH PLASKOW

Decentering Sex

Rethinking Jewish Sexual Ethics

M y purpose in this chapter is to sketch an agenda for a Jewish feminist sexual ethics that, as my title indicates, has a major paradox at its core. Sexual ethics is necessarily *about* sex: sexual ideologies, sexual norms and behaviors, the shifting and conflicted attitudes toward sex in the history of a particular religious tradition, and questions of authority and the transformation of tradition. The very act of writing about sexual ethics, whatever the content, by definition places sexuality at the center of interest and discussion. Yet, there are many reasons to question and even undermine the centrality of sexuality as a topic of religious concern. Private sexual behavior is given too much weight, both in our society at large and as a subject of religious debate. Too much is heaped upon it, both as an explanation for our social ills and as the center of our personhood. *Why* address sexuality at all, then; and how can one formulate a sexual ethic that decenters sex? Is it possible for a sexual ethic to focus on the sexual ideologies that are part of our social fabric, rather than on the rights and wrongs of individual sexual behavior? Whatever the final answers to these questions, I want to explore the two opposing impulses that animate this project: the impulse toward creating a sexual ethic and the impulse toward decentering sex.

The Positive Impulse toward Creating a Sexual Ethics

My commitment to rethinking Jewish sexual ethics stems from several sources. The simplest is the gap—indeed, one might say the abyss—between contemporary practices and traditional sexual mores.[1] The last thirty-five years have seen enormous changes in sexual behavior and values that affect virtually all Americans—if not in terms of their personal conduct, then in terms of that of friends or children, or simply what is in the newspapers and depicted in the movies and on television. Yet, for many Jewish (and other religious) communities, traditional values, as ideals, remain intact. The biblical book of Leviticus says, "You shall be holy, as I the Lord am holy," and, at least in the Jewish context, the *content* of that holiness has barely begun to be subjected to serious scrutiny. A number of Christian denominations set up commissions and task forces on sexuality in the 1970s and 1980s and over many years now have issued substantial reports trying to formulate sexual norms for the contemporary context.[2] But, for reasons that are not altogether clear, Jewish groups have turned to the topic of sexuality hesitantly, reluctantly, and only very recently.[3] As a result, individuals have had to choose whether to be holy or not to be holy— and most seem to have chosen not to be holy—but there has been little communal effort to redefine sexual holiness.

The failure to address the discontinuities between traditional and contemporary sexual values is problematic for a number of reasons. Sex is not the only or the most critical area in which people need to think about ethical decision-making, but it is an important area of human experience, and one in which some guidelines are necessary. The enormous variety in forms and values in human sexual expression cross-culturally points to the need for frameworks within which people can think and make decisions about sexuality. Despite what the old song says, sex is not just a matter of "doing what comes naturally." We always require, and indeed always find ourselves in, some context within which we negotiate this area of our lives. As things now stand, however, many Jews who try to integrate their Judaism into their daily experience don't even make the attempt when it comes to sexuality. This means that they are left without meaningful guidance from tradition in a significant area. It also means that at least some of the large numbers of synagogue members who find themselves or their children living at odds with traditional norms feel ashamed, and/or angry, and/or isolated.[4] They experience themselves as abandoned by institutions that ought to serve as sources of sustenance.

It is not simply or primarily the problems of individuals that draw me toward writing a sexual ethics, however, but the broader issues of the social construction of sexuality and the ways in which sexual norms and family structures intersect with and constitute power relationships in society. As someone who has long been interested in the feminist transformation of Judaism, I have often been struck by the centrality of anxiety about and control of women's sexuality to women's subordination.[5] Wherever we look in Jewish sources, it is clear that the regulation of women's sexuality is absolutely fundamental to women's oppression. A primary purpose of biblical law concerning sexuality, for example, is to ensure that a man had male heirs he knows are his. Thus adultery, for the Bible, is defined as sex with a married woman. The man who has sex with another man's wife steals from her husband his rights and honor, while the wife violates her responsibility to her husband by giving away what belongs only to him. Both parties are stoned to death. But a married man who has sex with an unattached woman suffers no such punishment. If the woman is an unbetrothed virgin, he has simply acquired another wife. Moreover, the man who even suspects his wife of adultery can subject her to the ordeal of the "waters of bitterness," a complex and humiliating ritual that was supposed to prove her guilt or innocence. There is no parallel ritual for the husband of a suspicious wife.[6]

In the Mishnah, an important second-century code of Jewish law that forms the basis for the Talmud, the attempt to control women's sexuality is vastly expanded. One of the six basic divisions or orders of the Mishnah is called "Women," and five of the seven sections of that division are devoted to laws surrounding the formation and dissolution of the marriage bond. Women pose a problem for the Mishnah precisely at those points of transition when they are about to leave the home of one man to take up residence with another. It is at these moments that "the wild and unruly potentialities of female sexuality" (to use Jacob Neusner's words) need to be regulated and controlled, that the woman needs to be reintegrated into some man's domain so that the social order will not be disrupted.[7] As a feminist, I am interested not simply in analyzing these mechanisms of control but in criticizing and overturning them. I want to formulate a sexual ethics in which women are sexual subjects rather than sexual objects, in which women—along with men—get to decide what questions are important to ask as well as how they shall be answered.

Analogous issues and questions of power can be raised about traditional norms from a critical lesbian or gay perspective. The control of women's sexuality in Judaism is far-reaching, but it is set in a framework of gender complementarity that both masks some of its worst features and attempts to soften their impact. The condemnation of male homosexuality, however, is direct and harsh. According to Leviticus 18, to lie with a man as one lies with a woman is an abomination. In the *Sifra*, a second-century collection of rabbinic commentaries on Leviticus, the rabbis extended this prohibition to sex between women, arguing that the "doings of the Egyptians" in Leviticus 18:3 refer to "a man marrying a man and a woman marrying a woman."[8] What does it mean to be a gay person in a tradition that anathematizes behavior that is a source of pleasure and intimacy? How does one read Leviticus every year as part of the annual cycle of Torah readings and still maintain any positive connection to the Torah and tradition?[9] What is the relationship between these prohibitions and the pervasive homophobia of both the Jewish community and the larger society?

Unlike the issue of control of women's sexuality, the subject of gay and lesbian rights has been the focus of much recent debate. Virtually every religious body in the country, including every Jewish denomination, is struggling with the question of homosexuality right now. But the issue is generally framed in ways that focus on gay and lesbian behavior rather than the norms that prohibit it—and in ways that deflect attention from the fact that traditional sexual values are breaking down for almost everyone. Lesbians and gays are treated as a distinct minority whose deviant conduct poses a unique challenge to tradition.[10] Whether that challenge is met through reaffirming traditional norms or reinterpreting them, lesbians and gays are still conceptualized as a "them" that the straight community needs to respond to. This one issue is thus forced to bear the whole weight of the crisis in traditional values, but precisely in a way that allows the problem to be projected onto an "other." I am interested in placing the issue of homosexuality in the context of a broader rethinking of sexual values in a way that is mindful of the connections between the control of women's sexuality and the condemnation of same-sex relationships.

The power relations inscribed in traditional sexual norms and their complex implications for the transformation of tradition were crystallized for me a few years ago by a very specific incident. After a lecture I delivered on sexuality at Pomona College in the spring of 1995, a woman approached me very upset. She was a member of a Conservative synagogue that, like many other liberal congregations, has abandoned the practice of reading the sexual laws of Leviticus 18 on Yom Kippur, substituting instead Leviticus 19 with its more general ethical injunctions. As a victim of childhood sexual abuse by her grandfather, the woman felt betrayed by her rabbi's decision to discard Leviticus 18 without congregational discussion. Grandfather/granddaughter incest is specifically prohibited by the chapter, and she wanted to hear her community state publicly the parameters of legitimate sexual relations on a day when large numbers of Jews gather.[11]

I remarked to the woman that it is not the purpose of the incest prohibitions of Leviticus 18 to protect the young and vulnerable. It is the honor of adult males that is being guarded through injunctions not to "uncover the nakedness" of those who belong to them. Yet even while I argued with her, I was aware that I was not really addressing the woman's pain and anger. The conversation with this woman did two things for me. First, it named yet another crucial group neglected by traditional sexual ethics. Jewish victims of incest and other forms of family violence not only have to contend with their abuse; they also need to wrestle with idealized images of the Jewish family that tell them they do not and cannot exist. Those who speak out about these issues are often treated as betraying the Jewish community by challenging its view of itself as immune to such problems.[12] Second, the conversation pointed me to a fundamental dilemma in the appropriation of tradition. On the one hand, to read Leviticus 18 on Yom Kippur is to read a text that may condemn particular forms of incest, but that in its construction of gendered and sexual hierarchies can be seen as supporting the larger context of abuse. On the other hand, to substitute a different Torah reading without explicit communal discussion is to abandon those who have suffered abuse to a realm of invisibility and silence.

In this context, in which neither reading nor not reading is an adequate response to the issue of sexual violence, the question becomes how to read, interpret, and appropriate tradition in ways that are transformative.[13] This question, which is equally applicable to lesbian and gay issues, sets the agenda for my sexual ethics. How does one remain in relation to the tradition and yet transform it? How does one write a sexual ethic that places at the center those who have been silenced or marginalized? How does one begin with the marginalized not to cordon off particular groups and issues but to focus attention on the social function of sexual norms and illuminate the broader questions at stake in rethinking Jewish understandings of sexuality?

Criticism and Construction

A sexual ethic that begins with the marginalized shares with liberation theology a commitment to the "epistemological privilege of the oppressed."[14] This principle says that those who have been marginalized or oppressed by a society or religious tradition often are able to perceive inadequacies in that society or tradition that are invisible, or much more difficult to see, to those who look from the dominant perspective. To my mind, a sexual ethic that strives to be in solidarity with those who have suffered from traditional values would necessarily have both critical and constructive dimensions. It would need to analyze traditional norms in ways that attend to the connections between different forms of sexual control and domination. And I would also have to propose a new set of values both in continuity and discontinuity with tradition.

The notion that those on the margins are potentially in a privileged position to see the deficiencies and injustices of the dominant ethical and religious system implies the necessity of suspicion or criticism as a central moment in the movement toward transformation. As Catholic feminist biblical scholar Elisabeth Schüssler Fiorenza has insisted throughout her work, feminist theology is always "a critical theology of liberation."[15] It always begins with an acknowledgment and analysis of the profound sexism of the Christian or Jewish traditions, at the same time that it seeks to move those traditions to a place of turning and renewal. The reason that criticism is essential to transformation is that, without it, the negative aspects of tradition are left to shape consciousness and affect our hearts and minds. In other words, were lesbians and gay men simply to lift up from the various strands in Jewish attitudes toward homosexuality the few voices that seem to celebrate same-sex love,[16] we would leave the homophobia of the dominant tradition intact to be enforced as a norm by others. Acknowledging those aspects of tradition that need to be repudiated and exorcised is part of the process of creating something new.

This task of criticism is very important, especially given the Jewish fondness for contrasting Jewish and Christian attitudes toward sexuality, and for depicting "the" Jewish view of sex as healthy-mindedly monolithic.[17] According to this serene perspective, asceticism has been an important value in Christianity, but it has never been part of Judaism. Jews view sex as an essential and ineradicable part of human nature. All Jews are expected to marry and have children. Within marriage, sex is for pleasure as well as for procreation. There is great freedom in permitted modes of marital sexual expression—as the rabbis say, a man may do anything he wants with his wife[18]—at the same time that the sexual rights of women are protected through Jewish laws requiring a husband to have sex with his wife at specified intervals. The Jewish understanding of sexuality, goes the argument, unlike more negative or ambivalent Christian views, is thus realistic, positive, and life-affirming.

The difficulty with this account is not simply that it hides the complex, conflicted, and changing nature of Jewish attitudes toward sexuality.[19] More important, it passes over in silence the huge and problematic assumptions built into the supposedly positive Jewish view of sex. As I suggested earlier, my primary motive in writing about sexual ethics is to explore the ways in which the frameworks human beings create for living our sexual lives inevitably express and reinforce the power differences in society. Since, in the Jewish case, all discussion of sexuality takes place among a small group of elite, male religious leaders, it is essential to look critically at what the rabbis take for granted in their debates about sexual behavior. From whose perspective are their assumptions about sexuality and sexual values formulated, and whose interests do they serve?

In my book, *Standing Again at Sinai*, I discussed some of the complicated history of Jewish perspectives on sexuality as they affect women. The rabbis, I argued, were deeply ambivalent about sexual desire. They called it *yetzer hara*, the evil inclination, and saw it as both necessary to the existence of the world and potentially disruptive and destructive. As an essential component of human personality, sexuality needed to be carefully channeled and controlled. But what were the mechanisms of that control and at whom was control aimed? On the one hand, men were perceived as more able to control themselves and were, therefore, responsible for reining in their urgent sexuality and avoiding occasions that might trigger inappropriate thoughts and uncontrollable passion. On the other hand, simply by virtue of existing, women were the ubiquitous temptations, the sources and symbols of illicit desire.[20] To speak of control was necessarily to speak of women—of the need to cover women, to avoid women, and to contain women in proper families where their threat was minimized if it could not be entirely overcome.[21]

Not surprisingly, this ethic of control of women intersects with other forms of sexual domination. For example, direct or indirect rabbinic discussions of various kinds of sexual violence are often more concerned with ascertaining the sexual status of an abused woman than in protecting her from harm.[22] Thus a Talmudic debate about a female child sexually violated before age three (three and a day was the age of consent) revolves around whether the child should be granted the marriage portion for a virgin.[23] Rabbinic discussions of rape specify the fines to be paid a father depending on whether his virgin daughter is forced or seduced.[24] They also consider whether a married woman who is raped is still permitted to her husband or must be divorced as an adulteress.[25] While, from a feminist perspective, the rabbis come to the "right" conclusions—they assign the child her marriage portion and permit the raped wife to remain in her marriage—the very terms of the conversation assume that women are sexual possessions rather than agents and persons.[26] Surely this assumption helps create an environment in which violence is thinkable and possible, even where it is not specifically condoned by particular decisions.

Another connection that needs to be explored as part of a critique of traditional Jewish sexual ethics is that between control of women and compulsory heterosexuality. Marriage is a primary mechanism in Judaism for channeling sexual desire. As the rabbis said, "He who has not married by age twenty spends all his days in the thought of sin."[27] Marriage is the context that legitimates sex and makes it all the delightful things that Jews are pleased to celebrate. But this means that outside of marriage lies the terrain of the forbidden—a whole realm of licentiousness and transgression that has to be carefully guarded against with well-defined constraints. Gayle Rubin, in her classic essay "The Traffic in Women," argues that, in traditional societies, the social organization of sex is built on the links between "gender roles, obligatory heterosexuality, and the constraint of female sexuality."[28] Gender roles guarantee that the smallest viable social unit will consist of one man and one woman whose desire must be directed toward each other, at the same time that men have rights to exchange their female kin in marriage that women do not have either in themselves or in men. While Rubin has since qualified this argument, contending that sexuality and gender are relatively independent vectors of analysis, her older essay still offers valuable insights for the Jewish context, in which an imperative to marry is part of a system in which women are acquired in marriage by men in a nonreciprocal way.[29] In the Jewish case, as in the societies Rubin discusses, gender complementarity supports the channeling of sex in marriage. A man who is not married is seen as less than whole, for only a man and woman together constitute the image of God. At the same time, the regulation of women's sexuality ensures that women are available for marriage to men who can be fairly assured that their wife's sexuality belongs only to them.

This brief discussion of some possible areas of feminist criticism of traditional Jewish sexual values suggests the potentially explosive nature of a feminist critique of tradition. Despite the deeply conflicting currents in Jewish attitudes toward sexuality; despite the efforts of certain rabbis to mitigate the worst abuses attending women's sexual subordination; despite differing rabbinic evaluations of the danger of homoeroticism,[30] sexuality is still the area in which feminists most often need to say that specific teachings are immoral or simply wrong. Feminist and lesbian and gay Jews working for justice in the Jewish and broader communities have committed themselves to certain fundamental principles that animate their struggles, and that must be formulated partly in opposition to traditional Jewish assumptions about sexuality. Some of these principles are: the insistence on the full humanity of women; the insistence that women are sexual subjects, not sexual objects; the rejection of violence in interpersonal relationships; an appreciation of the complexity and malleability of human sexuality and of a variety of forms in which it might express itself; and the valuing of mutuality over domination.

As these principles indicate, the point of criticism is not simply to call attention to the places where the tradition requires changing, but also—and more importantly—to articulate an alternative set of values developing out of communities of the marginalized. While these new norms emerge partly in opposition to the injustices of tradition, they are also shared by and rooted in it. The fact that Judaism itself originated in the experience of a small and oppressed people means that numerous Jewish sources speak from the perspective of the outsider or the powerless. "Be kind to the stranger, for you were strangers in the land of Egypt" is an ethical injunction that appears many times in the Torah and that has resonances way beyond it. Jewish tradition thus offers starting points for internal self-criticism and correction that cohere with and invigorate the feminist project of bringing voices from the margins into the conversation about sexuality. The imperative "be kind to the stranger" suggests that the adequacy of a sexual ethic must be measured partly by the degree of its inclusiveness. Does it allow "strangers"—that is, those made "other" by traditional sexual values—to participate in formulating Jewish sexual norms and to enjoy the riches of pleasure and sexual connection as they help to define them? Does it serve the interests of one social or religious group, or does it seek to extend the social and religious supports for achieving and sustaining intimacy to an increasing number of persons?

Such concern for the marginalized cannot be lifted up as the pure and uncorrupted core of Judaism that represents its true and authoritative voice, because opposing values are also thoroughly traditional. But the centrality of this concern does suggest that Jewish feminists are as much products as critics of our tradition. A Jewish feminist sexual ethic involves a complex and continuing dialectic among criticism, retrieval, and construction. It must address the damage done by dominant norms, seek to articulate the alternative norms in the name of which the old are criticized, and explore the ways in which these alternative norms are in continuity and discontinuity with tradition.

Decentering Sex

All of these issues that are part of rethinking Jewish attitudes toward sexuality, however, ultimately pertain to the constructive task of creating a new ethic. Even criticism is simply a way of clearing ground in order to make way for something new. Neither criticism nor construction of itself addresses the necessity to decenter sex, to displace it from its position as a central subject of interest and attention. My desire to decenter sex, which is both a motive for writing about sexuality and in tension with it, revolves around the inflated significance given personal sexual behavior, in a general way by the media, and by many types of academic, religious, and political discourse. I think of this impulse to decenter sex as having a number of different levels with differing degrees of significance, with some more easily assimilable than others into a sexual ethics.

Perhaps the simplest reason to decenter sex is that sexual ethics is too often approached as a specific and isolated subject. When issues of sexuality are discussed in religious contexts, it is quite extraordinary how often a handful of texts are cited and argued about, over and over, as if they were the only sources relevant to shaping norms around sexual behavior. In the Jewish community, for example, debates over homosexuality have often revolved around two verses in Leviticus and rabbinic commentary on them, while Christians add to the scanty Old Testament resources a third verse in Romans.[31] This approach not only overlooks the possible positive witnesses to homoeroticism in the stories about David and Jonathan, for example, or Ruth and Naomi, but, much more important, ignores the host of other injunctions and narratives in the Bible about forming ethical relationships, creating community, and ensuring social justice.[32] This approach fails to view sexuality as just one dimension of human relationship, embedded in a constellation of familial, interpersonal, and communal connections that shape, support, or deform it. Instead, sexuality is seen as a peculiar problem for ethics, a discrete and troublesome domain requiring unique regulation. It would be possible, of course, to write a sexual ethics in which sexual norms are seen as applications of broader values for relating to the world and other people.[33] But there is also a way in which writing about sexuality unavoidably reenacts singling it out as a special issue and problem.

Another, more pressing, reason to decenter sex is that we are bludgeoned with it constantly in our society. Sex is constructed as the escape from and compensation for all that ails us. The less satisfaction we find in work, the less meaning and rest in our leisure, the less compelling our sense of social obligation, and the less fulfilling the bonds of community, the more desperately we turn to sex to provide the pleasure and connection missing in other areas of our lives.[34] We are all expected to be having sex, good sex, a lot of sex, sex with simultaneous orgasms, with—or without—toys, sex in conformity with whatever fashion prevails at the moment. Our national obsession with sex, the constant images of sex coming at us from the media, act both as sources of persistent pressure and as yardsticks measured against which many must find themselves wanting. To write a sexual ethics would seem to reinforce this pressure and this privileging of sexuality, to once again lift it up as a uniquely significant aspect of human experience.

Rather than privileging sexuality in this way, it might be more useful to recognize that sex plays vastly different roles in the lives of different individuals, and at different moments and stages over the course of an individual lifetime. For many people most of the time, sex may not be a central life issue. This recognition is an important corrective to a lot of feminist theory about sexuality, which has tended to depict sex either as the chief source and instrument of the subjugation of women or as a special site for achieving autonomy and pleasure.[35] While both of these perspectives can contribute important insights to a sexual ethics, neither has dealt with sex as ordinary or routine. But probably most sex is neither as abusive as radical feminists would imply when they define sexuality as the fundamental locus of women's oppression, nor as ecstatic and transgressive as pro-sex feminists would hope when they call for the freeing of erotic desire from a long history of persecution.[36] Woody Allen once quipped that "99% of life is just showing up."[37] We may need to lower that percentage a little when we are talking about sex. But if we look at the most recent major study of sexual practices in the United States, among the vast majority of adults who are married or in long-term relationships, about 35% have sex with a partner two or more times a week, nearly 30% have partnered sex a few times a year or not at all, and the remaining 35% have partnered sex once or several times a month.[38] These figures raise interesting questions both for feminist theory and a sexual ethics about how to think about the meaning and role of sex in the overall context of a life.

Reflections on everyday sex are particularly appropriate in the Jewish context, for there are many areas of life in which Judaism has attempted to sanctify the routine. (Male) Jews are commanded to pray three times a day, whether they "feel like it" or not, in order that the experience of daily prayer may provide a foundation for encounter with God. While most required prayer may be hurried and uninspired, the practice of regular prayer opens up the possibility for spiritual moments that would not be experienced in the absence of the habit. It is interesting to speculate on whether the Talmudic laws concerning *onah*, which discuss the sexual obligations a husband owes his wife, have as part of their purpose the routinizing of sex as a component of the marital relationship. It may be that Jewish feminism, building on the insights of a tradition that has attempted to sanctify everyday experience, can make a special contribution to sexual ethics as an ethics of the ordinary. And yet, as I have suggested already, to focus on sexuality, even in its ordinariness, would seem to lift it up as nonordinary, to insist on its importance.

This issue of the place of sex in the context of a life takes on added significance when viewed from the somewhat different perspective of a feminist emphasis on embodiment. In 1993 Christian ethicist Mary Pellauer published on article on "The Moral Significance of the Female Orgasm," in which she attempted a phenomenological description of her own orgasms, and then tried to find an ethical language for speaking about orgasms. The strongest normative claim she makes in her essay is this:

> A good sexual experience is a source of worth and value to the participant(s). To touch and be touched in ways that produce sweet delights affirms, magnifies, intensifies, and redoubles the deep value of our existence. Ecstasy spills over onto the world outside the bed, not accidentally but intrinsically. It awakens rejoicing, but more, wonder and reverence, the poignant astonishment that we live, that anything at all is here, that life can enfold such bursting joy.[39]

This statement, which I find very powerful as an antidote to religious anxiety about and devaluation of sex, fits in with broader themes in feminist work. From the publication of *Our Bodies, Ourselves* in 1971, a major strand of feminist thinking has insisted on the importance of embodiment as integral to human selfhood. Rather than responding to women's historical relegation to the body by denying the significance of bodily experience, many feminists have refused a dualistic version of selfhood in favor of a more integral understanding of body/self. This theme has been particularly central to feminist work in religion, which has responded to the mind/body and male/female dualisms of the Christian tradition by strongly valuing embodiment.

I read Pellauer's affirmation of orgasm in the context of this focus on embodiment, as connecting the intense bodily pleasure of orgasm with a more generally enhanced appreciation of embodied life. To be fully, ecstatically, present in our bodies, she argues, increases our attachment to and our stake in life in the world. But is sex the only or even the most important arena in which we experience and affirm our embodiment? In 1994 I taught a seminar on the theology of sexuality at Harvard Divinity School, for which one of my students, Carol Schacet, wrote a final paper on the "Challenges Posed to a Theology of Sexuality by Women in Sport." She argued that women's participation in sports challenges rigid gender constructions and assumptions about the female body *and* provides new data for a theological understanding of embodiment and ecstasy. Speaking from her experience as a softball player, she provided an analysis of the joys of the game remarkably analogous to Pellauer's description of orgasm. Catching a sharply hit ball on a fly or placing a sizzling line drive into a gap, she argued, one can feel completely at one with and aware of one's body—free, powerful, and connected to the divine.[40] For her, *softball* is the place to live fully, to stretch one's body and capacity for joy, and to learn not to settle in the rest of one's life.

Schacet's paper leads me to ask from another angle: why privilege sexuality, in this case as the place we experience our embodiment most richly and fully? We might say that just as sexuality is only one topic in an ethic of *relationship*, so it is just one subject in an ethic of embodiment. How wonderfully rich it would be to develop accounts of the many ways in which we can live our embodiment deeply—through sex, sport, singing, music, dancing, playing, eating (this is not an exhaustive list)—and to examine what they have in common and how each is unique. It may be that, given the pervasiveness of sexual abuse and domination in women's lives, it is easier for many women to experience ecstasy on the ballfield or in dance class than it is in bed. It seems that trying to highlight the goods involved specifically in sexuality, as opposed to locating sexuality within the rich range of embodied experience, inevitably feeds into the pressures surrounding the quest for "good sex" in our society. However nuanced one's account, however one may simply be trying to provide alternatives to traditional religious values, it is almost impossible not to add to the cultural overvaluation of sex.

All of these reasons to decenter sex, however, and I find some of them very compelling, pale when we consider the project of writing about sexual ethics in the context of contemporary public policy debates. We live in a political culture in which "sexual immorality" and the "breakdown of the family" are being represented as the causes of all that ails us as a nation, and in which religious arguments continually are cited in the public arena to legitimize particular forms of family and sexual behavior.[41] In this situation, in which the New Right claims a monopoly on Christian moral values and biblical interpretation, it is particularly urgent that progressives bring to the public debate a critique of religious authority and an understanding of the complexities and contradictions of family and sexual values *within* each religious tradition. At the same time, however, *to enter into debates about these values as if they were the key to our nation's future is already to give up the major part of the battle.* There is far more at stake in arguments about family and sexual issues than competing visions of personal morality. The more fundamental question is whether the central problems facing our society are problems of individual behavior or problems of social injustice.

In February 1996 the Lakeshore Avenue Baptist Church in Oakland, California, was expelled from its regional organization for welcoming gays and lesbians as members of the congregation. How, asked the pastor in dismay, did fewer than ten verses on homosexuality "become the sum and substance of (Christian) faith," over which no compromise is possible?[42] How did these few passages come to outweigh the hundreds of verses on social justice that run through both Testaments? Clearly, issues of sexuality and family are highly symbolic. They are condensed codes, not only for a particular social and political agenda, but also for a host of social ills far less simple to delineate or easy to control. Rather than joining the debate about sexuality, then, shouldn't feminists try to decode this symbolic speech, to address the deeper social problems and tensions masked by a focus on private behavior? Doesn't the notion of a sexual ethics support the continued equation of morality and sex, as if sexual issues were the most pressing moral issues facing the nation?

Disentangling the connections between sexuality and other social issues is no simple project, because the symbolic meanings borne by sex are continually shifting. Race, gender, and class are all sexualized in our society, and shifts in power around these axes shape and are shaped by sexual discourses. As Hazel Carby and Jacqueline Dowd Hall point out, at the end of the nineteenth century, appeals to conventional codes of sexual morality were used to justify a reign of political terrorism and economic oppression against blacks.[43] The image of the black male rapist lusting after white women served as an excuse for the enforcement of racial hierarchy through lynching any black man for any supposed crime. The black man's foil was the white woman, constructed as untouchable sexual property, in Hall's words, as "the ultimate symbol of white male power."[44] The white woman's supposed frailty and need for protection helped provide the ideological underpinnings for lynching, at the same time as her symbolic power as object of rape effectively rendered invisible sexual violence against black women. The fact that accusations of rape were made at all in only one-third of lynchings was entirely irrelevant to this complex weave of sexual and racial ideology. The social function of the "southern rape complex"[45] (to use Hall's words) as a tool of sexual and racial suppression was far more salient than the facts of the murder of black men and the sexual abuse of black women.

Clarence Thomas, before becoming a Supreme Court justice, depicted his sister as welfare queen, providing a more recent example of the interstructuring of sexual and racial symbolisms in a way that bears little relation to reality. When Thomas depicted Emma Mae Martin as a deadbeat on welfare who, unlike him, had not had the drive and energy to get ahead, he was trading on the powerful image of the black welfare mother with many children, each with a different father, who drains the income of hard-working citizens by rejecting work for welfare. The fact was that his sister was on welfare only temporarily, while she nursed the aunt who normally cared for her children and worked at two minimum-wage jobs.[46] But this reality, while closer to the profile of the average woman on welfare, holds much less power than racial and sexual stereotypes that evoke images of sexual immorality and wantonness and mask the cycle of poverty and the dearth of decent jobs.

While sexual issues often stand in for or are interwoven with racial antagonisms and hierarchies, racial issues are not the only ones masked by a focus on personal sexual behavior. Kristin Luker's book *Dubious Conceptions: The Politics of Teenage Pregnancy* highlights the ways in which anxiety about teenage mothers distracts attention from a wide range of social issues. While the teenage pregnancy rate actually reached its peak in the 1950s and was declining when the "problem" of teenage pregnancy was officially discovered in 1975, the so-called epidemic conveniently explained what Luker called "a number of dismaying social phenomena," including growing "signs of poverty, persistent racial inequalities, illegitimacy, freer sexual mores, and new family structures."[47] In other words, the rhetoric around teenage pregnancy partly displaces a whole array of concerns about changing sexual and family values that affect everyone, not just teenagers, and partly offers simple solutions to a range of social problems that are difficult to address or even define. Again, as Luker says, "In contrast to complicated, expensive, and structural changes that would improve the distribution of advantage in American society . . . doing something about early pregnancy seems very attractive."[48]

Recentering Sexuality

Yet, if these examples point to the ways in which a focus on private sexual behavior can serve as a substitute for addressing serious social dilemmas, they also indicate that sexual ideologies are an essential element in the construction and maintenance of unequal power relationships. A fixation on sexual issues allows those in power to maintain that power by constructing problems of structural inequality as problems of private virtue. But the sexualization of race, gender, and class is not incidental to these hierarchies; it is not an "add on" that disguises or justifies them after the fact. Rather, it is an important way in which they are articulated and maintained.

In relation to the "southern rape complex," for example, what is masked by accusations of rape against individual black men is both racial hierarchy and violence and the sexual ideologies that help to justify that violence and hold it in place. In accepting her role as sexually vulnerable southern lady whose violation had to be avenged by male relatives, the white southern woman acquiesced both to her part in racial bloodshed and to her own subjugation to the white men who supposedly gathered to protect her. The construction of black women as "Jezebels," as women who could never be raped because they were always ready and willing to have sex, was also a crucial part of this drama. It served to render black women invisible, placing them on the margins of the social system, where they were fair game for sexual abuse that also served to bolster racial and sexual hierarchies.[49] The sexual rhetoric surrounding lynching thus played a crucial role in defining power relationships in a social system in which racial and sexual hierarchies intersected with and supported each other in complex and sometimes subtle ways.

The Thomas/Hill hearings in 1991 indicate how this enmeshment of racial and sexual ideologies continues unreconstructed. The specter of Anita Hill and Clarence Thomas confronting one another in front of a national television audience provided the American public, in Toni Morrison's words, an "unprecedented opportunity to hover over and cluck at, to meditate and ponder the excesses of black bodies."[50] Because the purpose of the Thomas/Hill hearings was unclear, and their nature and legal status was shrouded in obfuscation and misunderstanding, they seemed to provide nothing so much as an occasion for reenacting the intersection of racial and sexual hierarchies. A black man and potential candidate for the highest court in the land, Thomas was being examined to see whether he fit the stereotype of the black male as sexually voracious. Yet in drawing on the historical stereotype of the black rapist to accuse the Senate of a "high-tech lynching," Thomas completely denied the fact that he was being accused, not by a white lynch mob, but by a black woman. The hearings thus placed Anita Hill in the "political vacuum of erasure and contradiction" in which black women, as the victims of intersecting racial and sexual oppressions, have traditionally resided.[51] That the real issues of male sexual power and prerogatives at stake in the case should have been "worked out . . . and inscribed upon the canvas/flesh of black people" was no accident. The hearings constituted—and provided the occasion for—another chapter in the long history of the sexualization of blackness. Had the protagonists been white, the president would most likely simply have withdrawn the candidate's name from nomination, and the public spectacle would never have taken place.[52]

This thorough entanglement of sexual, gender, and racial issues in U.S. political life is part of the same dynamic of the sexualization of power differences that I discussed in the first part of this chapter. Although I focused there on the sexual dimensions of women's subordination, women's inferiority within Judaism is certainly not *limited* to the sexual sphere. On the contrary, traditionally, women were excluded from the central institutions of Jewish religious life, the synagogue and the house of study, and it is these exclusions that feminists have chiefly addressed. But the religious marginalization of women is systematically related to the control of women's sexuality, so that the two issues cannot really be separated. The exemption of women from study and public prayer "frees" them for marital and childrearing responsibilities, while the relegation of women to a spot behind the *mechitzah* (separation between women and men in a traditional synagogue) is justified by the demands of modesty and the dangers of sexual temptation. The gendered division of religious and other forms of labor also supports the necessity of heterosexual marriage, which in turn enables a man to perform his religious obligations and ties a woman to the sexual realm.[53]

The pervasive interstructuring of issues of sexuality with other forms of hierarchy points to the need for refinement of the notion of decentering sex. Sex as an issue of individual satisfaction and private morality may require decentering. But addressing and deconstructing the sexual ideologies that are interstructured with and support social inequality is crucial to creating a more just society. It is important, in this context, to distinguish between two terms I have been using interchangeably through most of this chapter—sex and sexuality. Sex can be defined as a series of behaviors centered around genital pleasure, while the broader notion of sexuality includes sex, but also refers to the ideologies and institutions that regulate and give meaning to such pleasure and that shape both individual sexual self-understandings and social power relations in any given time and place.

This differentiation makes it necessary to revisit and nuance a number of issues I touched on earlier with regard to decentering sex. My contention, for example, that, for many people, sex is not a central life issue must be understood in the context of the distinction between sex and sexuality. While the importance of sexual activity may vary considerably in the lives of different persons and over the individual lifespan, no one can escape the social meanings granted sexual activity, the sexualization of social hierarchies, or the hegemony of the heterosexual family as the central institution of sexual life. Thus it is important to decenter sex and, at the same time, recenter sexuality, deconstructing and restructuring the sexual ideologies and institutions that shape our self-understandings and social relations. This same distinction helps clarify the *difference* between sex and softball—and music or dancing, or various other endeavors through which we can experience our embodiment. While it is necessary to develop accounts of the many ways in which persons can live their embodiment fully on an individual level, on a social level, it is sexuality and not softball that is a central axis for structuring power relations.[54]

In light of these considerations, it would seem that the most effective way for a sexual ethic to decenter sex is to insist both on the distinction between sex and sexuality and the relationship between them. Instead of approaching sexual ethics as, first and foremost, the ethics of interpersonal sexual relationships, the ethicist must direct primary attention to the ideological and institutional frameworks within which interpersonal sexual values are contested and negotiated. It is these frameworks that shape the real-life meanings of particular norms, and it is all but impossible to infuse new meanings into traditional values without transforming these frameworks. Thus, "faithfulness" within the context of patriarchal marriage means that the wife is having sex only with her husband. The double standard, enshrined in the biblical understanding of adultery as sex with a married woman, supports male control of women's sexuality without imposing reciprocal obligations. But even within the context of this standard, only certain women were permitted to be faithful. Slave marriages were not legally recognized, and slave women were the sexual property of their masters, who frequently raped them and forced them to bear more slave children, even while the same master might jealously guard the faithfulness of his own wife.[55] The Jewish value of *shalom bayit* (peace in the home) has operated in a similarly one-sided way, placing on women the responsibility for maintaining family harmony. The wife who seeks to leave an abusive marriage, or who tries to get a rabbinic court to force her husband to divorce her, is often told that, for the sake of *shalom bayit*, she should try again; the burden is on her to put aside her own interests and personal safety and preserve the family.[56]

But in addressing a social situation in which these values have been used to reinforce unequal power relations, it is insufficient simply to argue that "what's good for the goose is good for the gander" and that the obligation of faithfulness or *shalom bayit* now rests on all parties alike. Traditional sexual norms were formulated in and take their meaning from the context of inequality, so that to question the context entails a fundamental rethinking of the purpose and substance of sexual norms.[57] This means shifting attention from the behavior of individuals, who must now justify themselves in relation to some particular set of sexual values, to the values themselves. The primary questions then become not how should individuals conduct themselves or, even, how do we adjust our sexual values to make them more generally applicable, but where do we get these values and what religious, social, political, and economic functions do they serve? Only in the framework of these questions can we examine particular norms to ascertain what their meanings have been, ideally, and as they have been realized in specific cultural and religious contexts riven by inequality. And only then, drawing on the epistemological privilege of the oppressed, can we ask how these same values might be understood were we to begin from the experience of the marginalized.

Conclusion

The project of writing a sexual ethics, then, is both important and strewn with pitfalls. On the one hand, the very act of working on this topic seems to acquiesce in and reinscribe the inflated significance granted sex in both the private and public arenas. Because doing sexual ethics has generally meant prescribing norms for interpersonal relationships, taking up the subject seems both to presuppose the special significance of sex as an arena for moral regulation and to separate it from other areas of personal and social interconnection. On the other hand, giving up the project of writing about sex—like quietly giving up the reading of Leviticus 18—not only abandons the many individuals forced to live with the consequences of an unreconstructed sexual ethic, but also fails to analyze the ways in which particular sexual norms intersect with and reinforce larger structures of injustice. The challenge, then, is to create a sexual ethics that walks a tightrope between deconstruction and reconstruction, between decentering sex and recentering sexuality. A Jewish feminist sexual ethics must find ways to stand in solidarity with the victims of a traditional sexual ethic, to recognize that issues of sexuality can never be discon-

nected from the broader issues of our existence in the world as embodied and interconnected persons, and to insist that the sexual ideologies that shape our social and
religious lives require to be examined and transformed.

Notes

1. Arthur Green, "A Contemporary Approach to Jewish Sexuality," in *The Second Jewish Catalog*, ed. Sharon Strassfeld and Michael Strassfeld (Philadelphia: Jewish Publication
Society, 1976), 96; Arthur Waskow, *Down-to-Earth Judaism: Food, Money, Sex, and the Rest
of Life* (New York: William Morrow, 1995), 243.

2. See, for example, United Church of Christ, *Human Sexuality: A Preliminary Study*
(New York: United Church Press, 1977); *Presbyterians and Human Sexuality: 1991* (Louisville, Ky.: Office of the General Assembly, Presbyterian Church, 1991). In the Catholic context, see Anthony Kosnick et al., *Human Sexuality: New Directions in American Catholic
Thought* (New York: Paulist Press, 1977).

3. The Conservative movement took the lead in 1994 with Elliot Dorff's pastoral letter
"This Is My Beloved, This Is My Friend," written for and with the Commission on Human
Sexuality of the Rabbinical Assembly. In 1995 the Reconstructionist Rabbinical Association
took up the issue of sexual misconduct among rabbis, passing "Breach of Professional Trust:
Sexual and Financial Ethics." Also in that year, the Central Conference of American Rabbis
(Reform) Ad Hoc Committee on Human Sexuality issued an interim report. Dorff's letter, at
seventy pages, is by far the longest of these reports, as opposed to the full-length studies cited
in n. 2.

4. Cf., *Presbyterians and Human Sexuality*, 1–2.

5. Judith Plaskow, *Standing Again at Sinai: Judaism from a Feminist Perspective* (San
Francisco: Harper Collins, 1990), 170–77.

6. Plaskow, *Standing Again at Sinai*, 172–73.

7. Jacob Neusner, *A History of the Mishnaic Law of Women*, vols. 5 Leiden: Brill, 1980),
271–72.

8. Rebecca Alpert, *Like Bread on the Seder Plate: Jewish Lesbians and the Transformation of Tradition* (New York: Columbia University Press, 1997), 29.

9. For an extended consideration of this question, see Alpert, *Like Bread on the Seder
Plate*, chaps. 2 and 3.

10. For example, when, in the course of the Conservative movement's debate about homosexuality in 1991–1992, Elliot Dorff called for a commission to place the issue in the larger
context of an examination of sexual ethics, both the congregational arm of the movement
and its seminary refused to participate in such a project.

11. I address this experience at greater length in "Sex and Yom Kippur," *Tikkun* 10, no. 5
(September–October 1995): 71–72, and "Sexuality and Teshuva: Leviticus 18," *Beginning
Anew: A Woman's Companion to the High Holy Days*, ed. Gail Twersky Reimer and Judith A.
Kates (New York: Simon and Schuster, 1997), 290–302.

12. Mimi Scarf, "Marriages Made in Heaven? Battered Jewish Wives," in *On Being a
Jewish Feminist*, ed. Susannah Heschel (New York: Schocken, 1983), 50–64; and Scarf, *Battered Jewish Wives* (Lewiston, N.Y.: Edwin Mellen, 1988), esp. chap. 6.

13. My "Sexuality and Teshuva" addresses precisely this dilemma.

14. See, e.g., Robert McAfee Brown, *Theology in a New Key: Responding to Liberation
Themes* (Philadelphia: Westminster Press, 1978), 60–62.

15. Elisabeth Schüssler Fiorenza, "Feminist Theology as a Critical Theology of Liberation," *Theological Studies* 36 (1975): 606–26; repr in her *Discipleship of Equals: A Critical*

Feminist Ekklesialogy of Liberation (New York: Crossroad, 1993). But this has been a consistent theme in all of Schüssler Fiorenza's work.

16. I have in mind the many medieval Jewish love poems celebrating relationships between men and boys. See Norman Roth, "'Deal Gently with the Young Man': Love of Boys in Medieval Hebrew Poetry of Spain," *Speculum* 57, no.1 (1982): 20–51 and "'Fawn of My Delights': Boy-Love in Hebrew and Arabic Verse," *Sex in the Middle Ages: A Book of Essays*, ed. Joyce Salisbury (New York: Garland, 1991), 157–72.

17. David M. Feldman's *Marital Relations, Birth Control and Abortion in Jewish Law* (New York: Schocken, 1974) is an excellent and widely cited example of this genre.

18. B. Nedarim 20 b.

19. See David Biale, *Eros and the Jews: From Biblical Israel to Contemporary America*. (New York: Basic Books, 1992); Daniel Boyarin, *Carnal Israel: Reading Sex in Talmudic Culture* (Berkeley: University of California Press, 1993); Michael Satlow, *Tasting the Dish: Rabbinic Rhetorics of Sexuality*, Brown Judaic Studies #303 (Atlanta: Scholars, 1995).

20. Satlow, *Tasting the Dish*, 13, 158–67.

21. Plaskow, *Standing Again at Sinai*, 178–85.

22. Bernadette Brooten, "Violence against Women in Rabbinic Literature" (unpublished paper delivered at the Claremont Women in Religion Conference, 1981), 3; Satlow, *Tasting the Dish*, 132–35; Rachel Biale, *Women and Jewish Law: An Exploration of Women's Issues in Halakhic Sources* (New York: Schocken, 1984), chap. 10.

23. B. Ketubot, lla,b.

24. Mishnah Ketubot 4:1.

25. B. Ketubot, 51b.

26. Rachel Adler, "'I've Had Nothing Yet So I Can't Take More,'" *Moment* 8, no. 8 (September 1983): 25.

27. B. Kiddushin 29b.

28. Gayle Rubin, "The Traffic in Women: Notes on the 'Political Economy' of Sex," in *Toward an Anthropology of Women*, ed. Rayna R. Reiter (New York: Monthly Review Press, 1975), 179–80.

29. Rubin revises her earlier position in "Thinking Sex: Notes for a Radical Theory of the Politics of Sexuality," in *Pleasure and Danger: Exploring Female Sexuality*, ed. Carole S. Vance (Boston: Routledge & Kegan Paul, 1984), 307–8.

30. Satlow, *Tasting the Dish*, 220.

31. See, e.g., Joel Roth, "Homosexuality," *Papers on Issues Regarding Homosexuality* (New York: Committee on Jewish Law and Standards of the Rabbinical Assembly, 1992), 4–23; Maurice Lamm, *The Jewish Way in Love and Marriage* (San Francisco: Harper and Row, 1980), 65–70.

32. Alpert addresses both of these issues in her *Like Bread on the Seder Plate*.

33. There are, of course, many ethicists who have done this. Examples include Margaret Farley, "An Ethic for Same-Sex Relations," in *A Challenge to Love: Gay and Lesbian Catholics in the Church*, ed. Robert Nugent (New York: Crossroad, 1983), 93–106, and Farley, *Personal Commitments* (San Francisco: Harper and Row, 1986); also Marvin Ellison, *Erotic Justice: A Liberating Ethic of Sexuality* (Louisville, Ky.: Westminster John Knox Press, 1996).

34. Cf. Beverly Wildung Harrison, "Sexuality and Social Policy," in *Making the Connections: Essays in Feminist Social Ethics*, ed. Carol S. Robb (Boston: Beacon Press, 1985), 85–86; and Rachel Adler, *Engendering Judaism: A New Ethics and Theology* (Philadelphia: Jewish Publication-Society, 1997), 126f.

35. There are many feminist writings on both sides of the "radical feminist" v. "pro-sex" debates. A representative anthology on the radical feminist side is Dorchen Leidholdt and

Janice G. Raymond, ed., *The Sexual Liberals and the Attack on Feminism* (New York: Teachers College Press, 1990). The most widely cited anthology on the pro-sex side is Vance, ed., *Pleasure and Danger*.

36. See Catharine MacKinnon, "Sexuality," in her *Toward a Feminist Theory of the State* (Cambridge: Harvard University Press, 1986), 126–54, and Rubin, "Thinking Sex," for central statements of each position.

37. Thanks to Sherry Israel for calling this remark to my attention.

38. Edward O. Laumann et al., *The Social Organization of Sexuality: Sexual Practices in the United States* (Chicago: University of Chicago Press, 1994), 88–89.

39. Mary Pellauer, "The Moral Significance of the Female Orgasm: Toward Sexual Ethics That Celebrates Women's Sexuality," *Journal of Feminist Studies in Religion* 9 (Spring/Fall 1993): 181.

40. Carol Schacet, "More Than a Game: Challenges Posed to Theologies of Sexuality by Women in Sport" (unpublished paper, 1995), 4, 15–18.

41. See, e.g., Ralph Reed, *Politically Incorrect: The Emerging Faith Factor in American Politics* (Dallas: Word Publishing, 1994), 29–32 and chaps. 6 and 13. It is striking that chapter 6 is subtitled "Family Breakup and Social Chaos." For an analysis of this rhetoric, see Paula M. Cooey, *Family, Freedom, and Faith: Building Community Today* (Louisville, Ky.: Westminster John Knox Press, 1996).

42. "Open Attitude on Homosexuality Makes Pariahs of Some Churches," *New York Times*, 8 February 1996, sec. A1, p. 5.

43. Hazel V. Carby, "'On the Threshold of Woman's Era': Lynching, Empire, and Sexuality in Black Feminist Theory," *Critical Inquiry* 12 (Autumn 1985): 268–70; Jacquelyn Dowd Hall, "'The Mind That Burns in Each Body': Women, Rape, and Racial Violence," in *Powers of Desire: The Politics of Sexuality*, ed. Ann Snitow, Christine Stansell, and Sharon Thompson (New York: Monthly Review Press, 1983), 333–37.

44. Hall, "'The Mind That Burns in Each Body,'" 334.

45. Ibid., 335.

46. Nell Irvin Painter, "Hill, Thomas, and the Use of Racial Stereotype," in *Race-ing Justice, En-gendering Power: Essays on Anita Hill, Clarence Thomas, and the Construction of Social Reality*, ed. Toni Morrison (New York: Pantheon, 1992), 201–2.

47. Kristin Luker, *Dubious Conceptions: The Politics of Teenage Pregnancy* (Cambridge: Harvard University Press, 1996), esp. chaps. 3 and 4; quotation on p. 86.

48. Luker, *Dubious Conceptions*, 75.

49. Hall, "'The Mind That Burns in Each Body,'" 331–33, 335, 339; Patricia Hill Collins, "The Sexual Politics of Black Womanhood," in her *Black Feminist Thought: Knowledge, Consciousness, and the Politics of Empowerment* (New York: Routledge, 1991), 163–79, esp. 174.

50. Toni Morrison, "Introduction: Friday on the Potomac," *Race-ing Justice*, xvii.

51. Kimberle Crenshaw, "Whose Story Is It Anyway? Feminist and Antiracist Appropriations of Anita Hill," in *Race-ing Justice*, 416, 403.

52. Morrison, "Introduction," *Race-ing Justice*, xvii, xix–xx; the quotation begins on p. xix. Cf. Karen Baker-Fletcher, "The Difference Race Makes: Sexual Harassment and the Law in the Thomas/Hill Hearings," *Journal of Feminist Studies in Religion* 10 (Spring 1994): 7–16.

53. Noam Zohar emphasized this systemic character of halakhic (Jewish legal) gender discrimination in his paper, "Women: A Talmudic Worldview" unpublished paper presented at the International Conference on Feminism and Orthodoxy, (16 February 1997).

54. To use Foucault's vocabulary, softball is not a discourse of power/knowledge. Michel Foucault, *The History of Sexuality: An Introduction* (New York: Vintage, 1980).

55. For a vivid description and condemnation of this practice, see Harriet Jacobs, *Incidents in the Life of a Slave Girl*, ed. Jean Fagan Yellin (Cambridge: Harvard University Press, 1987).

56. Martha Ackelsberg, "Jewish Family Ethics in a Post-Halakhic Age," *Imagining the Jewish Future: Essays and Responses*, ed. David Teutsch (Albany: SUNY Press, 1992), 155–56. Cf. Susan Aranoff, Rivka Haut, and Honey Rackman, "The Agunah: J'Accuse" (unpublished paper delivered at the International Conference on Feminism and Orthodoxy, 16 February 1997).

57. See, e.g., Adler, *Engendering Judaism*, chap. 5.

2

CHRISTINE E. GUDORF

The Social Construction of Sexuality

Implications for the Churches

A shared understanding of sexual values, roles, categories, rules, and norms has disappeared in the United States. This disappearance is rapidly advancing on the developing world as one part of the tidal wave of postmodernism. The disappearance of consensus around sexuality in our society is partly a result of the process of colonization of all areas of human life by the capitalist economy and its rationalizations. The capitalist economy has emphasized greater worker mobility and consumerism as the measure of both personal satisfaction and fulfillment of family obligation and has gradually required more work hours in order to sustain the American family's standard of living. At the same time, automation, increased foreign industrial and technological competition, and the export of production to low-wage areas has created a permanent labor surplus and many low-wage, temporary, or seasonal service-sector jobs insufficient for family support. These trends created pressures for smaller family size and more mobile worker families and the need for second (wives') salaries in working- and lower-middle class families. This in turn impacted the roles of women and men in the various racial/class sectors. Unemployment rates also increased, especially among minority groups, and the degree of support available to the family from extended kin and lifelong neighbors was lowered. All of this has affected attitudes toward sex, love, marriage, family, and parenting.

The disappearance of social consensus about sex was also a result of the simultaneous erosion of hegemonic control by white male elites in civil society. Their hegemony was increasingly challenged on all fronts by an array of new voices, including those of women, blacks, Hispanics, gays, and lesbians. Previously silent challenger groups were no longer willing to accept sexual—or cultural, political, or economic—roles defined by, and in the interests of, white male elites. In attacking the legitimacy of traditional forms of patriarchal control, challenger groups also attacked the sacredness of the patriarchal, biblically-legitimated ethic that had validated the elites. The sexual double standard, in which Christian sexual rules were normative for all subjugated groups but under which (white) male violations were largely invisible, was an early target. Though liberal feminist reformers, for example, tried to hold the elites responsible to the inherited Christian norms, theirs was a losing battle for two reasons. First, socio-political-economic power still largely remained in the hands of the white male elites, as other white feminists and many nonwhite feminists pointed out. Secondly, frequently the inherited Christian norms themselves reflected elite privilege. For these reasons, the norms themselves and the authority upon which they were based came under attack.

Eventually new groups arose on the Right to defend the endangered "universal" norms and values: the Moral Majority, fundamentalists, conservative evangelicals, and, increasingly today, militant conservative groups. Previously silent groups defending traditional "universal" values and norms became active. They became suspicious of the traditional elites on whom they had earlier relied to defend and protect inherited values and norms. Those elites, closely tied to the very market forces that now undermined the traditional sexual norms, were no longer reliable defenders of the traditional norms.[1]

Patriarchy and Social Hegemony in Sexuality

Today sexuality has become a focal point in the ongoing historical struggle for hegemony. On the one hand we have a nostalgic call, in both the churches and the nation as a whole, to reconstruct a single universal sexual ethic, to recreate a national consensus around tried and true (patriarchal) moral/religious values in sexuality. On the other hand, we have a plurality of voices reminding us that the sexual freedoms and rights of non-elites have had to be extracted with great suffering out of the supposed harmony of that past "consensus" that, even in the short history of this nation, has included exclusive male control of the person and property of wives and children, the separation through sale of African-American families, and proprietary rights to the sexual and reproductive faculties of female and male slaves, not to mention multitudinous forms of exclusion and discrimination based on sex, many of which still linger in attenuated forms. The new voices form a postmodern chorus insisting that any call for shared standards is a call to impose norms on the weak by the powerful.

The appeal of the call for shared moral norms, and shared sexual norms in particular, is powerful among the great majority who drift between nostalgia for universal norms and respect for pluralism. The appeal of traditional shared norms is even powerful to some within groups long colonized by patriarchal elites. The power of this call is partly based in colonized mentalities, in historical vestiges of past subjugation wherein the subjugated adopted as their own the values of the dominant elites.[2] For example, some women raised to find their identity and pride in their service of husband and children still find traditional sex roles, values, and norms a source of comfort and security, even though such women may reject individual aspects of traditional roles or norms, such as Catholic teaching on contraception or men's exemption from all childcare and housework, due to their own situation as working wives.

But I suspect that the appeal of this call is not only rooted in identification with traditional elites, but also in human relationality. A nostalgia for greater consensus in sexuality, a yearning for order, for peace, for social harmony—these are real. While there is a certain truth to the view that such yearning for peace and harmony can be a yearning for and an invitation to slavery, there is also a dialectic within both human history and individual life between activity and reflection, between the creation of new institutions and structures and the emergence of new social patterns of mutual interaction around them. Social theory of the last decades has attempted to find ways to integrate a micro-focus on the individual, on freedom and agency, on face-to-face relationships, with a macro-focus on structures, social process, groups, and social constraint, recognizing that both agency and structure, micro- and macro-levels, are real and important aspects of human social life and community. As individuals we make free sexual decisions, but we do so within a social nexus that has shaped our understanding of ourselves, others, and human sexuality itself, and those decisions we make involve social-sexual institutions such as marriage, heterosexual and homosexual cohabitation, and celibate religious communities.

During extended social crisis, human groups and societies come under great strain and often become willing to settle for less than justice in order to obtain a breathing space and some semblance of normality. This is as true of social crises over sexual justice as it is of crises over economic or electoral justice. While this willingness to compromise justice for "peace" is often exploited and manipulated by elites to buy compliance from groups protesting their subjugation, it is not in itself, it seems to me, a moral defect. Moreover, I suspect that the human attraction to order is one basis for much of the rejection of postmodernist arguments that human diversity precludes any capacity of human rationality to procure substantive agreement among individuals or groups.[3]

The basis of this predilection for order seems to be human relationality and the social process within which individual persons become human. It is the underlying order in human society that allows the world of the human infant to be intelligible; that intelligibility is what allows the child to learn independence. As the linguistic turn in late modern/postmodern thought has made clear, the order and structure within a given language are in many ways a map of the world in that society, organizing, interpreting, and even evaluating reality. Humans cannot be human without relationship to other humans, and the ways of interacting with other humans, such as language, have certain inner structures that predispose humans to seek patterns and order and to rely on them for fulfilling tasks.

Seeking a Christian Postmodern Sexual Ethic

If the Christian Right has been at the center of the political debate about sexuality in contemporary society, liberal Protestant discourse has been at the front of religious/

theological treatment of sexuality in postmodernity. This has been in some ways a continuation of liberal Protestantism's historical role as spokesperson for American religion, a role increasingly called into question today by liberal Protestantism's dwindling numbers. But the greater challenge to liberal Protestant theology has been the struggle to disassociate it from its historic alliance with Enlightenment rationality and, ultimately, market capitalism. By the mid-twentieth century liberal churches had been displaced from their role as arbiter of the hegemonic elite by the forces of the market.[4] Yet traditional liberal emphasis on individual rights and liberties continues to inform, for example, liberal Protestant treatment of sexual justice for women, gays, and lesbians, and to undergird attacks on traditional patriarchal sexual norms. Many liberal Protestant theologians look with great suspicion on the communitarian debate[5] but have difficulty locating in their tradition adequate grounding for a sexual ethic that goes beyond liberal individualism's inadequacy for sustaining human community.[6]

My own perspective for seeking a postmodern Christian sexual ethic reflects an American Catholic perspective. Catholics in the United States were historically among the critics and victims of WASP elites but now are divided between those Catholics who have in the last two or three generations assimilated into the white professional-managerial class and those who are the heirs of the traditional Catholic working-class ethnic enclaves. Historically, though American Catholic immigrants were victims of nativist exclusion and discrimination in the United States at the hands of Protestant elites, many were not unmarked by their own much longer and more developed history of Catholic/Christian European social and political hegemony, which has both similarities and dissimilarities with that of liberal American Protestants. Thus while Catholic moral theory has an inherent suspicion of unfettered individualism and has focused more than Protestantism on the common good and has been more suspicious of capitalism, its history also reveals the use of communitarian, universalist, and harmonious-order themes to mask domination and exclusivity. My references to, and reliance on, the Catholic tradition and its concepts, therefore, result not from belief in its superiority to, or its less compromised status compared to, other traditions, but from the fact that it is mine.

The Social Construction of Sexuality

Until the last few decades, human sexuality was usually understood as a fixed phenomenon. It was thought to endure over time in roughly the same form, with the same properties. But recently we have come to see in sexuality, as in other areas of human existence from forms of energy to the organization of space, that our categories for classification are not naturally occurring, but the result of human artifice. We talk now of paradigms for organizing our knowledge, and of paradigm revolutions,[7] for we have realized that often many aspects, even what we identified as the "essence," or center, of an object or event were actually characteristics of our experience, possibly even of our brain structures, rather than aspects of the reality we were attempting to understand. Essentialist understandings of humans have often been oversimplifications of reality. Past treatment of gender, for example, oversimplified by ignoring contrary (non-patriarchal) existing patterns of organizing gender and by identifying sex and gender among humans. Once constructed, this patriarchal understanding of human gender was imposed on other populations of mammals (e.g., apes), who in turn became evidence for this pattern as universal and normative—as God's will expressed in creation.[8]

A full-bodied essentialism in sexuality is impossible today because it so clearly denies the relationality and historicity of human persons, as well as ignoring what we have learned about the medium (here the human brain and senses) being the message itself. We know that humans not only require relationship to become capable of human behavior (from speech to capacity for nurture), but that human self-understanding and consequent behavior have changed with historical culture shifts, as the concept of the individual and the consequent concept of individual rights illustrates.[9]

The most difficult task in rethinking sexual ethics in this society concerns constructing any agreed-upon meanings in sexuality. The more a society agrees on the meanings of sexuality, the clearer the social expectations regarding sexual behavior can be. Such clarity and agreement tend to lower levels of both anxiety and victimization. To speak of meanings in sexuality is not to revert to essentialism, because the meanings can—and must—be consciously constructed by consensus. At the same time, the complexity of social construction, human historical unconsciousness of the process of social construction, and continuing resistance to the notion of sexuality as socially constructed all press for attempting to build on whatever usable basis we find in sexuality as presently constructed. We are simply at this time more capable of modifications than complete redesign; there are too many unknown connections and consequences.

The shift from essentialism in sexuality has presented the Catholic church with more serious difficulties than those facing Protestant churches, for Catholic treatment of sexuality has been grounded not in Scripture, where Protestant ethics is largely based, but rather in a natural law attempt to discern from the patterns in creation the intentions of the Creator. Catholic natural law interpretations have traditionally been physicalist, relying on biological determinism and stressing reproductive anatomy over the intellectual, psychological, emotional, and spiritual understandings of the person. Physicalist approaches to natural law are most vulnerable to both political critiques of essentialism and the scientific/social research that underlies them. While there were no basic differences in traditional Catholic and Protestant conclusions about the sexual nature of humans, and both Catholics and Protestants had to grapple with biblical patriarchy, Catholics found that revising sexual ethics required rethinking both scriptural revelation and the revelation derived from natural law. However, because of historic reliance on natural law and the resulting absence of debates over inerrancy, verbal inspiration, and literal interpretation, there has been less trauma for the Catholic church in reinterpreting Scripture on sexuality.

A natural law approach to sexuality is redeemable within a critical constructionist framework, but only with the sacrifice of the physicalism and the addition of a great deal of complex internal dialectic. One great advantage of a natural law approach is that it gives a theological basis for using the sciences as a central resource for constructing a Christian sexual ethics, for biological and social science have become the primary methods for discerning divine intentions within an evolving, dynamic creation. Understanding creation in terms of a process initiated and overseen by God sets the stage for the social construction of sexuality as neither a usurpation of God's right, nor a denial of divine intentions, much less as an irreligious, secular task, but as one aspect of the larger task of Christians to create ourselves and our society in the likeness of the Kingdom of God that Jesus announced.

The social construction of human sexuality, and all of human "nature" itself, does not imply a total plasticity. There is a wide variety of influences, some countervailing, that together produce human sexuality in individuals and societies. The role of individual choice varies from situation to situation depending on historical, cultural, and material factors. While some factors, such as biology, influence sexuality in all human communities, the degree and direction of influence will vary with individual differences in sex, in hormone levels, in genetically founded differences in the brain, in general health, as well as with culture and individual choice. Biology does not seem to be determinative aside from basic sexual dimorphism, though it plays an important role in predisposing populations and individuals to certain types of behavior.

For example, we know that there is a correlation between higher levels of androgen and assertive, even aggressive behaviors. This correlation is present in both men and women: raising the androgen level in the individual raises the level of assertion/aggression (both verbal and physical) that is displayed. Yet, inexplicably, women's *verbal* assertiveness and aggression occurs at levels similar to men's despite women's lower level of androgens, while men's higher level of androgen seems to (predictably) produce much higher incidence of physical aggression in men as a group. Biology does not have the last word even in this corner of human sexuality, for Peggy Reeves Sanday, and before her Margaret Mead, studied and classified human societies along spectrums extending from peaceful to violent socio-sexual interaction, regardless of the fact that male and female hormone levels are relatively constant along culture divisions.[10] Some cultures have overridden most or all of any biological predisposition toward aggression in males, and a few have socialized women to resemble the more typical male pattern in aggression.

Thus irenic cultures are rare,[11] aggression is much more commonly male than female,[12] and aggression and violence by men are most common among those men whose androgen levels are highest.[13] Cultures without (male) violence have expended a great deal of social energy in overcoming/resisting a biological predisposition to violence in young males; this energy is therefore not available for other communal needs. Ability to explain how biology may predispose humans and cultures to particular social patterns of behavior does not preclude the existence or the exercise of free will among individuals within the society. Just as cultures need to expend larger amounts of social energy to achieve higher levels of resistance to hormonal predisposition to aggression, so for individuals the cost of resisting strong cultural pressures will be higher than the cost of resisting low cultural pressures, but it remains possible. Many persons in Europe and North America today successfully avoid familial and social pressures to procreate; in sub-Saharan Africa the pressure to have children is much higher, thus childlessness is predictably rarer. Both individual Africans and Americans have free will and are responsible for their sexual choices. But the costs are different. In this, as in other areas of human life, we are discovering that all freedom is relative, and various types of freedom are more limited in some social locations than others.

In the same way, the Catholic church has been finding out anew the varied costs of a priestly vow of celibacy in different cultures. Vocations to the priesthood have always lagged in cultures where marriage and paternity defined wholeness, adulthood, and social status. But in the twentieth century the church is learning that the costs of celibacy have escalated in the very postmodern societies that used to supply many clerical vocations and reach beyond the rate of clerical vocations to within the clergy itself. As traditional communities gave way to anonymous urban centers, competitive economic patterns, and mobile populations, interpersonal intimacy came to be virtually restricted to sexual relationships. Celibacy in late modern/postmodern society is now linked to emotional isolation and is consequently associated with higher than normal rates of depression, alcoholism, broken vows, and emotional disturbances.[14] These problems have no inherent connection with celibacy but attend celibacy within a particular sociocultural interpretation of marriage and family.

Sexual orientation is an aspect of sexuality that seems similarly complex. Though the ancient Greeks and Romans observed some of the basic patterns in human sexual partner preference and speculated as to the etiology of those patterns,[15] the concept of sexual orientation is a contemporary construct created to account for specific patterns observed today. Those patterns include: (1) enduring individual patterns of partner choice (same sex, other sex, or partners of both sexes); (2) distributions of humans along a (Kinsey[16]) spectrum between exclusively heterosexual and exclusively homosexual sexual desire and behavior; and (3) very low success rates achieved in voluntary efforts at reversing homosexual orientation once fixed. (Attempts at reversing heterosexual orientation have not been studied.) The concept of orientation has been useful in challenging earlier, unproven assumptions that heterosexual attraction is normal and homosexual attraction is deliberate perversion. Nevertheless, there are continuing disputed questions, such as differences between the sexes in patterns of sexual orientation, where to fix the borders between bisexuality and both homosexuality or heterosexuality on the Kinsey spectrum, and the consequent degree of exclusiveness of these orientations.

In terms of the etiology of sexual orientation, it has become clear that biology does play a role in sexual orientation. Bailey's twin research has shown that where one sibling is homosexual, identical twins have the highest likelihood of being homosexual, other siblings a lesser likelihood, and adopted siblings a still lesser likelihood, while all three groups have higher than random likelihood.[17] If genetics *determined* sexual orientation, then *all* the identical twins of homosexual persons would have homosexual orientation as well, which is not the case. Since identical twins are more likely to share a homosexual orientation than are regular siblings, and regular siblings more likely than adopted siblings, then there must be a genetic predisposition. But family environment (learned behavior) must also play a significant role, since Bailey's adopted siblings demonstrate significantly more correspondence with a homosexually oriented sibling than does the general population. Other studies have shown that persons with homosexual orientation as adults were significantly more likely to have demonstrated nonconformist gender patterns as children.[18] But as with other suggested causes, nonconformity was only present in some, not all, persons with homosexual orientation, just as some children with gender non-conformity become heterosexual as adults.

Clearly, the etiology of sexual orientation is complex. It is made even more impenetrable by the unreliability of cross-cultural statistics regarding orientation. For example, many societies in the world claim to have no homosexual persons, despite strong reservations among social scientists concerning the impact of repression on overtness. Even where there is some openness about homosexuality, as in the United States, social and economic discrimination against homosexual persons makes obtaining an accurate population frame from which to select a representative sample extremely difficult.

This research on orientation presents severe difficulties for Christian churches' traditional condemnations of homosexual behavior. Churches that have dealt with the research data, the liberal Protestant and the Catholic churches, have concluded, in accordance with traditional understandings of sin as necessarily voluntary, that homosexual orientation itself cannot be sinful if it is not chosen.[19] Treatments of homosexual *behavior* vary, with the Catholic statement of 1986 clarifying that "although the particular inclination of the homosexual person is not a sin, it is a more or less strong tendency ordered toward an intrinsic moral evil; and thus in the inclination itself must be seen as an objective moral disorder."[20] The implication seems to be that homosexual orientation is objective, but not subjective, sin. At the other end of the Christian spectrum of opinion, the United Church of Christ has decided that if homosexual orientation is not chosen, it is not sinful, and acting on it should be subject to the same moral rules to which heterosexuals are held.

Resources for Christian Sexual Ethics

Traditional Christian resources for ethics can be reinterpreted in ways that are adequate for a socially constructed sexual ethic. The Methodist "quadrilateral" resources for Christian ethics—Scripture, tradition, reason, and experience—are perhaps the most useful and comprehensive contemporary sources. How each of these sources is understood and used will, and should, vary according to the circumstances of the communities active in the construction of the sexual ethic.

Scripture

While there are still many Christians who assume that a usable sexual ethic can be lifted entirely from the Bible, this is a distinct minority position among Christian churches. Even among many who view the Bible as *the* source for Christian sexual ethics, superficial inquiry often induces a defensive shift to a multisource stance. Explorations of the translations of Hebrew and Greek words for sexual acts, sins, and categories of persons, as compared to other uses of those terms in the text and in other contemporaneous texts, undermine any simple extraction of sexual ethics from Scripture. Some biblical stories and laws (e.g., concerning Lot's seduction by his daughters, Tamar's seduction of Judah, patriarchal polygyny, the buying and selling of women, marrying of rapists and their victims, concubinage, the stoning of adulterers) demand explanations as to why some biblical texts on sexuality are normative and others are not. Finally, questions such as whether biblical attitudes are normative, and if so how marital pronatalism in the Bible, for example, can be jettisoned, serve to multiply the sources claimed as revelatory.[21] Few Americans share the biblical understanding that women were made for procreation, which, as the primary purpose of marriage, should be maximized and not obstructed.

In a socially constructed Christian sexual ethic, the role of Scripture is to give us stories about what kind of persons we should be, stories about how easy it is to, and in what ways we, fall short of God's call, as well as stories that assure us of God's continuing grace and forgiveness. Scripture is only indirectly a guide for behavior, sexual or otherwise.

Reason

Protestant theology and ethics have been shifting from the Reformers' stance on reason, which rejected reason as a reliable source/tool for ethics and theology and pronounced it instead totally corrupted by the sin of the Fall. This stance was a reaction against the corruptions that had crept into the Catholic tradition, in which reason, in the particular form of casuistry, served more to dismiss ethical rigor than to preserve it from legalism. But the historic association between Protestantism and Enlightenment thought, and later between Protestantism and scientific modernity, has created a general acceptance in the United States of reason as a source for Christian ethics in general. On the Catholic side, reason—though not the more skeptical version of scientific reason—has always been a part of the natural law discernment of Catholic ethics. Reason is necessary if experience is to be valuable in the work of ethics.

Experience

Experience is perhaps the part of the quadrilateral that has been most drawn into the center of the ethical enterprise. Scripture and tradition, are, in fact, both interpretations of past human experience of the divine. Modern historical sensibility not only suggests that God's revelation in history has been interpreted and recorded in different forms, beginning with Scripture, then in various creeds and liturgical, theological, and ethical practices and in the histories of Christian communities of the past. Modern historical sensibility also suggests that God's revelation continues into the present, not only in the teaching authority of the churches, but also in the material world of creation and in the experience of individuals and communities of the present. Just as all scientific data comes to us interpreted by the human brain and senses, so all revelation comes to us in various interpreted forms, whether in the present or the past.

The insistence on collective and individual experience as a source for discerning divine revelation has escalated since the time of the Reformers, as various marginalized groups within Christianity have claimed the right of interpreting Scripture and tradition and have disputed the interpretations of the ruling elites within church and society. In the twentieth century, women, African Americans, Latin Americans, South Africans, various Asian groups, and the poor in general have claimed their own reasoned experience as tools for interpretation of divine revelation.

It is often assumed that diversity is so great among humans that the gulf between one person's experience and another's precludes any rational discourse aimed at discerning concrete common conditions for human flourishing. This is, in some ways, a contemporary version of the early Protestant rejection of corrupted reason. Today, in conservative Protestant congregations, this attitude discourages dialogue with other groups and encourages an inward, separatist focus, with or without an accompanying emphasis on proselytization. In liberal Protestant churches, insistence on the dignity of the person is sometimes interpreted to mean that all must be allowed to speak, but agreement will be only procedural, not substantive. Respecting the voices of others does not require engaging them in dialogue based on their particular experience, certainly not with the expectation of reaching any common agreement as to human goods, however partial, but only agreement as to procedural norms such as politeness toward the voices of others.

One of the strengths of the Catholic tradition is its insistence that human experience involves common goods that are embedded in a universally accessible natural law. But Catholicism's long history of using analogical reason to discover the concrete conditions for human flourishing has sometimes predisposed Catholics to propose their own Aristotelian-Thomist tradition as the basis for dialogue.[22] This is especially problematic in sexuality, where so much of the Aristotelian-Thomist tradition is permeated by sexism, a fear and repugnance of pleasure, and mistaken biology. It seems to me that any particular method for applying analogical reasoning to human experience must be carefully presented not as the authoritative method to be adopted, but as one of a series of extremely early and therefore flawed prototypes that have required and still require modification in order to equitably and adequately include the varieties of human experience and groups.

The late modern emphasis on the sciences in the work of ethics reflects a further turn toward experience and characterizes both Catholicism and Protestantism. In Catholic natural law thought, the sciences, both social science and natural science, have become central tools for discerning in natural law God's intentions for us and our world. Most Reformers rejected natural law as impossible to discern due to the corruption of reason in the Fall, and the Reformed tradition suspected "nature" of being aligned with Satan as a source of deception and temptation of the senses (with later dire consequences for the environment).[23] But their increasing reliance on science to understand both ethical motivation and consequence in the last century has brought many Protestants to what is, in effect, a general natural law stance. Contemporary Christians, Catholics and Protestants alike, are brought to a natural law–like approach not because of its role in past tradition, but because of (1) increased confidence in human discernment regarding creation given the new tools of science; and (2) an understanding that vastly expanded scientific knowledge of the world is not necessarily self-explanatory but requires disciplined, rational analysis that can interpret, using analogy, what contributes to and what detracts from human flourishing. The sciences cannot settle value questions in sexuality, but reasonable discourse on the data of the sciences can designate the ends of the spectrum within which the answers as to values may be found. To select specific answers we must resort to applications of reasoned analogy to other aspects of human experience.

Tradition

Tradition is a broad term that means different things within different Christian denominations. Scripture itself is one important part of Christian tradition. Other relatively uncontested parts of the revelatory Christian tradition are the early creeds and the teachings of the Fathers of the Church (including their differences and disputes with each other). Individual denominations generally recognize their own institutional history, creeds, and ecclesiology as aspects of the revelatory tradition.

Not everything that is historically part of Christian tradition is or should be regarded as revelatory. In the area of sexuality, the tradition of Christianity, including much of Scripture itself, is contaminated with patriarchal[24] attitudes and customs that subordinate women, children, and persons of other races and religions, denying them the human dignity that is the foundation of the Reign of God Jesus announced. Some basic requirements for tradition to be revelatory are that it must proceed from the consensus of the faithful, be generally compatible with the rest of Christian tradition proceeding from Jesus Christ, and be ordered to the good of the entire community and all of its constituent parts. Recourse to Christian tradition in the construction of a contemporary Christian sexual ethic requires a constant and critical vigilance in discerning pollutants such as patriarchy, racism, sexism, and anti-sexual dualism from the living water of revelation.

Challenge to the Churches

Many in the churches have refused to accept the social construction of sexuality. Their chief objections are not to the evidence for social construction itself, but to what they perceive as the consequences of accepting social construction: a relativizing of sexual morality, the end of moral standards, and teaching in sexuality. Social construction, they believe, will make any code of sexual ethics impossible: "If," they say, "sexual behavior results from the social interaction of many different causes, of which the human will is only one, how can humans be held responsible for their sexual behavior? What is the point of trying to teach that some acts—or even some relationships—are right and others are wrong when the role of human choice is so reduced in any situation?"

Social construction of sexuality *is* a challenge to any and every set of sexual norms pegged above the minimal lowest common denominator norms necessary for human survival. Sexuality stands today where civil government stood centuries ago during the erosion and collapse of belief in the divine right of kings to rule. Then the question was: How can we have social order if God did not appoint a ruler for us? Today it is not so very different: How can we have any meaningful sexual order in society if our inherited norms were based neither in nature as created by

God nor in God's scriptural revelation, but rather arose in a dialectic in which humans had a significant role? Can human groups respect values, customs, and rules once we realize they were articulated by humans?

Minimalist norms of behavior—criminalization of rape and child sexual abuse, for example—can and will be agreed upon in the name of human dignity and enforced so that humans can live in social groups. Minimalist social sexual norms today must include both basic parental responsibility for offspring and steps toward the elimination, even a reversal, of population growth, as well as forbid the irresponsible spread of sexually transmitted diseases, rape, sexual harassment, and other forms of non-consensual sex, including sex with children or the otherwise incompetent. These lowest common denominator sexual norms aim at the survival of the biosphere and the protection from abuse and neglect of human individuals and the bonds that connect them. With regard to these norms, the churches will need to make clearer than in the past their repudiation of past pro-natalism and their support for population reduction.

Some of these norms will be embodied in criminal law, others in social programs and education, but all should have the full force of the society behind them. Legal regulation of human behavior can only teach us to recognize disvalues. Law is a very clumsy tool for teaching positive values. Most Americans agree that law is not a good tool for discouraging adultery, sex between twelve year olds, unprotected sex, or illegitimate births, though the majority see these as not only less than socially ideal, but even morally problematic.

The immediate challenge that the social construction of sexuality presents to the churches is whether the churches can resist the liberal capitalist influences that promote, in the name of individual freedom, the reduction of behavioral norms to the lowest common denominator applicable to all cultural groups, associations, and societies. While all societies must demand that members do no harm to others, Christian ethics issues a perennial call for a willingness to sacrifice in discipleship toward others. But the churches' biggest challenges will be (1) accepting responsibility for constructing a sexual ethic for humans rather than displacing responsibility for human codes onto God; and (2) recognizing that what Christian faith and tradition contribute to the construction of a sexual ethic is not specific sexual rules, but the concept of behavioral limits based in concern for the dignity and welfare of all persons, for justice between groups, and for love of neighbor and the common good.

The churches need to make the case that past religious sexual norms have not been built on any unchanging code of revelation, but on the attempts of societies to interpret the concrete sexual conditions of human flourishing—God's will for the human community—in particular socio-economic-political circumstances. These norms, even within Christianity, have changed somewhat through the centuries and need to continue to change. It is vital that the churches acknowledge that the exercise of what they have often called "discernment" of natural law or scriptural teaching is truly human construction, regardless of how much it utilizes what we have discerned from these and other sources that have their origin in the divine.

Human sexuality has the potential to meet a variety of human needs and desires, but these varied potentials, many of which have been recognized and/or utilized in human history, are not the same as inherent meanings in sexuality. Furthermore, all of the needs and desires that can potentially be satisfied in sexuality can also be satisfied by other means. For example, sex can be an avenue to emotional intimacy, but it can also occur between strangers and be bought and sold as a commodity. Similarly, an individual's sex can determine virtually all of their roles, traits, and self-identity in one cultural system and can be relatively incidental to most of these in another cultural system. Some groups understand sex as synonymous with sexual pleasure, while the experience of other groups leads them to associate sex with shame, pain, and degradation. The desire to create, which sexual procreation satisfies for many, can also be satisfied through art, or business, literature or engineering, as well as by various kinds of childrearing, just as the desire for intimacy, which some satisfy in sex, can also be satisfied in intense friendships, and the desire for physical pleasure in a good massage. Which human needs and desires sex satisfies in any situation must be negotiated between religio-cultural, socio-economic, and individual pressures and preferences. There is no one universal binding form of sexual relationship or activity for all humans.

Christianity does not contribute specific sexual rules to a sexual ethic. Instead, it contributes the concept of behavioral limits based in human dignity, justice, love of neighbor, and the common good, which are not specifically sexual concerns, but Christian concerns in all areas of life. Christianity does not have—and never should have had—any one specific interpretative framework for sexuality. Although Christianity has had a 2,000-year history of largely anti-sexual, misogynist, material/spiritual dualism, this historical tradition is eroding (finally!). When this historical dualist tradition is dismissed, there *is* no Christian interpretation of sexuality. According to the gospels, Jesus had virtually nothing to say about sexuality other than a prohibition on divorce as a victimization of women in his society.[25] The New Testament has very little to add beyond testifying to the ongoing conflict in the early community between early patterns of sexual egalitarianism and increasingly strong patterns of conformity to cultural patriarchy.[26] The church's turn toward asceticism beginning in the second century, however it may have been motivated by a desire to free persons from the oppression of then-contemporary marital roles,[27] became responsible for a great deal of both anti-female and anti-sexual attitudes in the church.

The churches need to explicitly teach that sexual pleasure, and bodily pleasure in general, is one important aspect of the individual well-being and therefore of the common good, though its pursuit is always limited by the call to justice, mutuality, and neighborly love. Pain is not good; pleasure is not bad; the body as well as the mind/soul reflects God's creative gift. But all cultures have not, will not, and should not deal with sexual pleasure in the same way. I suggest that in our culture, sexual pleasure understood holistically needs to be redeemed as a source of social and personal interaction that benefits the common good and is independent of the market that is colonizing human life. Perhaps the most valuable aspect of sexual pleasure in this age of fragmented human persons is the one that much of the Christian tradition denied: it is *human* in the holistic sense. Sexual pleasure has the capacity to involve the senses, the emotions, the intellect, and the very soul of the human when it is shared in love.

My own suggestion is that the churches should seize, correct, and build upon the implicit model of sexual ethics found in some parts of secular society. In this model, marriage is an intimate, sexually exclusive, and ideally permanent union of two persons in love (who may or not desire children and may or may not share the same sex). Though marriage would be the most complete form of sexual relationship, less permanent, affectionate, contraceptive but also intimate and sexually exclusive, unions would also be recognized as mature responsible unions that, like marriage, can support and serve the common good. More casual sexual unions, if they are contraceptive, disease-safe, honest, and mutually respectful, could be accepted as morally inferior but not sinful, and not completely avoidable among the young. At the same time, any morally responsible sexual activity requires a degree of self-knowledge, sensitivity to others, and maturity that is impossible for very young persons. Such a model, implicitly found in more mainstream literature, film, and television, corresponds to findings of sociological surveys in the United States which report that while cohabitation has reached new heights, the majority are clear that it is not a replacement for marriage, but a step toward, or a test of, a possible marital relationship.[28] The same is true for most sex in dating—it is understood as part of a general search for the right mate with whom one will have an intimate, exclusive, and permanent relationship and ultimately marriage.[29]

But sexuality is not the only, and probably not the most important, aspect of human life. In our society, interpersonal needs of individuals that used to be filled by a nearby extended family and permanent neighbors have increasingly fallen to the nuclear family to fulfill, and especially to marriage, overburdening it to the point of frequent rupture. Persons without sexual relationships are assumed to be unhappy, unfulfilled, lonely, relationally isolated, poorly adjusted, and depressed. Celibacy is increasingly viewed as unnatural and even perverse. If sexual relationships are not to be completely overburdened, churches should support the cultivation of non-sexual forms of intimate relationships, continuity in relationships, and respect for celibacy.

In contemporary Western sexuality perhaps the most central specific value clash between Christianity and the larger culture involves the commodification of human sexuality. In Christian thought, all forms of human relations participate in the dignity of human beings and therefore cannot be legitimately reified or commodified. Where sex is bought and sold, so will human persons be treated. Where sexual procreativity is bought and sold, so will human persons be. And the human persons so victimized are invariably the weakest members of the society. Sexual objectification is the basis of the commodification of sex and the root of harmful stereotypes, many of which originate in admiration (in René Girard's thought, mimetic desire).[30] Women and male homosexuals have been the most common objects of sexual objectification. Women have been objectified either as objects of sexual pleasure or tools for reproduction, and gay men have been objectified as both totally defined by their sexual activity and as feminine (despite the fact that these two types of objectification usually result in conflicting understandings of gays as super-sexed *and* sexually passive!). The only method I know of controlling sexual objectification—for it cannot be eliminated—is to constantly focus on the diversity of concrete reality. A cure for the effects of too many beautiful people in advertising, television, or movies is to go to a gym and observe the multitudes of very real, sweaty people with bulges, lines, pores, and thinning hair, and relearn human diversity.

Emphasizing diversity as the cure for objectification and stereotyping is also relevant to the treatment of sexism in the churches. Christian sexual ethics must treat women and men equally in terms of rights and responsibilities, without imposing an unrealistic sameness of treatment. Men's and women's investments in pregnancy, for example, are not the same, but both must be treated with respect for their level of investment. Changes in this area of social thought and policy must be tentative and experimental, as the contemporary revolution in the roles of women has only begun and can take different legitimate shapes in different religious and cultural groups. Such redefinitions in sexual identity here and in other cultures also have tremendous relevance for correcting and deepening understandings of both homosexual and heterosexual orientation and interaction.

Conclusion

If human society is to do more than survive, if it is to fulfill the possibilities for flourishing collectively and individually, then it needs more than corrections of past teaching from the churches. The churches must call us to a vision of the "good life" that is richer and more compelling than the consumer version, embodying not just a basic respect but a reverence for the human person and for all human interactions. These visions are at the heart of religion.

If ever there were a period in which it should be easy to make ordinary persons distinguish not being abused from being treated with respect and reverence, it must be now, when so many social interactions are with impersonal functionaries. The triumph of formal rationality in our experience grounds an increase of isolation, depression, and ennui amid record consumption, as well as a callousness and obliviousness toward the materially deprived. These attitudinal afflictions in turn set the stage for the desperate contemporary quest for entertainment and badges of uniqueness. But these afflictions may also set the stage for rebellion, for the construction of collective norms self-consciously erected within a teleological process in the interests of a more humane society. The task of the churches here is to turn people's attention from the purported symptoms of social disintegration to the truly problematic causal trends that impede movement toward the vision of the Reign of God—the center of the legacy left Christians by Jesus Christ.

This is a huge agenda, and yet the various issues involved in it are so interlocked that piecemeal approaches are difficult. For the liberal Christian churches who have already taken some of the steps I have outlined, there is less to lose, for many of them have already lost large numbers of young families and look out on greying congregations. For the conservative churches, there is more risk, for much of their appeal has been the clarity and certainty of their teaching: their insistence that moral norms, especially sexual norms, did not need to be rethought, only enforced. Experimentation and tentativeness in a sexual norm will not, therefore, be easy to sell either for the Catholic church or for Protestant evangelicals and fundamentalists. And for both liberal and conservative churches, the generations who have drifted away from Christianity over the last three or four decades will be extremely difficult to reclaim. But the alternative to recognizing the social construction of sexuality and attempting to influence that construction through a broad-based social discourse informed by Christian values is the churches' eventual social irrelevance. In so potentially powerful an arena of human life as sexuality, the social irrelevance of religion is a bleak, if not terrifying, prospect.

Notes

1. The struggle for control of the Republican Party since the early 1980s has been the most public area for observing this change. By the Bush presidency it was clear that the Christian Right had lost its bid for control of the party: the so-called "moderates" were unwilling to commit themselves to resisting the economic tides that had created new economic roles for women and smaller families. Their refusal to make anti-abortion and anti-feminism the priority issues of the party signified this.

2. On this topic there is perhaps no better American source than Malcolm X, who taught that the worst kind of Negro slavery was the mental slavery that characterized blacks who loved their white oppressors because they had been brainwashed into believing everything white was better (see *The Autobiography of Malcolm X* [New York: Ballantine, 1964] or James Cone, *Martin and Malcolm in America* [Maryknoll, N.Y.: Orbis, 1991], chap. 4).

3. See, for example, the first three chapters of Lisa Sowle Cahill's excellent *Sex Gender and Christian Ethics* (New York: Cambridge, 1996), in which she refutes Lyotard by insisting that human experience, even amid diversity, is sufficiently analogous to allow agreement on the basic conditions necessary for human flourishing. I do not, however, agree with her proposal of the Aristotelian-Thomist approach to experience as a model for joint exploration of human experience. One cannot simultaneously approach groups subordinated for millennia, whose subordination was legitimated by this model, and seriously expect to further open and free communication with them by proposing the Aristotelian-Thomist model as the basis for discussion of experience.

4. See Elizabeth M. Bounds, *Coming Together, Coming Apart: Religion, Community and Modernity* (New York: Routledge, 1996), chap. 1, for an acknowledgement and review of this process.

5. Again, see Bounds, *Coming Together, Coming Apart.*

6. This is how I interpret the book authored by Don Browning, et al., *From Culture Wars to Common Ground: Religion and the Family Debate* (Louisville: Westminster John Knox Press, 1997). The book places the contemporary debate on the family firmly within a completely Protestant American history but then turns to a mix of social scientific perspectives and Roman Catholic theological and ethical resources with virtually no recognizably Protestant additions. Yet the authors are all identified as Protestant and liberal by occupational association if not by home church.

7. Thomas Kuhn, *The Structure of Scientific Revolutions* (Chicago: University of Chicago Press, 1962).

8. See Donna Harroway's brilliant exploration of gender and race in primatology, *Primate Visions: Gender Race and Nature in the World of Modern Science* (New York: Routledge, 1989), and also Harroway, *Simians, Cyborgs and Women: The Reinvention of Nature* (New York: Routledge, 1991).

9. Thomas Hoppe, "Human Rights," in *The New Dictionary of Catholic Social Thought*, ed. Judith Dwyer (Collegeville, Minn.: Liturgical Press, 1994), 457–60.

10. Margaret Mead, *Sex and Temperament in Three Primitive Societies* (New York: Morrow, 1963); Peggy Reeves Sanday, "The Socio-Cultural Context of Rape: A Cross Cultural Study," *Journal of Social Issues* 37 (1981): 5–27.

11. See, for example, the distribution of cultures in Sanday's research on sexual violence.

12. See Eleanor E. Maccoby and Carolyn N. Jacklin, *The Psychology of Sex Differences* (Berkeley: Stanford University Press, 1974), 227–47, esp. 242.

13. Maccoby and Jacklin, *Psychology of Sex Differences*, 246.

14. For example, see Philip Jenkins, *Pedophiles and Priests: Anatomy of a Contemporary Crisis* (New York: Oxford University Press, 1996), and Eleanor Burkett and Frank Brunni, *A Gospel of Shame: Children, Sex Abuse and the Catholic Church* (New York: Doubleday, 1992).

15. See William Schoedel, "Same Sex Eros: Paul and the Graeco-Roman Tradition" (paper delivered to a conference at Brite Divinity School, Fort. Worth, Tex., Sept. 1996, and his appendix of translations of Pseudo-Aristotle [*Problems*, 4.26], Caelius Aurelianus [*De morbis chronicis* 4.9, 131–32], Parmenides [*On Nature*], Lactantius [*De opificio dei*, 12–13], and *De Victu* [1.28–29]).

16. Alfred Kinsey et al., *Sexual Behavior in the Human Male* (Philadelphia: Saunders, 1948), 648.

17. J. M. Bailey and R. Pillard, "A Genetic Study of Male Homosexual Orientation," *Archives of General Psychiatry* 48 (1991): 1089–96; J. M. Bailey, et al., "Heritable Factors Influence Sexual Orientation in Women," *Archives of General Psychiatry* 50 (1993): 217–23; J. M. Bailey and R. Pillard, "The Innateness of Homosexuality," *Harvard Mental Health Letter* 10 (1994): 4–6.

18. J. M. Bailey and K. Zucker, "Childhood Sex-Typed Behavior and Sexual Orientation: A Conceptual Analysis and Quantitative Review," *Developmental Biology* 31 (1995): 43–55; A. Bell, M. Weinberg, and S. Hammersmith, *Sexual Preference: Its Development in Men and Women* (Bloomington: Indiana University Press, 1981); R. Greene, *The "Sissy-Boy" Syndrome and the Development of Homosexuality* (New Haven: Yale University Press, 1987).

19. See the Congregation for the Doctrine of the Faith, "1975 Declaration on Certain Questions Concerning Sexual Ethics," in Anthony Kosnick et al., *Human Sexuality: New Directions in American Catholic Thought* (Mahwah, N.J.: Paulist Press, 1977).

20. Congregation for the Doctrine of the Faith, "Letter to the Bishops of the Catholic Church on the Pastoral Care of Homosexual Persons, " in *The Vatican and Homosexuality*, ed. Jeannine Grammick and Pat Furey (New York: Crossroad, 1988), 1–10

21. The Old Testament is clearly pro-natalist, with the primary purpose for both women and sex being procreation in marriage. The New Testament, unlike the Old Testament, does not regard marriage (implicitly understood as procreative) as normative, but neither does it alter the existing understanding of procreation as the principle purpose of marriage.

22. See, as noted above, Cahill's *Sex, Gender and Christian Ethics*, which makes a compelling case for the need for a dialogical method based on analogical reason applied to human experience but suggests Thomas as a methodological model.

23. See Catherine Keller, "The Lost Fragrance: Protestantism and the Nature of What Matters," *Journal of the American Academy of Religion* 65, no.2 (1997): 355–70.

24. Patriarchal here refers to a system of social order in which a select group of males controls women, children, subordinate males of their own group, and entire populations of other groups. Early patriarchal systems involved male heads of families controlling other extended family members, slaves, and servants; later forms include not only household or clan

rule, but also colonial, postcolonial, and contemporary postindustrial forms of social organization in which small groups of homogenous males control larger heterogeneous social units.

25. Matt. 19:6 or Mark 10:9.

26. Virtually all of the discussions of sex and gender that arise in Acts and the epistles are either mentions of the practice of the earliest church (the references to Phoebe, Priscilla, Mary Magdelene, Junia, and their leadership functions; the baptismal formula of Gal. 3:28) or exhortations to drop such countercultural practices and adopt the Roman household codes (Col. 3:18–4:1; Eph. 5:22–6:9).

27. Peter Brown, *The Body and Society: Men, Women and Sexual Renunciation in Early Christianity*. (New York: Columbia University Press, 1988).

28. By 1993 3.5 million couples were cohabiting in the United States, a 120% increase over the previous decade, and a 700% increase over 1970 (S. Nock, "A Comparison of Marriages and Cohabiting Relationships," *Journal of Family Issues* 16 [1995]: 53–76; R. Famighetti, ed., *The World Almanac and Book of Facts* [New York: St. Martin's Press, 1995]). There is, however, some evidence that cohabiting relationships as tests do not necessarily produce more permanent marriages. While a number of studies show no impact of cohabitation on subsequent marriage, either for better or for worse, some studies, most recently, show that cohabitation before marriage produces higher failure rates and lower rates of marital satisfaction.

29. Ninety percent of adults in the United States still marry, some more than once, and the majority of cohabiting individuals also marry (Robert Crooks and Karla Baur, *Our Sexuality*, 6 ed. ([Pacific Grove, Calif.: Brooks-Cole Publishing, 1996], 389).

30. René Girard, *Job: Victim of His People* (Berkeley: Stanford University Press, 1987).

3

KATHLEEN M. SANDS

Public, Pubic, and Private

Religion in Political Discourse

In recent decades, religion in America has gone both public and pubic, not only for the Right, but for the wide swaths of the "middle" who live under the dispensation of "family values." This image of religion in America, of course, is distorted: it leaves out the diversity of belief and unbelief, and the diversity—not to say pitched battles—*within* most religious groups on matters social and sexual. Religious progressives, in particular, are missing faces in snapshots of the national "family." And that is not simply due to the shortcomings of religious progressivism itself. The effective identification of religion with social conservatism rests on economic and ideological forces that are global in scope, as other essays in this volume ably document. But precisely because the course and character "religion" are bound at every point to the political economy, to query this category may allow us to imagine a public ethic that is less fixedly pubic and a religious discourse that is more authentically public.

Curiously, both secular liberals and conservatism (religious and social) tend to presume that sexuality and reproduction, primarily of the strictly conventional sort, are the central concerns of religion. The difference is that while secular liberals, precisely for this reason, want religion consigned to the "private," conservatives for the very same reason are calling religion out of its private enclaves, to restore the supposed foundations of social life. Progressive religion, still more curiously, combines these approaches. With respect to sexuality and reproduction, it tends to speak the language of secularism, but when it comes to economic, social, and political issues, it prophesies boldly in the public square. However, progressive religion does not offer clear accounts of why the sexual aspects of religious ethics, in particular, should not be "imposed" in public. Nor has it adequately explained why the social aspects of religious ethics should be "imposed" on citizens in a democratic polity for whom the highest standards of religious ethics are supposed to be voluntary.

In fact, and this lies at the center of the riddle, "religion" is bound to not one but two sorts of "privates," not only to sexuality but also to private property, and through it to every sort of "public." This second marriage is more secret, for private property, under the aegis of secularism, is distinctly *not religion*. Therefore, it is not socially accountable in the ways religions might require; economic justice becomes charity; and charity, as the provision of 1996 (discussed below) puts it, is a "choice." But this exemption from accountability also makes private property like religion; no more than religious beliefs do economic motives need to justify themselves publicly or in terms of a common good. Economic privates, in this sense, enjoy both the legitimations of the private and those of the public. And religion plays a central role in constructing each sort of legitimation, because the definition of "religion" simultaneously delineates what is "not religion"—notably, the state, the market, and the academy. Each of these realms is said to be open to all rather than restricted, based on rational procedures and mechanisms rather than on tradition or revelation, driven by choice and desire rather than by rules, rituals, and authority. Finally, and this draws the circle into a knot, the structures of sexual life, while ostensibly given to the custody of religion, are profoundly imbricated with these public realms. How family is defined, for example, decisively influences the access of women to political and economic power; and the tolerance (or intolerance) of sexual difference profoundly affects whether gay and lesbian people can participate in democratic processes.

In these ways, the division between religion/not religion, like that between private/public, legitimates what lies on both sides of it. Rather than invoking these distinctions to resolve public issues, the distinctions themselves must be carefully interrogated. Whose "privates" are covered and whose are exposed by these divisions as they currently operate? Who is called to public account and who is not? Who gets to own their "privates" and whose privates are owned by others? Whose private views and interests sit unnoticed in the public arena, and whose raise a stir?

This essay will interrogate the category of "religion" under two crossed spotlights, one trained on the right to sexual dissidence and the other on poverty, social provision, and the right to work. In the first case, progressive religionists tend to retreat from public ethical discourse on secularist principles. Here I aim to show how the religious/secular division serves conservative ends, and how progressives, both religious and not, may lay claim to the public power now monopolized by conservative religion. In the second case, progressive religionists are already taking ever more active public roles but also risk becoming agents of conservative sexual mores and hence a conservative political economy. Here my aim is to suggest how progressives might exercise this public leadership in ways that, rather than consigning social provision to charity, calls citizens and government to their appropriate responsibilities.

Religion and Gay/Lesbian Rights[1]

Progressive Perspectives

Reviewing the range of American religious views concerning homosexuality, what stands out immediately is the depth and intensity of disagreement, not only between but within religious bodies. Popular representation to the contrary, *there is in fact no single or coherent "religious" position on homosexuality in America.* It is true that the two largest denominations in the United States—Roman Catholicism and the Southern Baptists, respectively—remain morally opposed to homoeroticism and politically opposed to gay civil rights legislation. But the religious picture in the United States includes far more than these two denominations, and even within these two the situation is more complex than one might guess from the media.

For example, the decriminalization of consensual same sex acts in private has been officially supported for decades by many religious groups. The United Church of Christ issued the first such statement in 1969; since then it has been joined by (among others) the Presbyterian Church USA (1970 and 1978), the Union of American Hebrew Congregations (1977), the Evangelical Lutheran Church in America (1970 and 1978), the Unitarian Universalist Association (1970), the Reformed Church in America (1978), and the Missouri Lutheran Synod (1981).[2] In many cases, this is linked with moral acceptance of homoeroticism in principle. Just as significantly, however, there are denominations, such as the Reformed Church and the Missouri Lutheran Synod, that support decriminalization while remaining firmly *opposed* to homosexual acts on moral grounds.[3] Though hardly a radical stance, decriminalization is nonetheless extremely significant as a political position, since anti-homosexual sodomy laws are still on the books in many states.[4] Moreover, in the infamous *Bowers* decision of 1986, the Supreme Court argued that homosexual sodomy could be criminalized because its moral proscription has "ancient roots"—further specified by Justice Warren Berger as "Judeao-Christian moral and ethical standards."[5]

In addition to supporting decriminalization, many religious groups urge their members to take active leadership in promoting the human and sometimes the civil rights of gay and lesbian people.[6] Again, this is especially striking when accompanied by disapproval of homoeroticism itself. The Church of the Brethren (1983), while morally opposing homosexual behavior under all circumstances, nonetheless pledged itself to "challenging openly the widespread fear, hatred and harassment of homosexual persons" and "advocating the right of homosexuals to jobs, housing and legal justice."[7] In October 1997 the Roman Catholic bishops wrote that "all of us must strive to eliminate any form of injustice, oppression, or violence, against [homosexuals]."[8] Even some extremely conservative denominations—for example, the Church of the Latter Day Saints—acknowledge that homosexuals have been subject to "bias" and "social injustice."[9]

Same-sex marriage is a particularly salient issue for religions in the United States, since the civil rite of marriage may also be a religious rite, as Rebecca Alpert discusses in this volume. In some cases—among them, the North Pacific Yearly Meeting, the Metropolitan Community Church, the Unitarian Universalist Association, and Reconstructionist Judaism—same sex marriage is heartily endorsed as both a civil and a religious rite.[10] In other cases, religious groups support same-sex marriage or its contractual equivalent as a civil right, even though the denomination itself is not prepared to perform these ceremonies as religious rites. The United Methodist Church, within the same declaration, asserted that homosexual practices are "incompatible with Christian teaching" and that it is "a clear issue of simple justice" to protect the rights of homosexual persons who have "shared material resources, pensions, guardian relationships, mutual powers of attorney."[11] Internally, however, the denomination remains intensely divided on whether clergy should perform same-sex marriage, with official governance bodies responding resoundingly in the negative.[12] Similarly, the Central Conference of American Rabbis (Reform) Judaism has publicly supported civil same-sex marriage and opposed the Defense of Marriage Act (1996) yet remains divided on whether rabbis may perform the ceremonies.[13]

The ordination of gay clergy, while a strictly religious matter, deserves mention as a particularly salient measure of religious diversity concerning homosexuality. This is certainly the issue on which it is most difficult for religions to "go all the way" in regard to lesbian and gay rights. Yet even in this area there is far more support for lesbians and gays than one would glean from popular representations. Unitarian Universalism, Reconstructionist Judaism, and the Metropolitan Community Church all happily ordain qualified homosexuals, without any demand for sexual abstinence. And, while many religious groups do have moral concerns about homosexually active clergy, most of these regard homosexuality as a more or less fixed condition. The denial of ordination on the basis of orientation alone would therefore seem unjust; the contested issue instead becomes whether a candidate intends to "practice" homosexuality after ordination. That has become the controverted question among Presbyterians, Episcopalians, United Methodists, in the United Church of Christ, and even in the Roman Catholic Church.[14]

In religious groups that continue to officially oppose homosexuality, internecine controversy typically persists, indicating that moral equilibrium has not yet been reached. For many denominations, an interim strategy is to devolve many policy decisions on homosexuality to the local level. Examples include the Presbyterian "More Light" churches, the "Open and Affirming" congregations within the United Church of Christ, and the "Reconciling Congregations Program" of the United Methodist Church.[15] The Episcopal Church in the United States, which includes many progressives, has had to contend with the condemnation of same-sex marriage by the Lambeth Conference and by a number of U.S. Episcopal bishops. The solution, for the time being, is that bishops are not censured for implementing same-sex marriage at the diocesan level. At the local as well as the national level, gay-affirmative laity have organized within virtually every religious denomination in the United States. The Catholic group "Dignity," founded in 1969, was one of the first, and it has been followed by dozens of others.[16] Such groups have now existed for decades, even in the face of official opprobrium, and are proliferating so quickly that it is virtually impossible to track them all.

Why, then, has this wide and turbulent range of views had so little public visibility? Why has it not become a stimulus for democratic debate about the politics of sexuality, the politics of religion, and the intersection of the two? Why does "religion" now function almost exclusively to authorize the repression of sexual difference, usually in fierce opposition to large segments of its own adherents? Again, the inefficacy of progressive religion is due to forces that are social, economic, and political, rather than simply ideological. We should not expect that these power relations will be transformed simply through adjustments of theology or political rhetoric. Nonetheless, the weak points of progressive religious ideology are also the points at which the impressions of these material forces are most clearly evident, and therefore the point where critical reflection has to begin.

I want to suggest three such weaknesses, which together illuminate the unique problematic of religion as a problem in American political discourse. First, many progressive religious positions on homosexuality rely on a dubious appeal to the notion of a fixed homosexual orientation—in other words, an argument from "nature." Secondly, this argument from "nature" is meant to minimize or obscure the challenges that sexual minorities might represent to hegemonic norms; hence it obstructs just the sort of public ethical expression and public ethical deliberation that are needed around controverted issues of sexuality. Thirdly, progressive religionists continue to rely on ideals of public and private that legitimate both the "religious" and the "secular" and that construct "religion" in a way that can only ratify, not critique, hegemonic norms. Finally, I will propose that the inscrutable category of religion be demystified, its inappropriate powers be deflated, and its appropriate political claims be extended to all communities of conscience—including those that support homoeroticism. On that basis, and only on that basis, I am suggesting, can a more rational, more ethical, and more democratic discourse about homosexuality in America be accomplished.

The Gay "Nature" Argument

Many progressive religious groups have founded their support for gay rights on the claim that some individuals are gay either by nature or by a disposition sufficiently fixed that it could be considered "second nature." In Bible-based theologies, this arguably implies that homosexuality is part of the creation that God declared "very good." Versions of this argument have appeared in the official declarations or publications of most religious groups or organizations that support gay rights.[17]

The nature argument does reflect the self-understanding of many who experienced homoerotic feelings well before they knew what those feelings were and even when they dearly wished such feelings would disappear. However, although for many individuals homoerotic patterns are *de facto* permanent, the attribution of this to a fixed or innate "orientation" is itself entirely historically contingent. The English term "homosexuality" has been in use for little more than a hundred years. Moreover, as most historians of sexuality today agree, the very notion of "sexuality" as a fixed and central component of "identity" is equally recent.[18] We should also bear in mind that the components of "sexual identity"—say, desire and fantasy versus sexual practice, or self-understanding versus social designation—do not always operate in concert. I could experience lesbian desires but not act on them, or engage in lesbian sex without desire; I could be thought of by others as lesbian but not so regard myself—or any other mix and match of "identity" pieces. What does it mean to speak of such a complex psycho-social reality as fixed or innate? In particular, what does it mean to say of a woman that she "could not be otherwise" than homosexual? That sort of self-description corresponds best to male sexual experience, in which the absence of erection is likely to bring "sex" to a halt, given how "sex" is likely to be defined. When asserted by a lesbian, "I cannot be otherwise" can bespeak a self-affirmation that is most salutary, or a suffering that is most genuine. Or perhaps both. Yet in either case it is constrained or enabled by social circumstance for women in very particular ways. As a glance through human history quickly reminds us, "sex" has not depended much on the desire or satisfaction of women—and for this, sadly, the species owes its females considerable gratitude.

Appealing to a fixed or innate homosexual orientation may seem expeditious also because it directly counters some of the most vociferous religious opponents of gay rights. For example, the Southern Baptist Convention insists that homosexuality is a "lifestyle" and hence a culpable choice.[19] However, this cannot be theologically checked by the assertion that homosexuality is innate or "natural," because in Christian theology, nature is regarded as "fallen." After the Fall, all creation—including human nature—is viewed as *disoriented* in relation to God.[20] That is why the Roman Catholic magisterium, although referring to a "permanent" or "constitutive" homosexuality for more than twenty-five years, has remained all the while a stalwart opponent of gay civil rights.[21] For official Catholicism, a homosexual constitution is one of the many "objectively disordered states" arising from "man's innate weakness following original sin."[22] It is cause for sympathy, not for blame, but also, most assuredly, not for celebration.

The designation of a homosexual nature, then, need not lead to support for homosexual lives, rights, or relationships. It can function in precisely the opposite way. By distinguishing the "condition" as involuntary from the acts as voluntary, a religious body can offer an acceptance to "homosexual persons" that it strictly withholds from "homosexual acts." And because the "acts" are not supported, neither are the persons when they "enact" their sexuality by living uncloseted lives. Unfortunately, it is just then that these persons need civil rights protection, because it is just then that they incur violence and discrimination.

"Nature," as the basis of rights, has a long pedigree within Western thought. For many gay civil rights advocates, religious and secular, it has the apparent advantage of linking homosexual civil rights with those of racial minorities. However, racial divisions themselves are hardly fixed and natural, as attested by the intensive legal and social means that have been deployed to *make and keep* the "races" separate.[23] Moreover, the analogy with race betrays the normative issues at stake in the gay rights debate by tacitly assuring the presumably heterosexual "majority" that homosexuality is not contagious and will not increase its numbers with social tolerance. To the conservative argument that activists are trying to "promote" homosexuality, one can then reply that it is no more possible to promote homosexuality than, say, to promote green eyes.

The heart of the conflict, however, *is* normative: it is about whether homosexuality is healthy or pathological, righteous or sinful, attractive or repulsive. And neither temporally nor logically does the normative evaluation of homosexuality simply follow from empirical or historical findings. Even Dean Hamer, a leading re-searcher in the ill-conceived search for a "gay gene," recognizes that a genetic dis-position toward homosexuality could be assessed as a pathological mutation just as easily as a normal variation.[24] Whether we are concerned about sex, race, or sexu-ality, normative judgments preexist and determine the empirical designation of fixed natures. "Naturally," the reverse seems to be true; this is precisely the ideologi-cal sleight of hand that makes biases based on supposedly "natural" features (such as sex, race, or sexuality) seem so compelling. But the dynamism of discrimination is not that people are treated badly because they belong to a particular class; that would presume that the class and its significance were simply given as neutral facts. As legal scholar Janet Halley has incisively argued, discrimination classes people in a particular way *so that* they may be treated badly, something the Supreme Court it-self has acknowledged in a much discussed 1938 case.[25] Constitutionally, Halley ar-gues, the question is whether law or policy are drawing a boundary against a group for purposes of discrimination. If so, *it is the boundary-drawing itself that is unjust.*[26]

Perhaps the greatest appeal of the "gay natures" argument is its congruence with popular gay rights discourse, in particular with the rhetoric of secular gay rights groups such as the Human Rights Campaign. Whatever political efficacy this ever possessed has been seriously diminished with the emergence of a kind of anti-gay ac-tivism that has recast homosexual civil rights as homosexual "special" rights. Al-though most of these activists belong to the Religious Right, it is well worth noting that their rhetorical strategy, which has been extremely effective, relies neither on re-ligious language nor on judgments about the fixity of homosexuality. Instead they argue, based on highly skewed data, that homosexuals already enjoy a disproportion-ate degree of economic and cultural power.[27] Whenever and wherever they live quiet (read: "closeted") lives, it is asserted, homosexuals already enjoy perfect social toleration. What "gay civil rights" demand is the right to publicly affirm homoeroti-cism as good (i.e., to live uncloseted lives) without incurring the social sanctions that would "normally" follow. And that, claim these activists, amounts to the "promotion" of homosexuality.[28] Whether homosexuality is a perversion or a disability, a willful choice or a desperate compulsion—is rendered, ingeniously, quite irrelevant. The point is that it is bad, and seriously so. To accept or even recommend a pathology is, after all, just as perverse as to recommend wickedness. Moreover, indifference to pathology is callous, and nonacceptance of a pathology, even on behalf of those who accept it for themselves, may seem deeply compassionate.

Normative Questions

So we are forced back to the very normative issues that the appeal to homosexual natures was meant to avoid. If sexuality is not "fixed" or immutable, then the un-closeted visibility of gay and lesbian persons does "promote" homoeroticism. For example, the high school student with an openly gay teacher may well find homo-sexuality more understandable and imaginable, even attractive and compelling. She may have, indeed, a greater risk/hope of "becoming gay." But the salient ques-tion is: why would that be bad? Why would an increased range of sexual inquiry and choice not be good for this student and for the rest of us as well? If homosexuality is not just a "given," but partakes of choice, then one *can* reasonably be asked to defend that choice—either its content or simply the value of its availability as a choice. Most startling of all, if homosexuality partakes of choice, then so does heterosexuality—and one must either defend *that* choice or explain why the absence of choice about heterosexuality is socially necessary or good.

But to say that sexuality does and should involve choice is also to say that the range of appropriate moral choice in sex itself is wider than convention and religious tradition would have us acknowledge. For example, as Christine Gudorf argues in this volume, homoeroticism and other contemporary trends underline sexual pleasure as a distinct good, in and of itself.[29] But if pleasure is given normative weight, then traditional religious criteria such as monogamy and procreation (which were not formulated to foster sexual pleasure!) cannot but be subject to reexamination. Moreover, homoeroticism and other forms of sexual dissent render more visible the *variety and incommensurability* of the various functions of sex. Sex can do many things besides stabilizing a nuclear couple for purposes of childrearing and/or relational intimacy. It can express love, enact aggression, share pleasure or withhold it, or enhance one's ego. It can enable survival, dominate or humiliate partners, foster intensity of experience, calm and comfort, betray or get even with a spouse or partner. It can make babies or make money, seal a commitment or explore fantasies. And so forth.

The ethical conundrum is not simply that the goods of sex may not go together in one particular type of sexuality—that procreation and love, or pleasure and procreation, may separate in a given instance or for a given population. The conundrum, first of all, is that these and other values that can be advanced through sex just do not go together in any intrinsic way. Sexual pleasure is not automatically or easily confined to the bounds of interpersonal commitment; the exigencies of survival may defy those of self-actualization within one's sexual life; the expression of love for a partner may not be accompanied by intensity of personal experience. If so, then it is extremely difficult, if not impossible in principle, for every instance of sex to accomplish every good thing that sex can do. The salient moral question then becomes, not whether all the putative goods of sex (say, love, pleasure, commitment, economic stability) fit in each and every sexual act or relationship, but rather whether those goods are present in the totality of a person or community's life. Moreover, the harms of sex, which can be substantial, are not easily separable from the goods. Worst of all, we do not always agree on which is which—not even with the person on the next pillow. If this points to the seriousness of sex as an ethical issue, it also shows how wide range of freedom is needed for citizens to envision and enact their own versions of sexual ethics.

To affirm sexual diversity and dissent is to recognize that people have distinct and often incompatible views of what makes a sexual life good or bad (or, at least, good enough or too bad). More than that, it recognizes that these disagreements may be both profound and legitimate. That does not mean that everything that can be done with sex ought to be done with it, either in personal life or in social life. Even libertarians agree that sex that involves violence or coercion should be proscribed by law and policy. And prohibitions of violence and coercion, while necessary for constraining harm through sex, are hardly sufficient as goods of sex. That is why it is important not to conflate sexual ethics with sexual regulation, as do many sex radicals. At the interpersonal level, we do well to reflect on how to conduct our sexual lives in ways that are gratifying and just—and most of us do badly when we do not so reflect. At the collective level, citizens do need to recognize that there are different accounts of the goods and harms of sex, to discern the arenas in which those purported goods and harms occur (i.e., whom they really affect and how), and to deliberate about the means appropriate within those different arenas. All this belongs to the realm of sexual ethics, and to the aspects of social ethics that bear on sex and reproduction. But only a small part of these ethics could be used to justify sexual regulation—only when it is established that public interests are at stake, when it is agreed what those public interests are, and when the interests are sufficiently vital to justify coercive measures.

This is where, politically speaking, the going gets particularly rough. For in addition to cultivating extremely different versions of what constitutes personal good and harm, Americans also hold disparate and dissonant versions of social life and the common good. Most progressives, like most libertarians, argue that law and policy ought to concern themselves only with constraining those harms that can be understood as violence.[30] I concur, not because there is no social interest in other goods and harms of sex, but because there are many and far more constructive ways for citizens to exert ethical influence upon each other than through political force. I would not concur, however, with the facile remanding of sexual matters to the "private," sphere, because discernment of the "public," the "private," and the appropriate relation between them must itself be a matter for democratic deliberation, as the aftermath of *Roe* (1973) and *Bowers* (1986) has made abundantly evident. The language of privacy, tolerance, inclusivity, and deregulation can function just as absolutistically as do conservative religious claims and can obstruct communication just as much.

One example of failed ethical deliberation is the way in which monogamy is sometimes invoked in debates about family and sexuality. Lasting and monogamous sexual relationships are of deep personal value to many Americans; while for many others this ideal may be descriptively or normatively inadequate. Ethical expression, debate, and experimentation concerning monogamy and non-monogamy are therefore appropriate and salubrious. It would be quite inappropriate, however, to appeal to monogamy as an argument either for or against gay *civil* rights. For example, in a televised debate with an anti-gay religious activist, Andrew Sullivan protested: "If I had a boyfriend and we actually had a loving relationship in our own home, you believe in upholding laws that would imprison us for that behavior."[31] It is true, of course, that gay and lesbian people are as capable of marital love as is anyone else. But what bearing should this have on the decriminalization of homosexual sodomy? Would straight citizens be willing to stake the privacy of their own bedrooms, their freedom from imprisonment, their bodily self-determination, and their intimate associations on how the majority of their fellow citizens assess the quality of their particular sexual relationships? When discussions go like this, it is a sign that something crucial is missing—on the one hand, discernment of the spheres of life that are at issue (e.g., interpersonal life vs. citizenship); on the other hand, robust debate about sexual ethics rather than the ritual invocation of moral conventions. Public discourse about sex and reproduction can and must be ethical discourse, but the ethics are those proper to the public sphere, discerning the common good and concerned with the quality of social life as a whole

The Public and the Private

As we have seen, progressive and moderate religionists tend to ally themselves with secularism on the question of gay rights, as on the question of abortion. Relying on the notion that certain ethical matters are private, they often fail to articulate the public ethic within which the "private" is delineated in this particular way.[32] They do not justify the availability of homoeroticism as a positive social good. Such as explanation could be possible even for denominations with moral compunctions about homoeroticism; there are many good reasons why a liberal democracy should tolerate a multitude of behaviors and an even greater multitude of beliefs that the majority of citizens see as wrong. For religious groups that find moral good in homoeroticism, it is important to articulate how those goods are also *social* goods— how, for example, the availability of homoerotic relations can contribute to gender equality and hence to the equality of citizens, or how same-sex marriage might contribute to the economic security of families.

The need for genuinely public progressive ethics has become much more pressing over the past two decades, as conservative religionists have imported their religious ethics ever more whole cloth into the public sphere. For example, the Southern Baptist Convention made its case against gay rights legislation explicitly in terms of religious authority: all homosexual practices "are sin and are condemned by the word of God"; members were therefore urged to actively oppose laws that "under the deceptive guise of human rights, have the effect of giving public approval to the homosexual lifestyle."[33] Arguing against proposed gay rights legislation, the Catholic bishops of Massachusetts lamented the "common perception in our country that whatever is declared legal, by that very fact, becomes morally right," substantiating this with reference to "the tragic abortion experience of the past ten years."[34] Cardinal Ratzinger, writing for the Vatican in 1986, put these vestigial theocratic aims in unmistakable terms, fulminating against "civil legislation to protect behavior to which no one has any conceivable right" and warning that, where such legislation is passed, we should not be surprised if "irrational and violent reactions increase."[35]

Citizens, given the legal latitude to reach different moral conclusions than do these religious denominations, obviously might do so. This alone is sufficient reason for legally constraining moral freedom, in the opinion of the Southern Baptist Convention and the Catholic hierarchy. How can a denomination oppose gay rights on grounds that are common neither to all citizens, nor to all religious denominations in the United States, nor even to a consensus of their own members? More to the point, how can these political positions be held by denominations that simultaneously and (let us grant) seriously claim to support religious freedom?

An answer may be found in a closer analysis of the "secular" public sphere. In his well-known study of the division of American religion along liberal-conservative lines, Robert Wuthnow found that religionists tend to become politically active only when they feel that the political sphere is violating their basic beliefs and values.[36] When mainline religion appears absent in the public arena, it is because the public sphere is already felt to covertly embody its central social norms. That may explain why conservative denominations act as if the "privacy" of their religion is somehow violated by religiously disobedient sexual beliefs and behavior, even when performed by citizens who are in no way under the authority of their religion—and especially when the dissident behavior or belief is protected under civil law.

Dominant groups, whether religious, social, or economic, experience their "privates" as extending well into the public; indeed, their "private" beliefs and interests tacitly constitute the public in fundamental ways. This tacit ownership of the collective "public" by particular "privates" can only occur because the public sphere does not accrue its fundamental coherence and stability by means of law and policy. On the contrary, the public is given shape and efficacy through conventions, norms, and values that "go without saying"—in other words, hegemonic norms. These unarticulated norms are exempt from the sorts of open inquiry, negotiation, and reason on which public life is supposedly predicated. Under the dispensation of secularism, religion too is exempted (or excluded, depending on one's viewpoint) from public inquiry, from the need to explain itself rationally or negotiate its claims in relation to others. In this way, religion becomes the perfect reliquary for hegemonic norms, ostensibly exerting no influence on public life but tacitly providing norms that serve *status quo* and that are never required to defend themselves. So when hegemonic norms are threatened—as they are in the debate about gay rights—"religion" is openly asserted as their basis, and the type of religion asserted will be authoritarian, absolute, non-negotiable, and intelligible only to believers. That is why counter-hegemonic views, such as support for gay rights, simply do not register publicly with the credibility and authority of "religion." In other words, it is not that opposition to gay rights gains its public authority by being "religious"; it is that views of homosexuality can only gain public authority as religious to the extent that they support the *status quo*.

Theorists of sexuality have a name for the private space that is really the hegemonic public space, the space where normative religion and normative sexuality are secretly joined—that is the "closet." As Eve Sedgwick has pointed out, the aim of the closet is less to make homosexuality invisible than to make *heteronormativity* invisible. Heterosexuality must appear as a natural state of affairs, rather than as a rule imposed by intimidation, coercion, and violence; only thus can it maintain an unexamined privilege.[37] As I argued above, this privilege, its coercion, and its violence are not undone by exposing the existence of sexual "minorities" who are "minor" exceptions to the norm but who do not contest the norm itself. In the same way, it is not enough to expose the existence of religious groups that support gay rights or the decriminalization of homoeroticism. The closet is not dismantled by "outing" the minorities, but only by "outing" the very norms that define these minorities as such. To "out" what goes as "religion" is to force it to come out from behind its *de jure* status as private and voluntary, and to expose its *de facto* status as public, political, and, to a significant degree, coerced.

When it comes to matters of sexuality, progressive religions generally do not "out" the dominant norms, because they are not prepared to question the context within which gay people are made into problematic minorities. Nor, evidently, are they prepared to question the construct of "religion," since often their argument on behalf of gay rights is simply that religious values should not be "imposed" in the public sphere. I would agree that a sexually capacious public sphere is a good in itself, and that our public sphere could and should be made more capacious. But this is different than implying, as appeals to religious and sexual privacy often do, that the public sphere can or should be sheerly neutral with respect to values. For one thing, this approach will always tend to reinforce conventional norms, because these are the norms that appear neutral—i.e., obvious and commonsensical—to most people. More profoundly, the problem is with the notion of secularism at work in this approach, which constructs religion as a composite of special exclusions and special privileges.

Secularists, including religious progressives on matters of sexuality, want the exclusions without the privileges—e.g., the disqualification of views from public discourse simply because they are religious. Conservatives want the privileges without the exclusions—e.g., the absolutizing of particular moral standards simply because they are religious. But these unique privileges and exclusions provoke and enable each other, together constructing the category of "religion" on which both conservative and progressive religionists rely for their peculiar legal and social standing. And "religion," as I have already suggested, validates that which is "not religion" as objective, inclusive, open, neutral, and fair. Religious believers and institutions, too, have much at stake in these realms that are "not religion," particularly in the market and state. Since the religion/not religion division, like the public/private division, serves the *status quo* on both sides of it, social critique and imagination will be inhibited by appealing to either.

Sexual Dissent and Religious Freedom

Once the argument about freedom of sexuality is understood not only as an argument from "privacy," but as a matter of public and political ethics, sexual dissidents can lay claim to the moral ground hitherto available only to religion. To put it differently, gay and lesbian rights would no longer have to be construed, in the manner of a naive secularism, as freedom *from* religion or ethics. Instead, the right to sexual dissidence could be understood as a freedom of conscience, speech, and association—in other words, as something very much *like* freedom of religion. This provides, as a first advantage, an alternative to the problematic "like race" arguments for gay civil rights. And, indeed, sexual differences are more like religious differences than they are like racial differences. Like religion, a sexual preference that is consistently affirmed and lived becomes central to one's self-understanding, behavior, style, and community—that is, to one's "identity." Also like religion (at least in the American context), choice and belief determine where you will land just as much, and maybe more, than does where you were planted by history or biology.

Recalling the positions of progressive denominations, it is clear that gay and lesbian rights are quite literally connected with religious freedom, since anti-gay law and public policy are in effect based on an illegitimate preference for one type of religious position over another. But the analogy goes farther, allowing us to name the "religious" functions that pervade the supposedly secular realm. Heteronormativity, in effect, is a religion—a set of beliefs, rituals, and moral commitments that explain and regulate the life of a community; this would be so even if heteronormativity were not underwritten by what is conventionally called "religion." Therefore, as historian Lisa Duggan not quite facetiously proposed, queer activists might well be "the new dis-establishmentarians, the state religion we wish to dis-establish being that of heteronormativity."[38]

Granted, sexual dissidents hardly agree with each other on everything, but nor do many religious bodies. In Duggan's words, sexual dissidents are connected by "a constellation of non-conforming practices, expressions and beliefs."[39] Inasmuch as they claim civil rights, sexual dissidents share the belief that it is right and just to publicly dissent from conventional sexual norms, and to do so without suffering undue sanctions such as the denial of physical safety, jobs, housing, or child custody. Anyone, straight or not, can join this "church." Anyone can believe that, in a democratic polity, the burden of proof must be upon those who would constrict the range of belief, association, and consensual sex, not upon those who would expand it. Anyone can believe that, because the goods that accrue to sexuality are so diverse, so incommensurable, and so central to human well-being, the world is a better place when dissident sexualities can be explored, fostered and, yes, *promoted*. But the right to promote these convictions does not depend in any way on whether sexual dissidents succeed in converting the world—any more than do the rights of Evangelical Christian or Quakers, Greenpeace or the National Rifle Association.

Construing gay rights in this way clearly connects these rights more with freedom of speech than with freedom of action. But this, argues Janet Halley, is appropriate in the post-Bowers era, when the Court has denied homosexuals freedom of action, even in private.[40] Moreover, freedom of speech is the key to exercising future influence over the laws that regulate behavior; it is the *sine qua non* of political participation. Since *Bowers*, the Court itself has recognized this right of political participation in striking down Colorado's Amendment Two, which would have preemptively disabled any future political activity by gay rights advocates.[41] Freedom of speech can also be a new basis for civil rights advocacy, Halley proposes. Because discrimination inhibits the free expression and hence the political participation of homosexuals, it can be argued, discrimination must be legislatively proscribed. It is worth noting, also, that the Court has also recently pared down freedom of religiously motivated action, when in 1997 it denied that religious freedom could justify violations of facially neutral law.[42]

The tensions and incoherences produced by the unique construct "religion" are not likely to be legislatively or judicially resolved in the near future. But they have at least begun to be widely recognized and, on the grassroots level, can be directly addressed. At the level of public discourse and political organizing, to dissolve the boundaries around "religion" would require progressive religionists and other gay rights advocates to welcome religion into the public conversations we create, but also to insist that religiously-based ethical claims be made intelligible and, like any other political claim, be subject to certain kinds of negotiation. It would call upon secular advocates, like religionists, to articulate their claims in terms of the common good and a public ethic. In so doing, they would finally lay claim to the public power hitherto monopolized by conservative religion.

The Welfare Debate

"Charitable Choice"

A new chapter for religion in the American public sphere was inaugurated in June 1996 with the passage of the Personal Responsibility and Work Opportunity Reconciliation Act (PRWORA). Defining poverty as fundamentally a matter of personal responsibility, the act aimed to reduce the "dependence" of poor families on government by discouraging "illegitimacy" and, via carrot and stick, transitioning poor parents into wage work. The stick is larger than the carrot, however. Any adult receiving assistance must be engaged, within twenty-four months, in an activity defined as work. Most often, these end up being minimum wage jobs, although certain unpaid activities such as community service may also count as work.[43] By the year 2002 states must show that 50% of all single parents and 90% of all two-parent families receiving aid are engaged in "work." And while data are kept as to the wages and benefits of recipients who are working, only random samples of such data are kept for those who, with or without jobs, go off the rolls. Clearly, the law is aimed primarily at the reduction of welfare rolls. Only in a secondary and contingent way is it concerned about whether poor parents actually get jobs, and its concern for viable wages and benefits ranges from transitory to nonexistent.

Even less is the law intended to ensure a minimal income for families. TANF (Temporary Aid to Needy Families) terminates the federal entitlement of individuals to cash assistance and stipulates that no individual may receive more than five years of aid in the course of a lifetime. States have complete flexibility in determining eligibility requirements and benefits levels. If states so choose they may legislate a "family cap"[44] or deny aid altogether to teenage parents. States may use TANF funds in any manner deemed consistent with the goals of TANF (e.g, reduction of "illegitimacy") and may transfer up to 30% of TANF funds to their social services or childcare block grants. In 2002, when current federal block grants end, states will be free to decide how and even whether to provide for the poor. At present, there is no telling what they, or the federal government, will do.

With the future presence of the public partner entirely in question, the law for the time being encourages social provision through "public-private" partnerships. It is in this context that "faith-based communities" have been invited to take an expanded role in social provision. The "Charitable Choice Provision" of the PRWORA is in one sense an antidiscrimination law; it stipulates that religious groups must be considered for contracts or voucher programs "on the same basis as any other non-governmental provider," provided that neither the Establishment clause, nor state provisions, nor the religious freedom of clients is compromised. In another sense, the discrimination now prohibited includes discretionary judgments that states, on the basis of complex judicial precedent, may well have felt obligated to make. For example, the provision not only allows religious providers to display religious symbols, but it also allows them to use a religious approach to assisting the needy, though clients cannot be made to actively participate in services and if they object to a provider's religious orientation they must have access to an alternative provider. Religious providers may not use contracted funds for sectarian purposes, but such restrictions do not apply under a voucher program.[45]

Doctrinaire secularists may be concerned that, as poor citizens rely on religious groups for survival, they will be subject to undue and possibly coercive religious influence. That is not the point of this argument. As a social services provider, religious groups may not be *especially* coercive; any provider, religious or not, will come to have undue and coercive power over poor citizens if poverty is redefined as a personal failing rather than a social responsibility. If poor women are pressured not to have children, scrutinized in their most intimate lives, or subjected to patronizing programs of moral reform—all of this will be no less oppressive or demeaning in settings where it is not "religious." Moreover, there are senses in which some religious providers may be especially suited to address the problem of poverty.

Progressive Religion and Social Provision

"Faith communities" include groups across the political spectrum, and, on this issue, the spectrum may be weighted to the Left. Progressive religious providers are often closer to poor communities than are secular agencies, and they are well acquainted with the damage poverty inflicts on the human spirit and community as well as on social and economic circumstances. They are equipped to organize communities rather than simply assist individuals, and many of them deliberately aim at building the political skills and "social capital" of poor communities.[46]

Progressive and moderate religionists also have the sorts of ethical framework within which poverty can be re-articulated as a social rather than a merely personal problem. Prior to the Personal Responsibility Act, dozens of religious groups laid out those frameworks, in statements insisting that the problem before America was poverty itself, not simply the welfare system.[47] Although many of these groups are prepared to partner with government for social provision, they insisted that government not abandon its part of this responsibility. As for "personal responsibility," they recognized work and family planning as incumbent on individuals but also urged government to shoulder its own proper burdens—e.g., legislating a minimum wage adequate to self and family support and ensuring the availability of health care and child care. Since 1996, many of these groups have been careful not to overlook the social and political aspects of poverty. The Campaign for Human Development, a project of Catholic Charities, is a good example; it has dispersed more than $500,000 in grants to support community organizing and citizen empowerment among the poor.[48] In early 1999 the Call to Renewal Conference brought religious agencies together to generate "public policy from below" aimed at eliminating poverty. Religious providers are also tracking the results of the new policies—for example, increased demands on food pantries and shelters, the percentage of former recipients who get jobs (about 50%), and the percentage of jobs with health benefits (about 25%).[49] In the future, religious providers might consider many other ways to put their social vision into action—for example, refusing to hire or place former recipients for less than a family wage.[50]

Nonetheless, progressive religionists can hardly view the current situation as a victory. During the legislative battle, the efforts of liberal religionists were mostly ineffective and in the end were reduced ultimately to the few concessions around issues such as the "family cap." In the near future, the risk of serious moral compromise or counterproductivity will increase, and the roots of those risks must be understood. Although there is no reason to specially exclude religious groups from assisting with social provision, it is important to ask why a new doorway in the supposed wall between church and state is opened just now and just for these purposes. Why is it now, as the problem of poverty is reduced to that of slashing welfare rolls, which is then reduced to an issue of sexual morality, that of "illegitimacy"—that the problem becomes newly "religious"? Why is it that now, as corporate capital grows ever more resistant to democratic controls, that social provision is transplanted to the child's garden of "charitable choice"?

Not withstanding the positive possibilities just enumerated, the political motives and outcomes of charitable choice may not be so sanguine. As if leaving a baby at the church door, government may be partnering with "faith-based communities" because these are the agencies that will be most morally unable to abandon the poor if it turns out that government is gone for good. And although progressive religionists try to emphasize social vision over sexual moralism, it is plainly the latter with which they have been publicly charged. How is "religion" being defined such that its *imprimatur* sticks only to the sexual moralism and not to the social vision? To refuse the charge of moralism and refute this definition of religion, it is not enough for progressives to merely downplay the sexual norms they are supposed to enforce. They have to understand and publicly articulate the way in which the social vision encoded in the term "illegitimacy" cannot be compatible with economic and political justice. The same applies to the questions of poverty and of work. If progressive religionists do not articulate the tensions between their own social vision and that which dominates the current political horizon, if they do not explicitly address the tensions and ambiguities within and between religious communities themselves on questions of economic, racial, and gender justice—then their public efforts can only work on behalf of those norms that "go without saying."

Religion, Women, and "the Family"

No tensions have been less adequately addressed than those surrounding welfare as a women's issue. As feminist thinkers have elucidated, childrearing is a form of social labor, a set of services upon which society absolutely relies, ordinarily performed by women and ordinarily unpaid.[51] To the degree that childrearing consumes their labor, women are made dependent on the financial support of men; marriage, in effect, becomes mandatory for them. This obviously compromises the reproductive and sexual freedom of women as individuals. But even disregarding the implications for the lives of individual women, it profoundly compromises the *citizenship* of childbearing women. Consigned to the "private," their access to economic, political, and social power becomes, at best, unsteady and inferior; at worst, entirely dependent on men. When the PRWORA pronounces that "marriage is the foundation of a successful society," it is presuming that this second-class citizenship of women does not count against social "success."

The sexual, economic, and political arrangements encoded in PRWORA's condemnation of "illegitimacy" are especially evident when one notices that the condemnation is not confined to teenagers or even to women in need of public assistance.[52] In other words, the issue of teen pregnancy is used to cover a general endorsement of the father-dependent family, and the enforcement of this patriarchal model is presumed to be the special province of "faith-based communities." In the last section I noted that once the hegemony of heterosexuality has been challenged, "religion" is openly invoked as its basis, despite the fact that citizens are supposed to be religiously free and despite the fact that there is not even a consensus among religious groups on this point. In a similar way, the married, heterosexual family is openly mandated by PRWORA as a condition of reproductive life, at precisely the point when this norm no longer fits the complex reality of American family life.[53] "Religion" is encouraged to execute this mandate because it is assumed that religions—at least, "legitimate" ones—exist fundamentally to conserve this and other hegemonic norms.

Ralph Reed complained of Aid to Families of Dependent Children (AFDC) that it made the state into the father.[54] In a sense, he was correct, but the point was to shore up the father-headed family, not to undermine it. AFDC (1961) grew out of Aid to Dependent Families (ADF; Title IV of the Social Security Act of 1935), which in turn evolved from state-level Mother's Aid laws. Both Mother's Aid pensions and ADF were entirely predicated on the economic dependence of women on men. They were intended for widowed mothers, husbandless through no "fault" of their own, and their purpose was to avoid or minimize the need for these women to work for wages. Moreover, these laws tied benefits to notions of motherly capacity, "racial welfare," and moral fitness that were intrusively monitored and that included such middle-class standards as chastity, church attendance, temperance, and "American" cooking.[55]

As many scholars have shown, these ideals of motherhood and family also expressed and sustained white racial domination. Of women receiving Mother's Aid pensions in 1931, 96% were white and 3% were black.[56] Under ADF, eligibility requirements were set by states, as a result of which discriminatory practices could continue at that level. Only in the 1960s and 1970s did African-American women enter the public assistance system in significant numbers, and that owed much to the organizing efforts of African-American women themselves through the National Welfare Rights Organization. AFDC was far more accessible to women of color than its predecessors had been, but unlike them it was distinctly not construed as a support for "good" wives and mothers. On the contrary, it came to be understood in terms derived from Daniel Patrick Moynihan's "Report on the American Negro Family," in which black families were cast as pathological due to their supposed "matriarchalism."[57] While Mother's Pensions had stigmatized African-American and other poor women for not staying home and rearing children, in the era of AFDC they would be stigmatized for doing just that. And while Mother's Pensions had denied them the supports that would have enabled them to stay at home with children, post-AFDC they were to be denied the conditions that would make it possible to sustain a family on wage work. Although criticized for "dependence," it would be in some senses more accurate to say that impoverished single mothers are stigmatized for their independence. Whether by choice or by circumstance, they are rearing children outside marriage, evidently (though not always truly) without the support or supervision of men. That has become socially intolerable, especially for African-American women, whose procreativity has for so long been placed at the sufferance of white men, as Traci West powerfully argues in this volume.[58]

Progressive and moderate religionists criticize the Religious Right's views of state and economy, but they have been far less bold in opposing conservative views of the family. In some cases, as Elizabeth Bounds shows with reference to the Evangelical Lutheran Church of America, that is because the middle-class nuclear family is tacitly assumed, although not actively defended.[59] Whatever the reason, it must be said that progressive religionists have not adequately voiced what is wrong with a society in which the cost of rearing children is the exclusion of women from public life and power. That they have either not undertaken this moral critique or have not declared it publicly cannot be unconnected with the fact that American religion today gains public authority almost exclusively when it serves as the guarantor of "family values." Progressive and moderate religionists know, tacitly or explicitly, that to speak against these social norms is to risk their authority as "religion."

The U.S. Catholic Conference (USCC) is a case in point. As if to underline their moral credentials in the welfare debate, the bishops' statement on welfare declared that "no institution is more committed to . . . marriage, family, responsibility, work, sexual restraint and sacrifice for children than our church." Despite their forceful argument that social and personal responsibility are complementary, the USCC was presuming a social order in which women are economically dependent on men. Individual responsibility was therefore thought to consist largely of compliance with the sexual and reproductive mores that uphold this particular social order. Sexual noncompliance, however, was the chief cause of social decay. For example, making teen pregnancy a root cause of poverty, they urged that it be fought "with at least as much vigor as we fight against teen smoking and substance abuse."[60] Because of their concomitant rejection of contraception and abortion, what the USCC says about teen pregnancy is also a statement about sex. From the get-go, sex is figured more a proclivity to addiction than an expression of health, affiliation, and liberty. Ethically, these assumptions are deeply problematic, both for their patriarchalism and for the ease with which they slip from serious social criticism to a sexually timorous moralism.

The targeting of teen pregnancy is not unique to Catholicism or indeed to the religious or political Right; President Clinton once labeled it "our most serious social problem."[61] In addition to their ethical shortcomings, such claims are also empirically dubious or simply incorrect. It is more accurate to say that poverty causes high rates of childbearing than to say that high rates of childbearing cause poverty, as has been widely and cross-culturally observed by scholars and policymakers alike. Moreover, as sociologist Kristin Luker shows, the "teen pregnancy" panic is predicated on misleading conflations of various categories, for example, birth rates and birth ratios, birth rate and pregnancy rate, teen motherhood and teen single motherhood, single motherhood and teen motherhood, single motherhood and unmarried motherhood. Contrary to political rhetoric, the birth rate among teens has actually declined dramatically and steadily from 1960 to present.[62] Single motherhood, however, has increased: one in three families is now headed by a never-married woman, according to Census Bureau statistics. But only one-third of those single mothers are teens. Due to the increase in cohabitation during these decades, and the fact that the welfare system itself has discouraged marriage, many unmarried mothers are not truly single but do in fact have partners who may assist them financially. Many single mothers are single due to divorce, and many are impoverished by divorce, while many other single mothers, including lesbian mothers, are able to support their children without any state assistance. All of these distinctions blur in the rhetoric of the supposed "teen pregnancy crisis" or "crisis of the family," which hides the profound lack of social consensus on the precise nature of the problem, the precise social interests at stake, and the appropriate solutions.

The most salient change in these decades is not a rise in teen motherhood as such, but a general decline in the marriage rate and a bifurcation of families into two kinds, reflecting the growing disparity between the affluent and the poor in these decades. In the affluent pattern, marriage is more common but is typically delayed, numbers of children decrease, and both parents are likely to work. In the poorer pattern, marriage rates decline, birth rates are higher, and childbearing is earlier.[63] Targeting "teen pregnancy" fudges on the question of whether the socially relevant concern is poverty or simply the maintenance of the two-parent family. More insidiously, it translates the causes of poverty from the economic and political realms to the realms of the sexual and renders this (mis)translation more plausible by naming a group (teenagers) over whose sexual behavior adult citizens arguably are entitled to some control. But the changed marriage rates and family patterns, like the changed economic circumstances, apply mainly to adult Americans. And since adults cannot as easily be represented as hormone-intoxicated, we have to ask why adults are making different choices than they used to, and take seriously these reasons.

Adult women, for example, are frequently choosing to delay marriage or not marry at all, to leave marriages in which they are unhappy or abused, or to live and rear children in same-sex couples. These choices are often constrained, sometimes extremely so, by the choices of men and by other external factors. For example, if William Julius Wilson is correct, marriage rates in poor African-American communities have declined as a result of job loss.[64] Nonetheless, the availability of contraception and the legality of abortion does increase the element of choice in women's childbearing.[65] Although there are still constraints on these choices, especially for poor and teenaged women, it is essential to regard all women as moral agents, striving within those constraints to make choices that are rational, practical, and principled. Among those considerations are all the factors, noted above, that count against the father-headed family or male-dominated marriage, as well as all those that count against middle-class marriage and family patterns for economically poor citizens.

Progressive religionists, in addition to facing these ethical and shortcomings and empirical distortions, have a responsibility to debunk the quasi-historical religious claims behind the father-headed nuclear family. The Religious Right would have us trace this social form, if not to Fred and Wilma Flintstone, at least to biblical times. But as Rosemary Ruether discusses in this volume, this model of family is no older than the nineteenth century. Even then, it pertained mainly to white and middle-class people; now, as noted above, it is not even accurate for them. Religious conservatives are certainly correct that patriarchalism is the assumed social world of the Bible, but it was enacted not through nuclear but through extended family forms—not a minor point given that extended family patterns today continue to be rendered invisible or made illegitimate by the nuclear norm. And, *contra* James Dobson, Christianity historically could not have had less "focus on the family." Until the Reformation (and for Catholicism, much more recently), Western Christianity saw religious celibacy rather than sexuality of any kind as the privileged expression of Christian spiritual life. Most significantly, patriarchalism is *now* widely questioned among religionists of every faith—just as are the racism, ethnocentrism, and imperialism that traditionally have characterized much human society and hence much religion. However these struggles for "religion" turn out, they must be recognized as real and utterly serious. In the meanwhile, religionists committed to gender and racial equality must therefore be very clear about what they are endorsing if and when they pledge support for "the family."

Religious Ethics of Poverty and Work

Progressive and moderate religious groups have emphasized that responsibility for poverty is at once individual and social. Though sound, this maxim is unilluminating unless one specifies what sort of society, and what sort of "individual," is presumed. Christianity, for example, has elaborated through most of its history a quite complex ethic of economic responsibility, but for the most part has not even aimed at the elimination of poverty as such, as Ruth Smith argues in an important essay.[66] Medieval Christianity posited that the non-poor and the voluntarily poor had a responsibility to give alms to those who were involuntarily poor. Unfortunately, the purpose of the almsgiving was to ensure the salvation of the *almsgivers*. And the beggar, in accepting these alms, was also accepting her own state of poverty as a part of this economy of salvation. Reformation Christianity, rejecting almsgiving as a spiritual "work," mandated a more genuine amelioration of poverty as a condition. Yet in dissolving the spiritual role of beggar, it also created a theological climate in which involuntary poverty could be read as personal vice or reprobation—in other words, distinctions between the "deserving" and the "undeserving" poor.

There has been much authentic *caritas* and even some radical movement for justice in this and other religious traditions on poverty. But to claim these strands, religionists must extricate them from histories that, in truth, contain much we should not wish to replicate. Most progressive and liberationist Christians know that, even as they assert the "preferential option for the poor" as moral doctrine. However, in the welfare debate they have not voiced these conflicts, present and past, very clearly or publicly. It is not hard to understand why, for to do so would again compromise the public power accruing to religion as the reliquary of unarticulated absolutes, and it is hard to relinquish absolutism when one's opponents are absolutists. A typical alternative strategy is to sacralize one's own position with an inspirational and indisputable religious ideal (e.g., the biblical God's interest in "widows and orphans"), without duly accounting for the fact that other adherents of the ideal appear to draw from it entirely different political conclusions.

Progressive religionists are seriously obligated to speak prophetically in and against their own histories on these matters, because it is in the context of these histories that poverty is being redescribed as more of a religious (and "personal") than political and economic problem. In the 1980s, along with the dramatic increase of street beggars in my semi-urban neighborhood, I was struck at how often those to whom I gave a bit of money would respond "God bless you." It was as if they were offering to reinstate the social contract of the Middle Ages, in which tokens of charity were offered to wrest God's blessing on wealth and to assuage the terrible dread that those who are not poor feel for those who are. The same social contract was iconographically represented by the African-American former welfare mothers who stood proudly at Clinton's shoulders as he signed the Personal Responsibility Act, as if by assuming "personal responsibility" they could erase the stain that public discourse had placed upon their moral reputations. Since that time, conservative religionists have kept up displays of moral reform by publicizing a steady stream of testimonials by former welfare recipients to the value of religious "tough love."[67] It is not hard to shame impoverished people for their poverty, but those who do should be ashamed to succeed. Poverty does damage spirit and community, but so does material comfort. And ugliest among the corruptions of comfort is the callous belief that poverty does not happen to good people.

Today, I would argue, the main public function of religion in regard to poverty is to render credible this belief, which despite its inhumanity functions as theological: that, with a few concessions to hard luck, *economic status depends fundamentally upon personal merit.* This, more than any "religious" claim, is the doctrine upon which the social order rests. Like most orthodoxies, it is enforced most cruelly just when people have most reason to repudiate it. Now, we should surmise, is one of those times for capitalism. One reason may be that global capitalism, while often said to increase the number of high-skilled jobs, adds most dramatically to the number of low-wage jobs.[68] Further, there is no question but that the low unemployment rate of recent years exerts an upward pressure on wages. Businesses interested in holding down the minimum wage therefore wish to increase the pool of unemployed low-wage workers. The reduction of the welfare rolls clearly supports these aims.

AFDC was widely criticized, and correctly so, for not sufficiently encouraging wage work. Progressive religionists, in their statements and policy on welfare, have supported the responsibility to work, adding that this entails a social obligation to provide the conditions under which wage work can be a viable means of self and family support. I would heartily agree that work is both a responsibility and a right. Indeed, if public policy proceeded upon these principles—and if child care were included within the category of work—the problems of social provision could be largely resolved. But if AFDC failed to support work and the Personal Responsibility Act succeeds, that is not because in 1961, Americans did not believe in a responsibility to work, whereas now they do. It is because neither in 1961, nor in 1996, nor since, have corporate interests been willing to support a *right* to work, and neither then nor now has the American public understood that the interests of corporate capital are not necessarily their interests. The Clinton administration has shown some sympathy to a right to work, but its efforts in this regard waned after its original health care proposals were soundly defeated. Since then its initiatives on behalf of the right to work have been far more modest, and its successes, such as raising the minimum wage, far from adequate. In the end, the only intimations of a right to work within the PRWORA are some limited child and health care benefits, largely transitional and based on governmental beneficence rather than on corporate obligation. It is not for nothing that the dismantling of public provision has been most vigorously championed by the most vigorous opponents of a family wage, national standards of health care, and national access to affordable child care; theirs has been the political victory.

For all the rhetoric of "personal responsibility," the forces that most powerfully determine work's availability, wage, and conditions could not be farther beyond the purview of poor people. Nor for that matter, the purview of "religion." Increasingly, they are beyond the ken of government itself. These are the portentous "signs of the times" that progressive religionists must read in terms of their best social visions. This is why "religion"—not the state and not the market—is now being privileged to handle the problem of poverty. The reduction of poverty from a problem of citizenship to a matter of charity, the shift from social analysis to individualized and sexualized moralism, the abdication of national accountability for local voluntarism—all this, far from putting people's lives back into their own hands, belongs to a large-scale and ever more rapid yielding of the social, economic, and political life to economic forces that are utterly and unaccountably "private." The problems encrypted in social provision are about the viability of democratic life in the face of these anti-democratic forces. It is not just for the sake of the poor, then, that progressive religion must refuse to confine itself to the moral or spiritual "parts" of life, the poor and vulnerable "parts" of society, or the "private parts" of individuals. It is for the sake of their own integrity as moral communities, and for the health of the political whole to which those communities belong.

Conclusion

These two cases lay bare the heterogeneity and historicity of religions as traditions that are subject to the ambiguity of all things human. In one sense, this undermines the authority that religions often claim as reliquaries of impenetrable absolutes. But that is the price of the ticket, since the "privilege" of absolutism cannot but provoke unique exclusions of religion from public and political life. What the ticket buys is not only fuller entry of religion into public life, but a public discourse in which all groups and persons—not just "religion"—are challenged to clarify their normative assumptions and to speak to the common good.

The fuller entry of religious groups into public life would not require a Rawlsian notion of "public reason" from which religious or ethical language as such is excluded.[69] However, it does ask of religious and other communities of conscience a sort of ethical bilingualism—that is, a tailoring of ethical warrants, scope, and sanctions to different dimensions of a group's existence. Although oversimplified, it is helpful at least to begin by distinguishing the existence of groups as *communities* in their internal lives and as *publics* in relation to the society as a whole. As communities, it is perfectly appropriate for religious groups to rely on authorities not acknowledged by other citizens, or to commit themselves to more totalistic visions, and more demanding principles than those constituting the political order. Religionists can invite other citizens to share their communities by accepting, in part or whole, their belief systems, social visions, or moral ideals. Leaving aside the question of which public works should be relegated to religion, religious groups that do offer public service should be free to predicate that service on their beliefs—for example, to predicate their social provision on ideals of radical economic redistribution, or of sexual morality, that are not shared by other citizens. That is even so when these works involve government funds, provided that the stated public mission is not compromised.

In these and other ways, religious groups can and should be free to testify publicly to their beliefs. But while testimony is the native language of communities, deliberation must be the public language of democracy.[70] Testimony is a prolegomenon to deliberation (and it is not only religious people who testify to their beliefs), because it enables other citizens to understand why the believer believes as she does. But it does not enable those others to understand why *they* should believe as the believer does, or which of her beliefs holds a claim on the public conscience. That requires deliberation, and to participate in democratic deliberation, religious groups (again, like believers of every political stripe) must make their positions intelligible to citizens outside their communities and engage in the sorts of compromise and negotiation appropriate to a democratic polity.

To those who conceive ethics as nothing but the implementation of absolutes, this sort of deliberation will not appear ethical at all. But for them nothing like a democratic ethic is really possible. For those of us who committed to a public sphere that is determined not just by power but by deliberation, negotiation, and consideration of the common good, public ethics can only be partial and provisional—partial in that it leaves the fullest elaborations of moral good to smaller spheres; provisional in that it is subject to change and renegotiation. That does not mean that such an ethic will have nothing to do with ethics as we know it individually, or with religion as we live it in our particular communities. On the contrary, it will mean that we are creating the specific kind of public ethics and religious dialogue that are appropriate to a pluralistic democracy.

As publics, the basic ethical warrant deployed by religious and other communities must be political—the right to democratic participation. "Radical democrats" note that the conditions of that participation are both formal and material. Formal conditions could include constitutional rights such as free speech and equal protection, as well as what Nancy Fraser calls "cultural recognition." Material conditions could include what she calls "economic redistribution"[71] and, additionally, social capital, laws, and policies that correct inequities. Gay and lesbian people, for example, need more than free speech. They need civil rights laws that protect that free expression from the extreme and undue sanctions to which society demonstrably subjects it. Impoverished citizens, analogously, cannot exercise political power unless they have access to decent education, civic organizations, and income beyond that which is necessary for bare survival. These citizens, like the rest of us, are entitled to free expression and association, fair and basic economic opportunity[72] as conditions for the possibility of meaningful participation in the political process. For some of us, advocating for and with these citizens will also be matters of love, compassion, or utopian vision. But when it comes to public ethics, those are not the basic principles at stake, and if we try to make them so, we effectively strip ourselves of any genuinely political warrants.

Whether religious or not, activists are always drawn to means that are less than deliberative and democratic. That is understandable, given that the material and formal conditions of democratic participation exist in dialectical relation, and that for so many the material conditions are needed so urgently. We may be tempted, for example, to rely more on financial clout than on deliberation or moral suasion for political influence; or to employ public rhetoric meant to shock, infuriate, or otherwise silence the opposition. This is not an argument against all such means; justice sometimes demands that we consider "any means necessary." But it is a clarion call to engage in a kind of public dialogue and deliberation that is rarely on the agenda on American publics, from left to right. Politics may be war by other means, but the less different are the means, the less genuine the politics.

Here, perhaps, religions do have something if not unique at least exceptional to offer to public discourse. Religions have—indeed they *are*—traditions of ethical debate within fundamental shared commitments. At least sometimes, they sustain community in the presence of conflict, conviction in the midst of doubt, ideals that outlive hypocrisy and failure. At their best, they may even know and share something of that love "which surpasses understanding"—and that, if not the foundation of public life, is for some of us its horizon.

Notes

1. It may be noticed that in this heading and at points throughout this section I sometimes use the term "homosexuality," sometimes the phrase "gay and lesbian," and sometimes the tag "sexual dissidents." When I use the categories "gay" and "lesbian," that is because these are the categories employed in the religious documents, legislation, and political discourse I am discussing, which ordinarily involve the notion of fixed sexual identities and usually do not include categories such as bisexual and transgendered persons, or other alternatives such as "sexual minorities" or "queers." To express my own view, I could use the term "queer," which is useful in that it connotes sexual nonconformity in general. However, it does not communicate well outside specific academic and activist communities. "Sexual minorities," while broader than gay and lesbian, is problematic because it carries analogies with race that are inappropriate (as I will argue). It also implies that only a minority of citizens have a stake in the social availability of a wide range of sexual choices, which I heartily dispute.

Since, as will be elaborated in this chapter, I regard sexual nonconformity as a matter of choice, preference, conscience, and political participation rather than a matter of innate or fixed "identities," the most precise term for the question in question is "sexual dissidence," a term coined by Gayle Rubin (see Rubin, "Thinking Sex: Notes for a Radical Theory of Sexuality," in *Pleasure and Danger: Exploring Female Sexuality*, ed. Carole Vance [New York: Routledge, 1984]). When I am referring to my own views, this is the term I will use.

2. For these and most other official religious statements on homosexuality in the United States, see J. Gordon Melton, *The Churches Speak on Homosexuality: Official Statements from Religious Bodies and Ecumenical Organizations* (Detroit: Gale Research, 1991). See also Jeffrey Siker, ed., *Homosexuality in the Church: Both Sides of the Debate*, (Louisville, Ky.: Westminster/John Knox Press, 1994), esp. 195–208.

3. In *Bowers v. Hardwick*, the Presbyterian Church USA went so far as to file a brief of *amicus curiae* at the Supreme Court on behalf of gay respondent Hardwick, even though Presbyterians themselves were and remain profoundly divided over the moral acceptability of homoeroticism.

4. There are nineteen anti-sodomy laws at the state level as of this writing, five of which pertain only to same-sex sodomy.

5. *Bowers v. Hardwick*, 478 U.S. 186 (1986).

6. Examples include the Union of American Hebrew Congregations (1987); the United Church of Christ (1975); the Evangelical Lutheran Church in America (1977); and the Presbyterian Church USA. See Siker, *Homosexuality and the Church*, and Melton, *The Churches Speak on Homosexuality*, for documentation.

7. Melton, *The Churches Speak on Homosexuality*, 87.

8. The U.S. Catholic Conference, "Always Our Children: A Pastoral Message to Parents of Homosexual Children and Suggestions for Pastoral Ministers" (Washington, D.C.: United States Catholic Conference, Office of Communications, 1997), 4.

9. Melton, *The Churches Speak on Homosexuality*, 362. These moral assertions may seem disingenuous when unaccompanied by support for gay civil rights legislation; more disingenuous still when accompanied by active opposition to civil rights legislation. But they also may express a denomination's sincere effort to differentiate religious ethics from the ethos appropriate to the political sphere. In any case, they deserve to be taken at face value, and they invite public accountability.

10. For statements on same-sex marriage by the North Pacific Yearly Meeting and the Unitarian Universalist Association, see Melton, *The Churches Speak on Homosexuality*, 145 and 269, respectively. For explication of Reconstructionist (and other Jewish) stances on same-sex marriage, see the essay by Rebecca Alpert in this volume.

11. Siker, *Homosexuality in the Church*, 208.

12. In 1996 the United Methodist General Council placed a prohibition on same-sex ceremonies within its "Social Principles." According to Reverend Jimmy Creech and other proponents of same-sex marriage, this should have had lesser weight than church law. In August 1998 the United Methodist Judicial Council invalidated this interpretation by declaring that Methodist clergy can be disciplined for performing these ceremonies. See "United Methodist Church Bans Same-Sex Unions," *Christian Century*, 115, no. 23 (August 1998): 775.

13. Again, see Alpert in this volume.

14. The Catholic situation is further complicated by the celibacy vow that, because mandatory for all priests, has not been an especially reliable predictor of sexual practice. The hierarchy appears to have a greater concern about whether gay priests will remain celibate, and that concern is not entirely inappropriate. The Catholic church does appear to have a higher percentage of gay clergy than the general population (15–20% by some estimates), a significant number of whom claim and enact this identity, at least within a gay circles (see Tim Unsworth, "Gay Priests," *National Catholic Reporter* 33, no. 21 [November 1996]:17).

Since Catholicism is officially committed to compassion for the homosexual condition, the hierarchy is loathe to reject candidates for homosexuality as such; however, gay candidates are often subject to greater scrutiny. In a recent investigation, the *National Catholic Reporter* found only one U.S. diocese (Omaha) that rejects openly gay candidates as a matter of policy. But many other dioceses have reservations about the capacity of gay candidates for celibacy and sometimes add provisos such as two years of prior celibacy, or no involvement with gay culture (see Robert McClory, "Some Seminaries Thrive, Others Struggle," *National Catholic Reporter* 33, no. 39 [September 1997]: 3).

15. See Melton, *The Churches Speak on Homosexuality*, 203–39, for documentation of the debate within the United Church of Christ from 1969 to 1985.

16. For example, the Episcopal group "Integrity," the United Church of Christ's Coalition for Lesbian/Gay Concerns, Lutherans Concerned/North America, a solidarity movement for Christian lesbians called "CLOUT," and a youth organization called Queer Young Christians. There is even a pro-gay evangelical organization, called Evangelicals Concerned, and an organization of gay and lesbians within Eastern and Orthodox Christianity, called "AXIOS."

For an account of intense intradenomination conflicts about homosexuality, see Keith Hartman, *Congregations in Conflict: The Battle over Homosexuality* (New Brunswick, N.J.: Rutgers University Press, 1996).

17. Examples include "Toward a Quaker View of Sex," Friends Home Service Committee in London (1963; referenced in Melton, *The Churches Speak on Homosexuality*, 199), which was very influential on Quakers and others in the United States; the Reformed Church in America (1978); Melton, 171); the Presbyterian Church USA (1970, 1979, and 1983; Melton, 147, and Siker, *Homosexuality in the Church*, 200); the Missouri Lutheran Synod (1981; Melton, 139); the Evangelical Lutheran Church in America (1978 and 1980; Melton, 120 and 127, Siker, 198); the Church of Jesus Christ of Latter Day Saints (1987; Melton, 364); the Episcopal Church in the United States (1979; Melton, 89, and Siker, 196).

The assertion that homosexuality is a fixed, innate, or even genetic condition is also central to the pro-gay arguments of many progressive or moderate theologians and ethicists. (See essays by John MacNeill, Chris Glaser, Victor Paul Furnish, Lisa Slowe Cahill, James Nelson, Chandler Burr, Virginia Ramey Mollenkott, and Jeffrey Siker, in Siker), *Homosexuality in the Church*.) For an extended form of this argument, see Patricia Beattie Jung and Ralph Smith, *Heterosexism: An Ethical Challenge* (Albany: SUNY Press, 1993), which not only argues that homoerotic acts are "natural" for gays and lesbians but that (in the absence of the charism of celibacy) it would be "unnatural and immoral" for them to engage in heterosexual acts (31).

Interestingly, some of the denominations that are most ethically at ease with homoeroticism have not felt so compelled to "fix" homosexuality as an orientation. The United Church of Christ, while referring (via Kinsey) to "the 10% of the population whose affectional or sexual preference . . . is predominantly toward persons of the same gender," did not specifically attribute this to an innate or permanent character trait. Instead the statement's focus was on the fact of discrimination, which may be provoked by "public revelation of even a single [homoerotic] experience" (1975, in Melton, *The Churches Speak on Homosexuality*, 205–6). The Unitarian Universalist Association described homosexuality, somewhat awkwardly, as "an inevitable sociological phenomenon"; its point, however, was that homosexuality is "not a mental illness" (1970, in Melton, 266).

18. For a lucid account of this debate, see David Halperin, *One Hundred Years of Homosexuality and Other Essays on Greek Love* (New York: Routledge, 1990), 15–40.

19. Melton, *The Churches Speak on Homosexuality*, 200–201.

20. The Evangelical Free Church (1978) put this very crisply when, in condemning

homosexuality, it wrote, "We are all subject to a variety of powerful *orientations* [emphasis mine] which have the potential for bringing forth sin" (ibid., 108).

21. In 1984, for example, the bishops of Massachusetts condemned the ridicule and ostracism of gays. But they did so in the context of a statement opposing the gay civil rights legislation then under discussion in Massachusetts that subsequently passed over their objections (see Roman Catholic Bishops of Massachusetts, "Statement on Rights of Homosexuals" [1984], in ibid., 37–45). Similarly, in October 1998, the Alaskan bishops publicly supported "Proposition 2," an ordinance that would preemptively invalidate same-sex marriage.

An interesting but unfortunately minor exception is Bishop Leo O'Neil of Maine, who agreed to support Maine's gay rights legislation of 1995, but only when it was amended to disclaim moral support for sex outside heterosexual marriage. In the spring of 1997, however, when the Christian Coalition and the Christian Civic League of Maine led a campaign to repeal this legislation, Bishop O'Neil remained neutral and the anti–civil rights campaign prevailed. See James Kales. "A Referendum in Maine on Gay Rights," *Commonweal* 121, no. 2 (January 1994): 7, and Chris Bull, "A Clean Sweep," *The Advocate* 738, no. 35 (July 1997).

22. Sacred Congregation for the Doctrine of the Faith, "Declaration on Certain Questions Concerning Sexual Ethics" (1975), and "Letter to the Bishops of the Catholic Church on the Pastoral Care of Homosexual Persons" (1986); see Melton, *The Churches Speak on Homosexuality*, 13 and 40, respectively.

This "acceptance" of the homosexual condition is commonly misconstrued as a statement that homosexuality is good or even neutral, as was the case with the media's reception of the U.S. Catholic Conference's 1997 statement "Always Our Children." The U.S. bishop's statement was gentler than the Vatican's in tone, partly due to its pastoral concerns, and relied heavily on the notion that homosexuality is a fixed and unchosen condition. However, the bishops emphasized that the statement "does not break any new ground theologically" and "is not to be understood as an endorsement of what some have called a 'homosexual lifestyle'" (1). Indeed, they could scarcely have represented the homosexual condition in a positive or neutral light, given that the Vatican's 1986 statement, which remains the fullest and most authoritative Catholic teaching on the subject, was provoked by the desire to refute this "misconception."

23. See Janet Halley, "The Politics of the Closet," in *Reclaiming Sodom*, ed. Jonathan Goldberg (New York: Routledge, 1994), 145–204, esp. 150–152.

24. Dean Hamer and Peter Copeland, *The Science of Desire: The Search for the Gay Gene and the Biology of Behavior* (New York: Simon and Schuster, 1994).

In fact, it could be added that the search for a gay gene is itself a product of normative assumptions (e.g., that homosexuality needs to be explained and justified in a way that heterosexuality does not). Only in the context of those assumptions could this research appear significant or even intelligible.

25. *United States v. Carolene Products*, 304 U.S. 144 (1938).

26. In a footnote of *Carolene*, which Justice Powell has called "the most celebrated footnote in constitutional law," Justice Stone wrote that judicial intervention is warranted when legislation denies "a discrete and insular minority" access to the political process. See Halley, "The Politics of the Closet," 145ff., for a full discussion.

27. See Didi Herman, *The Anti-Gay Agenda* (Chicago: University of Chicago Press, 1997). Herman names this new anti-gay tactic "Rights Pragmatism" and offers a critical analysis of its demographic claims about homosexuals.

28. Nan Hunter dubs this the "No Promo Homo" argument. Cited by Lisa Duggan, "Queering the State," *Social Text* 39 (1994): 11.

29. See Christine Gudorf's essay in this volume and also *Body, Sex and Pleasure: Reconstructing Christian Sexual Ethics* (Cleveland: Pilgrim Press, 1994).

30. Beverly Harrison makes an excellent ethical case to this effect in her essay "Sexu-

ality and Social Policy," in *Making the Connections: Essays in Feminist Social Ethics*, ed. Carol Robb (Boston: Beacon Press, 1985), 83–114. Sisela Bok makes an equally strong general case for ethical "minimalism" in law and public policy in *Common Values* (Columbia: University of Missouri Press, 1995).

31. Sullivan's opponent was Janet Folger of the Center for Reclaiming America for Christ (*Nightline*, 30 July 1998).

32. For example, in 1978 the Reformed Church in America wrote that sexual conduct "is primarily an ethical question and not the concern of criminal laws"; therefore, "legislation specifically directed toward homosexual persons is unnecessary and constitutes a prejudicial attempt to legislate private morality" (Melton, *The Churches Speak on Homosexuality*,172). Similarly, the Missouri Lutheran Synod's statement of 1981 attributed a morally educative role to law, yet also noted that "not all matters of morality are fit subjects for legislation," only those that "impinge on the common good." Whether homosexual acts in private do so impinge, they added "is difficult to judge." That they were nonetheless willing to support the decriminalization of homosexual sex (as previously noted) is somewhat perplexing. However, the statement continued on to assert that even if consensual same-sex activity were to be decriminalized, "The state would still have a legitimate interest in protecting children from homosexual influence in the years when their sexual identity is formed" (Melton, *The Churches Speak on Homosexuality*, 130).

33. Ibid., 201. This statement was issued in 1980; similar statements were issued in 1976, 1977, and 1985.

34. Ibid., 39.

35. Congregation for the Doctrine of the Faith, "Pastoral Care of Homosexual Persons" (Ibid., 43).

36. Robert Wuthnow, *The Restructuring of American Religion* (Princeton: Princeton University Press, 1988).

37. Eve Kosofsky Sedgwick, *The Epistemology of the Closet* (Berkeley: University of California Press, 1994).

38. Duggan, "Queering the State," 9.

39. Ibid., 11.

40. Moreover, Halley notes, that since free speech is a condition for the possibility of political participation, the Court "repeatedly states its protection of free speech as arising not from rights vested in individuals, but from a collective right we all share to participate in the wars of political truth" ("The Politics of the Closet," 183).

41. 000/US/94–1039. Interestingly, while gay rights advocates in the Romer case relied heavily on the idea of a fixed or innate homosexual orientation, that was not central to the Court's reasoning. Instead, the majority's concern was for the integrity of the political process, which it realized is fundamentally corrupted when a group is delineated for the specific purpose of exclusion.

42. *Boerne v. Flores* (1997), which struck down the federal "Religious Freedom Restoration Act" of 1993 (000/US/95–2074).

43. In addition to community service, work is also defined to include unsubsidized employment, subsidized public or private employment, on-the-job training, education directly related to a job, high school or GED education, work experience, job search and readiness training, up to twelve months of vocational training, and providing child care for another recipient who is engaged in community service. (See Section 104 of the Personal Responsibility and Work Opportunity Reconciliation Act.)

44. Though the family cap measure within the PRWORA was defeated, this means only that such a cap would have to be legislated at the state level, but is not enforced from the federal level.

45. For these and other issues related to Charitable Choice, see the January 1997 "Guide to Charitable Choice," published by the Center for Public Justice (Washington, D.C.), and the Christian Legal Society's Center for Law and Religious Freedom (Annandale, Va.).

46. Social capital refers to the sorts of norms, connections, and interpersonal confidence upon which social organizations rely, and which has been said to be declining with the decline of civic life in America. See Robert Putnam, "Bowling Alone: America's Declining Social Capital," *Journal of Democracy* 6, no. 1 (January 1995).

47. Statements were issued by, among others, the Evangelical Lutheran Church of America and the Central Conference of American Rabbis, and the U.S. Catholic Conference. The National Council of the United Church of Christ in the USA produced a statement that was endorsed by more than twenty-five religious denominations and organizations, including the American Baptist Churches USA, the Episcopal Church, the United Methodist Church, the National Council of Jewish Women, the Presbyterian Church (USA), the Union of American Hebrew Congregations, the Unitarian Universalist Service Committee, the American Friends Service Committee, and the National Council of Churches.

48. For purposes of this section, I will characterize the Roman Catholic position as moderate, in that it combines the conservatism of Catholic sexual ethics with the progressive tendency of Catholic social ethics. The views of the U.S. Catholic Conference may prove to have a particularly large social impact, because Catholic Charities is the largest nongovernmental social service provider in the United States.

49. These job placement and health benefits estimates were the informal consensus of participants in the Call to Renewal Conference. For information on a study of hunger by Catholic Charities, see "Hunger on the Rise," *America* 178, no. 3 (January 1998): 1.

50. Due to the new system of provision, religious and other private agencies soon may find themselves in a new and awkward relationship with the minimum wage. State subsidized jobs are among the permitted means for placing welfare recipients in jobs, and states employing that means are likely to do so through agencies with which they already have contracts. Thus, religious social service agencies may be availed of minimum wage workers at no cost to themselves, and the numbers of available subsidized workers will no doubt increase as time limits for employment come due. At that point, providers will either be forced to actively resist or, by nonresistant compliance, to accept the minimum wage.

For a discussion of subsidized workers and other challenges before faith-based providers, see Mary Jo Bane, "Faith Communities and the Post-Welfare Reform Net" in *Who Provides?*, ed. Mary Jo Bane and Brent Coffin, forthcoming.

51. For an excellent discussion of welfare policy and, more broadly, American politics in light of this insight, see Constance H. Buchanan, *Choosing to Lead: Women and the Crisis of American Values* (Boston: Beacon, 1996).

52. For example, states that show a reduction in illegitimacy are eligible for a federal funding bonus; nothing in the provision would exclude from the ranks the "illegitimate" those children born to and independently supported by adult single mothers.

53. On the changing realities of family life in the United States, see the essay by Rosemary Ruether in this volume.

54. Ralph Reed, *Active Faith: How Christians Are Changing the Soul of American Politics* (New York: Free Press, 1996), 78.

55. There is a rich body of historical and political literature on social welfare for mothers, its social aims and assumptions, and its differential effects by race and class. One good collection is Linda Gordon, ed., *Women, the State and Welfare*. (Madison: University of Wisconsin Press, 1990). For discussion of the moral regulations associated with aid, see especially the essay by Barbara Nelson in that volume.

56. This is according to a 1931 study by the Children's Bureau of the U.S. Department of Labor, cited by Barbara Nelson in "The Origin of the Two-Channel Welfare State" in *Women, the State and Welfare,* 151, n. 75.

57. Patriarchalism is not the only way to run a society, Moynihan conceded, but it is the way ours is run; moreover, "It is in the nature of the male to strut." A plethora of cognitive, moral, and social deficiencies, he argued, could be attributed to the "matriarchalism" of the African-American family. See Daniel Patrick Moynihan, "The Negro Family: The Case for National Action" (Washington, D.C.: Department of Labor, Office of Policy Planning and Research, 1965).

It should be noted, however, that in addition to his patriarchal moralism, Moynihan's analysis had a social prong. Since white society was responsible for the plight of the black family, he argued, it was obligated to support public assistance to these families. As time would tell, the racist and moralistic side of Moynihan's analysis could be entirely severed from his social analysis, the latter being largely absent from the PRWORA.

58. For a thoughtful discussion of welfare policy in relation to controlling the fertility of African-American women, see Susan L. Thomas, "Race, Gender and Welfare Reform: The Antinatalist Response," *Journal of Black Studies* 28, no. 4 (March 1998): 419–46.

59. See Elizabeth M. Bounds, "Welfare as a Family Value: Conflicting Values of Family in Protestant Welfare Responses," in *Welfare Policy: Feminist Critiques,* ed. Elizabeth Bounds, Pamela Brubaker, and Mary Hobgood (Cleveland: Pilgrim Press, 1999).

60. U.S. Catholic Conference, "Moral Principles and Policy Priorities on Welfare Reform," *Origins,* 30 March 1995, 675 and 676.

61. William Jefferson Clinton, State of the Union Address, January 1995. It is also worthy of note that Clinton called upon church and community leaders to resolve this problem.

62. Birth (or pregnancy) rates compare number of births (or pregnancies) to a numerical constant (1,000 women). Ratios, on the other hand, compare two events—e.g., the number of "illegitimate" births per the whole number of births in a given period. Ratios therefore fluctuate in terms of two variables; rates in terms of only one. For example, illegitimacy (for all women, adult and teen) will appear to have increased much more (about a 250% increase) if we look at its ratio per 1,000 births, than if we look at its rate per 1,000 women (a 70% increase). Like other women in America, teens who do give birth are less likely to marry than they were two or three decades ago. But that does not mean that teens are more likely to give birth. Contrary to political rhetoric, the teen birth rate has decreased substantially: in 1960, it was 91 per 1,000; in 1970, 70 per 1,000; in 1990, 60 per 1,000. The teen pregnancy rate has increased, but significantly less than has teen sexual activity. See Kristin Luker, *Dubious Conceptions: The Politics of Teenage Pregnancy* (Cambridge: Harvard University Press, 1996), 195–201 and 229, n. 12, for detailed presentations of this and related data.

These figures are not meant to gainsay the fact that teen sexual behavior has changed in these decades. Today, far more teens are sexually active and become pregnant, while far fewer marry. But it is not at all self-evident how we should interpret these changes, the social interests at stake in them, or the appropriate solutions. For example, is teen sexual activity taken as intrinsically problematic and, if so, why? If the objections are fundamentally moral, on what basis can they be imposed as law or policy upon other citizens, adult or minor? If there are social interests at stake in whether teens have sex, or become pregnant, or have abortions, it is important to clarify the precise nature of those interests. If poverty is the chief social concern, it must be asked whether poor teenagers, who comprise the great majority of teen parents, would actually be significantly better off economically had they delayed childbearing. Studies have shown that more than 80% of teens who become pregnant were poor or nearly poor before they became parents. Moreover, while middle-class young women can expect that delaying childbearing will bring social gains, poor teens know that "postponing their first birth is unlikely to lead to a partnership in a law firm," as Luker puts it (106 and 107, n. 80).

How these questions are answered determines what sort of problem "teen pregnancy" is taken to be, which in turn determines which solutions seem appropriate—e.g., abstinence education or fuller sex education, making reproductive services available, or simply addressing the underlying conditions of poverty.

63. Ibid., 81–108.

64. William Julius Wilson, *When Work Disappears: The World of the New Urban Poor* (New York: Knopf, 1996).

65. Here we have to note that abortion, while legal, is unavailable to many American women and particularly to teenagers due to several factors, including aversive court decisions, the physical intimidation of providers, and the denial of government funds. In addition to the factors discussed by Wilson, these are important constraints upon the reproductive freedom of poor women, especially poor teens.

66. Ruth Smith, "Salvation and the Need for Poverty," in *Welfare Policy: Feminist Critiques*.

67. See for example Carl Dudley, "Essential Conversions: The Welfare Revolution," *Christian Century* 114, no. 28 (October 1997), Barbara von der Heydt, "Tough Medicine for Welfare Moms," *Policy Review* 83, no. 16 (May/June 1997), or any number of issues of *Christian America* (a publication of the Christian Coalition). Dudley's article is a good illustration of Ruth Smith's observations about the dangers of classical Protestant beliefs about wealth and poverty. He writes that "unemployment offends God, for it is, the Reformers thought, the misuse of a divine bequest."

68. For a detailed discussion of this point, see Mary Hobgood, "Poor Women, Work and the U.S. Catholic Bishops: Discerning Myth from Reality in Welfare Reform," in *Welfare Policy: Feminist Critiques*.

69. John Rawls, *Political Liberalism* (New York: Columbia University Press, 1993).

70. Cf. Amy Gutmann and Dennis Thompson, *Democracy and Disagreement* (Cambridge: Belknap Press of Harvard University Press, 1996).

71. For essays by Fraser and others on radical democracy, see *Radical Democracy: Identity, Citizenship and the State.*, ed. David Trend (New York: Routledge, 1995). See also Nancy Fraser, *Justice Interruptus: Critical Reflections on the Post-Socialist Condition* (New York: Routledge, 1997).

72. The notions of "basic opportunity and "fair opportunity" are borrowed from Gutmann and Thompson but are not meant to endorse the particular content they ascribe to each.

Families and Family Values

Historical, Ideological, and Religious Analyses

ROSEMARY RADFORD RUETHER

Church, Feminism, and Family

Contrary to what American Christians generally assume, there has not always been a positive relation between the church and the family in the Christian tradition. Indeed, through much of Christian history there have been suspicious views of the family in relation to the church, fed particularly by the assumption that the highest vocation of Christians is the chaste single life.

Church and Family from the First to the Fifteenth Centuries

In the New Testament Jesus tells his followers to put aside loyalty to father and mother, spouse and children to come follow him (Matt. 10:37–39; Luke 14:26–27). Paul grudgingly concedes the right of Christians to marry, but as a second-rate option. He believes that truly committed Christians should remain unmarried in order to devote themselves exclusively to God and the coming of God's Kingdom (1 Cor. 7.7).

Later writings in the New Testament, such as 1 Timothy, represent a shift back to more traditional Jewish and Greco-Roman views in which the patriarchal slave-holding family is the normal Christian lifestyle and is presented as the model for the church. Women are to be eliminated as preachers and church leaders, and male heads of family are to be chosen as the best candidates for bishops and presbyters (1 Tim. 2:11–3:13). The author of 1 Timothy asserts this view against other groups of Pauline Christians who disparaged marriage and allowed women to minister.[1]

This conflict continued in the early centuries of the church. In much of popular literature of the second to fourth centuries conversion to Christ means putting aside the demands of the family. This was particularly explosive for women, who understood this message as a mandate to reject arranged marriages and leave parents and husbands to take to the road as itinerant preachers. In the *Acts of Paul and Thecla*, a second-century Christian writing, Thecla is converted to Christianity by Paul, rejects her fiancé and leaves home to preach the Gospel. She is pursued by her mother and her fiancé, as well as the governor, who seek to punish her by throwing her to the lions. But she is miraculously saved, not once but twice, and emerges triumphant, even baptizing herself. The story ends with Paul reappearing to commission her to return to her hometown to preach the Gospel.[2]

Stories of such women are repeated over and over in Christian literature into the Middle Ages as exemplars of Christian piety. In the late fourth century the Roman matrons Melania and Paula the Elder, wealthy propertied women, leave their children behind and travel to the Holy Land to found monastic communities for women.[3] In the Middle Ages hagiographic stories exalt women who reject marriages arranged by their parents in favor of a vocation to celibacy and the monastic life.[4] It was assumed that church leaders were to support women against their families in such cases. Marriage was seen as a spiritually inferior vocation. The fully dedicated Christian was celibate.

In the early Middle Ages the church had to come to terms with Germanic patterns of the family that allowed polygamy and easy divorce. The church's struggle to Christianize these Germanic peoples included a struggle to reshape the family. Marriage became defined as a sacrament and thus fell under the jurisdiction of the church and its ecclesiastical courts, rather than being, as before, a secular contract between families. Through the right to confer valid marriage and hence legitimate children, the church enforced monogamy and prohibited divorce and marriage between several degrees of kinship.

Medieval and even modern Catholicism followed the views developed by Augustine in which sexual pleasure even in marriage was seen as sinful, allowable only for procreation, but birth control and abortion were ruled out.[5] Married couples who follow these church rules can receive the sacraments and expect eventual salvation, while those who violate them are sinners cut off from the church and God. But the highest and best vocation for men and women is the celibate life.

The later Middle Ages saw an increasing subordination of women in society and the church. In the early Middle Ages a woman who inherited land was accounted a feudal lord in her own right, sovereign over her own territories and their inhabitants. The late medieval and early modern periods saw the restriction of political rights attached to landed families and the development of new state structures of government from which women were excluded.

In the church abbesses as female heads of monastic communities lost their independence and were increasingly subordinated to outside male ecclesiastical control. Education shifted from the monasteries to the universities, which women were barred from attending. Female options, whether in the family or the church, became a shrinking realm, and women were increasingly powerless and dependent.[6]

The sixteenth to eighteenth centuries would also see women continually lose ground as independent artisans and healers. Female guilds in textiles, beer brewing and printing declined, and it became more difficult for women to inherit guild membership in skilled crafts from their husbands. Healing arts, pharmacy, medicine, and midwifery became redefined by education and certification, and women were excluded from obtaining these credentials. Thus it became more difficult for a woman to maintain herself economically outside of marriage.[7]

Church and Family in the Reformation

The sixteenth-century Protestant Reformation capitalized on these trends in family and society in the early modern period. The Reformation churches rejected celibacy as a superior vocation for Christians and virtually mandated marriage for ministers. This had a positive effect of raising the status of marriage, but it also eliminated the alternative vocational options for women. Women could no longer choose between marriage and monastic life, where they might receive education and opportunities for leadership within a female community. Marriage and childrearing were their sole destinies.

Women did not always leave their communities willingly, and Protestants became militant in forcing convents to close. A great number of female vocations, associated both with various kinds of female communities, including grassroots groups, such as Beguines, as well as with Catholic worship (e.g., candlemaking), were thus lost to European women. Thus women's economic possibilities shrank dramatically in the Reformation era.

The Reformation churches emphasized the household codes of the later books of the New Testament, which demanded that slaves obey their masters, wives their husbands, and children their parents. For the Reformers this patriarchal hierarchy was God's will and order of creation for the family and society. Calvin reaffirmed the traditional Catholic teaching that woman was created subordinate in the original intention of God. This subordination has worsened and must be enforced coercively as punishment for woman's rebellion against God's commandment, whereby sin and death came into the world.[8]

Puritan writers on the family walked a narrow line between elevating women's spiritual and social status as a wife and subordinating her to the male authorities of the family, church, and state. They taught that the husband is the head of the family, and his wife's head as well. She should obey him in all things, even if he is harsh and tyrannical. Yet husband and wife are also defined as co-partners in family governance over children and servants, economic production and management, although the wife is understood as "junior partner" or "vice-regent" in these roles.[9]

The Puritans writers on "domestic economy" assumed a preindustrial farming or artisan family that owned its own means of production. Husband, wife, children, servants, or other dependents were the labor force in this household economy. When the husband was absent, either through travel, outside duties, or death, the wife was head of the household and manager of the household economy. Thus it was assumed that she must have much the same skills to do so as he. She must be both an obedient and also a competent helpmeet to her husband.

The Puritan emphasis on women's subordination and obeisance to her husband was in conflict both with this demand for competence and capacity to manage the family economy herself and also with the Puritan affirmation of the right of independent conscience of every Christian. These contradictions in Puritan ideology came to a head in the second half of the seventeenth century in New England.

The Puritan congregations that migrated from England to America possessed a high number of strong, independent women who had defied the persecution of the Anglican establishment to opt for Calvinist conventicles. Some were independent property-holders and heads of households. The conflict with Anne Hutchinson and her followers, then with Quaker women preachers, and finally the witch hunt at the end of the century all focused on older, independent women. The women singled out for attention were those who defied the Puritan concepts of women as quiet and obedient helpmates to their husbands, subordinate to the rules and teachings of ministers and magistrates, receivers and not teachers of the Word of God.[10]

Thus Puritanism is a two-edged legacy in American society. One side points toward individualism, equal worth before God, and the partnership family, while another side enforces the patriarchal family, strict male-headship over women and children, and woman-blaming for all that goes wrong in family and society.

The Feminization of Church and Family in the Nineteenth Century

In the eighteenth and nineteenth centuries the Western family began to be reshaped by new economic patterns. The extended household with relatives and servants shifted to the nuclear family, consisting only of parents and children. A sharp division emerged between the private sphere of unpaid female housework and childrearing and the public realm of male paid work, reflecting the effects of industrialization on work and family. Industrialization collectivized productive work outside the family. Fewer and fewer families owned their own means of livelihood, whether as farms or workshops. The food and goods consumed by families more and more were produced in factories or in corporate farms.

As industrialization advances, the home, and women's work in the home, loses more and more productive functions. Soap and candle making, poultry raising, and growing vegetables, fruit, and herbs disappear. Women not only no longer spin or weave to make cloth, but they also no longer buy cloth to make their own clothes, a skill still common when I was a child. Even food is bought more and more in a prepared form, even ready cooked, rather than prepared from "scratch."

The role of the home, and women, shifts from being a primary producer of much of the food, clothing, medicine, soap, candles, and baskets used or consumed by the family, and co-manager of the household economy, to being shopper, housekeeper, and primary parent, nurturer of husband and children, totally dependent on money brought back from paid labor from outside. Residual unpaid housework loses its status as work and is defined as "non-work" over against paid work outside the family. With the loss of a servant class, the housewife in middle-class families becomes the cook, launderer, and house cleaner. Expanding "labor-saving" household equipment is counteracted by raised standards of cleanliness and expected varieties of food, clothes, and amenities to keep women's housekeeping work extensive.

The nineteenth century saw the secularization of public life. Politics, education, and business separated from religious sanctions. The church is relegated to the realm of private life and thus is associated with the privatized sphere of women and family life, rather than with the public life of men. Women are defined as the mainstay of religion. Whereas medieval Christianity had defined women as less spiritual and more sexual than men, nineteenth-century bourgeois religion sees women as more "naturally" religious and moral than men, morality itself being redefined as more emotional than rational. It is now a woman's job to "uplift" her husband morally and nurture piety and morality in her children, under the direction of the male ministry.[11]

Bourgeois cultural ideology links femininity, domesticity, and piety. Good (i.e., white, married, middle-class) women are seen as naturally passive, altruistic, self-sacrificing, emotionally sensitive, morally "pure," asexual, and religious, while men are by nature more sexual, aggressive, competitive, and rational. Men are fitted by nature to the rough competitive secular world of war, politics, and business, while women are unfit for this public realm. This split of feminine and masculine "natures" for women and men corresponds to the split spheres of privatized family and paid work, reinforced by the secularizing of the public realm and the privatizing of religion.

The male minister becomes something of an anomalous or "liminal" figure in this system. Culturally linked with the family and women, he is also still seen as belonging to an elite, educated, male profession, although one with declining political and economic status. The male ministry has guarded this male status jealously, being the last profession to open to women in the twentieth century. Today there are increasing numbers of women in the ministry. Many theological schools have more than 50% women students. Yet this entrance of women into ministry is often construed as causing the decline of the status of the ministry, failing to recognize the older and deeper roots of this "decline" in the changed relation of the church and religion to public power.

Victorian patriarchal culture ratified the separation and complementarity between male and female, public and private, work and home. Middle-class women in the mid-nineteenth century were faced with a new set of contradictions. With less and less productive functions within the home, women had far less work to do there, and the abundance of cheap servants meant that the menial tasks of the household had not yet shifted to the backs of wives and daughters of the male head of family. Yet they were barred from higher education and interesting professions. The single, middle-class women had almost no way of making a "decent" living independently.

It is important to realize that this ideology of masculinity and femininity was created by and for the white middle class. It had little relevance to the reality of black or immigrant working-class women, most of whom had to combine low-paid work as tenant farmers, factory workers, or servants in other households with housework and childcare. The middle-class ideology of femininity and the luxury of being a "full-time housewife" was one to which the working-class woman was taught to aspire, but in circumstances that made it difficult for her to do so, thus denying her the respect accorded to the "lady."

The Victorian feminist movement that arose in the 1830s and grew in the second half of the nineteenth century, leading in 1920 to the suffrage amendment that granted women citizenship, was fed by the frustrations felt by white, middle-class women at their confined opportunities. The relation of the white, middle class–led suffrage movement to black and working-class women was not always positive. Some women suffrage leaders acceded to the disenfranchisement of blacks and immigrants and touted votes for (their kind of) women as a way of assuring the rule of the white middle class. Politically active working-class women were often suspicious of the suffrage movement and saw their interests more in the union movement to improve the conditions of labor for working men and women.[12]

Yet the rights that would be won by passage of the Women's Suffrage Amendment in 1920 would be won for all women, for all women were barred from the rights of citizenship. The women's movement fought for "eighty years and more" to gain for women not only the vote and the right to run for political office, but also the rights to hold property, higher education, and entrance into the educated professions.[13] Nineteenth-century feminists fought for women's rights by building on rather than rejecting the Victorian female culture of the family. They claimed the ideology of women's superior moral nature as maternal and used it to justify the need for women to move into the public sphere in order to moralize and "uplift" it.

They turned the patriarchal ideology of separate female and male natures around and asserted that if women were the more virtuous sex, then these virtues were too good to be kept at home. Women's "mother-nature" needed to be employed, not only to shut down bars and brothels, but also to clean up political corruption, improve sanitation, lessen crime, and put an end to war. In 1920 it was assumed that the woman's vote would be not only a vote against liquor, but also a peace vote. To men who argued that women could not be citizens because they did not bear arms, feminists like Jane Addams argued that women's entrance into politics meant replacing war with arbitration as the better way of settling international disputes.[14]

Feminism, Faith, and Family in the Twentieth Century

The collapse of the ideology of Victorian feminism in the 1920s was partly due to its own success. Women won the vote and access to higher education and professions. The "new woman" of the 1920s was embarrassed by her mother's militant feminism, moralism, and utopian religiosity. She wanted to prove that women were equal to men by competing in the world of secular male culture. She wanted to claim her sexuality and be partners with men in the give and take of public institutions. She wanted to speak no longer of women's rights or women's nature, but of human rights and human nature, to be a universalist rather than be tied to a separate gender identity. Above all, she no longer wanted to use the language of utopian religiosity, but the language of the social sciences. She still believed in values, but the language for this should be scientific, not religious.

Only gradually did the contradictions between women's new rights and their actual opportunities become evident. The Depression drove many women out of skilled professions. Business and government agreed that what jobs there were should be reserved for men. World War II brought many working-class women into heavy industry, but they were let go again after the war was over. By 1960 it appeared that the bright promises of the 1920s had come to naught. Proportionately, there were fewer women with Ph.D.s, fewer women ministers, doctors, lawyers, professors, and lawmakers than forty years earlier.[15]

It was not until the 1960s that a new feminist movement arose in the United States, awakened by the civil rights movement and an era of critical consciousness about American society. The way Victorian feminists appropriated and transformed familial ideology was no longer conceivable for those of the "second wave" of feminism. Instead the family was seen as the prime cause of the defeat of women's hopes. Women could not realize their potential in society as long as they were still tied to childbearing, childraising, and housekeeping as their primary responsibilities. Women who had B.A.s and even master's degrees from elite colleges found themselves confined to gilded cages in suburbia doing the work their grandmothers would have given to maids and nannies.

The problem of breaking out of the "feminine mystique" that idealized suburban housewifery was seen as a problem of the educated middle-class woman.[16] Yet all women who held paid jobs outside the home shared a similar problem, although with very different resources for solving it. The employed woman competed with her fellow male worker on the job with a hidden handicap. While being responsible for the same work as the male employees, sometimes even held to higher standards of competence than he, she also must rush about after work to shop, clean, cook, wash clothes, and care for children, while the male in a traditional marriage had a wife who did these things for him. Employed women worked a double shift, her paid job and her unpaid domestic work. The combination of the two kept her at the bottom of the job ladder.

The ideology of women's subordinate and auxiliary relation to men in the family also dictated the sort of work that women were more likely to be able to do in the paid labor force. They were more likely to work typing letters than dictating them, cleaning offices than managing them, to be a nurse rather than a doctor, a dental technician rather than a dentist, to teach primary school children rather than college students. And they could do these things only if they also did all the housekeeping and childraising. At the same time, the "working mother" was blamed for all social "evils," from homosexuality to juvenile delinquency. Going psychological wisdom taught that strong women make weak men.[17]

The feminists of the 1960s called for women to get out of the family and reject their confinement to these traditional female roles. But what they meant by "getting out of the family" was unclear. Did it mean not marrying at all, or divorcing to become single professionals? Did it mean forming female-bonded relations? Did it mean seeking egalitarian partnerships of men and women to support each other in their careers as well as housework and childraising? Feminists might mean some or all of these.

While earlier feminism had claimed the language of both religious and family values, especially motherhood, as a base for extending women's roles into the public world, the second wave of feminism seemed to have only negative views of religion, family, and traditional sexual morality. This left a vacuum into which the Religious Right would move to claim to be the true representatives of morality, religion, and family.

The claim to represent "family values" became, and continues to be, the base for a right-wing crusade against feminism, gay rights, abortion and sexual education, gun control, affirmative action, ultimately against all efforts at social reform for great economic and social justice—labeled "liberalism," or the "L word"—and in favor of a jingoistic nationalism, white supremacy, and patriarchal family and social order.

In an increasingly virulent atmosphere of culture wars, a military adventurer like Oliver North can position himself as the "family values" candidate, while Hillary Clinton is labeled by the Religious Right as a "radical feminist witch" with pointed hat, riding on a broomstick, despite her focus on such "feminine" issues as health care and child welfare. All of this means that more genuinely progressive solutions to dealing with gender, race, and class inequities, endemic poverty, worsening ecological crisis, and many other pressing issues of American and global society are driven off the map of public discourse.

What has happened to American women after thirty years of feminist struggles for greater gender equality, dogged by patriarchal backlash? On one level it seems that feminism has had considerable success in opening up middle and upper middle professional employment to women. Women doctors, lawyers, professors, ministers, and business leaders have expanded in numbers. But the progress of an elite group of women in professional employment must be weighed against the larger picture of increasingly unequal distribution of wealth in the last twenty years. The rich have gotten richer, the poor have grown in numbers, and the middle-income group has shrunk.[18]

The United States has the most polarized income distribution and the largest number of people without health care coverage of any industrialized nation. It has also suffered significant deindustrialization in areas such as steel production. Well-paying blue-collar unionized jobs have declined and a small sector of high tech jobs has grown, but the main job growth is in low-paying service jobs, often part time and without pensions or health benefits.

This shifting economic situation means that the male "family wage" has become a thing of the past for most families. The second female income is no longer a luxury, much less a feminist issue, but a necessity for low- and middle-income families. Two-income families with children struggle to have adequate time with children or even with one another. Yet the political leaders that trumpet "family values" are hostile to any of the kinds of reforms that might make it more possible for parents to actually share childcare, while maintaining employment adequate for family support.

This also means that, of the growing sector of women raising children alone, 60% are likely to be in poverty. Single mothers are caught between low pay for most jobs accessible to women and the high costs of childcare. The self-righteous call to "abolish welfare as we have known it," signed into law by President Clinton in the months before the 1996 election, is forcing poor women with children off public assistance. But even low-paid jobs available to them are in short supply and often don't pay enough to allow for childcare necessary for them to work. Welfare reformers have yet to realistically face this contradiction.[19]

Other sectors of society also are falling into poverty: the elderly, disproportionately female, without family support systems, as well as the mentally and physically ill, the drug-addicted, and the chronically unemployed who make up the increasingly numbers of the homeless.

Where does this leave us in terms of any possibility of working for a more egalitarian society for men and women? First we need to be clear that feminism is not the cause of the crisis in the family. The crisis in the family is caused by a patriarchal ideology of female subordination and separation of men and women into mutually exclusive spheres of childraising and paid work, forged in the Victorian age, which never worked for poor people and now no longer works for the middle class.

Those who claim to restore this Victorian middle-class pattern in the name of "family values" may win the backlash vote, but they will contribute nothing to actually getting at the underlying problems that are causing this crisis: namely, the inability of most families both to support their families economically and to have time to raise children and build family life. No amount of rhetoric that ignores the actual causes of this crisis and fails to construct concrete measure to alleviate the contradictions between economic maintenance and family life will have any relevance in lessening it.

What are some of the ways of genuinely alleviating this crisis? First, equality of men and women in family and society must be fully accepted. This means constructing both family systems and work patterns in which women can take their place in public society and men also can carry an equal share of childcare and housework. This cannot be done with the present pattern of "full-time employment." It must become possible for couples to work shorter and more flexible hours to have time for family life, while maintaining an adequate family income. The stress between work and childrearing must also be alleviated by subsidized childcare available either in the workplace or in neighborhoods where people live.

If two-parent, two-income families struggle with intractable contradictions between work and family life, this is immeasurably worsened for the under-employed and unemployed and the single mother. A society genuinely interested in families must find a variety of creative strategies to distribute adequate economic means and social support systems more adequately across the whole society. This calls for a fundamental questioning of the present economic system that concentrates 37% of the wealth in the top 1% of the population, while the lower 30% fall into poverty even with a fulltime job.

Does religion have a positive word to say about this crisis of economic inequality, gender inequity, and embattled family life? The identification of being "religious" with patriarchal subordination of women and the untenable call to return to the Victorian family can only exacerbate the crisis. Christians need to recognize the changing patterns of family life, as well as the complexity of their own historical relations to the family. The Victorian family idealized by the Religious Right has little in common with the teachings of Jesus, or even the sort of family envisioned in 1 Timothy.

Religion can make a positive contribution to the crisis only when it rediscovers the prophetic call for justice and allies itself with women and with the poor in supporting a more just society in which it can become possible for both men and women to work, to be active in society, and also to love and to care for children in a way that brings all of these parts of lives into coherent unity, rather than setting work and public participation in contradiction with the home. One awaits a new progressive movement in our society that can revive hope for more just conditions of viable family life in which the best of religion and social science, faith and feminism, can join hands.

Notes

1. Dennis MacDonald, *The Legend and the Apostle: The Battle for Paul in Story and Legend.* (Philadelphia: Westminster, 1983).

2. "The Acts of Paul and Thecla," in *Ante-Nicene Fathers*, vol. 8, ed. Alexander Roberts and James Donaldson (New York: Scribner's, 1897), 487ff.

3. Rosemary Ruether, "Mothers of the Church: Ascetic Women in the Late Patristic Age," *Female Leadership in the Jewish and Christian Traditions*, ed. Rosemary Ruether and Eleanor McLaughlin (New York: Simon and Schuster, 1979), 71–98.

4. Eleanor McLaughlin, "Women, Power and the Pursuit of Holiness in Medieval Christianity," *Female Leadership*, 99–130.

5. Susan Wemple, *Women in Frankish Society: Marriage and the Cloister*, 500–900 A.D. (Philadelphia: University of Pennsylvania Press, 1983).

6. Shulamith Shahar, *The Fourth Estate: The History of Women in the Middle Ages* (New York: Methuen, 1983).

7. Merry E. Wiesner, *Women and Gender in Early Modern Europe* (New York: Cambridge University Press, 1993).

8. John Calvin, commentary on Genesis 1–3. See also John L. Thompson. "*Creata ad Imagien Dei, licet Secundo Gradu*: Women as the Image of God According to John Calvin," *Harvard Theological Review*. 81, no. 2 (1988): 137–38.

9. See, for example, Edmund Morgan, *The Puritan Family* (New York: Harper and Row, l966).

10. Carol Karlsen, "The Devil in the Shape of a Woman: The Witch in 17th Century New England" (Ph.D. diss., Yale University, 1980).

11. See Ann Douglas, *The Feminization of American Culture* (New York: Avon, 1977); also Barbara Welter, ed., *Dimity Convictions: The American Woman in the Nineteenth Century* (Columbus: Ohio University Press, 1975).

12. Aileen S. Kraditor, *The Ideas of the Woman Suffrage Movement, 1890–1920* (New York: Doubleday, 1971).

13. Elizabeth Cady Stanton, *Eighty Years and More.* (New York: Harper, 1898).

14. Jane Addams, *Newer Ideals of Peace* (New York: Macmillan, 1907).

15. Lois Scharf, *To Work and to Wed: Female Employment, Feminism and the Great Depression* (New York: Greenwood Press, 1982).

16. Betty Friedan, *The Feminine Mystique* (New York: Norton, 1963).

17. For the shaping of the ideology of the dangerousness of women's sexuality and power by the medical profession, see G. J. Barker-Benfield, *The Horrors of the Half-Known*

Life: Male Attitudes toward Women and Sexuality in Nineteenth Century America (New York: Harper, 1976).

18. See Andrew Winnick, *Toward Two Societies: The Changing Distribution of Income and Wealth in the United States since 1960* (New York: Praeger, 1989).

19. Rebecca M. Blank, *It Takes a Nation: A New Agenda for Fighting Poverty* (Princeton: Princeton University Press, 1997).

5

JANET R. JAKOBSEN

Why Sexual Regulation?

Family Values and Social Movements

W hat are "family values"? Invocations of "family values" have become virtually ubiquitous in mainstream U.S. political discourse, so much so that their meaning has become "common sense." There is apparently no need for anyone to specify what is meant by the term and from its various and sundry uses it can mean anything and everything. Such elasticity and elusiveness in meaning is often the case with powerful symbols, and the political power of "family values" was more than evident in the Republican victories in the 1994 congressional elections. Although this historically important victory was not followed by the election of a Republican in the presidential elections of 1996, it did bring about a Republican control of Congress that signaled the denouement of both the New Deal and Great Society programs as frameworks for federal government in the United States Moreover, much of the rhetoric of the 1994 victory was taken up by candidates across the political spectrum, such that in the 1996 elections "family values" was espoused by both political parties.

Talk about "family values" often takes place through the invocation of the "traditional" family. But when did this family, the one named "traditional," exist? All kinds of authors, including Betty Friedan in *The Feminine Mystique* (1963), the book that supposedly opened the path to the second wave of feminism, assume that it was the 1950s.[1] Women stayed home. They cared for the home, and the husband, and the children. Women were housewives . . . in the suburbs. This picture of 1950s "tradition" is also somewhat mobile, however. In Bob Dole's acceptance speech at the 1996 Republican Convention, it is transposed to Depression-era rural Kansas. The relative affluence of Betty Friedan and the women with whom she went to college is assumed to be a form of life so traditional as to go for working people as well. The extended and complex families that made possible rural life as well as urban working life and even life in urban poverty[2] disappear in favor of a nuclear family enclosed within the particular walls of single-family property ownership. Thus, the "traditional" family has a virtual existence and yet its invocation has quite definitive material effects, providing the impetus, for example, for the 1996 "welfare reform" bill.

Similarly, in the 1994 elections, talk of "family values" was a primary discursive fund for the campaigns. Interestingly, the document that proved to be a stroke of political genius during the campaign, the "Contract with America," was afterward paired with a sibling, the "Contract with the American Family." The relationship between these two documents can tell us much about the workings of "family values" in contemporary U.S. politics.

On the face of it, the documents themselves are not particularly illuminating in terms of a coherent explanation of "family values." The "Contract with the American Family" includes initiatives like an end to public funding for PBS. Now, why exactly is this a "family value"? Granting even that the families in question are the white, middle-class, Christian nuclear families in conservative political discourse like Bob Dole's, Sesame Street seems ultimately more valuable to families than the violent schlock of commercial cartoons, particularly given Dole's apparently deeply held objection to violent cultural production *á là* his attack on Time Warner with regard to rap music.

I would suggest, however, that it may be precisely the incoherence of the position articulated by Dole that makes it work so effectively. The need for the two "Contracts" to be separate from each other, even as they are interrelated, may indicate a type of relation in which the loose networking of potentially contradictory terms works to strengthen rather than weaken the network as a whole. Specifically, the articulation of a conservative fiscal agenda geared to end "big government" in the "Contract with America" and a conservative social agenda, which might, in fact, intensify government regulation of social relations, including sexual relations, in the "Contract with American Family" allows the potentially uneasy or even incoherent alliance between economic and social conservatives to function effectively.

"Family values" works so powerfully because it condenses both social and conceptual relations, thus, making it a particularly polyvalent and potent symbol. Each of the terms is packed with a number of meanings, and, thus, the best way to understand the workings (if not the meanings) of "family values" is to consider the complexities condensed within each of the terms and elaborated by their conjunction. In particular, by giving "values" the appellation "family," it is possible to invoke "religion" without having to name it as such. As Robert Baird argues, after the enlightenment, talk about "values" becomes a primary way of talking about "religion."[3] Because religious "values" can be a set of reasonable principles, it can make sense to continue to talk about religion "within the limits of reason alone." In the contemporary U.S. context, beyond the obvious organizational ties between political advocates of family values and Christian-identified political groups, the terms "family" and "values" can, in precisely this manner, invoke (without naming) "religion." Thus, talk of family values engages the complex relationship between the religious and the secular, between myths of "America" as a secular and also as a specifically "Christian" nation.

Talk that conjoins "family" and "values" also contributes to a reworking of the relationship(s) among the economy, the state, and the American "nation." Under current economic conditions, the state's role has become complicated because it must now embody a transnational form of American-ness, American only insofar as transnational corporations are also U.S. corporations. Thus, interestingly, the U.S. government is sometimes seen as operating in a manner that is "un-American." In this climate, the "family" is being constructed as a site that, if it is made to embody American "values," can also embody the nation.

Thinking about the meaning of "family," of "values," and of the conjunction between them can tell us a great deal about contemporary politics. Why has "family" been taken up as such a central site of specifically public (rather than private) concern? And why has the concern for "family" been so closely tied to sexual regulation, to, for example, anti-homosexual activism, and to major shifts in federal programming like "welfare reform" articulated through concern about "unwed" or "teenage" mothers (both codes for young, poor women of color)? What prompted the contemporary focus on "values"? Why does having "values" imply conservative sexuality, such that for America to have "values" the government should be dedicated to, for example, the "defense of marriage"?

Because of the acceptance of "family values" as somehow expressive of "common sense," the question of why and how social movements become invested in sexual regulation is rarely asked. Yet, historically, the contemporary, "nuclear," form of "family" that is touted as definitive of "values" has not always been the norm, nor have social movements always been invested in the particular forms of sexual regulation that are articulated in contemporary American politics. Assumptions about Christianity are part of what fuels the idea that Christian-identified political movements, at least, should be concerned with sexual regulation. And yet, in the complex history of Christianity, both the importance and the forms of sexual regulation have varied extensively.[4] Even when a Christian interest in sexual regulation isn't assumed, the explanations of its contemporary political force are not fully adequate. One frequently offered theory is a variation on the claim that the process of secularization in the modern period, particularly the disestablishment of religion in modern democracies, has led the areas of social life over which religion can lay claim to be increasingly restricted to the private sphere of domestic or family relations.[5] While this explanation has some persuasive aspects, it also seems to give short shrift to the ways in which sexual regulation is a public activity. The issue is not simply the contradictions of a public that supposedly "values" a right to privacy and free expression, while sodomy is criminalized and censorship around sexual images rife. Rather, religion has been reasserted as a specifically public phenomenon through discourses of sexual regulation. Out of that move to (re)publicize religion a number of public policy issues have become directly linked to sexual regulation.

Yet, it is not always conservative political movements that are concerned with either "values" or sexual regulation. Talk of "values" has become a very popular word in feminist and lesbian ethics in the past decade, precisely as a contrast to the discourse of "norms" that is often perceived to be irrevocably implicated in disciplinary practices. "Values" are thought to open up a positive ethics of the good that can undercut the connection between ethics and normativity. Thus, in *Lesbian Ethics*,[6] Sarah Hoagland discards norms in favor of an ethics based on the creation of "new value" in the hope of disengaging from a dominant "ethics of control," specifically male control of women and lesbians. Obviously, however, in its right-wing usage, "family" is attached to "values" in order to reinstate the connections between "values" and the norms of heterosexuality and gender dominance.

This struggle over the potentially progressive or conservative meaning of "values" has taken up a complicated relation to sexual regulation within feminist movement itself. Within the second-wave feminist movement, some of the most vociferous and difficult arguments have been over what relationship feminism should have to sexual regulation. Second-wave feminists very early on focused on sexuality as one of the sites of women's oppression. They became specifically concerned with two main issues: (1) the ways in which legitimated sexual relations in church- and state-sanctioned marriage establish a sexual division of labor and structure patriarchal domination; and (2) the ways in which male sexual violence against women, both within and outside of marriage, works to subdue and contain women who might resist patriarchy. This analysis of sexuality as a conduit of domination led to feminist resistance along two main tracks: (1) a focus on liberating women's sexuality from male dominance, often through a focus on women's sexual autonomy and pursuit of their own pleasures; and (2) efforts to put an end to sexual violence against women. Each of these tracks has a potentially regulative aspect to it[7] that may have been present from the beginning, but in the late 1970s and through the first half of the 1980s the relative breadth of early tactics began to solidify into a strong focus on sexual regulation in campaigns against pornography, butch-femme and sadomasochistic sexual practices. Eventually feminist analyses of and activism around issues of sexuality polarized into what became known as "the sex wars" between sides that were often articulated as an opposition between "anti-violence" and "pro-sex" movements.[8] These two poles, addressing the potential "pleasures and dangers"[9] of women's sexuality, were sometimes conceptualized as mutually relevant, but the shift toward regulation split them into opposing topics.

Why did this shift toward sexual regulation occur at this moment in feminist movement? Like religious conservatism, feminism has always had an investment in sexuality, but at this specific historical moment, that investment became intensely focused on regulation. Thus, I'm interested in revisiting the "sex wars," not to rehash old oppositions but to raise some questions about how the opposition between the potentially interrelated issues of pro-sex and anti-violence was created and why "sex" became an issue of "war" in feminism.

Thinking through the historical example of why feminist movement became invested in sexual regulation may also open the door to a broader explanation of how sexual regulation works in contemporary U.S. politics for conservative movements. By inserting an analysis of feminist concerns with sexuality into an analysis of the conjunction between "family" and "values," I hope to interrupt the reduction of "values" to the appellation "family" and open new questions for progressive social movements about their own investments in a politics of sexuality.

Feminism

The question that makes a study of the feminist "sex wars" of the late 1970s and early 1980s relevant to an analysis of contemporary sexual regulation as promoted by conservative Christian groups is: Why did a shift away from diverse and complex responses toward the issues implicated in women's sexuality and toward sexual regulation occur at this moment in feminist movement? A number of theories have been suggested.[10] In her history of second-wave feminism, *Daring to Be Bad*, Alice Echols suggests that pornography served as an issue that could potentially unite a women's movement whose fragmentation along the lines of dominant social division—race, class, and sexuality—was becoming apparent.[11] If there were one issue that all women faced it was sexual violence, and thus the fight against pornography could transcend women's (potentially fragmenting) "differences." This scenario demonstrates the workings of a political theory that emphasizes the necessity of unification and understands alliances as transcending, rather than working through, differences. Thus, the regulatory aspect of the movement came to the fore as differences among women were recognized by the predominantly white feminist groups whose history Echols portrays. Audre Lorde offers an alternative, although related, perspective on this question. Lorde questions whether the entire fight that was the "sex wars" was, in fact, a displacement from the issues of difference and domination that white feminists hoped to transcend: "When sadomasochism gets presented on center stage as a conflict in the feminist movement, I ask what conflicts are *not* being presented?"[12] Particularly when read in conjunction with Echols's critique, Lorde's question raises the broader issue of why the "sex wars" erupted at a specific moment in feminist movement. In particular, these claims suggest that feminist movement was at this time enacting its own family drama, the drama of sisterhood. In this drama sexuality was not just a random "displacement" from issues of race and class (and note that this example reverses the classic Freudian displacement where "sex" is what is displaced). Rather sex became "hot" specifically as a conduit for regulating gender, race, and class relations without having to address directly the potentially explosive issues of difference or fragmentation, thereby maintaining the domestic fiction of unified sisterhood.

How can the regulation of "sex" work to regulate other forms of social relations, particularly relations that are imagined along the lines of "kinship" like sisterhood? To state, for example, that the "sex wars" took place within a context of racism is not simply to alert us to white supremacy, but also to the fact that discourses of sex are (in this context) always already racialized. In this context women of color are already characterized as both "sexually deviant" and as "sheer sexuality," as nothing but their sexuality (hence literally as embodying deviance and nothing else). A discourse is, thereby, established in which efforts to control "sexuality" are also efforts to control women of color (who are nothing but sexuality) and these efforts constitute a reaction in which women of color must deny (their) sexuality in order to resist this control.[13] Thus, internal regulation of sexual relations among white women may serve simultaneously to establish a racial border that defines who is in the feminist "family." The ever-vigilant focus on this internal regulation limits discursive production around kinship relations that cross the racial border, in this case "sisterhood" that includes either the discussion of the connections between race and sexuality or the production of cross-racial alliances.[14]

Internal sexual regulation can also reinforce class hierarchy, hence the focus in the "sex wars" on class-coded practices such as butch-femme. Working-class women's perspectives were frequently excluded from these debates, and class as a category of analysis that might challenge the structure of debate or the focus on sexuality was most frequently ignored. Very few of the contributions to anthologies like *Take Back the Night, Coming to Power*, or *Against Sadomasochism* even mention class or present a detailed analysis of class in relation to sexuality and fewer still bring together issues of race and class in relation to sexuality.[15] These exclusions led writers like Dorothy Allison,[16] Joan Nestle,[17] Cherríe Moraga, and Amber Hollibaugh[18] to point to the ways in which debates over "sexuality" can also reproduce dominative class politics. For example, each of these writers mentions the connection between dominant middle-class values of purity and disembodiedness and arguments against butch-femme or s/m (sadomasochism). As Moraga and Amber Hollibaugh note,[19] the criticisms of butch-femme in the early 1980s anthologies tend to ignore the historical emergence of these identities within communities of lesbians of color and white working-class lesbians. Moraga and Hollibaugh argue that butch-femme relationships come under attack because of their obvious interest in sex, an interest that is construed as low class.[20] John D'Emilio and Estelle Freedman[21] note that middle-class lesbians often found the erotic energy of the bar (the site of visible butch-femme cultures) threatening.[22] Lapovsky and Davis present a more complicated picture of the relations between working-class and middle-class lesbians in the 1950s, but they are clear that the question of "sexual style" was closely tied to the elaboration of class-based discourses.[23]

Just as the "sex wars" could displace anxieties over race and class differences, they could serve to displace the challenge of lesbian sexualities to dominant feminist movement. Lesbians have historically held a complicated place within feminist movement. Heterosexism and homophobia were recurrent issues within feminist movement,[24] but as Paula Webster suggests, "Lesbians were [also] asked to carry the banner of 'good sex,'" meaning that they would have to "leave their more complex feelings at the door."[25] Yet, once again the ties between carrying the banner of "good sex" and race/class relations must be kept in mind, since within a context of race and class stratified discourse, separating good girls from bad along the lines of sexuality could also distinguish good girls from "degenerate races"[26] and "low class individuals." And, as Mosse points out within the racialized discourse of degeneracy, it is frequently incest that causes "mongrelization," thereby, implying that sex within the feminist family of sisters must be only the most pure to avert the slide into degeneracy.

Thus, the underlying forces that drive sexual regulation may not be about "sex" *per se*. Rather, sexual regulation can provide an effective site for the regulation of both individual and social bodies, and in so doing it works to regulate social relations along the lines of gender, race, sex, and class. This argument has a number of implications. Analyses of sexual regulation will only be useful if placed in the broader context of multiple social relations, and, similarly, politics that resist sexual regulation will only be effective if they also address this broader context. Thus, it is not surprising that despite its hopes, the anti-pornography movement did not succeed in either transcending race and class barriers or even in unifying feminists in opposition to pornography. The focus on unity instead produced even greater divisions. This implies the need for alliances across social divisions as well as organizing that directly addresses issues of sexuality. In particular, in developing a radical politics of sexuality it is important to question the ways in which norms of "whiteness" or "middle-class" status can be implicitly established as the center of "sexuality." As Hortense Spillers points out, talk of sexuality, even radical sexuality, can simply work to (re)produce "culture in its dominative mode."

Family

What can this analysis of feminist movement tell us about Conservative Christian–identified political movements that are, when taken at face value, the polar opposites of secular feminist movements? Indeed Christian-identified conservative political groups have in part formed both their identity and their political power through opposition to feminist issues like reproductive rights and freedoms. I would suggest, however, that "family" operates as a condensation of multiple social relations in much the same way that "sisterhood" did for feminist movements.

In her article, "Thinking Sex: Notes for a Radical Theory of the Politics of Sexuality," Gayle Rubin argues that sex has become weighted with "an excess of signification."[27] Thus, Rubin poses the question of why it is that "sex" can come to carry all kinds of different meanings. It can, for example, come to be a paradigmatic marker of "values" in general. In "Thinking Sex" Rubin is shifting her own analysis away from the question of her earlier work in the "The Traffic in Women: Notes on the 'Political Economy' of Sex."[28] In this earlier article, Rubin argues by using Claude Lévi-Strauss's analysis of kinship relations that (hetero)sexuality is fundamentally about exchange relations among men in which women are the items exchanged. Rubin shifted her analysis, in part, because she wanted to show some of the limits of a feminist theory that tended to conflate gender and sexuality.[29] Insofar as feminist theory made all sexuality about gender relations, it thus couldn't fully explain, for example, the social struggles over various sexual minorities. Rubin is interested in asserting the need to analyze "sex" as a specific axis of experience and political struggle that is related to, but not the same as, "gender." This article has often been taken as a foundation for a "lesbian and gay" or "queer" studies that is also related to, but autonomous from, feminist or women's studies.[30]

In her 1994 article, "Against Proper Objects," Judith Butler argues that it may be time to reconsider the relationship between these two axes. In particular, Butler argues for a reconsideration of kinship relations that has become less commonplace in various theoretical fields given historical shifts away from kinship as the encompassing site of either gender or sexuality and intellectual shifts from the structuralism of Lévi-Strauss to post-structuralist theories, particularly the theories of sexuality offered by Michel Foucault. Foucault has argued that "sexuality" as a discourse of the nineteenth and twentieth centuries is deployed in contrast with, but also on the basis of, the deployment of alliance through kinship and law. Foucault writes:

If the deployment of alliance is firmly tied to the economy due to the role it can play in the transmission or circulation of wealth, the deployment of sexuality is linked to the economy through numerous and subtle relays, the main one of which, however, is the body—the body that produces and consumes. In a word, the deployment of alliance is attuned to a homeostasis of the social body, which it has the function of maintaining; whence its privileged link with the law; whence too the fact that the important phase for it is "reproduction." The deployment of sexuality has its reason for being, not in reproducing itself, but in proliferating, innovating, annexing, creating, and penetrating bodies in an increasingly detailed way, and in controlling populations in an increasingly comprehensive way. . . . It is not exact to say that the deployment of sexuality supplanted the deployment of alliance. One can imagine that one day it will have replaced it. But as things stand at present, while it does tend to cover up the deployment of alliance, it has neither obliterated the latter nor rendered it useless. Moreover, historically it was around and on the basis of the deployment of alliance that the deployment of sexuality was constructed.[31]

The question that Foucault leaves open is the specific workings of systems of kinship and alliance that may be covered up, but are neither obliterated, nor rendered useless, by sexuality. This question is particularly important for understanding the relations between gender and sexuality. Rethinking this connection offers the opportunity to reconsider the tangle of relations between individual bodies that produce and consume and are incited and effected in so doing by the discourse of sexuality and the ways in which those bodies are still tied alliances and kinship through both law and economics. Butler makes the important point that "to claim that [sexuality and kinship] ought to be thought in relation to one another is not to claim that sexuality ought to remain restricted within the terms of kinship; on the contrary, it is only to claim that the attempt to contain sexuality within the domain of legitimate kinship is supported by moralizing and pathologizing discourses and institutions."[32] Thus, if we are to understand the stakes in debates over "family values" it is important to think about how regulating sexuality is entangled with maintaining something that might be called "legitimate kinship."

Foucault is making an important distinction between the productive, but nonetheless still disciplinary, mechanisms of incitement that form the discourse of "sexuality" and the repressive enforcement of sexual regulation through kinship relations. The disciplinary discourse of sexuality is not the same as sexual regulation. Foucault argues that sexuality is deployed through interconnected micro-level incitements of desire. Thus, desire itself is what leads the body to participate in the disciplines of sexuality. For example, women who participate in the disciplines of beauty often do so out of a sense of social enforcement, but they also often do so out of a sense of desire, of wanting to be beautiful, of enjoying the pleasures of shopping or the rituals of a daily regime. These incitements of desire are not the regulations of social prohibition, although they may be intertwined with such prohibitions, just as there are sanctions for women who do not desire and refuse to participate in the requirements of beauty; nor are they, like kinship, established through law. It is the force of law that is entailed in the focus on "legitimacy." Sexuality does have the potential to escape the restraints of the law, but the work done by "family values" is precisely to enforce a relation between sexuality and kinship through the regulatory language of values. The very need to assert "family values" as a defining discourse of sexual regulation in U.S. politics demonstrates that sexuality has to some extent escaped from the definitional discipline of kinship, but this disarticulation is by no means fully accomplished: hence the political struggle.

For the Christian-identified radical right (hereafter referred to as the "Right") this political struggle is an attempt to enclose the modern discourse of "sexuality" within legitimate kinship.[33] The Right undertakes this project through a discourse of "return," a return to conservative sexual values, a return of "America" to its "Christian roots." If Foucault is correct, however, the Right is actually trying to establish a new regime in which the modern discourse of sexuality as it has been distinguished from kinship is enclosed within a particular form of kinship—nuclear family life. This "family" is named as "traditional" but is actually most relevant in the post–World War II economic situation. The stakes for progressive social movements in the battles over family values are in Butler's terms not over "kinship . . . [as] identified with any of its positive forms," but over kinship as "a site of redefinition which can move beyond patrilineality, compulsory heterosexuality, and the symbolic overdetermination of biology."[34] Thus, for the various sides in this conflict, the stakes are over how to establish a *new* relation between kinship and sexuality in the postmodern situation, including the postmodern economic situation. Finally, because "sexuality" as analyzed by Foucault is itself a discourse of productive regulation, Rubin's hope in developing a radical theory of "sex" is not simply to establish a "sexuality beyond kinship," [35] but to establish the possibility of "sex" that is not determined by either "sexuality" or "kinship," that is rather open to various "bodies and pleasures."[36]

Foucault's advice for where to begin an analysis of alliance and sexuality thus remains a useful starting point for working out the specific stakes of family values: bodies, both individual and social. Because bodies literally are the site of intersection for various social relations—gender, race class, as well as sexuality—sexual regulation can carry the stakes for these various relations and the social differentiations upon which they depend. The differences and dominations that mark gender, race, and class relation frequently operate by denying this intersection and separating bodies from each other. The regulation of sexuality allows for these intersections to mobilize without being named. Thus, regulating sexuality becomes a means of regulating a number of social relations.

Enclosing sexuality within kinship allows for a multi-axis regulation that is one of the ways in which sexuality becomes weighted with excessive meanings. If legitimate kinship defines legitimate sexuality and is restricted to the "traditional" (nuclear) "family," then the possibilities for a sexual desire outside of dominating social relations can be strictly regulated. The patriarchal gender relations of "traditional" marriage can be articulated not as male domination, but as "values." The early second-wave feminist concerns about the structures of both marriage and sexuality can, thus, be simultaneously undercut. In this sense, the anti-feminist and the anti-homosexual agenda of the Right are directly linked, and both are condensed into talk about "family values."

"Family values" then becomes a means of publicly regulating much more than what goes on in private. In fact, "family" operates as the center of a matrix that regulates the broad set of social relations that differentiate and define the "public." For example, historically in the United States, race relations have been established through a complicated conjunction of sexuality and kinship. Kinship supposedly establishes racial identity in a relatively straightforward manner, but historically this assumption of direct kinship-racial relation has been complicated by sexual and kinship relations across racial borders that are both induced and actively denied. Abdul R. JanMohamed's analysis of sexuality "on/of the racial border" begins to chart some of these complexities by rejoining the white family drama of father, mother, and child with its "open secret" of kinship across racial borders in the history of the United States.[37] "Sexuality on/of the racial border" is structured by and structures a series of kinship relations that require a double form of sexual regulation. Legal regulation within the white community ensures kinship relations that reinforce internal gender and class hierarchies, thus creating appropriate families and continuing family control of property. The racial border is sexualized, just as sex is always racialized—in other words, legitimated sex between white men and white women creates "whiteness," while non-legitimate sex across the border is denied, in both the sense of being silenced and of being restricted. Given this racialization, regulating sex becomes a way of both creating and maintaining the power dynamics of race.

JanMohamed points out that historically, within this system, racism is maintained by white patriarchs' ability to cross this border and forcibly "appropriate" women's sexuality, while denying or punishing any other form of border-crossing; hence, the strong legal (and extra-legal in the form of lynching) penalties for cross-racial sex that were rarely if ever applied to white men's rape of black women. The border allows for the denial of kinship between, for example, white and black children of the patriarch. Crossings of the racial border become "open secrets" that cannot be openly discussed because to do so would "undermine the socio-political impermeability of that border" and force the admission that race relations lie at the heart of the (supposedly race-less) white family,[38] and thus also at the heart of "family values."

On this reading, race is, in fact, central to the gender dominance that "family values" so obviously articulates. The control of white women within the confines of legitimacy and through the "threatening protection"[39] of the lynching narrative and the violent control of African-American women through cross-racial rape are equally central to this family drama and its "values." Thus, as Susan Fraiman points out, rather than creating an "interracial fraternity" among men, the cross-racial structure of gender dominance connotes "a struggle to preserve racial hierarchies among men which does not exclude so much as rely upon the feminine as a switching point."[40] Thus, the obvious gender regulation of a "family values" that calls for particular gender roles is also productive of racial hierarchies even without so naming them.

Similarly with class: if, as Foucault argues, alliance is deployed in the service of property and inheritance, as alliance and sexuality become related in a complicated fashion in the modern period, sexuality is tied to the economy in multiple ways. Beyond the ways in which the discourse of sexuality constitutes a body that as producer and consumer is tied to and disciplined by economic relations, the continuation of alliance relations implies that inheritance and property are still connected to marriage, family, and sex. Moreover, when modern narratives of class mobility beyond the inheritance structure becomes possible, the category of "respectability,"[41] where respectability means first and foremost sexual respectability, becomes the ordering discourse of that mobility. Thus, respectability becomes the category that ties alliance and sexuality together, so that legitimate sexuality can still be tied to the law and the distribution of property. "Family values" is, then, a new articulation of respectability as a reassertion of legitimacy and kinship in relation to a sexuality oriented to production and consumption. In the terms of "family values," sexual "orientation" becomes so important because while sexuality may be part of the marketplace, producing bodies that both want to labor as producers and participate in the market as consumers, the category of the "family" needs to mediate the value and values of this sexuality in terms of legitimacy.[42]

Mosse also connects the establishment of middle-class more of respectability primarily to the project of modern nation-building. Interestingly, then, in Benedict Anderson's[43] (1991) trifold analogy of "kinship," "religion," and "nationalism" as levels of identity so naturalized that everyone "has" one, the religious, specifically Christian, discourse of "family values" works to reinstate Christianity as the regulating discourse of not just family, but also nation. Sexuality is often taken to mark the moral health of the "nation" as a modern social unit, but the connection between "sex" and the "nation" is often simply assumed. Didi Herman has, for example, identified this type of assumption in right-wing congressman William Dannemeyer's 1989 book, *Shadow in the Land: Homosexuality in America*. Dannemeyer writes that "the United States is surrendering" to the homosexual threat to "our civilization" such that "'we don't even know we've been conquered."[44] A loss of "sexual values" is, thus, tied to a loss of the American nation itself. This connection between values and nation allows talk that conjoins family and values to operate as a site for reworking nationalism under conditions of the transnationalization of capital. Thus, as Foucault suggests, uses of the body and of sex become tied to issues of the economy through a number of circuits in the complex relation of alliance and sexuality. Individual bodies (and their sex) are implicated in the economy as producers, consumers, and as symbols of relations between national and social bodies.

Here, then, we see some of the stakes for the Right in claiming that threats to "family values" are also threats to the nation, if not all of Western civilization. If kinship structures are part and parcel of gender, race, class, and national structures of domination, then efforts to regulate sexuality by keeping it within the confines of legitimate kinship are also efforts to regulate gender, race, class, and nation. This broad regulation of social relations explains what is meant by "family values" and how "sex" becomes burdened with overrepresentation through the discourses of both alliance and sexuality. Within this framework, the seemingly hyperbolic claims of Christian ministers, among others, that homosexuality can end "Western civilization as we know it" make sense. For example, William Bennett argues in the right-wing Christian videotape "Gay Rights, Special Rights" that all civilizations must reject homosexuality for the purpose of maintaining reproduction. Given the fact that underpopulation is not a contemporary problem or even a threat, such claims are nonsensical when taken at face value (unless one believes that if homosexuality is allowed at all, the vast majority will choose it, something Bennett would certainly want to deny). For those on the Christian-identified political Right, however, if sex becomes a site for (re)Christianizing America, then homosexuals would threaten Christian religious identity, the national identity of the United States, and the tie between Christianity and "America."

For radical social movements, particularly those concerned with a radical politics of "sex," the stakes are about the possibilities of creating spaces for bodies that are not overdetermined by the disciplinary mechanisms of either sexuality or alliance. In his later work, Foucault hopes, as does Rubin, to remove sex from both of these discourses. As Foucault says:

> For centuries we have been convinced that between our ethics, our personal ethics, our everyday life, and the great political and social and economic structures, there were analytical relations, and that we couldn't change anything, for instance, in our sex life or our family life, without ruining our economy, our democracy, and so on. I think we have to get rid of this idea of an analytical or necessary link between ethics and other social or economic or political structures.[45]

Simply asserting the autonomy of sex does not make it so. Butler makes the point about elaborating the relationship between radical sexuality and feminist movement is precisely to take into account the ways in which "psyches bear" the "traces of kinship."[46] Moreover, a feminist analysis suggests that it is women's bodies, in particular, that can become the conduits for the various relations and dominations circuited through sexuality and enacted as sexual regulation. The economic relations of sexuality and alliance are particularly inscriptive for women's bodies because other avenues of economic and social relation are more restrictive for women. Hence the Right's simultaneous investment in antifeminist issues is a means of reinforcing the tie between sex and the economy. If we are to share in the various hopes named by Rubin, Foucault, and Butler for sex as a "practice of freedom," we must understand how the Right constructs the relationship between economic value and the discourse of "family values." This relation can be further explored through an analysis of the two "Contracts"—with America and the American family.

Values

So, what does this analysis tell us about the Christian-identified radical Right and why we are currently seeing such vociferous efforts to regulate and control sexuality in the name of "family values"? The preceding analysis suggests that the campaign for family values is not just about regulating "homosexuality." Naming the "American dream" with the tag "family values" is fundamentally about ending (the dream of) the Great Society as established by the social movements of the 1950s, 1960s, and 1970s. What we are seeing today is not just right-wing backlash against the greater visibility of lesbians and gays, nor the necessary outcome of a conservative

Christian theology (after all, the Catholic Alliance, auxiliary to the Christian Coalition, and the Catholic Bishops actually disagree on a number of issues).[47] Rather, the current campaign is part and parcel of efforts to make sexual respectability and "traditional" family structure into discourses that can regulate race and class relations, thus reinforcing efforts to gut the civil rights and social welfare bills of the 1960s and, finally, reasserting Christianity as the defining discourse of the nation.

If the discourse of "family values" is an effort to regulate a broad number of social relations, then resistance is likely to be most effective by making the connections among the various aspects of the right-wing agenda. Making such connections would, for example, place the "Contract with the American Family" in the context of the larger political and particularly economic agenda of the "Contract with America." The two contracts were self-consciously split by Republican Party strategists so that the "Contract with America" could be pitched as fiscal policy and, therefore, as socially "moderate," while the "Contract with the American Family" is pitched as presenting social issues. Thus, the split between the two Contracts opens possibilities for managing the potential contradictions between fiscal and social conservatives, a politically important task given that the alliance between them provides the political power of contemporary conservative politics. Because the two contracts are divided, fiscal conservatives can support the balanced budget, tax cuts (primarily in the capital gains tax), and small business incentives without having to actively identify with an agenda focused on religious expression, school choice, restrictions on abortion, and anti-pornography legislation. Similarly, social conservatives can support these latter measures while distancing themselves from complete freedom of the market, which might produce pornography because it "sells." The explanation, then, for the fiscal and social conservative alliance is not that they are the "same," but that they work together. In fact, the disjunction between them is precisely why they "work." To be allied is not to come to a consensus, to agree, but to work in and through and to depend upon "differences." The "Contract with America" and the "Contract with the American Family" are two separate documents because their separation enables them to speak to different sites in the political landscape, while their connection enables conservative dominance.

In the preamble to the "Contract with America," the two sides of this conservative agenda are placed side by side in a promise to bring about a change that would "be the end of government that is too big, too intrusive, and too easy with the public's money. [This change] can be the beginning of a Congress that respects the values and shares the faith of the American family." In the middle of each Contract are crucial points that provide the links to solidify the alliance. The middle of the "Contract with America" promises "an anti-crime package . . . to keep people secure in their neighborhoods and kids safe in their schools" and "The Family Reinforcement Act" and "American Dream Restoration Act," to give tax cuts that "reinforce the central role of families in American society." Similarly, the middle of the "Contract with the American Family" promises a "Family-Friendly Tax Policy" and measures to "Punish Criminals, Not Victims." The differences between the two Contracts are, however, also critical to their working together.

The first legislative initiative of each Contract expresses its main point. In the "Contract with America," it is "The Fiscal Responsibility Act," promising a balanced budget and line-item veto "to restore fiscal responsibility to an out-of-control Congress, requiring them to live under the same budget constraints as families and businesses." In the "Contract with the American Family," it is the "Religious Equality Amendment" to "restore" "voluntary, student- and citizen-initiated" religious expression in "non-compulsory settings such as courthouse lawns, high school graduation ceremonies, and sports events."

These separate but connected agendas of the political Right articulate a connection between economic value and moral or religious values. The "Contract with America" places family values in the context of economic reforms that would allow for more corporate freedom in the operation of the marketplace, strengthen "flexibility" in corporate regulation, place limits on punitive damages and product liability in lawsuits, and provide for specifically private insurance for elder care. These reforms are tied with a reassertion of U.S. nationalism through the military, a reassertion that is addressed to contemporary economic conditions under which capital has become fundamentally transnational. "The National Security Restoration Act" would not allow U.S. troops to be under United Nations command and would "restore" military funding "to strengthen our national defense and maintain our credibility around the world." Here the tie between military "credibility" and U.S. credit in the (international) market asserts the importance of U.S. nationalism despite the transnationalization of capitalism. Under these conditions, the state's role as a central site of nationalism has become complicated because it must now embody a transnational form of American-ness, American only insofar as transnational corporations are also U.S. corporations. The working alliance with the other side of the conservative agenda as articulated in the "Contract with the American Family" can, however, help to manage this contradiction by reworking the relationship(s) among the economy, the state, and the American "nation." In this climate, the "family" is being constructed as a site that can come to embody the nation precisely because, under the discourse of family values, it embodies "American" values. Thus, in the "Contract with the American Family," the United Nations is mentioned under provisions "protecting parental rights." The Christian Coalition explains its opposition to the UN Convention on the Rights of the Child as follows:

> The Coalition urges Congress to reject the U.N. Convention on the Rights of the Child because it interferes with the parent-child relationship, threatens the sovereignty of U.S. law, and elevates as "rights" such dubious provisions as access to television and mass media.[48]

To protect the sanctity of the "American family" from threats by supranational politics and (international) mass culture is also to protect "the sovereignty of U.S. law."

The "Contract with the American Family" further manages the contradictions of a "free" market that could undercut "American" sovereignty or more accurately dominance, by placing "freedom" in a religious context. The Contract connects religious "freedom" to a set of conservative moral values, named "family." The connection between religion and "family values" is based on the assumption that without appropriate and public "religion," moral values are not sustained either. Thus, the relationship between value and values is further complicated by the relation between the "religious" and the presumably "secular" in American life. Beyond the obvious ties between political advocates of family values and Christian-identified political groups, the terms "family" and "values" can invoke religion even when religion is not specifically named. Thus, talk of family values engages the complex relationship between the religious and the secular, between myths of "America" as a secular and also as a specifically "Christian" nation. The split between the secular and the religious as it developed in the modern period was often articulated as about establishing a site of "freedom" from religious "dogma." This freedom from religion included economic freedom from ecclesiastical authority, instituting the market as a site of economic activity outside of the oversight of the church.[49] Once the market is established as a secular realm, however, religious values continue to be invoked to temper the socially corrosive effects of the market. Moreover, in their reformed Protestant form, religious values can also be invoked to provide the moral incentive for participation in the market in the form of a "work ethic." As with the attempt to place sexuality within the confines of legitimate kinship, part of the struggle waged by the Christian Right through the assertion of values is to place market "freedom" within the context of Reformed Protestantism. The Christian Coalition has, in fact, had difficulty in its attempt to form Catholic and Jewish alliances precisely because the values that the Christian Coalition names as "Christian" or as "religious" are a particular version of Protestantism.

This connection between market–Reformed Protestantism and the "secular" has important implications for how both religious freedom and religious pluralism are understood and enacted. If "values" is a secular site at which various "religious" traditions might be articulated, then either the differences or the similarities among traditions might be made prominent. The effort to make the secular a site that articulates, without naming, market–reformed Protestant "values" is an effort to erase potential differences. Thus, making market–Reformed Protestant "values" the quintessentially "American" values is to make them the publicly acceptable articulation of all "religions." In referring to "religious" expression in relation to "courthouse lawns, high school graduation ceremonies, and sports events," the "Contract with the American Family" is naming sites for lawsuits that have prevented specifically Christian expression, without making this Christian content explicit or without referring directly to lawsuits that have been brought by offended Jews or Muslims who felt that American public sites should not be marked as specifically Christian.

Not only must "family values" be placed in its context as Christian, the unnamed version of Christianity—market–Reformed Protestantism—invoked by "family values" enables the working alliance between conservative economics (value) and conservative social programs (values). Thus, the split between the two Contracts that enables some people to identify with only one side or the other of the conservative program is linked together through the connection between (economic) value and (religious) values.

This working alliance between the two Contracts allows the Right to pursue an agenda of gender, race, class, and sexual regulation without ever having to name it as such. For example, despite the Right's seemingly incessant focus on homosexuality, often the first issue named in fundraising letters for conservative organizations like the Family Research Council, the Christian Coalition's talking points on the "Contract with the American Family," do not mention homosexuality at all. The

Christian Coalition does enumerate the points in the Contract that would "restore respect for human life" and restrict pornography, but women and homosexuals are nowhere mentioned as the targets of such initiatives. Moreover, welfare cuts, arguably the most extensive and effective of the social regulatory measures, are not mentioned in the "Contract with the American Family." According to the division between the two documents, cutting welfare is primarily a fiscal act that has some social effects but is not really relevant to the protection and promotion of the "American family." Rather welfare cuts promote "personal responsibility," the individual responsibility to act within the confines of the free market.

Resistance

This reading of the broad context invoked by the simple phrase "family values" has important implications for social movements that work to resist sexual regulation. If social movements, like the Right or even certain strands of feminist movement, turn to sexual regulation in order to regulate a number of social relations, and if "family values" connects Protestant moral values to a program of economic value, then resistance to these discourses requires a similarly broad-based response. My suggestion is that Christian-identified, right-wing discourses in favor of sexual regulation, particularly the discourse of "family values," be read and responded to as not simply about sex. Anti-homophobic movements, for example, would do well not to isolate talk about family values as if it is simply homophobic or heterosexist discourse. Moreover, replicating the discourse of "family" within the context of "lesbian and gay" politics in a bid for inclusion in dominant cultural and social structures can also replicate the various social hierarchies condensed within the symbol of "family values." Similarly, feminist movements need to take care that their own concerns about sexuality not be articulated as singularly about gender relations, rather than as about the intersection of a network of social relations. "Family values" provided the legitimating discourse for both the Defense of Marriage Act *and* the welfare reform bill in the summer of 1996. This connection did not, however, materialize an alliance between advocates of "gay rights" and of "welfare rights," and the resistance to each bill on its own was ineffective.

The division between "moderate" fiscal conservatives and more radical social conservatives is, however, accepted by many dominant "lesbian and gay rights" groups, including the Human Rights Campaign (formerly the Human Rights Campaign Fund), which made a donation to Bob Dole's campaign in order to empower "moderate" republicans over "conservatives." This strategy was undertaken in the name of creating a "broader" lesbian and gay movement, meaning one that extends beyond the radical Left. My analysis of "family values" indicates, however, that the effort to broaden the movement to include Bob Dole also effectively narrows it to exclude potential allies while leaving intact the conservative alliance. By accepting the claim that the conservative fiscal agenda is not relevant to social issues like lesbian and gay rights, anti-homophobic movements come to speak mainly for those white, middle-class men of privilege who are just like Bob Dole, "but for" being gay, while they exclude all those queer bodies that are regulated by budget cutting and welfare reform as well as by "homophobia." If, however, the Human Rights Campaign wants to create a "broader" movement, it would need to hold conservative politicians responsible for both sides of the conservative agenda. The "Contract with America" and the "Contract with the American Family" work precisely by presenting their agenda as separate issues, and then holding the agenda together through a discourse like "family values." If "family values" can legitimate sexual regulation through both fiscal and social legislation, through both "welfare reform" and bans on "gay marriage," then attempting to address social issues of sexual regulation, while ignoring its fiscal component, is unlikely to dislodge the current dominance of "family values" in any meaningful way. Taking on "family values" in its various permutations would broaden "lesbian and gay" movement well beyond a single-issue focus on "homosexuality." More importantly, such breadth of analysis and agenda would clarify the stakes for queers as well as straights in the entire right-wing agenda, showing how "family values" provides the punitive discourses about women, poverty, race, and sexuality that short-circuit counter-claims for economic and racial, as well as sexual, justice.

Notes

1. Betty Friedan, *The Feminine Mystique* (New York: Penguin, 1963).

2. Carol Stack, *All Our Kin: Strategies for Survival in a Black Community* (New York: Harper and Row, 1974).

3. Robert Baird, *Inventing Religion in the Western Imaginary* (Princeton: Princeton University Press, forthcoming).

4. See, for example, Carolyn Walker Bynum's work on the importance of food symbolism in medieval Christianity, *Holy Feast and Holy Fast: The Religious Significance of Food to Medieval Women* (Berkeley: University of California Press, 1987). Also see Beverly Harrison's history of Christian perspectives on abortion, *Our Right to Choose: Toward a New Ethic of Abortion* (Boston: Beacon, 1983).

5. For example, conservative U.S. Christian efforts to control gender roles, particularly in relation to sexuality, can be read as offering an area of control that structural economic shifts in gendered work patterns have denied. For useful sociological analyses of these issues, see Nancy Ammerman, *Bible Believers: Fundamentalists in the Modern World* (New Brunswick, N.J.: Rutgers University Press, 1987); and Judith Stacey, *Brave New Families: Stories of Domestic Upheaval in Late Twentieth Century America* (New York: Basic Books, 1990).

6. Sarah Lucia Hoagland, *Lesbian Ethics: Toward New Value* (Palo Alto, Calif.: Lesbian Studies Institute, 1988).

7. The first project potentially includes regulation of women's sexual relations with men, eventually producing a focus on political lesbianism as "feminism's magical sign"; the second project potentially includes regulation of depictions as well as acts of sexual violence. See Katie King, "The Situation of Lesbianism as Feminism's Magical Sign: Contests for Meaning and the U.S. Women's Movement 1968–1972," *Communication*, 9 (1986): 65–92.

8. For example, initial guerilla tactics aimed at proliferating images of sexual violence and the objectification of women (campaigns that expressed wariness about state intervention and censorship) solidified in the 1980s into anti-pornography campaigns that eventually led to efforts to enact civil ordinances against pornography in Minneapolis and Indianapolis in 1983 and 1984 and to Andrea Dworkin's testimony in favor of regulation before the Meese

Commission on Pornography in 1986. Similarly, the 1982 Feminist IX Conference, "Towards a Politics of Sexuality," held at Barnard College, intended initially to be a broadly-based discussion of various aspects of women's sexuality along the lines of both "pleasure and danger," became instead a pitched battle where some feminists sought to regulate the presence of others, particularly the potential participation of members of the Lesbian Sex Mafia. Thus, movements against pornography and lesbian butch-femme and s/m practices became part of an intense move toward sexual regulation.

9. Carole S. Vance, ed., *Pleasure and Danger: Exploring Female Sexuality*, 2d ed., with a new introduction by the editor (London: Pandora Press, 1992; originally published 1984).

10. Some theorists argue that the turn toward a strict anti-pornography campaign was a response to the intractability of male violence. Early activists often felt that if the problem of male violence was exposed, the code of silence around rape and incest broken, then male sexual violence could not be sustained, or at least not sustained at such horrific levels or with such prevalence. By the late 1970s, a decade into these efforts, it was apparent that much more was required. Pornography became the visible, commercialized, and potentially containable expression of this deeper problem.

11. Alice Echols, *Daring to Be Bad: Radical Feminism in America 1967–1975* (Minneapolis: University of Minnesota Press, 1989). Echols states, "By invoking traditional ideas about women's sexuality and manipulating women's anger at pornography, anti-pornography feminists hoped to unify the movement and expand its base. For them pornography was the issue that could transcend race, class, age, sexual preference, and even ideology" (289).

12. Lorde continues, "Is this whole question of s/m sex in the lesbian community perhaps being used to draw attention and energies away from other more pressing and immediately life-threatening issues facing us women in this racist, conservative and repressive period." While Lorde is responding specifically to the increasingly visible pro-s/m movement, a positioning indicative of her role in the anti-pornography movement, her critique can be read as a criticism of the "sex wars" in general since the focus on s/m is maintained as much by anti-pornography and anti-s/m struggles as by sex radical defenders and practitioners of s/m. In Robin Ruth Linden et al., eds., *Against Sadomasochism: A Radical Feminist Analysis* (San Francisco: Frog in the Well, 1982), 68.

13. Evelyn Hammonds, "Black (W)holes and the Geometry of Black Female Sexuality," *differences: A Journal of Feminist Cultural Studies* 6, nos. 2–3 (Summer–Fall 1994): 126–39.

14. These problems have led later theorists to argue that the very structure of the "sex wars" was racist. In her review essay "Feminism and Sexuality in the 1980s," B. Ruby Rich notes that "the ethnocentrism of the sexuality debates remains acute . . . in terms of a sexuality constructed to exclude the experiences and perspectives of so many women of color" (*Feminist Studies.* 12 [1986] 525–63, 869). In *Coming to Power* for example, there are no lesbian of color contributors (see Samois, *Coming to Power: Writings and Graphics on Lesbian S/M* [Boston: Alyson Publications, 1987; originally published in 1981, repr. in 1982]). As Lisa Walker notes, within this type of dominative cultural production, when women of color aren't directly excluded, "[they] become essentialized as authentic subaltern identities" (Lisa M. Walker, "How to Recognize a Lesbian: The Cultural Politics of Looking Like What You Are," *Signs: Journal of Women in Culture and Society* 18, no. 4 [1993]: 869). This essentialism reinforces white domination as positions established by women of color are invoked by white women in order to claim the "other side" is inherently racist, while challenges by women of color to the categories or structure of debate are obviated. See also Jackie Goldsby, "Queen for 307 Days: Looking B(l)ack at Vanessa Williams and the Sex Wars," in *Sisters, Sexperts, and Queers: Beyond the Lesbian Nation*, ed. Arlene Stein (New York: Plume, 1993).

15. Laura Lederer, ed., *Take Back the Night: Women on Pornography* (New York: William Morrow, 1980); Samois, *Coming to Power*.

For example, in "Racism and Sado-masochism: A Conversation with Two Black Lesbians," Darlene R. Pagano opens her interview with Karen Sims and Rose Mason by making direct connections between a white, working-class position and that of black lesbians: "When I first started trying to answer of the sadomasochism arguments, I was with other working-class women, and we said, 'Can you imagine trying to talk about this at home?' . . . And when I went to my Third World friends and said, 'Would you like to be included in this book we're trying to get together?' a couple women when this was first coming up said, 'That's not my issue whatsoever, that's for white people to deal with.'" This mention of class, effectively appropriated into race, is the only reference to class in Linden et al., *Against Sadomasochism* (99). In *Take Back the Night*, class is rarely mentioned; when it is, it is to point to another example of the way pornography eroticizes power relationships. In this text, class is almost always tacked on to examples that invoke racism or anti-Semitism (37). In *Coming to Power*, there is not much overt mention of class; at one point in an interview, Chris asks: "Do you want to talk any about class and sex?" Sharon initially responds by saying no, but then goes on to talk about how it is one more thing that she and her lover have in common—they are both working-class dykes and that makes them comfortable (55). They go on: "That we're both big and strong had something to do with being working class. And physicalness, being more physical. Bear: The only big women that I've been lovers with have been working class. I think I'm attracted more to working class women, partly because of the verbal thing, being able to communicate" (60). While they don't explicitly connect class to the critique of s/m, their argument about physicality seems to lead in that direction.

16. In Vance, *Pleasure and Danger*, 103–114.

17. In Ann Snitow et al., eds., *Powers of Desire: The Politics of Sexuality* (New York: Monthly Review Press, 1983), 468–70.

18. Ibid., 394–405.

19. Ibid.

20. Ibid.

21. John D'Emilio and Estelle Freedman, *Intimate Matters: A History of Sexuality in America* (New York: Harper and Row, 1988), 291.

22. Sue Ellen Case also notes that as lesbians moved up the economic ladder, they tended to forgo role-playing, a move that may, in fact, be connected to passing: to achieve class privilege, one must not be visibly lesbian. In Henry Abelove, David Halperin, and Michele Aina Barale, eds., *The Gay and Lesbian Studies Reader* (New York: Routledge, 1993).

23. Elizabeth Lapovsky and Madeline Davis, *Boots of Leather, Slippers of Gold: The History of a Lesbian Community* (New York: Routledge, 1993).

24. Jill Johnston, *Lesbian Nation: The Feminist Solution* (New York: Simon and Schuster, 1973).

25. In Vance, *Pleasure and Danger*, 386.

26. George Mosse, *Nationalism and Sexuality: Middle-Class Morality and Sexual Norms in Modern Europe* (Madison: University of Wisconsin Press, 1995).

27. In Vance, *Pleasure and Danger*, 279.

28. Gayle Rubin, "The Traffic in Women: Notes on the 'Political Economy' of Sex," in *Toward an Anthropology of Women* ed. Rayna R. Reiter (New York: Monthly Review, 1975), 157–210.

29. See Rubin's interview with Judith Butler, "More Gender Trouble: Feminism Meets Queer Theory," *differences*, 6, nos. 2–3 (Summer–Fall 1994): 27–62, for a description of Rubin's understanding of the relationship between the two articles.

30. "Thinking Sex" is, for example, the first article in *The Lesbian and Gay Studies Reader*. Butler, however, wants to emphasize the relationship between "Thinking Sex" and a

concept of sexual minorities that is not fully encompassed by "lesbian and gay," thus marking the import of "Thinking Sex" as extending, at least to "queer," as well as "feminist" studies. See Judith Butler, "Against Proper Objects," *differences: A Journal of Feminist Cultural Studies* 6, nos. 2–3 (Summer–Fall, 1994): 1–26.

31. Michel Foucault, *The History of Sexuality, Vol.1: An Introduction*, trans. Robert Hurley (New York: Vintage Books, 1980), 106–7.

32. Butler, "Against Proper Objects," 15.

33. I use the term "Christian-identified radical right" to avoid a series of analytic reductions in terms like the "religious right." The reductive nature of such appellations tends to the claims of the Right—that to be religious is to be Christian is to be a right-wing Christian. While "Christian-identified radical right" may be a more accurate phrase, it is also cumbersome. Thus, I also use the shorthand version of the "Right."

34. Butler, "Against Proper Objects," 14.

35. Ibid.

36. Foucault, *History of Sexuality*, 159.

37. Abdul R. JanMohamed, "Sexuality on/of the Racial Border: Foucault, Wright, and the Articulation of 'Racialized Sexuality,'" in *Discourses of Sexuality: From Aristotle to AIDS*, ed. Domna Stanton (Ann Arbor: University of Michigan Press, 1992), 94–116.

38. Ibid., 104.

39. Minnie Bruce Pratt, "Identity: Skin Blood Heart," in *Yours in Struggle: Three Feminist Perspectives on Anti-Semitism and Racism*, Elly Bulkin, Minnie Bruce Pratt, and Barbara Smith (Brooklyn: Long Haul Press, 1984).

40. Susan Fraiman, "Geometries of Race and Gender: Eve Sedgwick, Spike Less, Charlayne Hunter-Gault," *Feminist Studies* 20, no. 1 (Spring 1994): 67–84, 76.

41. Mosse, *Nationalism and Sexuality*.

42. See Gayatri Spivak's "Scatter Speculations on the Question of Value" for an explication of the affective investments in labor, of the ways in which the body desires to "consume the affect of labor itself," thus constituting labor as "affectively necessary" (in *In Other Worlds: Essays in Cultural Politics* [New York: Metheun, 1988], 162).

43. Benedict Anderson, *Imagined Communities* (London: Verso, 1991; originally published in 1983).

44. Didi Herman, *The Antigay Agenda: Orthodox Vision and the Christian Right* (Chicago: University of Chicago Press, 1997), 63–64.

45. Foucault, *The Foucault Reader*, ed. Paul Robinow (New York: Pantheon Books, 1984), 350.

46. Butler, "Against Proper Objects," 15.

47. New York Times, 5 November 1995, Sec.

48. Christian Coalition News Release, 17 May 1995.

49. John Guillory, *Cultural Capital: The Problem of Literary Canon Formation* (Chicago: University of Chicago Press, 1993), 328.

6

REBECCA T. ALPERT

Religious Liberty, Same-Sex Marriage, and the Case of Reconstructionist Judaism

The performance of the marriage ceremony by clergy provides an interesting location for a discussion of the ways in which religious claims on sexual practices
are played out in the public sphere in the United States. Clergy routinely perform
the civil function of marriage, which is delegated to them by the state. "By the
power vested in me by the state of____/and by my religious denomination, I now
pronounce you husband and wife" are words included in wedding ceremonies performed by clergy. This speech act, accompanied by the signing of appropriate licenses, makes the clergy person an agent of the state. Civil and religious marriage
in the United States are thus linked together.

This connection would be unremarkable, except in cases where the religious
institution or the state approves of a type of marriage that the other rejects. Of
course, clergy are not compelled to perform any marriage that their denomination
deems inappropriate. Clergy routinely refuse to perform intermarriages, for example, although the state permits them to perform any marriages, even if both participants are outside their church. But clergy also perform ceremonies that may be acceptable to the denomination, but not legal according to U.S. law, for example,
those that are at too close a degree of consanguinity, or polygamous unions. Another example of marriages that, although to date illegal, have been deemed acceptable to some denominations is the category of same-sex marriage.

Same-sex marriage has come to public attention in the United States recently
because of the current case pending in Hawaii, *Baehr v. Lewin*. A gay couple in
Hawaii went, by their own report quite innocently, to file for a marriage license.

When their request was denied, they brought the matter to the courts, which determined that because Hawaii's constitution has an equal rights clause, it would be sex and gender discrimination to deny same-sex couples the right to marry. The case has gone through several appeals and is now to be decided on appeal by the Hawaii Supreme Court. So far, court rulings have favored the couples that have joined this suit.

In response, a comprehensive reciprocal partners benefits bill was passed by the Hawaii legislature, in the hope that this would satisfy advocates of same-sex marriage. Hawaii is also planning a vote on a constitutional amendment that would redefine marriage as the union of a man and a woman. Other states and the U.S. Congress have already passed "Defense of Marriage" legislation that gives them the right not to recognize same-sex marriages should the Hawaii case stand as law and that explicitly defines marriage as the union of a man and a woman.[1] Whatever the result of the Hawaii case, and similar cases in Vermont and Alaska, same-sex marriage is now on the public policy agenda of the United States, and the question of same-sex marriage must be considered by concerned citizens.[2]

Much of the legal debate about same-sex marriage ignores the religious dimension and concentrates on arguments related to definitions of marriage, gender and sex discrimination, and the reciprocal rights and responsibilities of states. Yet marriage is an important religious issue, both because the state supports religious marriage and because religious communities have a stake in defining public policy about marriage from a moral perspective. In a pluralistic society, each religious group must have the right to determine who is eligible for marriage in that religion. For these reasons, it is imperative that the issue of religious freedom be considered part of the public policy debate on this issue.

As would be expected, there is strong religious opposition to same-sex marriage. Some denominations, for example the United Methodists, have banned ministers from performing these ceremonies, while individuals from these denominations, such as the Reverend Jimmy Creech, have gained national attention by challenging these rulings. Colleges with religious affiliations have refused same-sex couples the right to use their campus chapels. Yet while we frequently hear about religious opposition to same-sex marriage, we rarely hear about those religious groups that have supported gay men and lesbians in their desire to have ceremonies to make public declarations regarding their long-term committed relationships. There is strong support in many religious communities for same-sex marriage, and religious leaders have taken the initiative themselves to perform same-sex ceremonies over the past decade. The Society of Friends, Episcopal priests, Reform and Reconstructionist rabbis, Buddhist priests, and ministers of the United Church of Christ, Lutheran, and Unitarian Universalist traditions have all performed ceremonies of commitment for gay men and lesbians, including public ceremonies involving hundreds of couples at national marches on Washington in 1987 and 1992. If religious denominations are willing to perform same-sex marriages they ought to have the right to confer the same societal benefits for those marriages as for those of heterosexuals. Despite popular opinion to the contrary, these religious ceremonies have no legal status because clergy only serve as functionaries, not arbiters of civil laws on marriage.

The connection between religious and civil marriage opens up the possibility for religious denominations to play a major role in this public policy debate. Rather than viewing these ceremonies as isolated "religious" events that have no bearing on public policy, religious denominational support of same-sex marriage creates an opportunity for progressive religious groups to express moral concern over this particular issue and to exert influence on public policy by demanding the right to perform same-sex marriages that have legal authority based on religious liberty.

Religious Liberty and Same-Sex Marriage

It can be argued that the free exercise clause of the First Amendment gives clergy the right to perform legally binding same-sex marriages as a matter of religious liberty. There are good reasons why religious denominations that support same-sex marriage might choose to make a claim that their religious liberty is being abridged because members of their faith community lack the right to legal marriage.

The free exercise clause suggests that the state must make accommodation to religion for a sincerely held and established religious belief, provided there is no compelling state interest in opposition. Same-sex marriage proponents have argued that the state has no compelling interest in prohibiting same-sex marriage. These marriages would harm no one in society, nor require any cost to the government. These marriages would even support government interests in the stability and support of children and provide an efficient way to distribute health care benefits. Same-sex marriage can also be shown to be a sincerely held and established religious belief. The case of Reconstructionist Judaism will illustrate this point.

Clearly, not all denominations in Judaism support same-sex marriage. To understand what makes same-sex marriage problematic in Jewish tradition, we must examine ancient Jewish understandings of same-sex relationships. In biblical law, male homosexual acts are prohibited, while such acts between females are not mentioned. In rabbinic law, lesbian behavior is considered a minor infraction, but not enough to disqualify a woman who indulges in these practices from marrying a priest, which would be the case if she would have been understood to have lost her virginity through a lesbian act. In other words, homosexual behavior was forbidden. It was not understood in terms of relationships, but as specific acts, at least as far as the law was concerned.

Another compilation of Jewish legal precept, *Sifra*, suggests an awareness of same-sex marriage in other cultures. A gloss on Leviticus 18:3 suggests an interpretation for what is meant to be prohibited by the commandment against "copying the practices of the land of Egypt." The commentary in *Sifra* defines these "practices" as "a man would marry a man, or a woman marry a woman." Homosexual marriage was unknown in Egyptian culture, so the reference was probably to Roman practices known to the author (second century BCE).

This evidence is sufficient to prohibit same-sex marriage for Orthodox Judaism, which follows a strict interpretation of Jewish law. Because of the differences in the ancient laws, which are stricter for men, Conservative rabbis have suggested the possibility of accepting same-sex marriage for women more readily than for men.

But in general non-Orthodox denominations include a doctrine of "tradition and change," which requires that the wisdom of contemporary times must be weighed alongside the dictates of ancient law. These denominations would therefore consider the purposes and values of marriage before deciding whether same-sex marriage would be acceptable.

The organization of reform rabbis, the Central Conference of American Rabbis (CCAR), made news at its 1996 convention by easily passing a measure supporting civil marriage for gays and lesbians and opposing any legislative enactment like the Defense of Marriage Act. Yet the CCAR did not vote in favor of religious marriage for gays and lesbians, but referred the discussion to committee, where it has languished for two years. The Union of Orthodox Rabbis immediately denounced the Reform initiative on civil marriage.

Reconstructionist Judaism

The Reconstructionist movement, which has long been in the vanguard on the issue of gay and lesbian rights, publicly supports civil and religious ceremonies for same-sex couples. *Shahar v. Bowers* cited the acceptance of same-sex marriage in Reconstructionist Judaism as support for a public employee who claimed that she was fired from her position because she participated in a same-sex marriage ceremony.[3] The official statement of the Reconstructionist Rabbinical Association has left willingness to perform religious ceremonies up to the conscience of the individual rabbi and expressed unequivocal support for efforts to legalize civil marriage for same-sex couples.[4] In Reconstructionist Judaism, same-sex marriage is understood as a religious value because it provides economic justice, creates stable, committed relationships, and fosters support for childrearing.

Marriage in Judaism has an economic basis. As witnessed by the Jewish marriage contract, the *ketubah*, marriage began as an exchange of property: a man would "give" his daughter in marriage to another man. Her economic value was determined by her sexual status (virgins were worth more than widows; virginity had to be substantiated or else the terms of the contract could be renegotiated). In exchange, the husband would provide the basic necessities of life for his wife, who was then his property.[5] While a notion of women as property is offensive to modern sensibilities, the Jewish marriage contract provided economic protection for women at a time when choices were limited. Jewish marriage contracts are clearly designed to establish economic well-being for the parties involved.

The political and economic emancipation of women over the past few centuries has changed the terms of the economics of marriage. With those changes have come a variety of changes in the Jewish marriage contract. While traditional Jews still use the ancient contract (which is the only contract valid in Israel), contemporary contracts have been written that omit any economic factors, assuming that women no longer need these ancient protections.

In contrast, civil marriage still has great economic significance. For many gay men and lesbians, the reason to fight for same-sex marriage is indeed economic. Married couples automatically share property and inherit from one another, are defined as next of kin in medical decision-making, are allowed to adopt each other's children, receive pension and health benefits, can file joint tax returns, and provide citizenship for immigrant spouses. The absence of these benefits has caused severe financial hardship to gay and lesbian couples. The traditional Jewish recognition of the economic basis of marriage gives validation to Reconstructionist support of gay marriage on the principle of economic justice.

Marriage in Judaism is also about love. It is an opportunity to give communal support to a committed partnership between two individuals. It is a chance to express faith in the relationship and in the community that supports it. Marriage celebrates the religious values of long-term commitment, faithfulness, and the willingness to share life's joys and sorrows. The nature of the commitment may no longer be about a woman's protection by and subservience to a man but rather emphasizes equality between the partners. Yet the committed nature of the relationship is paramount and enforces deeply held religious values.

There is no difference, in the case of these religious values, between heterosexual and same-sex marriage. The partners pledge the same commitment to love and devotion, in the presence of a loving community. And there is no evidence to show that the intent to make a lasting commitment is different in either case. Same-sex couples seek to be married within the Jewish tradition for the same reasons that heterosexual couples do: they see this public declaration of their commitment in religious terms. Same-sex couples know that the state does not at this time validate their marriages, but they want to be considered married in the eyes of God and the Jewish people. They are looking to invest the ceremony with religious meaning. The principle of religious equality espoused by the Reconstructionist movement requires that these expressions of love be given the same societal validation, regardless of the genders of the partners involved.

Reconstructionist Judaism rejects differences based on gender in the wedding ceremony. Rings and vows are exchanged by equal partners, both parties sign the marriage contract, and they are often pronounced life partners rather than the traditional husband and wife. Often, both partners break a glass at the conclusion of the wedding. This egalitarian approach defines a marriage ceremony that is a transaction of interdependence between equals and removes any assumption that those equals must have different genders.

The other main purpose of marriage from a Jewish perspective is to control and encourage procreation. In today's society procreation outside of marriage is not stigmatized as greatly as it once was, although single mothers still receive serious approbation from society. Married people without children are also more common, and childlessness within marriage is more acceptable. But Jewish communal values are strongly pro-natalist. The shrinking of the Jewish community through the Nazi genocide on the one hand and factors of assimilation on the other produce a strong communal value in support of having and raising children. The Jewish population has remained stable over the past few decades. Jews form a very small percentage of the world population. The threat of extinction makes Jewish leaders passionately committed to population growth, despite larger societal concerns.

While many people assume that same-sex marriages are childless, this is far from the truth. Stereotypic notions of gay antipathy to children are slowly being eroded. The availability of children for adoption to single parents (and even to gay couples), the growing awareness and acceptance of alternative insemination methods, and the presence of children from previous heterosexual unions make children commonplace in gay and lesbian communities. In the Jewish community in particular, one can speak of a gay and lesbian baby boom.[6] Gay and lesbian Jews are often attracted to involvement in the Jewish community because of their desire for children. And this desire is often connected to a wish to marry, for legal protection for children if for no other reason.

Same-sex marriage promotes "family values"—pro-natalism, communal involvement, monogamy. It is an issue of economic justice and gender equality. It is an issue of public policy that directly involves clergy, and individual clergy already perform ceremonies of commitment for same-sex couples that have yet to be recognized by civil law. These factors establish a warrant for Reconstructionist Judaism to define same-sex marriage as a deeply held religious belief, and on that basis to claim the right to perform same-sex marriages as a dimension of religious liberty. Similar arguments could be made by other denominations that have publicly performed and supported same-sex marriages.

A Religious Liberty Approach to Same-Sex Marriage

Legal scholars interested in same-sex marriage have been reluctant to argue for same-sex marriage based on this strategy. Their reluctance stems from several factors. They are skeptical about using religious arguments for determining public policy. Efforts to establish the right to marry based on religious liberty have failed in the past. And recent court rulings have begun to place limits on claims of religious liberty. Yet it is precisely for these reasons that this strategy should be employed, in order to challenge restrictions on religious liberty and the role of religion in public life.

Many liberal religious denominations are reluctant to demand public policies that recognize their religious beliefs. In recent years, progressive religious people have been reticent to involve themselves in the public policy debate, while conservative religious people have spoken out strongly and decisively, powerfully influencing policies governing issues like abortion and gay rights. Perhaps the progressive voices have been silent because they believe that these are issues of privacy. Or perhaps they have forgotten the role that progressive religious voices played in issues like civil rights and U.S. interventions in Latin America. Or perhaps it is because of their understanding of the doctrine of separation of church and state.[7] This reluctance is particularly misguided in the case of marriage where religious leaders are given the authority to preside over a civil function. Furthermore, a religious liberty argument does not suggest that a particular religion's values be universally accepted; only that their values are recognized as valid and given respect in the public sphere.

A religious liberty argument also assumes the right of religious people to express their values in the public arena. It is an abdication of responsibility for religious leaders not to speak out about moral issues. The anti-establishment clause in the First Amendment suggests that no particular religious belief should have the authority of state power. It nowhere implies that those with moral values based on religious commitment should not make a persuasive case in the public arena in favor of those values. It only suggests that no particular religious group has the power to determine public policy based on their beliefs. A democratic system requires the full participation of all its citizens in the making of public policy. And moral considerations cannot be omitted from democratic deliberation if we are to make policies that promote liberty and justice.[8]

Free Exercise and the Right to Marry

The courts' rejection of free exercise arguments for polygamy in the past suggest that compelling state interest outweighs religious liberty as it relates to defining a right to marry. But there have been challenges to this judicial perspective,[9] and it is not unreasonable to argue that the 1878 ruling on polygamy should also be reconsidered as an abridgment of religious liberty. Constitutional law professor Mark Strasser points out that Native American polygamous unions have been recognized by some states under full faith and credit.[10] Whether or not there is a compelling state interest against polygamous unions should not necessarily determine whether there is a compelling state interest in prohibiting same-sex unions, however. These unions should be viewed on their own merit on the basis of religious liberty strongly supported by religious values.

Another argument against this strategy is that recent court decisions have begun to limit religious liberty, as in *Employment Division v. Smith* (1990), which prohibited religious use of peyote by Native American churches.[11] Constitutional scholar David Kairys suggests that this Supreme Court ruling has set a precedent that limits free exercise in the case of non-majoritarian and unpopular practices and cautions us to be concerned about these limitations on religious freedom that the conservative Court has begun to enact.[12] A religious liberty case on same-sex marriage would give supporters of a broader reading of religious liberty an opportunity to articulate their arguments publicly and a chance to raise the right for individuals to have their religious beliefs and practices accommodated by this society, even if these are not the beliefs and practices of the majority.

Other Religious Strategies in Support of Same-Sex Marriage

In addition to making the religious liberty argument, religious groups might also employ other strategies to support same-sex marriage. Public protest and resistance would give religious people opportunities to express outrage about the injustice of the laws and attitudes that prohibit same-sex couples from marrying. They would demonstrate the prophetic function of religion: to show a society that its laws are unjust and must be changed.

There are several situations that might call forth such strategies. For example, legislators have proposed arresting clergy who perform same-sex marriages in states where these ceremonies are not legal. Clergy who would submit to arrest for performing a same-sex marriage could challenge this proposal. Such acts of civil disobedience would surely bring attention to this issue. Religious denominations could also consider challenging the Defense of Marriage Act in court because it too could be viewed as religious discrimination against denominations that recognize same-sex marriages. Public support (in the form of friends of the court briefs) for the case that Robin Shahar has brought to the Supreme Court is another vehicle for making religious voices heard on this issue. And religious groups could be writing letters to the editor and opinion columns in the press to express their view that same-sex marriage is a matter of religious liberty. Several groups have generated "Declarations of Support" for same-sex marriage, garnering hundreds of signatures. Supportive clergy could also perform highly visible same-sex ceremonies on college campuses where there has been controversy over the use of chapels for such ceremonies, for example at Emory College, which ruled that same-sex marriages could be performed in their chapel only by clergy whose denominations supported these ceremonies. Clergy might also consider a more radical strategy suggested by Rabbi Jane Litman, who refuses to sign any marriage licenses for heterosexuals until same-sex couples are given the right to marry.

Together, these strategies for same-sex marriage based on religious liberty and in opposition to religious discrimination are critical for religious denominations to pursue. Such an approach, based on religious values like economic justice and support for building family networks, would strengthen the position of liberal religious groups in their efforts to take a role in deliberations over public policy. It would support the idea that religious liberty needs to be broadened in scope rather than limited in our society. And it would establish the right to marry as a significant dimension of religious liberty. By publicly advocating same-sex marriage through legal and political strategies, religious denominations could create new possibilities for conversations in the public sphere that acknowledge the crucial role of religious ethics in determining public policy.

Notes

1. For an overview of the legal issues related to same-sex marriage and the Hawaii case, see William Eskridge, *The Case for Same-Sex Marriage: From Sexual Liberty to Civilized Commitment* (New York: Free Press, 1996), and Mark Strasser, *Legally Wed: Same-Sex Marriage and the Constitution* (Ithaca, N.Y.: Cornell University Press, 1997).

2. For articles about this debate, see two anthologies: Andrew Sullivan, ed., *Same-Sex Marriage: Pro and Con, a Reader* (New York: Vintage, 1997); and Robert M. Baird and Stuart E. Rosenbaum, eds., *Same-Sex Marriage: The Moral and Legal Debate* (New York: Prometheus Books, 1997).

3. *Shahar v. Bowers* 70 F.3d 1218, 1223 (11th Cir. 1995). The ceremony in question was performed by Reconstructionist rabbi Sharon Kleinbaum. Shahar lost the case at the federal district level but has decided to appeal to the Supreme Court. If the Court decides to hear the case, religious discrimination will be part of the argument presented by Shahar's lawyers, as it was at the lower levels.

4. *Homosexuality and Judaism: The Reconstructionist Position*, the Report of the Recon-

structionist Commission on Homosexuality (Wyncote, Pa.: Reconstructionist Rabbinical Association, 1993), 40–41.

5. Judith Wegner, *Chattel or Person? The Status of Women in the Mishnah* (New York: Oxford University Press, 1988).

6. See Christie Balka, "Thoughts on Lesbian Parenting and the Challenge to Jewish Communities," *Bridges* 3 (1993): 57–65.

7. See Robert Booth Fowler, *Religion and Politics in America* (Methuchen, N.J.: American Theological Library Association and Scarecrow Press, 1985), 175.

8. For a thorough discussion of the need for moral values in public debate, see Iris Marion Young, *Justice and the Politics of Difference* (Princeton: Princeton University Press, 1990); Sissela Bok, *Common Values* (Columbia: University of Missouri Press, 1995); Amy Gutmann and Dennis Thompson, *Democracy and Disagreement* (Cambridge: Harvard University Press, 1996); Elizabeth Mensch and Alan Freeman, *The Politics of Virtue.*(Durham: Duke University Press, 1993).

9. Mark Strasser, *Legally Wed*, points out that William O. Douglas, in his dissent in *Wisconsin v. Yoder* 406 U.S. 205, 247 (1972), commented that this decision would eventuate in overturning *Reynolds v. United States* 98 U.S. 145 (1878), which banned polygamy (65 n. 87).

10. Strasser, *Legally Wed*, 113.

11. The U.S. Congress responded to this case by passing the Religious Freedom Restoration Act (RFRA, 1993). The Supreme Court reiterated its position in *Boerne v. Flores* (1997), which ruled that Congress exceeded its power in passing RFRA. RFRA was problematic legislation, as it shifted the burden of proof to the states to show compelling interest, rather than on the challenger to prove discrimination.

12. *Employment Division v. Smith* 494 U.S. 872 (1990). For a full discussion of the implications of this case for religious liberty of non-majoritarian traditions, see David Kairys, *With Liberty and Justice for Some: A Critique of the Conservative Supreme Court* (New York: Free Press, 1993), chap. 4.

Sticks and Stones

The Language of Public Debate

TRACI C. WEST

The Policing of
Poor Black Women's
Sexual Reproduction

In popular political rhetoric about social problems in this nation, the sexuality of poor black single mothers who receive welfare is labeled a major threat that endangers the moral health of society. Politicians, academics, and media pundits who contribute to the shaping of public policy often make dramatic claims that stigmatize the procreation of poor black single moms. Thus, the nature of poor black female identity comes to be seen as an appropriate object for public scrutiny, debate, and regulatory experiments. The rhetorical assaults on these women and girls license vicious, state-sponsored, material assaults on them in both direct and indirect ways.

A careful investigation of how and why the sexual behavior of this particular population is declared a national crisis provides insight into the subjugating character of American moral discourse. Through such moral inquiry, we glimpse the peculiar racial-gendered dynamics involved in a nationally orchestrated process of inventing a cultural anathema. Unfortunately, it is invented at the expense of women and children who suffer under the most extreme poverty conditions that our society produces. Examining the specific terms of the rhetoric is helpful in deciphering how the social violation of women, expressed as the public demeaning of women, is couched in an acceptable veneer. I investigate this damaging process by focusing on a representative sampling of statements and arguments advanced by public leaders and in popular media. In particular, those discussions of federal welfare reform that center on the topic of "illegitimacy" serve as the primary source for my analysis.

In addition, many of the claims that are made about contemporary black women invoke recurrent historical depictions of them. Recognition of this tradition of stigmatization deepens one's insight into the context and basis for the ideology about black women's immorality that infuses the more recent rhetoric. This overall decoding project yields clues about how some of these public assaults on poor black women and girls might be thwarted. It points us toward some strategies for shifting the moral discourse by undermining the objectification of poor black single moms.

In this discussion, I seek to chart and critique the distinctly ideological nature of popular political constructions of poor women, rather than offer a study of poor women's lives. The dominant ideology that is described here is devised to serve the political interests of its authors rather than the women and girls who are objectified in its characterizations. Unfortunately, the brokers of power who invent these political constructions are distinctly unconcerned with the human dignity and worth of the population occupying the focus of their attention. This indifference is evidenced by the insistent propagation of narratives that are deeply disrespectful and endangering to those women's dignity and survival. The transforming of fictive characterizations that entrap and damage the lives of women and children into public policy not only constitutes a corrupt process of social control but poses a real threat to society.

The "Illegitimacy" Threat

In the 1996 "Personal Responsibility Act," the initial section, "Reducing Illegitimacy," begins in an auspicious fashion: "It is the sense of the Congress [of the United States] that marriage is the foundation of a successful society"[1] A second statement added immediately following this one asserted: "Marriage is an essential institution of a successful society which promotes the interests of children." In those few words the authors of the bill signal their definition of a woman's choice to birth and mother children without being wedded to a man as socially transgressive behavior. This welfare reform bill was introduced during the 104th Congress as a centerpiece of its "Contract with America" plan. As this legislation illustrates, political leaders at the highest levels of government have devoted much of their energy and time to highlighting "illegitimacy" as a historic crisis confronting the nation. Black women will be singled out in this effort, their sexual reproduction designated a unique cultural menace.

The social offense that is constructed here can be defined in the following way. The identified culprits are women who engage in heterosexual liaisons, become pregnant, and then choose to give birth to and raise their children. These women are considered to have produced "illegitimate" children if they are not partnered to a man in a relationship that has been validated with a state-issued license. If these women are sufficiently impoverished that they need financial assistance from welfare programs, the eligibility of their sexual and maternal behavior for condemnation intensifies exponentially. In popular political rhetoric, the notion of "illegitimacy" is a useful recipe for linking together blacks, women, welfare, and sexuality, to identify a national phenomena of rampant immorality.

The Purported Enormity of the Crisis

Avowals about the tremendous import and proportions of the problem of "illegitimacy" seemingly justify the cloak of urgency that is often repeated in the media. Epitomizing this viewpoint are statements like the one published in the *Wall Street Journal*, written by Charles Murray, a proponent of the innate intellectual inferiority of poor blacks.[2] Murray asserted: "Illegitimacy is the single most important social problem of our time—more important than crime, drugs, poverty, illiteracy, welfare, homelessness because it drives everything else."[3] Even in the aftermath of the Republican welfare legislation cited above, which granted the issue of "illegitimacy" such primacy, the conservative popular magazine *National Review* similarly claimed:

> Illegitimacy is arguably America's greatest social problem. Yet nobody is willing to do anything about it. The welfare bureaucracy's historic response to public dissatisfaction has been to make window-dressing reforms that pose no threat to its power and indeed enhance it.[4]

This editorial also encapsulates prevailing sentiment about illegitimacy, establishing its primary status among social problems, endemic link to welfare policy, and significance as a "public" concern. The tone offered here represents another frequently sounded general theme that calls for a firm, tough approach to "illegitimacy" that has heretofore been lacking. Apparently, what is fundamentally needed to effectively respond to the problem of illegitimacy is someone in government who has the backbone to definitively defeat the "power" of the welfare bureaucracy, for that bureaucracy purportedly generates the "greatest social problem" in America.

It has been pointed out by liberal welfare reformers that the term "illegitimacy" offensively characterizes an "innocent" child's personhood.[5] This argument implies that it is more appropriate to label the mother's "non-innocent" behavior, as in the preferred term "out-of wedlock births." Even if one accedes to this rhetorical effort to guard the innocence of the offspring of single moms, the problematic nature of the term "illegitimacy" should be understood more broadly. There is more connoted in this language than a reference to an "illegitimate" child. As employed in the federal welfare bill cited above and influential media such as the *Wall Street Journal* or the *National Review*, "illegitimacy" signals a large antisocial entity that spawns other social ills. This entity must either be "reduced" (1996 "Personal Responsibility Act") or emptied of its "power" (the *National Review*). The term "illegitimacy" presupposes the existence of a moral/social standard that does not need to be described or explained. This tacit standard subsumes women's sexual reproductive behavior, categorizing and interpreting it as wrong. The term itself helps to reduce women, to empty them of their "power" (read personhood). Carrying no direct reference to the humans involved, it spotlights some thing or group of things that commit "illegitimate" acts. Of course, the femaleness of these transgressing things is retained. We know that "illegitimacy" is not something of which men are guilty. In part, we know this because the term is either used interchangeably with or defined as out-of-wedlock birthing. Moreover, not all women are thingified[6] in this way. After all, even within the ranks of women who commit "illegitimacy," those mothers who have the financial means to avoid welfare assistance are not actually included under this regulatory action. By labeling "illegitimacy" as the problem, the Congress and its supporters in the media can mask the fact that they are really only targeting poor mothers who engage in this phenomena called "illegitimacy." Especially when "illegitimacy" is attached to the similarly encoded term welfare, we come to appreciate that it is poor women, poor black women particularly, who are so easily reduced.

The mindset exemplified in the *National Review* presumes the appropriateness of the federal government's role in unseating the supposed powerful hold that "illegitimacy" has over this nation. The article suggests that there is a "dissatisfied public" expecting the government to respond to the problem. This particular kind of family problem necessitates strict government control. There is also an unequivocal presumption that, with motivated leadership, legislation and bureaucracy linked to welfare are the appropriate venues for making the needed changes. It seems natural that the problems of these families—"female-headed" families—must be regulated by manipulating their access to resources such as food, housing, and health care.

An alert also was sounded by President Clinton when preparing to begin his second term in office, he dedicated his very first radio message of the new year (1997) to the subject of "teen pregnancy." In this speech he warned that there was a lot more for his administration and the nation to do in order to make the American dream a reality for all citizens in the twenty-first century. He noted that "we still have some pretty big problems in our society. None stands in our way of achieving our goals for America more than the epidemic of teen pregnancy."[7] The ensuing references in the radio address to the poverty conditions of teen mothers and to the welfare that they receive made it clear that the sexual reproduction of poor girls was the main subject of his concern. Their sexual behavior prevents the nation from moving ahead to achieve its goals in the twenty-first century.

Unlike the gloomy outlook of other alarmists, Clinton conveys a sense of hope and efficacy when he boasts in this same speech about the "executive action" he took to deny welfare benefits to "young mothers" who do not remain in school. Punitive manipulation of access to the funds needed to support the livelihood of poor mothers and children is seen by the president as an outstanding achievement. The president reiterates a familiar linkage in popular rhetoric about the key social problems facing the nation. Crime, welfare, and out-of-wedlock births are collectively cited as the most pressing national issues, with teen pregnancy (a subset of the out-of-wedlock birth issue) being described as the number-one problem. This selection of references places the onus on a particular marginalized population, targeting, in a thinly veiled way poor, urban, racial minorities. In explaining what impedes the progress of this nation, President Clinton selects problems of some of the very poorest communities. He lumps together certain features in the lives of differing members of those communities under the category of irresponsible behavior and designates poor teenage mothers as the preeminent impediments.

When the president of the United States argues that the power to hinder this nation's progress rests primarily upon the sexual reproductive behavior of the most economically and socially disenfranchised group of girls in American communities, a highly distorted notion of reality is portrayed. It is precisely the depth of their so-cial vulnerability that makes the girls such accessible subjects for this distortion. Ad-ditionally, the selection of their sexual reproductive behavior creates an ideal tool for shaming and silencing them as well as any potential dissenters from this con-structed reality. Placing mothering behavior in the same context as "other" shame-ful behavior such as crime, equates or at least directly relates the birthing and rais-ing of children by these girls with the victimizing of others by means of assault or the taking of life and property. The connection with such criminality annuls any claims poor women and girls might have to being "innocents."

The president's depiction completely reverses the reality of where social power is actually concentrated and how it is normally exerted in American society. It hides the truth that power over other citizens is principally wielded by those who are the most economically advantaged and whose identities are granted privileged status in our society. Instead, we are led to view those who struggle from the bottom of the social and economic pyramid of benefits and status in this culture as exercising the highest degrees of social influence over this nation's future. The existence of potent institutional social forces is neglected, in favor of placing the onus upon the control of personal behavior by selected low-status individuals. The fiction is further se-cured by severely limiting conceptualization of social problems to one small sector of the population. President Clinton's construct ensures that the myriad of social problems concentrated in other economic groups besides poor females are ex-cluded from popular vocabulary and perceptions. And, this technique of spotlight-ing poor women and girls tacitly renders invisible *actual* crimes related to sexuality committed by other groups, such as sexual abuse by male professionals of female co-workers and clients.

The Black Face of the Problem

When considering the rhetorical construction of the imperiled plight of this nation due to the proliferation of single moms on welfare, the recurrent characterizations of blacks must be noted. The issue of welfare policy has provided a platform for using black women as principle icons for what needs reforming and who needs to exercise "personal responsibility." When President Clinton signed the 1996 "Per-sonal Responsibility and Work Opportunity Reconciliation Act," he was flanked by two black female former welfare recipients, Penelope Howard and Janet Farrell. They literally functioned as exhibits personifying the societal problem that this leg-islation was meant to address. Clinton pointed the women out in his speech at the signing ceremony, notifying his audience that these kinds of women are, in fact, ca-pable of personal responsibility and of actually working.

The governor of New Jersey orchestrated the same type of display during her televised 1997 "State of the State" address. At a previously agreed-upon moment in the governor's speech, Monica Jones, a former welfare recipient who was sitting the audience, stood up. In the midst of discussing her welfare reform achievements and proposals, Governor Christine Whitman raised a pointed finger toward the stand-ing black woman. Governor Whitman described Monica Jones as formerly on welfare but now usefully employed, now *helping* her "own community." For political leaders of this nation to persuade the public that economic problems related to poverty are merely matters of deficient moral fiber among welfare recipients, the visual identification of a black woman serves as one of the most potent tools available.

In addition, as a national "illegitimacy" crisis is dramatically announced and depicted, blacks are described as the ones who lead the way down this supposed path of disaster. One is reminded with monotonous frequency by politicians and news reporters often in connection with discussions of welfare, that "illegitimacy" is a dominant factor in black communities.[8] Sometimes this trend is delineated as mainly prevalent among the black poor, and sometimes not. Whether named as the disintegration of black families or the crisis of multiplying African-American "female-headed families," the existence of single black moms seems to be an especially conspicuous "epidemic" for mass media and policymakers.

The increasing illegitimacy rate among African Americans is the very first citation in the "Reducing Illegitimacy" section of the "Personal Responsibility Act" of 1996. I hasten to add that this example is followed by a statistic about the growing illegitimacy rate among whites. In a later paragraph, the act states the "fact" that the likelihood of a young black man committing a crime increases substantially if he is raised "without a father." This notation about the adverse consequences of black single motherhood is placed under the "Reducing Illegitimacy" heading. As such "illegitimacy" and single black motherhood are seen as part of the same socially destructive manifestation. Also, the absence of a statistic about crime and the sons of white single mothers conspicuously supports the ideological agenda of maintaining the primary connection of crime, blacks, illegitimacy, and black single mothers. Maintaining this linkage solidifies an image of these categories as an equatable, interdependent cadre and as a predominant, multi-pronged moral contagion.

The racialized structuring of this rationale portrays a country that consists of two cultures: one black, one white. According to this view, "illegitimacy" and its concomitant depravities have already overrun black culture and are beginning to take root in the white community.[9] But why is race being discussed at all? Stated differently, why has race been defined by national leaders as the most salient feature for culturally analyzing the procreative behavior of poor women and girls? Also, are we to infer that racial/ethnic groupings other than blacks and whites are insignificant in their rates of "illegitimacy"? Or, are other groups purposely deleted from the social spectrum of American society when "personal responsibility" legislation is being devised? If so, why?

William Bennett, former Bush administration drug czar, helps clarify why blacks are singled out. Echoing a similar sense of urgency as other political leaders, Bennett points out in his testimony before a 1995 House subcommittee considering welfare reform legislation: "Illegitimacy is the single most destructive social pathology in modern American society"[10] He cited that bell weather announcement of the dysfunctional, disintegrating Negro family—the 1965 Moynihan Report— and noted how the problem has only gotten worse in the ensuing thirty years. The Moynihan Report, entitled "The Negro Family: The Case for National Action,"[11] was the centerpiece of Bennett's argument about the momentous proportions of the crisis that confronts us. Recalling this report on the Negro family aids us in recognizing "the ruinous social slide" on which our country has embarked over the last three decades. Bennett ominously warns:

> This rapid, massive collapse of family structure is without precedent among civilized nations. Our country cannot sustain it; no country can. The American public in general—and the black community in particular—would surely give its collective eye teeth to wake up one morning and again face the "frightening statistics" of 1965.[12]

In such espousals of the threat that illegitimacy represents, blacks serve as the prime object-lesson for the nation on moral decline. In part, they are such an accessible example because their social behavior has historically been so closely studied and debated. Hence, social scientific "proof" of their destructive patterns is readily available in documents such as this 1965 report on the Negro family, prepared by a former Harvard University political science professor acting in his role as a senior policy adviser to the president. Because of an extensive history of public assertions and records documenting their base tendencies (which I discuss in more detail below), the invocation of blacks summons familiar images and connotations of moral depravity. In public rhetoric, a reference to black behavior often serves as a handy symbol for demonstrating the intransigence of moral turpitude in the general society.

In the Bennett thesis (invoking the Moynihan thesis), black girls and women commit pathological behavior in their perpetuation of "illegitimacy." Sustaining such pathological behavior, i.e, rising illegitimacy rates, is untenable for a civilized nation and inevitably leads to a dire fate for "our country." In this world of reversed truths, birthing—the spreading of life—is considered the spreading of pathology, of disease. And, it is a disease with catastrophic potential.

This dismal scenario is summarized by economics professor, Glenn C. Loury as he testified at the same session of congressional hearings as Bennett. Loury advocated the restoration of moral teaching for the black community to help stem the tide of "illegitimacy problems and family breakdown." Such moral teaching, he argued, could occur most effectively through religious institutions. Without this restoration, "The behavioral problems which Moynihan first noticed thirty years ago will persist, threatening the survival of the republic."[13] Loury offers a note of hope by proposing moral leadership in the black community as the antidote to the menacing sexual and mothering behavior that infects it. Since he identifies them as the most promising source of help, Loury even suggests that checks be sent directly to churches, so that they can "help the women change their lives." According to Loury, churches can do this by saying to the women: "John over here is living the right way, Judy over here is living the right way, we want you to be able to do that too."[14]

Some state leaders and clergy are quite receptive to the idea of churches playing this kind of role with poor women. The governor of Mississippi, Kirk Fordice, launched a "Mississippi Faith and Families Project" aimed at getting churches to adopt a welfare recipient. This governor, in a state where most of the welfare recipients are black mothers, felt that such a plan "could remove all of Mississippi's families from the welfare rolls in twelve years."[15] Churches are seen as uniquely suited for providing the "tough love" that is needed. Reverend Ronald Moore, pastor of two local churches in the historically black National Baptist denomination, asked to be the first to sign onto the Fordice plan. Several Mississippi churches have reportedly made getting off welfare either a church membership criterion or a goal.[16] Since poor black mothers on welfare are assumed to be inherently immoral, some policymakers enlist the church to act as moral enforcer to redeem them, which after all is the proper business of the church. In this way, the church works for the state, relieving them of economic responsibility while functioning as an instrument that directly reinforces in the minds of the affected women their personal blameworthiness for their economic plight.

Poor black females disproportionately serve as the poster children for moral decline. Finding them guilty of committing significant pathological acts and culpable for monumental social destruction justifies, indeed warrants, social control, punishment, and further castigation.

Gettin' Paid for It!

The tethering of illegitimacy to welfare invites indicting judgments of the sexual morality of poor women and girls in multiple ways. In prevailing rhetoric, the term "welfare" has come to refer to a cultural phenomena, rather than a government program that responds to particular subsistence needs of citizens. It has come to indicate a cycle of dysfunctional behavior, much like the term illegitimacy. Thus, the social significance of welfare and illegitimacy are conflated and described as attributable to personal behavior. They are seen as equatable matters of deliberate, personal choice by certain women and girls. Note that this redefinition removes any focus on poverty from the discussion.[17] The economic disenfranchisement and brutal realities of poverty are eclipsed by the image of a behavioral phenomenon called "welfare," which individuals choose to engage in, because of their own characterological flaws. [18]

In another version of this recasting of systemic economic problems, poverty may indeed be mentioned, but only to be labeled as a consequence of morally bankrupt individual choices. President Clinton, for instance, makes such a link in a speech given to leaders of the black Protestant denomination the Progressive National Baptists. In this speech, he pronounces that it would be viable to cut the poverty rate by more than 50%, if, in part, "Teenagers who are unmarried didn't have babies."[19] The message to the black religious leaders gathered in the audience is: if you want to diminish the poverty that ravages many of your communities, get teenage girls to make different personal choices. If anyone who heard this 1995 speech failed to recognize this rationale as something to be taken seriously, they learned to do so later. By 1997 this principle had been transformed into federal law. As he boasted in the 1997 radio address mentioned above, Clinton enacted welfare legislation to penalize teenage girls and their children by denying them all subsidies for their survival if they do not meet certain conditions about where they can live and about school attendance. The law also encourages states to end cash payments altogether to girls who have children outside of marriage.[20]

Within the logic of this constructed scenario of a combined lifestyle of welfare dependency and "illegitimacy," all possible explanations for why these issues persist in poor communities and how they can be disrupted stem from character deficiencies. Impugning presuppositions about the morality of the poor women and girls who "choose" welfare and illegitimacy as a way of life constitute both the cause and effect of this "national crisis." To expose the specific types of personal defects that are assumed here is to help unravel the overarching and distorting ideologies that are culturally operative.

Those who accept the idea of "personal responsibility" as the crucial issue for crafting public policy related to poverty emphasize the economic link between welfare and illegitimacy. As William Bennett testified before Congress, "Welfare is illegitimacy's life-support system."[21] In this view, welfare is understood as making illegitimacy economically viable. This scenario effaces the prima facie worthiness of poor families for health, housing, and nutrition benefits that enhance and enable their survival. The focus on "illegitimacy" identifies the alleged sexual misbehavior of poor women and girls as the key criteria for consideration when judging their eligibility to receive public monies. The government policy debates conducted within this framework conceive of the women as merely breeders of pathology, namely of "illegitimacy," who receive monetary inducements for functioning as such.

In his testimony before the 1995 congressional hearings on welfare reform, activist scholar Father Robert Sirico succinctly articulated the moral problem related to sexuality that proponents of this view seek to address. Sirico explained, "Removing subsidies will discourage promiscuity. . . . We cannot guarantee perfect results, but we can stop subsidizing the current crisis."[22] Ending this government program is seen as a means for creating sexual discipline among poor females. It remains unclear, however, why these women and girls are considered "promiscuous," that is, guilty of entering into sexual liaisons with many men and thus violating standards of reputed, proper female sexual activity. Is it because they are single with children? If multiple sexual liaisons with men and not singleness is at issue here, do not middle class married women with children from previous marriages also represent a "promiscuous" menace to society? Why aren't middle-class women such as these, who bear children from multiple sexual liaisons, also publicly stigmatized as "promiscuous"? Why doesn't the state seek to regulate *their* "promiscuity" by denial of mortgage tax credits or student loans for the children borne out of that "promiscuity"? How does the state choose which "promiscuous" mothers will be subject to public debate and regulation? Nevertheless, it is abundantly clear that the prevailing, operative ideology warrants manipulation of funding for the food and shelter of the poor based on the assumption that the moral characters of potential recipients are corrupted by their engagement in sexual promiscuity. As media culture critic Caryl Rivers bluntly summarizes, "The image of the black woman as whore is a subtext of the war on welfare. What enrages many people is the idea that tax dollars are subsidizing black sexuality."[23] However, this idea may not always be buried in subtext.

Some proponents of regulating poor women directly assert that poor women and girls engage in this phenomena of illegitimacy for the purpose of attaining welfare money. Representative Tom Delay (R-Tex.) pointedly explains at a Republican press conference on welfare:

> The number one issue in welfare [is] the enabling of illegitimacy in this country. Welfare is a major enabler of illegitimacy, and current policy presents young girls with a terrible deal. They make the best proposition that a young woman under the age of eighteen can make. If you'll just have a baby out of wedlock, taxpayers will guarantee you cash, food stamps, medical care, and a host of other benefits.[24]

The language of Representative Delay and of other proponents of this view evokes the image of prostitution. The state "propositions" poor girls, who accept the deal and then go out and engage in sexual activity, producing offspring in order to receive payment. In Delay's scenario, it is as if the state acts as "pimp," inviting the girl into this way of life, and then sees to it that she gets paid. Especially with respect to younger poor girls, it is taken for granted that cash is the primary motivation for sexual/procreative activity.

Using terminology that relies on these very assumptions, Congressman James M. Talent (R-Mich.) spoke of "the seductive potential" of cash benefits for poor young women to have out-of-wedlock births in his testimony before a House sub committee considering welfare reform.[25] President Clinton, in the previously mentioned speech to the National Progressive Baptists, also insisted that there is a need for a clear signal to young people that a welfare check is not granted so that "you can go out and perpetuate" having babies without being married.[26] Some policymakers even admit that this connection between welfare benefits and "illegitimacy" is not supported by research data but are still undaunted in claiming it as a recognizable truth anyway. Under the Reagan administration, the report from White House Working Group on the Family stated:

> Statistical evidence does not prove those suppositions [that welfare benefits are an incentive to bear children]; and yet, even the most casual observer of public assistance programs understands there is indeed some relationship between availability of welfare and the inclination of many young women to bear fatherless children.[27]

The reasoning demonstrated here is that despite evidence that proves our assumptions false, we still know that they are true. Why are poor young girls depicted through so many statements and inferences by national leaders as "going out" and doing "illegitimacy" for cash? Why does this cultural image of girls who procreate for money "fit" so easily as a convincing portrayal of this population?

In addition, the idea of mothering or the desire to be a mother is erased from the spectrum in this analysis. Instead, the mothering of children by poor females signifies only "illegitimacy"—that thingifying phenomena that purportedly only generates "other" pathologies. Also, the caricature of girls greedily viewing the performance of "illegitimacy" or the birthing of out-of-wedlock children as an opportunity to make money implicitly asserts that some advantaged lifestyle will be gained by this practice. There is a complete misrepresentation of the quality of life that is ensured by the "host of benefits" referred to by the congressman. All of the grinding economic and stressful emotional realities that poor moms face are expunged from the picture and are replaced by a dehumanizing portrait of a girl in search of cash who has found a way to thrive both sexually and economically.[28]

Congressional representative Delay calls for a definitive solution to the problem that poor women's fertility represents in his normative vision for society. He contends that:

> We must encourage responsibility. The birth rate among welfare recipients should be zero. Research shows conclusively that no intervention program, not parenting classes, family planning, education, job training, work experience or counseling can have even a modest impact on making young, unwed mothers financially independent of welfare.[29]

According to this political leader, responsible behavior for women who are poor is to choose to forego their sexual reproduction. In fact, at this Republican congressional press conference, Delay, just prior to this call for zero birth rates, boasts of the recent passage of his amendment to create a federal "abstinence program" for "these young women." This law was an incremental advancement toward his intent to establish a federally mandated means for eradicating all sexual behavior by poor women and girls. Presupposing the inherent immorality of poor females "naturally" leads to this potentially eugenic formula for state policy. This supposition fosters in the public mind the possibility of considering both heterosexual intercourse by poor females as criminal behavior and procreation by the poor as something that needs to be outlawed. Law professor Beverly Horsburgh identifies the same exploitative consequences of animal analogies used by members of Congress for welfare recipients in her critique of how welfare rhetoric stigmatizes black women. Horsburgh argues, "Negative, dehumanizing rhetoric likening the poor to animals in cages distances society from identifying with the intrinsic personhood of welfare recipients facilitating social tolerance of more explicit eugenic measures."[30]

The social acceptability of forced sterilization for poor women is also furthered when measures against procreation and abortions by poor women come together,[31] as they do in the 1996 Temporary Assistance for Needy Families (TANF) program. States are required to set up goals and programs to reduce "illegitimacy" and are awarded hefty sums if they successfully simultaneously decrease their abortion rates.[32] The legal apparatus has now been erected to encourage and sanction state-sponsored sterilization of poor women.

What is the overall significance of the depiction of "illegitimacy" as a crisis, besides the creation of a gateway for curbing and punishing the sexual and procreative rights of poor women and girls? The patriarchal goals of controlling women sexually and of restoring or reinforcing male control of families and communities are less than subtle in this approach. As James Q. Wilson explained in his testimony at the 1995 congressional welfare reform hearings, "But once you have created a neighborhood in which all or most of the children are growing up in single-parent mother-only families, you are creating a neighborhood with men but no fathers. As a result the social control that all communities try to maintain is weakened, because the people who primarily provide that order, fathers who take responsibility for their children and their neighborhoods, are absent."[33] The absence of father-ordered communities and families indeed threatens traditional means of social control.

The motivation behind the deliberate choice to concentrate policy debates about poverty issues on the sexual reproduction of poor women and girls also has to be considered. This choice of emphasis and its expression through the use of such racialized images and coding is quite revealing. It exposes the sexual interests of the individuals who make that choice. Politicians and media could have, for instance, centered their investigation on the link between the poverty conditions that women and girls face and the quality of educational opportunities that are available to them. Their preferred choice of topic allows them to engage in a dialogue that is extremely loaded with images of female sexuality. The constructions of poor black females in terms of uncontrolled sexual reproductivity, promiscuity, and an unstoppable drive to take money for sexual reproduction and then the emphatic avowals about the need to take charge, to definitively assert control over this spreading, driving, persisting phenomena may simply betray the sexual fantasies and fixations of the political rhetoricians. Who knows? For the white male elites involved in this policymaking process, their agitation and insistence on the need to assert control over black female bodies could arise from their collective unconscious memory. Perhaps these white males are partly motivated by the memory of several hundred years of exercising complete domination over black female bodies that were legally defined as chattel. This unconscious memory of the unbridled authority to mandate whatever sexual/procreative functions they desired of those enslaved black female bodies might fuel the simultaneous sense of frustration and entitlement that propels the "welfare reform" agendas described above. Who knows?

Moral Devaluation of Black Women as a Familiar Paradigm

How does explicit governmental control of black women's procreation become so palatable as normative policy in this culture? What makes ideas about poor black women's propensity toward immorality seem like such a valid and plausible presupposition in the American psyche? The acceptability of these notions rests upon familiar, deeply embedded methods of socially constructing black women. The well-established pattern of creating and propagating distorted images of black women in U.S. history lends resonance to rhetoric about welfare mothers. This cultural echo provides credibility to demeaning stereotypes and precedent for invasive state policies.

Slave plantation owners were probably some of the first American architects of plans to regulate black women's birthing and mothering using material means for manipulation. As a sympathetic slave mistress, Frances Kemble explained about incentives for slave women who become pregnant: "Certain additions of clothing and an additional weekly ration are bestowed upon the family. . . . The more frequently she adds to the number of her master's livestock by bringing new slaves into the world, the more claims she will have upon his consideration and good will."[34] Mrs. Kemble's description of slaveowner expectations concerning what motivates slave women toward sexual reproduction prefigures ideology about "welfare mothers" who will bring babies into the world for "a host of benefits." This type of planning offers more important insights about its authors than its targets. The plantation owner schema demonstrates the deep historic roots in white cultural attitudes of the capacity to view birthing and mothering as an economic tool for amassing one's own power and wealth. It helps elucidate the "welfare reform" logic of trying to eliminate women's procreation when the interests of white economic elites are no longer being served by the offspring of those females who are relegated to the lowest socioeconomic spheres in the culture.

Dating back to the antebellum period, pronouncements about the sexual immorality of illegitimate births by black women could be found in public debates about national policy. In the abolitionist newspaper *The Liberator*, William Lloyd Garrison, a leader in the antislavery movement, highlights the often involuntary lack of "chastity" among black slaves and its moral implications for the nation:

> There are in this country a million females who have no protection for their chastity, and who may be ravished by their masters or drivers with impunity!! There are born every year more than SIXTY THOUSAND infant slaves who are *illegitimate*! a large proportion of whom have *white fathers*—some of these are the most distinguished men at the south—who sell them as they would pigs or sheep!! *Is this not perdition upon earth*—A BURNING HELL IN THE VERY BOSOM OF OUR COUNTRY—A VOLCANO OF LUST AND IMPURITY, *threatening to blast every plant of virtue, and to roll its lava tide over all that is beautiful to the eye, or precious in the sight God?*[35]

Though they are construed as victims by Garrison, black women who gave birth to "illegitimate" children are publicly associated with impurity and implicated in endangering a Godly society at this early point in their history as part of the United States.

Historian Beverly Guy-Sheftall details a discussion about black women's sexual immorality that took place during the postbellum period in the northern newspaper *The Independent*.[36] One southern white woman who wrote to this newspaper in 1904 found it inconceivable that any black woman could be described as virtuous and believed black women to be the "greatest menace possible to the moral life of any community" in which they reside. Also in 1904, a northern white woman wrote in an attempt to be charitable, blaming the prejudice of "the white man" for "the worthlessness" and "depravity of the blacks." Guy-Sheftall recounts the discussion of another southern white woman writing to the paper in 1902, who indicated:

> that though she has spent thirty-five years in the South, she has met only one chaste black woman. All of her female servants had illegitimate children and were born out of wedlock themselves. Furthermore, slavery cannot be blamed for the immorality of black women, which is an innate trait that education cannot alter.[37]

As is evident from these examples, there is a long tradition of alleging and chronicling black women's propensity to bear "illegitimates" through sensationalized examples displayed in the American print media. In addition, the 1902 claims about the inherent, recalcitrant moral inferiority of black women that no educational program can modify bears uncanny resemblance to Congressman Delay's emphatic assertion that no government program could impact young welfare women's attachment to the cash for illegitimate babies proposition that the state was offering.

Black women's sexually immoral characteristics have been presented as fact by historians and sociologists throughout most of the lifespan of those academic disciplines in the United States. Antislavery historian Arthur Calhoun explained that because of the brutal sexual practices of slavery, slave women's "female honor" was wiped out.[38] His 1917 *A Social History of the American Family* described how the "negress" manifested "spontaneous sensuality" and the "promiscuities of chatteldom."[39] Historiographer Patricia Morton gives the following concise summary of one of the dominant images of the black woman in similar white-authored historiography during the age of Jim Crow:

> She asserted herself so unrestrainedly that she seemingly could overpower the white man's will to resist her allure. . . . Cast in the image of Eve, the black woman was assigned responsibility for the downfall of the manhood of both races. As the "bad black mother," she apparently fertilized the seeds of savagery in generations of black children, while also neglecting and abusing them.[40]

This account underscores not only the themes of sexual promiscuity and deficient mothering, but also the assertion of black women as culpable for the general downfall of "man." Historians of the early twentieth century helped to initiate the link between black women's sexual behavior and the fate of the society that is later found in 1990s "welfare reform" rhetoric. Sweeping generalizations in historiographical literature attributing blame for the social plight of the nation to the sexuality of socio-economically marginalized women have been given social scientific credibility for more than a century.

The work of sociologist E. Franklin Frazier is a prime example of black-authored social science emphasizing and tracing patterns of black female degeneracy. His 1939 *The Negro Family in the United States* included documentation of the "immoral sex conduct" and "matriarchal" tradition of black women.[41] These depictions contributed quite significantly to the claims in the 1965 Moynihan report, which was invoked by witnesses such as Bennett and Loury in their 1995 testimony before Congress. Frazier charted the supposed dysfunctionality of Negro families from slavery to their post–World War I migrations into northern urban settings. According to this sociologist, for black women, in their rural southern "peasant" incarnations, illegitimacy was considered harmless behavior, a view generally supported by their small communities. As the women moved into contact with "the outside world," this need to gain "satisfaction of their undisciplined impulses" became part of the "general disorganization of family life" that afflicted Negroes in more cosmopolitan settings.[42] Frazier's study documented the unchecked, out-of-control nature of poor black female sexual reproductivity.

Frazier conveyed a general disappointment about the lack of efficacy in the influence of the black church for curbing illegitimacy. Although he saw the church as the key institution with potential for impacting the problem of illegitimacy among Negro women, even its capacity to do so is hampered by the intransigence of female immorality. Frazier noted that the Negro community "expresses its disapproval of moral delinquencies almost exclusively through the church."[43] The "effectiveness of the church as an institution of control over sex behavior" depends on families and other community members.[44] Especially among the poor, the "illiterate peasants," the church inevitably fails to counter women's "normal behavior."

In addition to scholarship proving black women's depravity and debates in the

newspapers about the precise root causes of that depravity, there were also more activist community efforts to control the women. In 1939 the Birth Control Federation
of America launched such an endeavor called the "Negro Project." Three or four
"colored Ministers" were specifically recruited to travel throughout the South advocating birth control among Negroes. The proposal argued, "The mass of Negroes,
particularly in the South, still breed carelessly and disastrously" and went on to
point out that the increase among Negroes "is from that portion of the population
least fit, and least able to rear children properly."[45] Margaret Sanger, a major birth
control activist of the period, wrote in a private communication to a colleague, "We
do not want word to get out that we want to exterminate the Negro population and
the minister is the man who can straighten out that idea if it ever occurs to any
of their rebellious members."[46] The pivotal role that the church played in black
communities was calculated into eugenicist plans regarding the women's sexual
reproduction.

It was argued by leading eugenicists of the 1930s that the birth control movement was needed to "prevent the American people from being replaced by alien or
Negro stock, whether it be by immigration or by overly high birth rates among others in this country."[47] At that 1994 Republican press conference on welfare, Senate
majority leader Robert Dole (R-Kans.) similarly connected the idea of a multiplying
"alien" population with those perpetrators of out-of-wedlock births. He said, "And
we also feel strongly that real reform should not reward out-of-wedlock births, and
that welfare should not be a magnet to attract aliens to the United States."[48] Thus,
in the understanding of this type of 1990s political leadership, welfare reform
should be used as a means to prevent the wrong people from multiplying. The argument fits within the tradition of 1930s birth control advocates like Sanger. Dole's
view would also probably hold that the nation should have heeded the warnings of
those like Sanger who foresaw negative population consequences resulting from the
relief programs of the New Deal. Regarding those relief programs she counseled
that "grandiose schemes for security may eventually turn into subsidies for the perpetuation of the irresponsible classes of society."[49]

The public and authoritative forms as well as the relentlessly condemning substance of this moral discourse mutually contribute to the demeaning of poor black
women. The historically uninterrupted process of repeating a litany of derogatory
sexual/procreative images helps to transform those images into recognizable "facts"
about the women. So, one need only point out a poor black female to summon the
"reality" of a host of moral failings and identify a challenging civic project.

On the basis of her own experience and those of her friends as black single
mothers who have received welfare, Barbara Omolade writes:, "Pitting themselves
against social agencies and public opinion—Black single mothers and their families
have something to offer us all. By daily demonstrating that they can survive and succeed without marriage, that they may even be better off without it, they challenge
the basic patriarchal ideal."[50] Can we learn from these women and join them in engaging in this sort of challenge? In order to thwart the entrenched patterns of stig-
matizing and policing poor black women's procreation, dramatic reversals in perspective and focus are needed.

When judgments are made about whose morality it serves the national interest to publicly monitor, the behavior and character of those who formulate public policy should be given primacy. It is the viewpoints of the president, members of Congress, selected academics, and members of corporate sponsored media that actually guide the direction of the nation. Then, would not their moral/sexual attitudes and behavior be most pertinent for gauging how the moral climate is set? To determine what norms of sexuality and family, in reality, inform the national agenda, the focus of scrutiny should be for instance on sexual harassment charges against male political leaders in the Senate such as Robert Packwood (R-Ore.); the charges of sexual harassment and extramarital sexual liaisons against President Clinton; William Bennett's deeper emotions and attitudes about his own single mom–headed family[51]; Glenn Loury's children from a woman he never married or his alleged physical assault of his extramarital female partner.[52] State-commissioned studies similar to the Moynihan report on how family values and sexual ethics evolve for these types of people are needed. The garnering of creative strategies and insights about how to improve and strengthen the "personal responsibility" of the elites who are the decision-makers in this culture has undisputable benefit for American society in the twenty-first century and beyond. I do not advocate the formulation of public policy on the basis of "personal" sexual behavior. But, if this formula is to be applied (as it has been), then we ought to scrutinize and regulate the "personal responsibility" of those who actually wield political and economic power in this nation, instead of targeting those with little or none.

Also, religious institutions are key in this task of rejecting status quo priorities for the assignment of moral insufficiency. Churches need to shift out of their chosen or co-opted complicity in cultural assaults on poor black mothers. Rather than working as instruments of the state to help degrade and blame women, churches ought to challenge the state, working in solidarity with poor black women and in behalf of their rights and dignity. In its internal practices, black churches in particular can dispute worn, fictive constructions perpetuated in the wider culture by creating traditions and language that celebrate and affirm the intrinsic value of poor women's motherhood. The church should be the one dependable place where the wholeness and inherent worth of black women's identities are reflected back to them; where the shaming distortions that surround them elsewhere in the culture are corrected. White Christians have one of the hardest yet most crucial tasks, of working with one another to develop strategies to exorcise themselves of their deification of a white supremacist ordering of social relations. Those who make the choice to undermine the privileges of whiteness that they are granted by the culture must institutionalize ongoing consciousness-raising and commitment-sustaining activities within their faith communities. Even if it is absent from every other community setting, their churches should be one place where whites can count on support in their struggle to refuse the enticement of maintaining the privileges of whiteness. Specifically, they should be bolstered in their efforts to reject devaluing views and exploitative relationships with persons relegated to the status of "the other" by popular culture and political leaders.

In the broader community context, church leaders together with other community activists must help formulate moral agendas that explicitly counter existing ones that spring from dehumanizing and objectifying assumptions about poor black women and girls. And, most important in the formulation of that agenda, economic change that redistributes wealth and resources, making dramatic readjustments in areas such as child care, health care, housing, wages and salaries, must be made a priority. Only a moral agenda that aims to substantively tilt the existing socioeconomic pyramid holding in place the poverty conditions that maintain a stranglehold on the lives of so many black women and girls will suffice.

Finally, on the one hand, the social and spiritual value of poor black motherhood has to be recognized and promoted in order to erode popular conceptions of these moms as female things that spawn social ills. Barbara Horsburgh recommends appreciation of the emancipatory, renewing, and redemptive qualities of poor black women's natality. She writes, "I propose that Black welfare mothers claim the right to natality—the source of human freedom and the birthright of each generation to begin life anew . . . freedom to bring forth newcomers and thereby participate in the resurgent recreation of the universe."[53] On the other hand, in addition to their right to natality, the right of these women to stigma-free sexual expression has to be asserted and protected. We need a moratorium on any further open debate about poor black women's sexual reproduction. There must be a permanent end to the practice of making poor black female sexuality and procreation an object for public titillation, denouncement, and regulation.

Notes

I would like to express my appreciation to Kyung-in Kim, Pauline Wardell-Sankoh, and especially to Jody Caldwell for their critical research assistance, and to Jerry Watts, who served as an invaluable dialogue partner on this project.

1. U.S. Congress, *Personal Responsibility and Work Opportunity Reconciliation Act*, 104th Cong., 2d sess., 22 August 1996, sec. 101-1.

2. Richard J. Hernstein and Charles Murray, *The Bell Curve* (New York: Free Press, 1994).

3. Charles Murray, "The Coming White Underclass," *Wall Street Journal*, 29 October 1993, sec. A14.

4. Opinion/Editorial, *National Review*, 8 April 1996, 14.

5. See statements by Children's Defense Fund advocates such as Deborah Weinstein: "It places a stigma on the child," quoted in Robert Pear, "G.O.P. Affirms Plan to Stop Money for Unwed Mothers," *New York Times*, 21 January 1995, sec. A9.

6. I am using Joel Kovel's notion of "thingification," which includes an understanding of the way that black bodies have been historically quantified and controlled in the United States. See *White Racism: A Psycho-History* (New York: Columbia University Press, 1984).

7. Bill Clinton, "Radio Address of the President to the Nation," St. Thomas, Virgin Islands, 4 January 1997.

8. For examples see George Will, "Voting Rights Won't Fix It," *Washington Post*, 23 January 1986, sec. A23; *ABC World News Tonight* "American Agenda" segment, 4 April 1992; Michele Ingrassia, "A World without Fathers: The Struggle to Save the Black Family," *Newsweek*, 30 August 1993; "The Facts of Life in the Inner City," *Nightline*, 8 May 1992; Robert J. Samuelson, "Should We Think the Unthinkable?" *Newsweek*, 13 September 1993, 43; Jonathan Alter, "The Name of the Game Is Shame: The New Reactionaries Are Those Who Excuse Teen Pregnancy," 12 December 1994, 40.

9. Charles Murray is the author of this viewpoint. See Murray, "The Emerging White Underclass and How to Save It," *Wall Street Journal*; *Philadelphia Inquirer*, 15 November 1993, sec A15.

10. House Committee on Ways and Means, *Contract with America—Welfare Reform: Hearing before the Sub-Committee on Human Resources, Hearing on Illegitimacy and Welfare*, 104th Cong., 1st sess., 20 January 1995, pt. 1 of 2, 159.

11. Office of Policy Planning and Research, U.S. Labor Dept., March 1965.

12. House Committee, *Contract with America—Welfare Reform*, 160.

13. House Committee, *Contract with America—Welfare Reform*, 146.

14. Ibid., 172.

15. Joe Maxwell "Real Welfare Reform: Mississippi's Challenge; Will the Church Be the Church?" *World* , 5 November 1994, as cited in House Committee, *Contract with America—Welfare Reform*, 538.

16. Maxwell, "Real Welfare Reform," cited in House Committee, *Contract with America—Welfare Reform*, 539.

17. Describing the key needs and issues that have to be addressed by "welfare reform," President Clinton argued: "We need to go after what is the real source of this problem, which is the inordinate number of out-of-wedlock births in this country." Interviewed by Ann Blackman and James Carney. In *Time*, June 1994, 28.

18. In her analysis of what she calls the "the war on welfare" that has emerged since the 1970s, Nancy Ellen Rose notes the deliberate decision by the advisers to the Clinton administration to choose to focus on eliminating welfare dependency rather than on eliminating poverty. This decision was made by David Ellwood and the White House Working Group early in the process of devising its approach to the issue. See Rose, *Workfare or Fair Work? Women, Welfare and Government Work Programs* (New Brunswick, N.J.: Rutgers University Press, 1995), 172.

19. "President Bill Clinton: Remarks to Progressive National Baptists Convention," Charlotte, N.C., 9 August 1995, *Dialog File 660: Federal News Service*.

20. *Summary of Welfare Reforms Made by Public Law 104-193*, 104th Cong., 2d sess., 6 November 1996, 18–19.

21. House Committee, *Contract with America—Welfare Reform*, 161.

22. Ibid., 214.

23. Caryl Rivers, *Slick Spins and Fractured Facts: How Cultural Myths Distort the News* (New York: Columbia University Press, 1996).

24. "Press Conference with Representative Bob Michel (R-IL), Senator Bob Dole (R-KS) and Others," Washington, D.C., 14 June 1994, *Dialog File 660: Federal News Service*.

25. House Committee, *Contract with America—Welfare Reform*, 534.

26. "President Bill Clinton Remarks to Progressive National Baptists Convention," Charlotte, N.C., 9 August 1995, *Dialog File 660: Federal News Service*.

27. Gary Bauer, "The Family: Preserving America's Future, a Report to the President from the White House Working Group on the Family" (1986), 24, as cited in Lucy A. Williams, "Race, Rat Bites and Unfit Mothers: How Media Discourse Informs Welfare Legislation Debate," *Fordham Urban Law Journal* 22, no. 4 (Summer 1995): 1159–96.

28. For real depictions of life-circumstances that are based on representative samplings of women and girls who live on welfare, see Mark Robert Rank, *Living on the Edge: The Realities of Welfare in America* (New York: Columbia University Press, 1994); Valerie Polakow, *Lives on the Edge: Single Mothers and Their Children in the Other America* (Chicago: University of Chicago Press, 1993); Jill Duerr Berrick, *Faces of Poverty: Portraits of Women and Children on Welfare* (New York: Oxford University Press, 1995); and Elaine Bell Kaplan, *Not Our Kind of Girl: Unraveling the Myths of Black Teenage Motherhood* (Berkeley: University

of California Press, 1997). For an extremely thorough and well-argued de-bunking of popular prejudices that masquerade as facts about poor teenage girls, see Kristin Luker, *Dubious Conceptions: The Politics of Teenage Pregnancy* (Cambridge: Harvard University Press, 1996).

29. "Press Conference with Representative Bob Michel (R-IL)," *Dialog File 660: Federal News Service*.

30. Beverly Horsburgh, "Schrödinger's Cat, Eugenics and the Compulsory Sterilization of Welfare Mothers: Deconstructing an Old/New Rhetoric and Constructing the Reproductive Right to Natality for Low-Income Women of Color," *Cardozo Law Review* 17 (1993): 566.

31. Horsburgh makes this observation about the confluence of political rhetoric against procreation and abortions by poor women, which unfortunately became an astute prediction about the forced sterilization possibilities that were opened up in the welfare law enacted after the publication of her article, 578ff.

32. *Summary of Welfare Reforms Made by Public Law 104-193*, 18–19.

33. House Committee, *Contract with America–Welfare Reform*, 152.

34. Frances Anne Kemble, *Journal of a Residence on a Georgian Plantation in 1838–1839* (New York: New American Library, 1961), 95, quoted in Paula Giddings, *When and Where I Enter: The Impact of Black Women on Race and Sex in America* (New York: William Morrow, 1984), 45–46.

35. William Lloyd Garrison, *The Liberator*, 21 February 1835, quoted in Hazel V. Carby, *Reconstructing Womanhood: The Emergence of the Afro-American Woman Novelist*, (New York: Oxford University Press, 1987), 35.

36. Beverly Gut-Sheftall, "Sinner or Saint?: Antithetical Views of Black Women and the Private Sphere," *Daughters of Sorrow: Attitudes toward Black Women, 1880-1920.* (Brooklyn: Carlson Publishing, 1990): 46–47.

37. "The Negro Problem," *The Independent* 59 (September 1902): 2224, 2228, as cited in Giddings, *When and Where I Enter*.

38. Patricia Morton, *Disfigured Images: The Historical Assault on Afro-American Women* (Westport, Conn.: Praeger, 1991), 30.

39. Arthur Calhoun, *A Social History of the American Family*, vol. 1 (New York: Barnes and Noble, 1960; orig. pub. 1917); vol. 2 (orig. pub. 1918), 243, 246, 292, as quoted in Morton, *Disfigured Images*.

40. Morton, *Disfigured Images*, 36–37.

41. E. Franklin Frazier, *The Negro Family in the United States* (Chicago: University of Chicago Press, 1966; orig. pub. 1939), 267, 102ff.

42. Ibid., 100.

43. Ibid., 98.

44. Ibid.

45. Linda Gordon, *Woman's Body, Woman's Right: A Social History of Birth Control in America* (New York: Penguin, 1976), 332.

46. Quoted in ibid., 332–33.

47. Ibid., 283.

48. "Press Conference with Representative Bob Michel (R-IL)," *Dialog File 660: Federal News Service*.

49. Gordon, *Woman's Body, Woman's Right*, 315.

50. Barbara Omolade, *The Rising Song of African American Women* (New York: Routledge, 1994), 78.

51. Bennett refers to the fact that he was raised by a divorced single mother in his 1995 testimony before Congress, House Committee, *Contract with America–Welfare Reform*, 160.

52. See Peter J. Howe, "Loury Bows Out of US Job Bid, Arraigned on Assault Charges" *Boston Globe*, 6 June 1987; Robert Connolly, "Harvard Prof 'Dragged Me Down Stairs,'" *Boston Herald*, 6 June 1987; Diane Alters, "Loury: Public View vs. Private Life," *Boston Globe*, 6 July 1987.

53. Horsburgh, "Schrödinger's Cat," 581.

8

MARY E. HUNT

Too Sexy for Words

The Changing Vocabulary of Religious Ethics

Efforts by the self-defined Christian Right to turn back social progress for women and sexual minorities include rhetoric that distorts the lives of their subjects. They would have every gay/lesbian pride march made up of bare-breasted women and men in leather chaps and would deem every woman who chooses an abortion a child murderer, if their videos and pamphlets represent accurately their positions. The success of these efforts at creating new meanings for words, especially at creating new ethical patterns with which I generally disagree, alerts me to the fact that ethical vocabularies change both with the use of words and the meanings given to them.

The changes are often well orchestrated. Many conservative religious groups realize that the power of naming, long touted by feminists as the ultimate religious power, is the name of the game. Of course some progressives have been equally dismissive of conservative views, something I try to avoid in the name of fair play. The aim of this essay is to look at this phenomenon in the increasingly pluralistic religious context that is the United States today and to offer constructive suggestions for how the ethical chasms that result might be bridged in the next century. Otherwise, I fear we are condemned to a power struggle based on caricature and intolerance all around.

I will do so in three steps. First, I will look at the contemporary context as it is shaped by globalization, pluralistic religious patterns, and changing sexual mores. Second, I will address the changing vocabulary itself as it has been instrumentalized in anti-gay videos and in the opposition to the 1993 Re-Imagining Conference. Finally, I will propose how people from various religions might work together to reweave an ethical fabric worthy of the history of a country founded on the principle of freedom of religion.

Contemporary Context

Globalization

Globalization is the "expansive evolution of systems such as economies, governments, media, culture and communications toward international integration and coordination."[1] In practice, globalization has all of the positive aspects with which scholars are so familiar—air travel, Internet access, and fax. But in reality, it literally cashes out to more decisions being made for increasingly larger sectors of the world by increasingly fewer people. Media manipulation of things sexual is a product of this reality in that media is bought and paid for by those who can afford it. Those with the means can leave their visual stamp on the culture and its psyche long after the television is turned off. That is the main reason why the Religious Right has put so much of its financing into media.

Globalization shows up most clearly in economic settings. For example, hourly wage laborers, the largest single and growing sector of the current U.S. economic boom (which by definition is a global phenomenon for which the collapse of the Asian market may signal a slowdown), are told what to do and exactly how to do it. They get no encouragement, indeed punishment, for creativity. This "guarantees" that every McDonald's hamburger will be the same throughout the world, with the tomato on top of the lettuce, and not the lettuce on top of the tomato. Various companies, like Nike for example, have budgets that are larger than the budgets of some developing countries. Some decisions made in those company boardrooms carry weight equal to those taken in the legislative arenas of some developing countries as transnational corporations rapidly join governments as seats of power. Market forces are such that the gap that used to exist between rich people and poor people is now the gap between those with investments and those without. These economic factors, woven together with racist and gender-based restrictions, condition which people can and cannot transgress sexual boundaries, for how long, and with what consequences. For example, as a white, middle-class, upper-educated lesbian feminist professional it is easier for me to live and work as I wish than it is for my colleagues who are women of color in a racist society, or for waitresses or teachers in Catholic schools. Hence, efforts that will remake the ethical fabric need to begin with this economic and political power dynamic.

Globalization is clear in technology, where there is a geometric increase in the speed and scope of those who are on-line and an equal and opposite disempowerment for those who are not. Air travel has increased far beyond the ability of medicine to keep up with the jet-speed spread of some forms of disease such as HIV/AIDS. These new circumstances set by globalization allow some of us to be closer, both literally and ideologically, to those who share our economic and educational privilege. But it can also mean an increase in the distance between near neighbors. The result can be increasing elitism, the negative side of globalization.

Globalization is a fact of contemporary life. It is within a globalized framework that sexual ethics, and discussion about them, take shape. While the focus of this analysis is the U.S. context, globalization means that decisions about behaviors and commitments, i.e., ethics, have far-reaching implications in countries whose people are not even in the conversation. The same market forces indicate that they will watch the movies, use the pharmaceuticals, and rethink their own cultural expressions in light of what hegemonic Western corporations offer. In my judgment, this ups the ethical ante for U.S.–based social ethicists. While ideally I would be about the business of critiquing business, in this essay I simply confine my analysis to the results of this dynamic for which I feel a special responsibility as a U.S. citizen.

Religious Pluralism

Though alleged by some to be increasingly secular, the United States is more religious in the odd quantitative sense that more religions shape it. Far from being the three-religion culture of old, the contemporary U.S. religious mix is best characterized by what Diana Eck, professor of comparative religion and Indian studies at Harvard University, calls diversity:

> America today is part of the Islamic, the Hindu, the Confucian world. It is precisely the interpenetration of ancient civilizations and cultures that is the hallmark of the late twentieth century. *This* is our geo-religious reality. The map of the world in which we now live cannot be color-coded as to its Christian, Muslim, or Hindu identity, but each part of the world is marbled with the colors and textures of the whole.[2]

Now in the United States, Diana Eck reports, there are "more Muslims than Episcopalians, more Muslims than Presbyterians, perhaps soon more Muslims than Jews."[3]

The impact of this increasingly complicated religious fabric for sexual ethics remains to be seen, but it must be taken seriously as a shaping force in the articulation of laws and customs. The very pluralization itself demands more sophisticated ways of handling ethics since teachings of no one, or even three, faith traditions will be sufficient to ground the discourse. Given the bellicose atmospheres within so many religious groups over sexuality, notably Roman Catholics on abortion and Presbyterians on ordaining homosexual ministers, I am pessimistic about the interreligious possibilities. Nonetheless, this is the current reality, and it demands of everyone a new stance. Perhaps, ironically, it will act as a corrective to the ways in which in-house religious debates have been conducted.

Changing Sexual Mores

Few social institutions have changed as markedly as sexuality in the second half of this century. From the women's movements and the so-called sexual revolution to the gay rights struggles and now the emergence of queer theory and practice, just the fact that we speak so openly about sexuality is new. What we say is still another matter.

Cultural battles rage from the legality of gay marriages in Hawaii to the limits imposed on surrogate parenting, from new reproductive technologies to the place of lesbian/gay people in the military. How sexual issues are problematized has been one of the triumphs of the Religious Right. Most people immediately associate such matters with private or bedroom morality, rather than thinking immediately of the socioeconomic causes and consequences. But same-sex marriages have significant implications for inheritance, insurance, and hospital visitation policies for everyone, not simply consequences in terms of the emotional well-being of lesbian and gay people. The rights of persons who are homosexual to serve in the military means the right to a job, indeed access to a career, and the ability to work toward a pension. Economic well-being of this sort is denied when sexual orientation is used to determine fitness for service, a consequence far more serious in practical terms than any sexual matter. Likewise, surrogacy is finally an economic matter as much as a biological one when we decide once more (as in adoption) as a society whether and when money can change hands when it comes to children.

It is these economic issues that fall by the wayside with the problematizing of sexuality in individualistic terms. Yet relatively few religious discussions have prioritized economic issues as part of the sexual debate. Progressive religious groups have fallen into the traps set by conservatives that narrow the focus either to economics or to sexuality, normally confining their concerns to the micro when it is the macro that rules. I suggest that either solo focus—sexuality or economics—is engaged in at our peril. The nexus of the two illuminates each dimension.

When it comes to discussions on sexuality, religious debates have been slow to keep up with the rapid pace and the changing face of scholarship. Learned opinions clash over the socially constructed and/or essentialist nature of sexuality, with remarkably little clarity, much less consensus, emerging. Studies on the hypothalamus of male homosexuals and the intricate workings of lesbians' inner ears offer scant insight into nature/nurture discussions. Nonetheless, they are important data for religious scholars because they shape public conversation and signal the direction of the discussion, however misguided they may turn out to be.

Meanwhile, the sexual landscape has changed in dramatic ways, despite conservative religions' wranglings. Young people report sexual encounters earlier than previous generations. Use of contraceptives is up; abortion rates show a slight downturn. Homosexuality, bisexuality, and transsexual/transgendered experiences are widespread and increasingly well accepted. But now the categories are shifting, with performance replacing essence as the crux of how we know who we are.[4] This muddies the ethical waters.

Rather than claiming that our sexualities are fixed at birth, some scholars note the fluidity of both sexual orientation and sexual activity. Heterosexual people become gay or lesbian, and vice versa, depending on whom they love. Bisexuality is generally accepted as real and not a stage. Transgender experiences are only beginning to surface in large enough numbers to make any, however tentative, generalizations. Still, most debates within religious groups are predicated on the notion that we are a certain way, with consequences following from such essentialism. It seems that so little is clear in this regard and that scholarship is changing so quickly that religions might make a real contribution by offering what they know best:

love, justice, tolerance, prudence, hospitality, welcome, ministry, and the like, all of which do not change with sexual identities.

The challenge for the next century is how to rethink these issues without reinforcing sex as something private after the fashion of the Religious Right. It is to discuss ethics in the light of changing understandings of sexuality, indeed when definitions are on the move at a rapid clip. Yet more difficult is how to do all of this without so desexualizing and destabilizing the discourse that conservative forces carry the day. Their clearly focused attention on sex and their rock solid discourse on morality yes/no, permitted/forbidden can be attractive for its clarity alone. But this particular clarity comes at a high price—that of judgmental ethics that eclipse the well-being of anyone who moves beyond the box of Christian-determined heterosexual patriarchy.

Changing Vocabulary

The ethical conversation starts, obviously, with words. However, constantly increasing speed of communication via fax, e-mail, interactive television, and ever changing cultural sets cannot keep up with the fact that some words change their meaning even before they reach their destinations. Such is the case in contemporary ethical discourse, where many of the words relating to sexuality, such as "gay," "lesbian," "married," "sodomy," "procreative," "recreational," "adultery", and "safe" are subject to changing meanings.

Most people used to know what they meant; now it is not so obvious. Take the word "procreative," for example. It used to mean heterosexual sex with the intention that the woman involved might become pregnant with the sperm of the man involved. Now this form of sexual relationship is but one of many ways in which new life is created, indeed one of many ways of being procreative. In vitro fertilization is, by definition, procreative. Lesbians who use donated sperm, which they transfer from test tube to woman, are acting procreatively. When they couple such action with intimate touching, it is not a stretch to call theirs procreative sex despite the fact that Catholic church officials do not have them in mind when they promote it. Hence, the word "procreative" has an expanded meaning that proponents of hetero-only sex do not realize when they tout it. Should we tell them?

Likewise, the definition of safe sex is changing constantly as more is known about sexually transmitted diseases, including HIV. What was considered safe ten years ago is simply no longer an adequate description for preventing the spread of these problems. While conservatives would argue that there is no such thing as safe sex outside of heterosexual procreative marital sex (an absurdity because HIV pays no heed to marriage licenses), sexual progressives distinguish between safe and safer. Absolutes and sex mix like oil and water, but in this case words used imprecisely can have deadly consequences. Who will write the dictionary entry?

This linguistic phenomenon of meaning morphosis plays a major role in religious debates about sexuality, which in turn shape U.S. society as a whole. My concern is not only *what*, but also *how* religious groups decide on meanings. How religions are used to shape the meaning of words and which religious people are given credence make all the difference. The divide between religion and society, church and state is increasingly thin, but the language and images are thickening as conservative theopolitical forces use the power of naming to define people and practices in ways very different from how the practitioners themselves would do. The question is whether, as part of the construction of the common good in the next century, we can reverse the trend toward caricature, especially by religious traditionalists, but perhaps at times also by religious progressives, and use religious resources to develop more adequate, accurate ways to talk about matters as common as sexuality.

Several examples of manipulation help make the case. The documentary *The Gay Agenda* made by opponents of the gay agenda features images and dialogue so far from the mark as to be unrecognizable. Made in the early 1990s as part of campaigns to discredit the gay movement, it features footage of the most flamboyant aspects of gay life, including parades and parties, as if that were all gay people do. Race is instrumentalized through the use of spurious coalitions of people of color who speak against gays when in fact tolerance in many such communities is well known. Anti-Semitism rears its ugly head through the use of Christian assumptions about moral norms; Christian images and symbols are assumed to be national symbols. To watch such movies is to assume that gay men kiss most of the day and all lesbians ride motorcycles. Images create the words that describe them.

Efforts to answer such portrayals point up the problems of power. Proponents of lesbian/gay/bisexual and transgendered civil rights turn the tables at our peril. The effort to argue on the basis of images presented, starting with the notion of an agenda, is doomed because the images speak to a public uneducated about the more nuanced aspects of contemporary queer culture—the bird watchers and marathon racers, the anti-abortion and pro-family forces. Furthermore, progressive gay groups cannot agree on much when it comes to strategy, so to impute an agenda is flattering but simply not accurate. Moreover, a clash of worldviews is at hand, not only different views on issues but whole different ways of seeing issues. In such a situation, merely answering arguments is doomed from the outset. At best, it will result in the inclusion of a few of us into a stratified society bought at the expense of the rest of us. At worst, with media money on the right side, other views stand little chance of a fair hearing.

Curiously, in the video it was obvious that the subjects of the documentary were having fun. There was the celebration of bodies that one sees at a queer parade, the use of costumes and make-up, all of which are portrayed negatively by the Right but which strike me as benign contributions to a more inclusive culture. Herein lies the trap: dammed if you do and damned if you don't. To deny that such images, indeed such people, are part of the large and diverse lesbigay community, as some buttoned-down types might, is to betray the whole. To lift them up as emblematic is equally problematic and self-defeating. I want to argue for the right to be flamboyant but resist mightily the notion that such is the heart of the matter when it comes to being lesbigay. What is needed is a strenuous reinterpretation of what is presented from the perspective of those involved or at least from the perspective of sympathetic observers who see the big picture.

The challenge is how to keep the doors of diversity open, how to keep things safe, non-abusive, and respectful without falling into the traps that result in gay bashing or worse. With the maturation of the movement for sexual diversity, people are able to affirm things and people they do not need to do or become. There are more than queer Republicans who live in monogamous relationships, work forty hours a week, and keep their grass mowed, but the very need to underscore that fact is what can lead to dividing queer from queer. I think religious voices can be helpful in preventing that. When progressive religious voices are granted a hearing as *religious*, there is an opening to other values and mores that might shape a more tolerant, welcoming social order both within queer communities and well beyond.

Another example of such instrumentalization is from the now famous Re-Imagining Conference that was held in Minneapolis in November 1993. This was a gathering of 2,300 mostly Christian church–affiliated women (and a few men) who came together in response to the World Council of Churches' Decade of Churches in Solidarity with Women. It was a weekend of lectures, workshops, rituals, artistic expressions, and strategizing, the culmination of meetings, events, and discussions in the first half of the decade. It was resourced by the work of feminist, womanist, mujerista, and other women who have been engaged in the deconstruction and reconstruction of Christian images, symbols, beliefs, and practices for decades. This, of course, is in itself a threat. Among the issues to be reimagined were work, family, sexuality, community, and church. Not surprisingly, the focus fell not so much on creation as sexuality, not so much on work as on Jesus and gender, though in my view the challenges in those areas were at least as foundational if not more so than the ones that caught attention.

Many speakers who are quite routine fare among professionals in the field, including a number of women theologians from around the world, were featured speakers. The vast majority of the participants went home enthusiastic but not awestruck, edified and not scandalized. A month later there began a barrage of articles and reports in right-wing church publications, then in conservative newspapers like the *Washington Times* (affiliated with the Unification church), and eventually in the so-called mainstream media, including *Nightline*, *McNeill-Lehrer News Hour*, and the *New York Times*.

Differences in ideology were expected in the media coverage, but the distortions fairly amazed. Rather than a church women's conference, one would think from the coverage that the Goddess Sophia had arrived with her female partner, made love in the aisle, and banished Jesus to the outer reaches of Hell. Organizers were not so naive as to expect that more conservative people would applaud, but they never anticipated the flow of misinformation and caricature that resulted from their attempt to make the point that Christianity has become, under feminist influences, more tolerant.[5]

At Re-Imagining, womanist theologian Delores Williams gave a brilliant, insightful presentation on Jesus. She was vilified in the conservative media for questioning the usefulness of the Doctrine of the Atonement, arguing that it reinforces notions of victimhood and surrogate suffering—a debate that has gone on for some time in feminist/womanist/ mujerista theological circles. Despite the fact that she was one of the few on the program who spoke about Jesus at all, she was singled out for ridicule, leading many to conclude that this may well have been a racist attack.

Facilitators of dance and movement were caricatured by the opponents of Re-

Imagining as liturgical police who forced participants to engage actively in gestures that accompany songs in modest dances around the tables. Their function could not have been further from that of *forcing* people. Rather, they were positioned strategically around the hall to model for and encourage those of us who are less skilled in such expressions. The police image would be laughable if it were not emblematic of the vicious distortions that opponents used to debunk the conference. Knowing that more people read and saw the opposition-fueled media coverage after the fact than were at the conference, one must conclude that history will record it more for the aftermath than for the event itself.

As in the case of the anti-gay videos, the most serious problem was the way in which such distortions set the agenda. Every ensuing discussion, every effort at explaining the conference had to begin by setting the record straight. Sometimes there was no such opportunity, with the result that the enduring images of the conference were actually constructed by people who were not there. Not surprisingly, much of the opposition was centered on things sexual—the panel on sexuality, prayers based on quotations from the Hebrew Scriptures that included references to the female anatomy, the presence of lesbian women in the absence (for a change in church circles) of opposition to our existence, and the almost exclusive use of female imagery for the divine. But in fact this was not sex or gender in itself, but sex and gender as constructed to privilege male economic, political, and religious power, which was problematized and in the process of being dismantled. No wonder there was backlash!

The backlash in turn distracted attention from other substantive matters at hand, including re-imagining family and community, and critical looks at economics and domestic violence. This successful right-wing strategy all but erased the innovative liturgies that carried the conference to new heights of ecumenical Christian cooperation, the spirit of hospitality that characterized the event, and the important critique by many participants of the lack of anti-racism work at such a predominantly white gathering.

The Institute for Religion and Democracy (IRD), a conservative think tank in Washington, D.C., provided the rhetoric for the opposition. Anti–Re-Imagining folks argued that what was at stake was not freedom of religion as such, but whether churches must countenance, much less pay for, such events that so contravene their theologies. It was an attractive line on the face of it, inviting churches like the United Methodists and the Presbyterian Church USA to rethink their financial contributions to future events like this. Many church staff members were subsequently cautioned against attending such meetings on their denominations' tabs. But in fact the ploy was more damaging because it effectively claimed the center of what Christian theology is, eliminating the many and varied voices that urge openness to new images, symbols, and interpretations that reflect more porous walls and more open doors in the effort to be religious in the increasingly globalized, religiously pluralistic, and morally more diverse culture in which we live.

These two examples of backlash are perhaps better referred to as whiplash, or the backlash against backlash, when video and other media are so deliberately distorted and used against progressives by well-funded, well-connected groups like IRD. They reflect what I have come to think of as a hermeneutics of hatred, a deliberate way of constructing frameworks so that people and ideas that some despise are projected in the dimmest light. Armed with this sort of set, many previously good things can be sullied: marriage vaunted for male-female partnering is anathema when proposed for same-sex couples; recreation urged upon a workaholic culture is wrong when it is sexual; procreation is suddenly proscribed when women do it with minimal male input. To turn words inside out, to reverse their ethical fortunes when they apply to some and not to others is to engage in a hermeneutics of hatred.

Imagery is imagery, but who owns the camera still determines which way the lens will be aimed and how it will be focused. When some own not only the camera, but in some cases of religious broadcasting also the network, new strategies may be necessary to level the ethical playing field. Otherwise, the hermeneutics of hatred will shape our ethical future.

Developing a Religiously Inclusive Common Good

The confluence of globalization, religious pluralism, and changing sexual mores with the kind of backlash I have described does not bode well for a religiously inclusive common good. On the face of it, the virulent battles within Christian denominations in a country that has been shaped in large measure by Christian hegemonic discourse would point toward an impending disaster on the ethical front. The same players, unable to deal justly with their compatriot coreligionists, show no signs of being adept in interreligious discussions.

Hence the need to consider proposals for how people from various religions might work together to weave an ethical fabric worthy of a country founded on the principle of freedom of religion. My contribution is a set of four suggestions, based on what has transpired of late in the rough and tumble of theopolitics—whether on abortion and family planning, homosexuality, the death penalty, or welfare reform—and beginning to lay a foundation for common work. The foundation for a strong ethical fabric includes economic and political as well as philosophical concerns.

1. *Representation on the principal's own terms.* The most pernicious problem in the videos and in the controversy surrounding Re-Imagining was the failure to argue the issues on their merits, instead caricaturing beyond recognition the people and matters at hand. This same dynamic is present in some of the debates over the use of religious garb, especially headgear, in schools and the military. Whether Muslim women in the chador or Jewish soldiers petitioning for the right to wear yarmulkes, the point is that an inclusive society can and must find ways for people to participate fully *on their own terms.*

Such arguments are never simple, but they are complicated by the failure to allow the principals to explain and contend on their own terms, not on terms set by others. For example, in the case of head coverings, the force of religious law and custom on its own terms must be measured against the good of discipline and order.

What is crucial is that the measure be set on the terms of the group at hand, not on some already established measure based on the force of law in another tradition. For instance, Muslim and Christian laws may differ not only in their content but also in the force they carry for their respective adherents. It is that difference and not just the difference in content that deserves respect. Arguments about content are well known, but we are far from being able to handle the constitutional and cultural intricacies that come with weighing how important an issue is within a tradition. To take a tricky example, opposition to abortion for conservative Catholics tends to be a very important article of faith. For more progressive Catholics it is not trivial but is by no means determinative of one's membership or standing in the Catholic community. How to adjudicate this issue is an ethical challenge that, until now, remains untouched despite the increasing pluralism of belief *within* particular communities of faith.

2. *Diversity within diversity.* Perhaps the central matter in all of this is determining what group or groups represent a given tradition in order to know with whom to negotiate. In the case of Re-Imagining, what was on display was a clear shift in power to a more diverse offering, with all of the attendant backlash from the institutionalized forms of various Protestant denominations. The fact that women theologians voiced new opinions and offered new images and symbols as bona fide members (and in some cases clergy) of their respective denominations was what caused the stir. The vocabulary was changing.

This is equally problematic among Roman Catholic women whose Women Church movement provides another face to Catholicism, among Jewish women whose Rosh Hodesh groups are the locus for experimentation, among Islamic feminists for whom the term is not a contradiction, and so on. Religious diversity is both an external (among groups) and internal (within groups) phenomenon. Many local councils of churches are becoming interfaith networks. As they do so, they need to take into account not simply the usual players, but those groups, both progressive and conservative, that claim an affiliation with the faith tradition.

Of course this is a logistical nightmare. How is the White House liaison to faith communities supposed to decipher which groups to invite, listen to, and otherwise pull into the discourse? WomenChurch Convergence has cordial ties with that office, giving the White House feminist faces and voices to associate with the religious category Catholic. How does an interfaith AIDS coalition cope with member groups that prohibit the use of life-saving condoms? The answers do not come easily but, given the future make-up of this culture, must come constantly.

3. *Assume the limits of our understanding.* Theologians of a certain age were trained as if religion in general could be understood through the lens of one faith tradition. Looked at deeply, religious experience of one stripe was considered a window on others. But that is no longer the conventional wisdom in an age of religious diversity when, as Eck made clear, to know one religion is to know no religion. Experts in the field must acknowledge that we need retooling in our respective disciplines to have the skills adequate to the needs of our society. Indeed, non-specialists, even more so, need to realize the partial nature of their knowledge.

This sets up a complex situation for religious education. Religious education, once the purview of religiously-based schools for adherents, needs to be redefined. Now what is necessary is the study of the many religions that make up our culture. Just as public school students already study the ethnic/racial groups that comprise their communities, so too will a carefully crafted, inclusive, and honest presentation of the religious traditions go a long way toward assuring the foundations of decent discourse. Wholesale adult education is also crucial in this regard, virtually on the level of computer training, which has emerged as a necessity in the last ten years. Adults need to rethink and relearn the nature and content of religions as they shape culture, since we now have whole generations unschooled both in what religions teach and, worse, how to talk about such differences in a civilized and respectful way.

Imagine, for example, a case study approach to learning about the world's religions. Comparing religious perspectives on abortion, homosexuality, or the death penalty would reveal differences both within traditions and among them. Students would emerge with a rich and full map of the religious terrain, something that would make them better-informed citizens.

4. *Revisit the notion of the separation of church and state.* The sacrosanct notion of a separation of church and state is problematized by this analysis. First, it is not church but religions that are separated from government. Changing the vocabulary is not trivial in this case. Does this separation exist in reality, or is it something that some religions are subject to and others not, as can be shown in instances of Christian hegemony? It is remarkable how recently (if at all) many people have noticed the need for diverse religious symbols and holidays rather than simply Christian ones. But this trend shows every sign of increasing, changing the question from separation of church and state to something more like the relationships between religions and government. Here the changing vocabulary helps to clarify the nature of the problem at hand and to level the ethical playing field. Though far from defining my own position on the separationism and accommodationism spectrum, I am increasingly clear about how to frame the problem, something that does not always warrant the critical attention of people on either side.

Conclusion

These four suggestions sketch some of the basic parameters for a society in which what ethicist Daniel C. Maguire calls the "renewable moral energy of religion"[6] can be sustained and increased. What begins in the effort to rethink sexual vocabulary and ethics offers a starting point for rethinking economic and political words and practices as well. Imagine how words like "just wage," "sufficient compensation," and "basic human needs" all are understood through a hermeneutics of hatred that applies not only to gay people but to poor people. The injustice that results from changing the vocabulary to suit the needs of those in power begs for more resources to assure the survival of people and a planet left to such devises. Images and symbols that include, sometimes transcend, and always leave open the possibility of change are necessary. These are typically religious. When put to this use, the remarkable power of religions to do their job—literally, to link people—becomes obvious and compelling in the development of the common good.

Notes

1. "Women's Lives in a Changing World," *Interhemispheric Resource Center Newsletter*, January 1995, 2.

2. Diana L. Eck, "Neighboring Faiths," *Harvard Magazine*, September–October 1996, 44.

3. Ibid., 40.

4. Judith Butler is helpful in this regard: "Gender is performative in the sense that it constitutes as an effect the very subject that it appears to express." See "Imitation and Gender Insubordination," in *Inside Out: Lesbian Theories/Gay Theories*, ed. D. Fuss (London: Routledge, 1991), 18.

5. Michael Norman, "Feminists Nurture a More Tolerant Christianity," *New York Times*, 11 April 1998, sec. A, pp. 15–17.

6. Daniel C. Maguire, "Population-Consumption-Ecology: The Triple Problematic," in *Christianity and Ecology*, ed. Mary Evelyn Tucker and John Grim (Cambridge: Harvard University Press, forthcoming).

9

L. WILLIAM COUNTRYMAN

The Bible, Heterosexism, and the American Public Discussion of Sexual Orientation

Although the United States of America has a long tradition of separation between church and state, this has never meant that religion is unimportant in our public discourse. The belief of some intellectuals, in the middle of this century, that religion was withering away among us has been disconfirmed; and there has never been any firewall between religious belief and public discourse. After all, public discourse in matters of importance must always be anchored, focused, and oriented by those things that the community or culture holds sacred: those values that seem beyond challenge and provide the foundation for resolving conflicts. In the United States, some of our sacred themes are rooted in democracy and in principles of free market capitalism; some in an older, more cooperative communalism still present, though fading, in rural areas; some in traditions of British common law; some in the Enlightenment; some in our particular national experience. But probably no single influence has been more important in establishing our sense of what is sacred than Protestant Christianity.

Protestantism has contributed in a variety of ways. Some of its traditional values have become secularized and no longer seem particularly religious to us—for example, its insistence on the individual person's duty and privilege to make decisions of fundamental importance about belief and action. But Protestant Christianity also remains powerfully formative for us as a religion. Public figures still appeal to Protestant values, not by citing the distinctive beliefs of particular churches, which would violate another sacred value of ours (the separation of church and state), but by appealing to the Bible, regarded by Protestantism as the fountainhead of religion. Protestantism is, in effect, the culture religion of the United States, with other religions defined as in some sense exceptional, even when, like Roman Catholicism, they have very large numbers of adherents.

To say that Protestantism is our culture religion is not the same as saying that it is always a majority religion. At times in our history, the majority has been nonreligious or at least uncommitted to organized expressions of faith. Still, popular preconceptions over the centuries have tended to identify "religion" with Protestantism in its varying forms. In the thirteen colonies, it took the form of the churches transported from Europe; by the late nineteenth and early twentieth centuries, the chief influence was the revivalist movement with its Prohibitionist offshoot. In the mid-twentieth century, the "mainline" denominations held sway, while the present scene has anointed the blend of fundamentalist and charismatic influences that characterizes contemporary televangelism and suburban megachurches. The assumption in each age is that the current anointed representative of Protestantism represents "traditional" Christianity and is therefore a suitable vehicle of traditional cultural values.

This reality creates a set of problems not always remarked upon or understood. It means that Protestantism in the United States has dual roles that may come into conflict with each other. On the one hand, it is a collection of rather diverse worshipping communities, voluntary organizations concerned with the common life of their constituents and trying to make their way in the great competition that is typical of American life. On the other, they are cultural institutions embodying a significant aspect of the "American tradition"—rather like the liquid in which the other elements of the American stew have floated and to which they have contributed without ever entirely losing their shape. Hence the genuine perplexity that many Americans have felt when the courts have prohibited Christmas observance, for example, in public schools. These observances were part of the public role of Protestantism, its function as culture religion; but it was difficult for many people to distinguish their abolition from an attack on the Protestant churches as a voluntary tradition, since the two roles are so entangled with each other.

For Protestant churches themselves, the line between their role as voluntary organizations, responsible only to their own traditions and membership, and their role as culture religion, maintaining the continuity of American traditions, has often been hard to find. I remember, for example, a Methodist bishop in the 1950s preaching at a Reformation Day service in Oklahoma City. His message, basically, was that Protestantism is democratic, as evidenced by the absence of strong Communist parties in northern Europe, while Roman Catholicism and Eastern Orthodoxy were deficient in this regard. An observance of Protestant origins easily became an occasion for the celebration of American culture religion. One might, indeed, argue that the mainline churches of the period sold their souls in order to serve the role of culture religion.

For the public at large in the United States, the question is: "When are specific Protestant churches acting as culture religion to the larger community and when are they advocating their more particular doctrinal or ethical stance?" Is abortion, for example, an ethical issue of concern to the larger public or is it the concern of certain religious groups that they are endeavoring to force on the larger public? For the churches themselves, the question is different. It is the question more formally established churches in the Old World have had to deal with, reframed for the

American situation: "When are we being true to the gospel and the traditions of faith and when are we being the mouthpiece of a set of cultural expectations which may even contradict that mission?" Thus, for example, the question of the Vietnam War proved very difficult for the major churches. It lacked the clearer justifications of World War II, but the churches had formed a habit of supporting what the government wanted in military terms and saw themselves more as defenders of the capitalist-democratic world than as moral critics of their own society.

None of this is to say that the American church-state system is intrinsically better or worse than any other. It is only to note the multiple opportunities for betrayal that it affords. We have entrusted a significant segment of our sacred principles to the care of voluntary organizations. The churches can fulfill this trust only by maintaining their own faith traditions—traditions that contributed to the making of the culture. Yet, they can be recognized as fulfilling it only if they satisfy the expectations of large numbers of people who have no active connection with their life. The twin temptations for American churches are either to corrupt the integrity of their faith traditions for the sake of power or to abandon the public arena in order to preserve the purity of their faith.

In Protestantism, much of this tension plays itself out around the Bible, since Protestant faith of all sorts maintains a strong commitment to Scripture, admittedly with a wide range of approaches and interpretations. In the beginning, at the time of the Reformation, this commitment to the Bible was revolutionary. Early Protestant leaders appealed to the Bible for the authority to overturn or reject many of the tenets and practices of medieval Western Catholicism. The Bible originally served Protestantism as the authority for subversion and reform of more contemporary church authorities. Its potential for disrupting contemporary consensus was its great value. At the same time, the reformers also began using the Bible as an authority for the codification of new doctrinal norms and behavioral systems, a process that became more and more central to Protestant theology once the battle with Rome had been fought to a draw and western Europe settled into a divided religious regime.

By this point, established Protestant churches no longer wanted the Bible read as a critique of existing institutions (which were, after all, now Protestant and claimed the Bible as their foundational authority). They wanted it read only to confirm the now codified forms of Protestantism. If dissenting groups such as the Puritans or Baptists in England did continue, for the time being, to read it in more disruptive ways, they, too, were generally prepared to convert it to an authoritative code when they could carve out their own realm, as in New England. This dialectic between the Bible as source of revolution and the Bible as source of law codes is apparently intrinsic to Protestantism. Needless to say, when Protestantism is acting as culture religion, it favors the Bible as law code.

Because of the centrality of the Bible to Protestantism, religious discourse in the United States always tends to take the form of discourse about the Bible. This does not necessarily mean, however, that the actual meaning of the biblical text is the primary point at issue. Protestantism as culture religion does not read the Bible primarily for its own sake or in the hope of new spiritual or religious illumination; and it certainly does not read it for its revolutionary potential. It reads it rather for legal purposes and to confirm existing presuppositions.[1] Indeed, one might say that the very purpose of a culture religion is to serve as a kind of chaplaincy to the status quo, a way of formulating its sacred themes. It will vary with, not against, the changes in the culture. Thus the mainline Protestantism of the 1950s served as chaplaincy to a status quo that was seen as internally complete and flourishing but threatened from without by godless Communism. The fundamentalist-charismatic Christianity of the 1990s, which serves a more divided culture, functions as chaplaincy to a status quo seen as crumbling from internal erosion and subversion. Both, however, essentially serve to sanctify the idealized familiar.[2]

Accordingly, the reading of the Bible in American culture religion (and therefore in American public discourse) typically follows the pattern that Peter Gomes has identified as "culturism." It accepts the status quo (in a somewhat idealized form) and assumes that the Bible *must* support a familiar and relatively conservative arrangement of social life. The only question for culturism, in approaching the Bible, is how to draw out of it something that will serve to confirm its presuppositions. As one looks back over the past couple of centuries in American public life, one finds that it has been relatively easy for American religious leaders to draw from Scripture support for such violent and sinful acts as the displacement of the Native American population, slavery, segregation (and its accompanying denial of rights to people of color), subordination of women, and denial of rights to homosexual persons. [3] Such a reading owes something, to be sure, to the fact that the biblical books were composed in a social context that was characterized by conquest, slavery, and patriarchal structures. Biblical writers sometimes support these practices, sometimes protest against them, but almost always assume them as usual. It is therefore easy to present the Bible as establishing such norms.

But, in another sense, what the Bible actually *says* is of no more than secondary import. The very function of a culture religion is to reassure the public that the idealized status quo is the divinely intended order of the world; and the public will typically be satisfied if its religious leaders can make even a meager case for claiming that the status quo reflects a biblical model. Public discourse, accordingly, has difficulty separating what the Bible says from what the culture religion says that it says. As long as the culture religion is doing its job of confirming the status quo, its interpretations will be accepted, at least initially, as self-evident. In the matter of sexuality today, just as in the matter of slavery in the nineteenth century, whatever the currently acknowledged representatives of Protestant Christianity say will be widely accepted as an accurate representation of the biblical witness. The Bible is conceived as quintessentially Protestant. Protestantism is the culture religion of America. The Bible and Protestantism are therefore assumed inevitably to agree with received opinion.

What actually drives most public claims about the Bible and homosexuality, then, is not careful reading of the Bible itself, but the heterosexism that is a part of our existing cultural presuppositions. Since the heterosexism of the public agrees with that of the spokespersons for the culture religion, no sense of discontinuity serves to alert the hearer to the possibility that the religious authorities might be misrepresenting the Bible. Even the weakest of citations will initially seem adequate to confirm the cultural status quo.[4] In the process, the Bible itself ceases actually to be an element in the debate, and only certain public representations about what the Bible says really count. The Bible's potential for disruption, so central to historic Protestantism, is lost entirely.

As I have already suggested, the fundamentalist-charismatic leaders of televangelism have become the principal representatives of Protestantism as culture religion at the end of the twentieth century. This is true not only among their immediate followers and supporters, but also in the broader communities of discourse represented, for example, by the media and the academy. Nominal Christians and nonbelievers often assume that the televangelists and their fundamentalist kindred represent "standard" Christianity. (In actual fact, their historical pedigree is short and their doctrinal preoccupations peculiar by most historic Christian standards.)[5] Thus, it is not merely conservative or right-wing Christians who take the televangelists' word about what the Bible says, but, to a great extent, the culture at large. It seldom occurs to anyone, friend or foe, self-described Christian or self-described secularist, to question whether the Bible has been accurately represented. While this speaks volumes about the power of Protestant Christianity as our cultural religion, it also implies a failure of Protestantism in its own terms, since it makes the Bible itself superfluous and deprives it of the power to trigger reform. Why even have a Bible, if one need only listen to what its anointed representatives claim that it says?

One of the sacred values of American culture, maintained by our romances and legends as much as by our culture religion, is heterosexuality; and it is fair to describe American culture as "heterosexist." When I speak of *heterosexism* here, I am following the lead of Patricia Beattie Jung and Ralph F. Smith, who see it as a set of presuppositions built into our view of the world:

> Heterosexism is a reasoned system of bias regarding sexual orientation. . . . By describing it as a *reasoned* system of prejudice we do not mean to imply that it is rationally defensible. . . . Rather we mean to suggest that heterosexism is not grounded primarily in emotional fears, hatreds, or other visceral responses to homosexuality. It . . . is rooted in a largely cognitive constellation of beliefs about human sexuality. . . . *Heterocentrism* lies at the heart of this system of prejudice. [Heterosexuality] is the measure by which all other sexual orientations are judged. All sexual authority, value, and power are centered in heterosexuality.[6]

Heterosexuality as a sacred theme of American culture is manifest in everything from Hollywood movies to law codes to the social organization of the American high school. Heterocentrism is key to our sexual morality. The culture religion therefore has a presumptive interest in defending it. But heterosexism was often largely unconscious until recent decades brought new challenges to it. These challenges have now brought heterosexism itself into conflict with other of our sacred values such as freedom, opportunity, and equality. This creates a problem for the culture religion. How will it defend the status quo in one respect without appearing to subvert it in others?

By appealing to the Bible—or rather making claims about what the Bible says on the subject of sexuality—the culture religion can endeavor to put the exceptions to the rule of heterosexuality outside the bounds of the culture. If homosexual, bisexual, and transgendered people can successfully be characterized as outside the range of permissible variation, then values such as freedom and equality will no longer apply to them. What emerges from this is a complex dynamic in which the culture debates how it will define humanness, sin, freedom, and related sacred principles. It is not, for the most part, a discussion of what the Bible itself actually says. Even within faith communities, the demands of the culture religion are so great as to make such discussion very difficult.

These dynamics may actually become more visible in a denomination that is not, at present, part of the anointed voice of American culture religion but that has been dealing with these issues longer than most others. My own denomination, the Episcopal Church, is a "mainline" denomination, part of the group of Protestant churches that held authority in the middle of the twentieth century.[7] It belongs to the Anglican tradition, which is related to Protestantism by its Reformation origins, but less inclined to treat the Bible as its sole authority. Still, it has had to incorporate the Bible into denominational discourse about sexual orientation. Over the past twenty years or so, it has moved first toward recognition of the issue of sexuality as significant and legitimate for study and, more recently, toward full affirmation of gay men and lesbians in its community life, at least in some places—a development fraught with anger and with a continuing potential for dividing the church.

The Episcopal church began with the heterosexist presuppositions common to the culture at large. Before the escalation of the controversy, heterosexism appeared most often, I think, in the form of a tacit acceptance of the presence of homosexual persons combined with an expectation that we would either be quiet about our identity or segregate ourselves into a limited number of inner-city churches. The church thus made limited toleration available to a group that was defined as being an exception to the heterosexual norm: they could be present as long as they were invisible. Twenty years ago, this tacit agreement "not to notice" our presence could claim the defense of naivete. Today, it still exists in some places, though it cannot claim to be quite as naive as before. There was a time when church authorities could simply claim not to "know" any gay men or lesbians, to have no notion that they might be represented among the Episcopalian faithful. That is now more difficult.

As discussion became more open, the claim to naivete that sheltered the agreement "not to notice" often became real hypocrisy. I recall a bishop in the mid-1980s, for example, who made public pronouncements of compassion about the disadvantages suffered by lesbians and gay men—problems of job security, housing, AIDS hysteria, and anti-gay violence. The same bishop, at the same time, used his influence to get a gay seminarian thrown out of the local seminary for the crime of flaunting his gayness. "Flaunting," in this case, consisted of the man's living quietly and monogamously with his life-partner. To make the whole case even more interesting, the seminarian did not belong to the diocese of the bishop in question, who need not have broached the issue at all; but the resulting publicity led to the seminarian's being rejected by his own diocese, which could no longer pretend not to notice that he was gay. The bishop had "outed" him.

At the time, the bishop insisted that gay and lesbian people were not being ordained in the Episcopal church and treated the seminarian's case as unique. But, not long after, he explained to a mutual acquaintance that he "lived in fear that the laity were going to discover how many of the clergy were homosexual." The real offense, in other words, was not being homosexual, but being openly homosexual. The bishop excused his gratuitous interference in the matter by referring to the heterosexism of the culture. Appeal to the cultural norm seemed to him adequate justification for his action. The bishop, who was well aware of the existence of gay clergy, assumed a public stance of surprise and made an "example" of a gay man who was relatively open in order to protect more closeted homosexual clergy or, more likely, the clerical institution as such from criticism. A kind interpretation would take this behavior as that of a mildly liberal prelate in a very conservative environment—constantly calculating how far he thinks he can go before his public will refuse to listen. But one might also describe it as an example of the culture religion justifying heterosexism by erasing visible anomalies.

Gradually, however, the issue of sexual orientation moved from being a matter of scattered "incidents" to being part of the public discourse of the Episcopal church. Gay and lesbian Episcopalians no longer agreed to remain invisible. Only at this point did those who rejected an openly gay-lesbian presence in the church begin to appeal to the Bible as the guarantor of the heterosexist status quo. The bishops of Province VII, in the west-south-central United States, created a statement that reasserted what they called the "biblical" standard of marriage between one man and one woman that is "in intention lifelong" and rejected all same-sex partnerships on that basis. This, of course, is a very difficult statement to reconcile with the biblical record, which nowhere insists explicitly on monogamy and which does not refer to "intention" in speaking of either marriage or divorce. The Episcopal church, like the culture at large, however, had already come to terms with the remarriage of divorced persons; and the bishops were, in effect, enunciating a standard based on existing ecclesiastical usage, not the Bible. They set forth, as the norm, serial (albeit reluctantly serial) heterosexual monogamy. Precisely because their declaration did express the existing cultural norm for most Americans, their peculiar claim that it was biblically founded seems to have passed without challenge. Heterosexism could thus represent itself as biblical doctrine without having to specify how that claim was grounded in the Bible or what was meant by it.

The bishops' self-styled biblical seriousness merely reflected cultural heterosexism, not any genuine interest in the Bible as such. Indeed, the right wing in the Episcopal church still refuses to come to grips with what the Bible actually says. Their arguments have consisted of repeating their own assertions *ad infinitum* while ignoring arguments from other perspectives. There is no evidence of any effort to examine the biblical texts with more integrity. It is easier simply to maintain the tradition of Protestant Christianity as culture religion, offering divine sanction to the existing cultural order. When the Episcopal church's General Convention mandated open discussion of these issues, most of the more conservative dioceses ignored the directive. Where a diocese of mixed character officially proceeded with dialogue, conservative congregations generally absented themselves. On the few occasions when I saw self-styled conservative Episcopalians participate, they did so only by reasserting their own position, never by reexamining the texts and responding to the challenges raised with regard to their interpretations.

The Bible, then, is cited constantly, both within and without the churches, in

our public discourse about sexuality; but it is not in fact getting read carefully or respectfully. This may sound like the professional complaint of a New Testament
scholar. Perhaps it is in part! There is a more serious matter, though, at stake here —
not neglect of scriptural scholarship, but abuse of Scripture itself and betrayal of the
Protestant faith tradition. We want the Bible to reconfirm for us what we have "always" thought and taught. We do not want to be troubled to rethink anything. We
are afraid of what might have to change if we should do so. This is a fundamental
betrayal of the Reformation, which could not have happened at all under these
conditions. If Protestants and Anglicans cannot trust the Bible enough to read it
honestly and without forcing it in a culturist direction, we may be functioning well
enough as servants of the culture, but we have lost our souls. This reflects not faith,
but the fear of losing our established position; and the Bible the churches are citing
is not the Bible at all, but a culturist representation of it.

What is required if one is to read the Bible in continuity with the Reformation's
rediscovery of its revolutionary capacities? One must take risks. One must place
one's cherished presuppositions at risk and read with an expectation that the Bible
may say something unexpected, even with an expectation that one may emerge
from the reading a different person. What the Reformers discovered in the Bible
was the power to convert, to transform the reader. The Bible, they found, was not
the creature of the culture religion of their own time but, if read respectfully and
nor merely to confirm existing presuppositions, might actually function as a critic
of it. And it was precisely this discovery that made Protestantism such a formative
influence on the culture of the United States. One may question how deep an im-
pression Enlightenment doctrines of the "Rights of Man" would have made on an
America that had not already been primed for them by Protestant insistence on the
importance of individual decision in matters of faith. Modern American Protestantism betrays its own roots when it settles into its role as culture religion and refuses any longer to grant the Bible the ability to surprise and transform.

This betrayal of the Bible in the name of the Bible works by overinterpreting, by
careless reading, by attaching arbitrary interpretations to the text and then presenting
them as if they *were* the text, by fragmenting the text and choosing from it only what
accords with one's point of view. It will be helpful to show by a couple of examples
how this betrayal works.[8] First—and rather briefly—the story of Sodom and Gomorrah (Gen. 19), so deeply entangled with later notions about homosexuality that the
English term "sodomy" derives from it. The representatives of the culture religion
still tend to claim that "the sin" of Sodom was genital acts between men. The text,
however, says little about what brings God's wrath on the city in the first place.[9] And
in describing the intentions of the men of Sodom toward the angelic visitors, it uses
an ambiguous verb ("to know"), leaving it uncertain whether the men of Sodom in-
tend sexual penetration of the strangers; if that is in fact what they have in view, then
the penetration would amount to rape of the visitors and therefore to violation of the
ancient laws of hospitality. "Hospitality" may have a relatively trivial ring in modern
English; and "the laws of hospitality" may sound like the province of Miss Manners
rather than of high ethics. In antiquity, however, given the lack of both national and
international protections for travelers, hospitality was a very serious—indeed, a fundamentally sacred—matter, not only in Hebrew but in other cultures.

What is contemplated, then, in the story of Sodom and Gomorrah is not consensual sex between people of the same gender, but rape of visitors who have thrown themselves on the conscience of the community by their mere arrival and who have become specifically the guests of Lot, himself a resident alien among the people of Sodom and therefore entitled to their protection. To use this story as biblical grounds for declaring consensual genital acts between two people of the same gender sinful is bizarre (as an increasing number even of conservative Christian leaders have begun to recognize).[10] Were a story about heterosexual rape used to claim that the Bible is opposed to heterosexual genital activity as such, the argument would be recognized at once as quite beside the point. The abuse of sexuality does not invalidate its appropriate use.[11]

The leap that allows a reader to interpret a story of same-sex rape committed on apparently defenseless strangers as a general prohibition of same-sex genital intimacy is strange enough to compel us to ask how people could have done it for so long without noticing the difficulty. The answer can only be that as long as the Bible is assumed to support the status quo, no further questions need be asked. In other words, the culture religion is not actually *reading* the Bible, but only mining it for confirmation of the status quo. Authentic reading, by contrast, implies respect for the text being read and some awareness of one's potential to misuse it. Respectful interpretation of a text requires clarity about the path from text to interpretation and some coherence or consistency of interpretive approach in order to protect the text from being merely a vessel for the reader's presuppositions. Otherwise, the Bible is deprived of its chance, so central to Protestantism, to challenge the prevailing view.

Another biblical passage often used to validate heterosexism is the creation narrative of Genesis 1–2. Since it is initially more plausible for this purpose, it deserves a more extended examination here. Broadly speaking, the claim of the culture religion is that the creation narrative implies that God intended all human beings to be heterosexual rather than homosexual. The argument is summed up in the fundamentalist slogan: "God made Adam and Eve, not Adam and Steve." To a large public, this slogan seems to embody a self-evident truth and an inevitable reading of Genesis. Once again, however, this assurance owes more to the heterosexist presuppositions of our culture than to a careful reading of the biblical text.

In its more cautious form, the culture religion's reading of Genesis runs something like this: the first creation narrative, in Genesis 1, says that the two sexes, male and female, are a basic given of humanity. Both were present from the first moment of creation and both reflect the image of God (Gen. 1:27–28). After creating the two sexes, God commands them to be fruitful and multiply, to fill the earth and subdue it. Thus, the first creation narrative links the existence of the two sexes closely with the human need for reproduction. The second creation narrative (Gen. 2) is distinct from the first, but related in its emphasis on the two sexes. It tells how God created Adam (Hebrew for "Human Being") from the dust, breathed life into him, and put him in the Garden of Eden.[12] Then it goes on to say that God recognized Adam's need for help or companionship (2:18). Since the animals proved not sufficient to this purpose, God put Adam to sleep, took a rib from his side, and fashioned it into the first woman. Thus, when God sought for Adam a uniquely suitable helper or companion, God created the first woman as complimentary to the first man. The narrative describes heterosexual intercourse as existing for this purpose and makes no direct reference to procreation.

The combination of the two creation narratives allows Protestants to see procreation and mutual support as the twin purposes of heterosexual intercourse. And the conclusion of the second narrative may then be read as making heterosexuality an exclusive pattern for humanity: "Therefore a man leaves his father and his mother and cleaves to his wife, and they become one flesh" (Gen. 2:24, Revised Standard Version). This, culturist interpreters claim, establishes a universal rule for human sexual behavior. Sex exists for the sake of both companionship and reproduction; and, in both respects, it "works" only by virtue of a certain complimentarity between male and female.[13]

A more extreme version of this interpretation actually finds a detailed prescription for modern Christian marriage in the verse quoted. It holds that the singular nouns ("a man . . . his wife") imply the monogamous union of one man with one woman, that "leaving father and mother" implies some kind of public ceremony, that the verb "cleaves" implies a lifelong connection, that "becoming one flesh" refers to the requirement of sexual intercourse to consummate marriage. They further affirm that the pattern thus established is exclusive and mandatory and that no other pattern is "natural" or morally acceptable. This pattern, in other words, has the force of *law*. In consequence of this argument, same-sex sexual acts must be seen as immoral in the same way as extramarital heterosexual unions, adultery, and polygamy.[14]

How credible is this interpretation, taken simply as an interpretation of Genesis 1–2 and abstracting from the heterosexist presuppositions that make it seem inevitable in our culture? Not very. For one thing, the conservative reading assumes that Genesis 2:24 constitutes a *law*. That is one possible reading of the verse. The leading verb, in Hebrew, is in the imperfect tense, a tense that we sometimes translate into English with a future and that was sometimes used in giving commands—such as "Thou shalt not kill. Thou shalt not commit adultery." However, the imperfect tense has other meanings, too. For one thing, it can describe repeated or habitual action. Thus, the translators of the Revised Standard Version (who were not, in their translation, well disposed toward gay or lesbian people) understood this verse not as a commandment, but as a description of the way things usually are in human society. They translated it, appropriately, with present-tense verbs: "A man *leaves* father and mother and *cleaves* to his wife and they *become* one flesh."[15]

This translation in fact fits the context of the passage best, for etiological narratives—stories about how things got to be the way they are—are quite common in these early chapters of Genesis.[16] The passage answers a widespread human question: Why do boys, who start out so dependent on their parents, grow up to become men and get interested in women (as the great majority do) and eventually form their own households? Because, in the beginning, the woman was taken out of the man and the man has wanted her back ever since. Such a story assumes that heterosexual coupling is the usual pattern, but it does not automatically reject other possibilities.[17]

It is easy enough to treat a pattern as "normal" without defining every departure from it as intrinsically wrong. In fact, the normal antonym of "normal" is "unusual," not "sinful." I may assume a college education as normal for young adults in my family, but I would not regard it as immoral if one of them made a mature decision to pursue another kind of livelihood and not go to college. The identification of a norm, then, implies the designation of other behavior as unusual, but not necessarily as immoral. We have no certain indication whether the author of Genesis 2 was thinking in terms of law or of norm. Yet, if it does incorporate a set of moral instructions it does so in ambiguous fashion. And, since Genesis is otherwise fairly clear on the few occasions when it is enunciating law, it is simpler to interpret the text as the kind of etiological story so common in this book.

But the issue is broader than this one verse, which is typically treated in isolation from the rest of Genesis 1–2—a kind of proof-texting, in other words. The culturist interpretation of Genesis 1–2 implies that the creation narratives embody an ideal plan for subsequent human life and that it is sinful for human beings to vary from this pattern. Is this assumption actually rooted in the Bible? Does the text itself suggest that humanity was expected to remain forever exactly as we were created? Or does it treat the created order simply as a starting point? Are we to understand that human beings sin whenever we vary from the original order of creation as described in Genesis? If we do read Genesis in this way, what kind of moral code will result?

Most critically, are the culturist interpreters prepared to follow the implicit logic of their argument? They cannot consistently claim that Genesis sets up an inalterable law about sexuality and then refuse to see the same process at work regarding other aspects of human existence. Otherwise, they admit that they are merely picking and choosing texts that support their preconceptions. Perhaps people reading Genesis 1–2 might come to their conclusions merely because they are used to heterosexism and assume that it must be grounded in Scripture and that this seems like as good a place as any. If the Sodom story and other real or apparent references to homosexuality in Scripture are, at most, inconclusive with regard to the modern issues, the creation narratives become correspondingly more important. But is the appeal to Genesis really any more sound? If we want to be *reading* scripture rather than abusing it for political ends, we should try to maintain some consistency of approach.

Let us, then, try the experiment of looking at the whole of Genesis 1 and 2 in the same way as the culturist interpreter reads 2:24. We shall treat each aspect of the original pattern of creation as establishing a kind of moral imperative and draw from that an ethic for human life lived in accordance with the creation narratives. This essay does not offer the space for detailed exegesis; but a random list, with verse numbers attached, will give us a picture of human life as it existed, according to Genesis, at the dawn of the world:

> we were naked and unashamed (2:25)
> we were vegetarians (1:29-30; 2:16)
> we spoke a single language (2:20)
> we observed the Sabbath (2:3)
> we ruled peaceably over the wild animals (1:28; 2:19–20)
> we needed companionship (2:18)
> we existed in two sexes (1:27; 2:21–23)
> we were commanded to multiply (1:28)

Since all of these are equally features of the original creation of humanity, a consistent ethic, based on the creation narratives, without screening the texts through culturist preconceptions, must include them all. Does this, in fact, offer us an ethic we are prepared to take seriously?

Most American Protestants would probably answer "no" without much further thought—but why? How does eating meat or wearing clothes differ, in terms of Genesis 1–2, from engaging in same-sex sexual acts? All are equally at variance with what it specifies as the order of creation. Many ancient and medieval Christians would have seen nakedness and vegetarianism as the really telling elements in the picture. In recounting the lives of saints, particularly of the great desert hermits, they liked to tell how the hermit lived on nothing but a little parched grain. They told of elderly saints who had been far from human habitation for so long that their clothes had all rotted away, leaving nothing but long hair or beard to cover them. They told about the friendliness of wild beasts, who became the saints' attendants.[18] A Christian ethic that prized, above all, simplicity, nakedness, and friendliness with the natural world might have much to commend it—at least in warmer climates.

Yet, some aspects of the original creation were modified within the Scriptures themselves. Thus, God made clothes for Adam and Eve after their fall (Gen. 3:21). God permitted Noah and his descendants to eat meat, though with the stipulation that they not consume any blood (Gen. 9:3–4). God created enmity between us and at least one kind of animal (snakes, Gen. 3:15). God destroyed the original unity of human language as punishment for the building of the Tower of Babel (Gen. 11:1–9). Moreover, in the New Testament, Jesus was apparently celibate, thus violating the requirements to multiply and to wed; and Paul, on his own authority, encouraged Christians to remain unmarried (1 Cor. 7:8–9, 36–38).

These examples show that humanity can vary a good deal from its created order and still remain human. These departures cannot have been intrinsically contrary to the purpose of creation. The wearing of clothes does not render us less human. (Some Christians, in fact, treat our original, created nudity as immoral.) The multiplicity of human languages may be inconvenient and troublesome, but it is not immoral. We are not entirely to blame if some animals are harmful to us. And most Christians in the modern West have come to the conclusion, whatever church hierarchies may say, that the command to multiply is an area where couples ought to exercise informed judgment. To diverge from the order of our creation, as given in Genesis, is not, then, intrinsically sinful. Indeed, one may very well live one's life as a fully-clothed, bilingual, municipal ratcatcher with only two children and not incur any moral blame thereby. To depart from the pattern of creation as laid down in Genesis is not intrinsically sinful.

Still, a culturist interpreter might argue that, while God or an apostle could modify the order of creation, once the canon of Scripture was complete, no more modifications were possible. Such an argument might carry weight if its exponents held to it consistently; but in fact no mainstream Christian does. For there are at least two elements in the original order of creation, as sketched above, that are repealed nowhere in Scripture, but that the vast majority of Christians nonetheless ignores entirely—one is the observance of Sabbath, the other is the question of the exact limits of carnivory. Sabbath (Hebrew *shabbat*) is not an arbitrarily chosen day of rest, but a specific day of the week, the 24-hour period from sunset Friday to sunset Saturday that God consecrated as a memorial of his own rest from creative labor (Gen. 2:3). The significance of the Sabbath is reconfirmed by its inclusion in the Ten Commandments. It is not by authority of Scripture but by tradition that most Christians have dropped observance of the Sabbath. Some have transferred the *term* "Sabbath" to Sunday, though the origin of the Sunday observance is in the celebration of the Resurrection, not in the Sabbath. But, of course, Saturday is not Sunday, and this is at most an allegorizing of the actual commandment in order to adapt it to existing usage. It is difficult to see how any Christian who ignores the Sabbath can go on to maintain that other elements in the creation narrative set up absolute and unalterable moral rules.

The same argument applies to the matter of eating meat not slaughtered in the kosher manner. As mentioned above, the created order of human life, according to Genesis, was vegetarian. After the flood, Noah and his descendants were given limited permission to eat meat, but only if all blood were drained from it. This exception is never altered in Scripture. It even appears to be reaffirmed in Acts 15:29. Yet, few subsequent Christians have taken it seriously. Even without specific warrant of Scripture, then, Christians have always felt free to develop and change the "order of creation" as they live out their faith.

If one wants to maintain that the original order of creation, as laid down in Genesis 1 and 2, is the foundation of Christian morality, then one ought to be consistent in interpreting these chapters. The culturist use of the creation narratives against homosexual persons falls to the ground because it fails the most basic test of consistency. Its proponents pick and choose which elements of creation they will take seriously and which they will ignore. If they wish us to believe that their arguments are founded in the Bible and not in cultural heterosexism, they will need to be more faithful in both their method and their use of the text.

I have been arguing that the role of Protestantism as culture religion in the United States means that any claim to biblical authority that supports the existing presuppositions of the culture will automatically be accepted, at least at first glance. Whether it represents a careful reading of the Bible is quite secondary. Those who claim biblical authority for attacking homosexual persons feel no need to present an authentically biblical argument—i.e., one that actually takes the texts of the Bible seriously—in behalf of their position. They need only announce the conclusion that the culture has previously agreed upon and claim biblical authority for it. For the most part, their claim will be accepted automatically. In the process, the Bible always seems to wind up on the side of the status quo.

The most effective antidote to this pseudo-biblical, heterosexist culturism would be a more careful reading of the Bible itself in the culture at large. The Bible does not, in fact, afford simple, clear blueprints for social order. Only by ignoring large portions of it can anyone claim that it does. The more carefully people read the Scriptures, the more evident this becomes. The Bible is an ongoing conversation in which one writer counters another. What is assumed as inevitable in one text is discounted in another. The authors of Job and Ecclesiastes, for example, counter the deuteronomic theology that permeates the books of Kings as well as

Deuteronomy itself. Paul, with his concern for the inclusion of unclean Gentiles, counters the concern for purity found in Leviticus. An honest and respectful reading of the Bible must begin by letting the texts say whatever they will, even if they do not agree with one another or give us the answers we expected. This principle of letting the Bible say surprising things is at the heart of the Protestantism that helped create American culture in the first place.

The healthiest change for American public discourse, then, might be for those who have dismissed the Bible as archaic and irrelevant, perhaps even oppressive and retrogressive, to reclaim a role in interpreting the Bible. Because of our Protestant heritage, the Christian Scriptures are part of our common cultural heritage as Americans, even for those who do not regard them as religiously authoritative. The claim of the currently anointed leaders of Protestantism to speak for the Bible can best be challenged if others—Protestants, other Christians, people of any religion and none—begin reading the Bible carefully themselves, so that they can participate as genuine partners in this aspect of our cultural debates.

Notes

1. I have argued elsewhere that the overcoming of this kind of reading-without-reading is the main purpose of biblical scholarship. See L. Wm. Countryman, *Biblical Authority or Biblical Tyranny?* 2d ed. (Valley Forge, Pa.: Trinity Press International, 1994).

2. Similar dynamics affect the work of other "priesthoods" of our sacred values, for example that of the sciences. See Stephen Jay Gould's remarks on the way Herbert Spencer was able to distort Darwin's thinking to make it a justification of the rampant social indifference of developing capitalism: "A Tale of Two Worksites," *Natural History* 6, no. 9 (October 1997): 18–29.

3. Peter Gomes, *The Good Book: Reading the Bible with Mind and Heart* (New York: William Morrow, 1996), 53–172.

4. One thinks, for example, of the case of Total Abstinence, which never managed to come up with a biblical argument for total abstinence as a moral imperative, much less for state prohibition of alcohol. Yet, many thousands of people were firmly convinced, without any evidence at all, that it was a biblical belief, simply because its chief advocates were church-based. Cf. Gomes, *The Good Book*, 75–83.

5. Bruce Bawer, *Stealing Jesus: How Fundamentalism Betrays Christianity* (New York: Crown, 1997), 77–129.

6. Patricia Beattie Jung and Ralph F. Smith, *Heterosexism: An Ethical Challenge* (Albany: State University of New York Press, 1993), 13–14.

7. I would describe the Episcopal church at present as an "elite dissenting" denomination. It stands outside the circle of the current anointed representatives of Protestantism as cultural religion; but it represents not a disadvantaged minority but one distinguished and marginalized rather by greater education and often higher social standing. It has not altogether shed its role as culture religion, even if it is now largely ignored by the media.

8. I do not pursue the five or six other texts cited against homosexual persons here, but I have dealt with them at length in *Dirt, Greed, and Sex: Sexual Ethics in the New Testament and Their Implications for Today* (Philadelphia: Fortress Press, 1988).

9. The interpretation that it was male-male genital sexuality emerges only about the beginning of the Common Era and is not found in earlier references to the story. See Countryman, *Dirt, Greed, and Sex*, 30–32, 61–64.

10. E.g., Marion L. Soards, *Scripture and Homosexuality: Biblical Authority and the Church Today* (Louisville, Ky.: Westminster John Knox Press, 1995), 15–16.

11. In other, more ascetic times, Christians could and did argue that the variety of dangers to which sex exposed persons (especially women) meant that all sexual activity was to be avoided. But, then, heterosexuality has not always enjoyed its unquestioned status among Christians. The dominant Christian attitude toward sexuality from the fourth century onward was that it held people back from salvation and was something to be surrendered or avoided by anyone with the courage to do so.

12. I follow the Hebrew text in using masculine pronouns for the undifferentiated Adam, but it is not entirely clear that he is male from the beginning in the sense he will be after division into two persons.

13. Thomas E. Schmidt, *Straight and Narrow? Compassion and Clarity in the Homosexuality Debate* (Downers Grove, Ill.: InterVarsity Press, 1995), 39–48.

14. John Stott, *Homosexual Partnerships? Why Same-Sex Relationships Are Not a Christian Option* (Downers Grove, Ill.: InterVarsity Press, 1985), 13–16.

15. Italics mine.

16. A few examples: origins of the Sabbath (2:1–3), of human antagonism toward snakes (3:14), of labor pain and the social subordination of women (3:16), of agriculture (3:19).

17. Cf. the Greek equivalent of it in Plato's *Symposium*, which allows for same-sex variations.

18. Alison Goddard Elliott, *Roads to Paradise: Reading the Lives of the Early Saints* (Hanover, N.H.: University Press of New England for Brown University Press, 1987).

Contested Issues in Law and Public Policy

DANIEL C. MAGUIRE

Religion and Reproductive Policy

The sexual is political. Every government knows that and every government addresses sex and gender issues. All social theorists take account of sexuality. No
realistic theory of economics, sociology, religion, history, or law could leave it untouched. Gender is part of the primordial experience of identity; it is also the primal socializing experience of an "other." If that gender relationship is skewed, it
will have an impact on how we relate to other others. Gender prejudice (sexism) is
thus the elemental distortion, the setting of one half of the human dyad against the
other; it is then the genetic paradigm for all forms of prejudice. In theological
terms, sexism is original sin and a pandemic root of mischief.[1] Sex also functions as
a mirror, an attitudinal showcase that reflects society's values and power assumptions. Major social revolutions come to grips with it since sexual attitudes reflect social arrangements to a degree. A military culture will not be sexually gentle.

Sex is also a social activist, a *maker*: it makes babies, friends, and enemies and is
a conduit for disease. It is, in a word, a thoroughly public reality. And yet, it is also
insistently private, personal, and intimate.

Talk of sex reflects this inherent contrariety. Sex-talk is a zone of contradiction.
Sex is idealized as the gateway to love and fulfillment, but it is also demonized as
dirty and impure. Sex is gentle but regularly commingled with violence. Religions
give it sacramental status in marriage and present it as an image of divine love but
then go on to define it as an impurity and as an impediment to holiness and ritual.
Amid this conceptual melee, youth are given colliding counsels: "Sex is dirty; save
it for someone you love."

Humans love their sexuality. Advertisers know that we will buy products cleverly associated with sex even if the product has no connection to sex at all. At the same time we are afraid of it. Most sexual ethics begins with the assumption that sex is *bad* unless . . . We do not dare start with the assumption that sex is *good* unless . . . Rightly or wrongly, we are afraid of its power, and so we fence it in with taboos and limits. Sex stands under social indictment as the cause of disease and over-population, of violence in the form of rape and harassment, obsession, and prostitution. Our laws treat sex like an errant force that needs social constraints. And to some degree that is true.

What is manifestly true is that sex is power. All the taboos and legal restraints of history testify that sex purrs like a kitten but has the strength of a tiger. Those whose passions are for power and control do not overlook sex, and they use it as a means of control. The use of sex as power by religions and the impact of that particularly on reproductive policy is the subject of this chapter. Sex is power. Religion is power. Historically, both have proved that they can move mountains. So when sex and religion get together, we are dealing with power *squared*. It is a fact of life to be dealt with that religion in its multiple forms is intricately woven into the history of reproductive ethics.

Religion and Social Analysis

Since much social criticism in the Western world ignores religion, and since many Americans indulge the illusion that we banished religion from public life with the First Amendment, a pause to see what religion is in order. Definitions are the paragon of all reality checks, and they are often bypassed in the rush to discussion.

Religion, I submit, is *a response to the sacred. Sacred* is the superlative of *precious*. We call sacred what we find uncompromisingly, ineffably precious. And since no one finds nothing sacred, religion is pan-human. If "the sanctity of life" had no meaning there could be no law; punishments and force alone would not maintain the fabric of social order.

What we call sacred varies. Sometimes sacred-talk leads to theism, sometimes not. Theoretical Buddhism and the Chinese religions are not theistic, yet they are deeply imbued with a sense of the sacred. Some native religions have a God figure, but often it is the ancestors who are more important in their sense of the divine. In other words, God is not the essence of religion; sacrality is.

And sacrality is power-packed. John Henry Newman said people will die for a dogma (religiously held convictions) who will not stir for a conclusion. This links with Camus's observation that people will not die for scientific truths—and with the poet Alexander Pope's view that the worst of madmen is a saint gone mad. All are making the same point. We are never more serious than when we treat of that which we call sacred.

Social analysis that ignores this fact of life is hallucinatory. *Religion, the Missing Dimension of Statecraft* is the telling title of a recent study from Oxford University Press.[2] The volume makes its point by way of cases, cases showing the bungling that occurs when the influence of religion is ignored in international political decisions. This common deficit is a cultural malady, not limited to international politics. All too much of Western thought is phobic on the subject of religion. If the literature of a period were to ignore all reference to love or sexuality we would accuse it of neurotic suppression for its slighting of such a central force in human personality.[3] Yet it is taken as normal when political and economic analyses of contemporary problems treat religion the way Victorian school marms treated sex. Any effort to consider human fertility, either to control it or to enhance it, will invoke the emotions of the religio-sacred. Policy discussions of reproductive ethics that avoid the religious dimension are limited. This essay will address that problem.

A final observation on religion and social realism—religion is not confined to what we call "religions." Crypto-religion is more common than institutionalized religion. Arnold Toynbee said we have not outgrown the primitive identification of the tribe with the divine, *Roma dea*. In modern, supposedly democratic nations he argues that "four-fifths of the religions of five-sixths of the population" is nationalism. As he puts it, the religion of the masses is but the "worship of the deified community concealed under the fine name of patriotism."[4] As I have written elsewhere, rechanneling the misplaced sacreds that roam through our political and economic processes "is not an option; it is a necessity for survival. The sacred—however described, theistically or non-theistically—is the motor of all major cultural reform. To try to change culture with mere rationality is like writing a love letter with mathematical formulae. You'll get nowhere."[5] The major social ills of our planet "will not be solved by mere rationality but only by truths that stir the flaccid collective will by touching the sacral core of human willing."

Nationalism, however, is not the only misplaced sacred or extramural religion. Indeed, it is yielding to a higher power. David Loy, a Buddhist economist teaching in Japan, points to a religion that is superseding both nationalism and the traditional "religions." Loy starts with a functional definition of religion: religion "grounds us by teaching us what this world is and what our role in that world is." Then he argues that traditional religions are fulfilling that role less and less. These influential functions are being taken over by a new belief-system, a new value-system, called market capitalism. "The collapse of communism makes it more apparent that the Market is becoming the first truly world religion, binding all corners of the globe into a world-view and set of values whose religious role we overlook only because we insist on seeing them as 'secular.'"[6] This system is telling us what is sacred, who and what matters, and by way of a vicious cycle of increasing production and consumption it pretends to offer a secular salvation. Economics is its theology; advertising its catechetics and preaching.

Religion in its myriad forms is a central fact of human social existence, from economics and politics to reproductive ethics. "Everything is full of Gods," said the ancient Thales. He had that right. Modern social analysts, take heed!

The Temptation to Tyranny

Religions, even those that began as breakthroughs of liberation, tend to tyranny. The instinct for power, which is stronger than the instinct for sex, prompts some within the religious group to set out to control everyone else . . . to control what they do and even what they think. Christianity's birth was attended by songs of freedom. "Where the Spirit of the Lord is, there is liberty."[7] One of the gospel texts that scholars feel might well go back to Rabbi Jesus is an attack on oppressive authority and a radical rethinking of authority in terms of service. "In the world, kings lord it over their subjects. . . . Not so with you: on the contrary, the highest among you must bear himself like the youngest, the chief of you like a servant. . . . Here am I among you as a servant."[8] This was a blunt and countercultural critique of the mode of government that prevailed in that society. But as Christianity got organized, the spirit of liberty gave way to the spirit of the Grand Inquisitor. The Inquisitor decides that only certain formulations do justice to the experience of the sacred. An orthodoxy is established, and contrary views are burned at the stake.

The Abrahamic religions, Judaism, Christianity, and Islam, are particularly prone to this fault. Indeed the Abrahamic religions are notoriously closed to dialogue about their beliefs. Among the classical civilizations of Greece and Rome, there was a kind of freewheeling democratic tolerance of diverse divinities and theologies. Herodotus (484–425 B.C.E.), evinced no sense of threat when he commented amiably that the Gods Amon and Horus that he met in Egypt were the equivalents of Zeus and Apollo from his native Greece. This same relaxed attitude is seen in Euhemerus (330-260 B.C.E.), who felt free to speculate that the Gods were simply historical persons who began to be worshiped after they died. Some of the Stoics could wonder whether the Gods might just be personifications of sea and sky and other natural forces and phenomena.

There was nothing freewheeling and tolerant about ancient Israel in this regard. Isaiah was not into genial dialogue with those who doubted that the Lord of the covenant had spoken to Abraham, Isaac, Jacob, and Moses. The Christian Paul said that even if an angel from heaven were to teach anything at variance with what he taught that even such a supernatural being should be banished as an "outcast" (Gal. 1:8). The children of Israel, Christianity, and Islam all displayed this rigidity throughout most of their history. Those who took a different view of things religious were candidates for rack and stake, with hell fires the eternal sequel to their gory demise. This overconfident dogmatism was an epistemological tone-setter in the formation of Western culture, and, as Daniel Pals writes, "came to dominate Western civilization throughout most of the medieval era."[9] And indeed as the West moved scientifically and philosophically from the medieval to the modern they did not easily shake off this habit of simplistic certainty. The current ill-defined "postmodernism" I dare to see as in large part a delayed adolescent rebellion against the pan-certitudinalism that the Abrahamic religions bequeathed to the Western world.

Pelvic Orthodoxy

The focus of orthodoxy enforcers is mutable. The inquisitors were not interested in Galileo's views on masturbation or birth control. Their orthodoxy concern was in the stars. Galileo would have no problem today. The focus has turned from astral to pelvic issues. The modern Christian inquisition will be heard from in the halls of legislatures if the issue is gay rights, sex education, erotic art, contraception, or abortion. And here another dimension of authoritarian religion emerges, its inherent fascism. The desire is not just to control the faithful but to subdue the entire polity. The abortion issue illustrates this mind-set at work. It was particularly evident at the United Nations Conference on Population and Development in Cairo in 1994.

At this major gathering, two of the Abrahamic religions, Christianity and Islam, after fourteen centuries of hostility became bedfellows, and noisy ones at that. The orthodoxy that bonded them was pelvic. The Vatican and conservative Muslims dominated and obstructed the discussion of family planning and abortion, and their strategic bickering about language slowed down the entire conference. I submit and have argued elsewhere that the concern that brought these two rivals together was not really abortion. Abortions had been going on for all the centuries of their coexistence, and it had ignited no ecumenical coziness. The threat that ignited their new unity was the rise of women, which threatens both of these robust patriarchies.[10]

The final Program of Action that emerged from this important world conference was weak on abortion and on family planning generally. A major reason for this was the newfound friendship between the Vatican and the conservative Muslims. The subject was handled skittishly throughout, even though among the 20,000 people who attended that conference, either as officials of nations or as members of Non-Governmental Organizations (NGOs), the openness to abortion as a possible moral choice for women was overwhelming.[11] Of course the support for contraception, which the Vatican also rejects, was literally overwhelming.

The Vatican's behavior before and at the United Nations conference in Cairo is a glaring example of sacralized political power in the realm of sexuality. There are two distinctive elements in this use of power: (1) the creation of a false orthodoxy; and (2) the attempt to impose this orthodoxy on publics that in no way affiliate with the religion. Complicating the situation is the fact that it is the most conservative views within the various religions that are most loudly proclaimed and presented as the only orthodox stand. This confuses not only the affiliates of these religions but also policymakers who mistakenly think that Catholicism, Judaism, or Islam are monolithic on issues of family planning when this is not the truth and never has been.

As I shall note, the Vatican is in a uniquely good position among religions to impose its will on non-adherents because of its fictional status as a state among states in the United Nations. It was able to obstruct discussions in Cairo because of the "gentlemanly" diplomatic customs that allow nations to press their concerns in that forum in the often unrealistic hope that they will not overdo it. It becomes even more difficult in national and international fora to deal with actors and interests that are draped in the mantle of the sacred. Their arguments that would otherwise be easily countered acquire a kind of immunity. It can seem like cultural insensitivity or cultural imperialism to do forthright battle with "religious" views. All of this gives the Vatican and other religious spokespersons in national and international debates an unfair advantage.

The question that presents itself is how to fight the efforts of world religions when they want to inflict their archaic natalist habits on a world with bulging populations, a world that is newly aware of the limits of growth. This is not to suggest that the religions of the world have nothing positive to offer to a sound reproductive ethics. They are not simply mausolea of archaisms. Each of them contains renewable moral energies and classical theories of justice that could enrich the debate on reasonable control of fertility. What makes the great religions of the world great is not their decadence, but that at their core they were revolutions of cherishing and compassion. They pioneered classical modes of human solidarity and reverence for our miraculous earth. One of the projects of the Religious Consultation on Population, Reproductive Health and Ethics at the present time is entitled *The Right to Family Planning, Contraception and Abortion in Ten World Religions*. This project will show that support even for contraception and abortion can be found in the classical sources of these religious traditions.[12] The world religions fully understood are not the natural enemies of reproductive rights.

Defending the Right to Contraception and Abortion

It is not surprising that the world religions are largely natalist since they formed in a world where death was more of a problem than too many births. In prehistoric times the estimated length of life, factoring in infant deaths, was eighteen years. In ancient Greece, it may have reached twenty years and in ancient Rome twenty-two years. In medieval Europe that estimate expanded to thirty-seven years and to forty-seven in the United States at the beginning of this century.[13] With figures like that one would not expect in the cultures that spawned the religions a preoccupation with limiting births. Birthing a child who survived into maturity was a feat, and the religions saw it as a gift of the Gods to be celebrated, not eschewed. With advances in medicine and nutrition, demography turned a corner. Many religions missed the turn, and yet they have survived as major cultural and political forces in the modern world.

I will suggest four strategies to counter unhealthy religious influences in family planning. These are: (1) present family planning as a "human right" as that term is used today; (2) unite conservatives and liberals in fighting the causes of unwanted pregnancies; (3) show that family planning can hold its place on the high moral ground to counter the so-called "pro-life" movement; (4) show that the traditions themselves contain moral support for family planning, including contraception and abortion.

1. *Family planning, including both contraception and abortion, is a human right.* The term "human rights" has become the keystone of international ethics. Some years ago, the term was thought less useful since. Westerners gave it an individualistic meaning, representing a claim one individual has on another without communal concerns factoring in. Other cultures found this egoistic and hardly moral. However, the term has been evolving into a more universally accepted ethical vernacular. The United Nations has led the way, starting with its Universal Declaration of Human Rights in 1948 and in 1966 by its Covenant on Civil and Political Rights and the Covenant on Economic, Social and Cultural Rights. Through the permanent UN Commission on Human Rights, subsequent documents have been issued on subjects such as genocide, racial and religious discrimination, and the

rights of children, refugees, and women.[14] The term "human rights" has acquired symbolic and political power as witnessed by the United Nations 1995 conference in Beijing, where the effort was made to cast women's rights specifically in terms of human rights.

This same effort should be made regarding abortion and contraception. The dignity of human life that undergirds all human rights claims cannot be honored if the means to fertility control are denied. Neither can respect for the miracle of life in the rest of nature be honored if the carrying capacity of the land is overwhelmed by human numbers. Human rights language should not be used as new packaging for libertarian individualism. Even at the Cairo conference, a libertarian spirit was visible, implying that nothing should interfere with a woman's right to reproduce. Individual human rights never exist independently of the needs of the common good, and the notion of the common good includes the good of our ecological setting and its carrying capacity.[15]

All the world religions claim to honor human rights. It is important in debate to present the right to family planning, contraception, and abortion as human rights grounded in the very sanctity-of-life and compassion traditions championed by the religions themselves. It is neither conservative nor liberal to misrepresent a rich religious tradition, to present it as one-sided when it is not. Information on family planning rights as grounded in those religions is important for on-the-ground workers in the related fields of population and ecology as well as for policymakers and journalists.

2. *Conservatives and liberals can unite in the cause of preventing unwanted pregnancies.* The subject of abortion is too often presented in terms of the fetus and not in terms of the woman. There is a way of uniting all factions when the question is posed not as *why are there x million abortions every year?*, but as *why are x million women pregnant when they do not want to be?* Aside from the most hardcore anti-contraceptionists, this approach allows for conversation among all parties. Who could deny that unwanted pregnancies are a tragic problem! If we could unite to limit the causes that precipitate or contribute to the epidemic phenomenon of unwanted pregnancies, the need for abortion would be limited. Abortion, after all, is never preferable to prevention. It would be good if no woman had to make the choice for abortion. But when a conflict situation arises, it is horribly imperialistic and invasive and indeed fascistic to deny a woman the right to make this choice.

Thus to some of the precipitating causes and social realities that influence this tragedy: poverty, lack of education, sexism, and lack of respect for the gift of sexuality.

First to poverty. "The poverty of the poor is their ruin," says the Book of Proverbs. Poverty produces social and familial chaos and makes reproductive planning extremely difficult. Also, poverty causes high mortality among children with the concomitantly perceived need to produce many so that some will live. Both conservatives and liberals should be able to agree that the relief of poverty is the best contraceptive and would prevent more abortions than any combination of stringent laws. [16]

The education of women is surely a goal that can be shared by both conservatives and liberals. Education is empowering, and empowered women are more likely to manage their reproductivity. This was strongly stressed at the 1994 United Nations Cairo conference on population. Religions should be able to unite in pressing for universal literacy. The result, intended or unintended, would be fewer unwanted pregnancies.

It would be difficult to deny that sexism causes unwanted pregnancies. To the question: "How do you make love to an inferior?" the answer would seem to be "carelessly." That leads to unwanted pregnancies. The argument must be made that religions that do not teach men to respect women are encouraging unwanted pregnancies and contributing to the high abortion rate. The Religious Consultation on Population, Reproductive Health and Ethics is working on a project entitled "What Men Owe to Women: Positive Resources from the World's Religions." Eleven male scholars are exploring their religious traditions, patriarchal and sexist though those traditions are, and finding powerful grounds for gender mutuality and respect. They are applying in a new and creative way the rich theories of justice that were developed in these religions but not applied to women. They and many other scholars in the traditions are proving that the assault on sexism can be reinforced by drawing from the very traditions that have sanctioned and encouraged sexism.[17] Again, the result would be to bring reason and mutual respect to fertility decisions as well as to bring harmony into the homes where children are born.

People across the political spectrum can see that deception and dishonesty about sexual decisions can lead to eruptive and unplanned sex. Humans tend to live in uneasy tension with their sexuality. Most cultures have strong anti-sexual biases. This sense of sex as impure and tainting finds its way into the world's religions, but it is not their only story. There are also celebrations of sex in these religions and creationist theologies see sex as part of the divine plan.[18] All of this gives grounds for a healthy and corrective view of sex as good. When reverence and appreciation replace shame and sick hostility to sex, reproductive behavior is more likely to avoid the violence of unwanted pregnancies.

3. *Family planning, including contraception and abortion, can claim a place on the moral high ground.* Too often religionists and others who oppose the right of a woman to choose an abortion present themselves as having an exclusive hold on the high moral ground. They are "pro-life," leaving their opponents implicitly characterized as deadly. Discourse must dare to highlight the fact that the anti-choice position is anti-woman. If more than 50 million women choose abortions annually, and if abortion is *tout court* evil and never justifiable, then these 50 million women are either demented or thoroughly evil. There is no benign alternative. Once you place abortion in the unjustifiable category where rape and genocide rightly belong—once you make them in the terms of ethics, *negative absolutes*—no decent person could so choose. Those who indulge in such ethical simplism and tabooism defame every woman who chooses an abortion in any kind of a conflict situation. There is no moral high ground in such an unnuanced and unparalleled indictment of a single gender. Nor is there in it any evidence of sound reason.

My critique here is directed toward those who are absolutists on the subject. By declaring abortion a taboo, they stand above the debate as though they were purists, not entertaining exceptions. Some, such as the late Cardinal Bernardin, become critical of all life-taking, calling their position "the seamless garment." In a similar vein we have seen Daniel Berrigan after a protest against nuclear weapons going across town to picket women entering an abortion clinic as though these issues were seamlessly knit into one. This conflational muddling violates a prime law of sound ethics: *make distinctions where there are differences.* Like most mistakes in ethics, this one is not just unfortunate; it is also cruel.

It does not serve clarity of thought to crunch disparate realities into a single judgment. Pregnancy is a unique human situation. No *man* encounters its like. The abortion decision is similarly unique; it is not like nuclear war, and no avowed love of life justifies conflating or confusing them. A woman bearing embryonic or fetal life faces an unparalleled situation, and moral choices regarding that situation are uniquely hers. Add to this the fact that women have served life well. If they had not, our species would not have survived. Men have been the main killers and warriors of the species; the Amazons were creatures of myth. It is a well-grounded ethical assumption that women can be trusted vis-à-vis life.

Those, unlike Bernardin and Berrigan, who espouse absolutism only on abortion, raise even stronger moral suspicions. Double standards are a symptom of chicanery, not a sign of moral high ground. Often in this group there is no disposition to picket nuclear weapons and no distaste for capital punishment. Many "pro-life" protagonists have great sympathy for "the just war theory." This theory states that the slaughter of war can be morally acceptable when the circumstances warrant it. The ethics here is situational and circumstantial. Yet, enter abortion, and there is no circumstance, no situation, no tragedy that could justify the abortion of a single embryo. There is no "just abortion theory" to parallel "the just war theory."[19]

Pope John Paul II indulges in this inconsistency in his encyclical *The Gospel of Life.* He is vigorously opposed to capital punishment and says that it can almost never be justified. Notice that. Not never. Almost never. In some circumstances it could be all right. Abortion, sterilization, and contraception however are pure never. The pope on sexual and reproductive issues departs from the Catholic tradition that recognized with Thomas Aquinas that practical moral principles are valid and applicable *"in pluribus,"* most of the time, but that they will experience *"defectus,"* deficiency in certain circumstances.[20] The exception can at times produce more good than the rule. There are good exceptions to good rules. To agree with that in most cases but not for abortion signals a double standard. Nothing reveals bias more quickly and more surely than a double standard. There is nothing uncivilized about pointing that out. Religious leaders operating in the public square are treated with excessive politeness. If they presume to enter public discourse in hopes of influencing public policy, their baggage should be open for inspection.

Those persons who are sensitive about abortion but admit exceptions, if only in instances of rape or the physical life of the mother, are doing ethics. They are in the debate. They have acknowledged the complexity of the issue and conceded that the moral value of the embryo or fetus can be outweighed in certain circumstances.

4. *The religions themselves support family planning.* As an example of religious support for family planning, I will show in some detail that Roman Catholicism, the

most vigorous and articulate critic of contraception and abortion, has a long and distinguished "pro-choice" tradition. Catholicism merits special consideration since its influence in countering family planning is enormous in so-called "Catholic countries" and because it has successfully reached out to conservative evangelical Christians and to conservatives in the other world religions, particularly Islam. It has taken on a leadership role in international reproductive politics.

Catholic and Pro-Choice

Although it is virtually unknown in much public international discourse, the Roman Catholic position on abortion is pluralistic, *normatively* and *statistically*. It has a strong "pro-choice" tradition and a conservative anti-choice tradition. Neither is official and neither is more Catholic than the other. The hierarchical attempt to portray the Catholic position as univocal, an unchanging negative wafted through twenty centuries of untroubled consensus, is dissolved by a chastening walk through history and a little sound theology. By unearthing this authentic openness to choice on abortion and on contraception in the core of the tradition, the status of the anti-choice position is revealed as only one among many Catholic views.

The Bible does not condemn abortion. The closest it gets to it is in Exodus 21–22, which speaks of accidental abortion. This imposes a financial penalty on a man who "in the course of a brawl" caused a woman to miscarry. The issue here is the father's right to progeny; he could fine you for the misdeed, but he could not claim "an eye for an eye" as if a person had been killed. Thus, as conservative theologian John Connery, S.J., said, "The fetus did not have the same status as the mother in Hebrew Law."[21]

Following on the silence of Scripture on abortion, the early church history treats it only incidentally and sporadically. Indeed, there is no systematic study of the question until the fifteenth century. The early references to abortion do not constitute a condemnation of abortion as homicide but as part of behavior that frustrates the procreative purpose of sex. They proceeded from the belief that sperm consisted of *homunculi*, little human beings, some of whom would grow into full-grown babies in the womb, the mother providing only the locus. Thus at times in the early centuries male masturbation was described as homicide. One early church writer, Tertullian, discusses what we would today call a late-term emergency abortion where doctors had to dismember a fetus in order to remove it, and he refers to this emergency measure as a *"crudelitas necessaria,"* a necessary cruelty.[22] Obviously this amounted to moral approbation of abortion in a conflict situation.

One thing that develops early on and becomes the dominant tradition in Christianity is the theory of delayed animation or ensoulment. Borrowed from the Greeks, this taught that the spiritual human soul did not arrive in the fetus until as late as three months into the pregnancy. Prior to that time, whatever life was there was not human. They opined that the *conceptum* was enlivened first by a vegetative soul, then an animal soul, and only when formed sufficiently by a human spiritual soul. Though sexist efforts were made to say that the male soul arrived sooner— maybe a month and a half into the pregnancy—the rule of thumb for when a fetus reached the status of "baby" was three months. Reflecting the pious belief in a res-urrection of the dead of all time at the end of the world, Augustine pondered if early fetuses who miscarried would rise with the rest of us in this grand finale of the revived dead. He said they would not. He added that neither would all the sperm of history rise again. (For that we can all be grateful.)[23] The conclusion reached by Latin American theologians in a recent study is this: "It appears that the texts con-demning abortion in the primitive church refer to the abortion of a fully formed fetus."[24] The early fetus did not have the status of *person*, nor would killing it fit the category of murder.

This idea of delayed ensoulment survived throughout the tradition. St. Thomas Aquinas, the most esteemed of medieval theologians, held this view. Thus the most traditional and stubbornly held position in Catholic Christianity is that early abor-tions are not murder. Since the vast number of abortions done today in the United States, for example, are early abortions, they are not, according to this Catholic tra-dition, murder. Also, all pregnancy terminations done through the use of RU 486 would not qualify as the killing of a human person according to this tradition of "delayed ensoulment."

In the fifteenth century, the saintly archbishop of Florence, Antoninus, did ex-tensive work on abortion. He approved of early abortions to save the life of the woman, a class with many members in the context of fifteenth-century medicine.[25] This became common teaching. For this he was not criticized by the Vatican. In-deed, he was later canonized as a saint. (Catholic bishops today might well begin their discussions of abortion with a prayer to St. Antoninus.)

In the sixteenth century, the influential Antoninus de Corduba said that medi-cine that was abortifacient could be taken even later in a pregnancy if required for the health of the mother. The mother, he insisted, had a *jus prius*, a prior right. Some of the maladies he discussed do not seem to have been a matter of life and death for the women, and yet he allows that abortifacient medicine even in these cases is morally permissible.[26] Jesuit theologian Thomas Sanchez, who died in the early seventeenth century, said that all of his contemporary Catholic theologians approved of early abortion to save the life of the woman.[27] None of these theolo-gians or bishops were censured for these views. Note again that one of them, St. An-toninus, was canonized as a saint. Their limited "pro-choice" position was consid-ered thoroughly orthodox.

In the nineteenth century, the Vatican was invited to enter a debate on a very late-term abortion, requiring dismemberment of a formed fetus in order to save the woman's life. On September 2, 1869, the Vatican refused to decide the case. It re-ferred the questioner to the teaching of theologians on the issue. It was, in other words, the business of the theologians to discuss it freely and arrive at a conclusion. It was not for the Vatican to decide.[28] This appropriate modesty and disinclination to intervene is an older and wiser Catholic model, but it was not the model em-ployed by the Vatican representatives who attended and disrupted the United Na-tions Conference in Cairo.

What this brief history shows is that there is ambiguity and pluralism in the Catholic theological tradition on abortion. The modern absolutism displayed in this century where abortion gradually came to be seen as "intrinsically evil" is a novelty. Clearly something else is in play. The sudden onset of such rigidity must hide some other power agenda, and I suggest again that it relates to the rise of women starting in the nineteenth century. At any rate, Vatican theology today gives a prominence in the definition of orthodoxy to issues of sexual and reproductive ethics that is not typical of the Christian tradition in healthier moments.

A final theological note. the history of Catholic openness to early and to some later abortions is virtually unknown in our time. This amnesia has been promoted by the rigidly hierarchical notion of church that has developed since the first Vatican Council, 1869–1870. This council, not without controversy among the bishops, declared the pope infallible in his teaching power. Since that time, official "Catholic teaching" has been interpreted by church leaders as the view currently held by the hierarchy. This is untraditional. Traditionally, Catholic teaching authority rested on a tripod that included the hierarchy, the theologians, and the *sensus fidelium*, the sense or belief of the faithful. Thus it was believed that the Spirit of God could manifest itself through each of these sources and that they could be mutually corrective.[29] The hierarchical trend (sometimes called "early Catholicism") was, of course, present in Christianity from the first century, mirroring the patterns of government in the Greco-Roman world. What is special about Christianity is the pioneering presence right from the start of more collegial and democratic concepts of authority that were countercultural to the dominant modes in that society. These breakthroughs were not merely imitative or reflective of the surrounding society. Thus they can stake a claim to being more distinctly part of the Christian revolution. The very discontinuity of these authority modes that did not "lord it over" people as others did is a badge of their authenticity. The current Vatican's anachronistic insistence on an absolute monarchy is a defection from the early Christian effort to pioneer more collegial modes of authority and governance.

In this context it is clear that when the Vatican refused to enter the mid-nineteenth century debate on a very late-term abortion to save a woman's life, it was acting on the earlier and thoroughly traditional theology of church authority. It referred to the teaching of the theologians who had a proper and acknowledged teaching role in the church. Thus there was no reason for the Vatican to enter into the dispute. It was being handled by the appropriate authority, the *auctores probati*, the tested authors, the theologians who were the recognized authorities in this matter.[30] With the declaration of the infallibility of the pope and with the onset of a frightening modernity, the church hierarchy repaired to a monopod notion of teaching resulting in a kind of creeping infallibilism that most people within and without the church today think to be the essential Catholicism. It is not.[31]

All of this subverts the Vatican's claim to represent *the* Catholic, or even *the* Christian view on abortion. The current Vatican's authoritarian and monolithic position on abortion and *a fortiori* on contraception has no standing before the bar of Catholic history. The twentieth-century Vatican is a misrepresentation of a Christian tradition that championed revolutionary and liberating modalities of authority. The position on abortion and contraception that this Vatican pressed onto the world scene at Cairo is also a caricature. For most of its history, Christianity treated the abortion issue with a respectful silence. When it did struggle with abortion, the church never agreed to one orthodox stance on it, even that part of the Christian church called Catholic. Whatever its imperfection and incompleteness, the traditional Catholic positions on abortion left room for differences and nuance. And the hierarchies and the Vaticans that preceded current church leaders approved of this. Again, those who speak now of "the Catholic view" on abortion, as though an unnuanced negative had floated serenely through twenty centuries of Christian history, are either uninformed or mendacious.

This is not merely "a Catholic discussion." If the Catholic hierarchy imposed their ecclesiology and controls on the willing faithful and left it there, it would be less significant. However, as illustrated at Cairo, the Vatican does no such thing. It takes its distorted and unrepresentative view of "the teaching of the church" on reproductive ethics and attempts to impose it on the world.[32]

And here is where the Vatican has become a unique example of the religious use of power in society. Vatican City is a small estate consisting of 0.44 square kilometers with some 400 citizens, mostly consisting of church officials. The Catholic church lost the papal states in 1870. In 1929 the Lateran Agreement signed by Italy and the Vatican finally settled that Rome was under the jurisdiction of Italy while the "State of Vatican City" was under the "sovereignty of the Supreme Pontiff."[33] When the United Nations was being constituted the Vatican made inquiries about becoming a member state. Among others, Secretary of State Cordell Hull expressed the view that Vatican City did not meet the requirements for admission. After a number of maneuverings, the Vatican succeeded under Pope Paul VI in getting status at the UN as a "non-member state" permanent observer. Switzerland is the only other entity with this status.

Hence the anomaly. Here is a small piece of property housing a church and offices of the Catholic hierarchy, an entity with no women or children, presenting itself as a state among states. It does not have a fully functioning government and depends on the Italian state for a number of services. Rather than a state it should be described as office space with a church. Modern states should be made of sterner stuff. There are no rules in the United Nations Charter for "permanent observers"; they cannot vote in the General Assembly, but they can participate in discussions. Even though none of the other world religions claim such status at the UN, the Vatican has not been bashful about seizing this opportunity and expanding its influence in the deliberations of the real states of the United Nations. The Cairo conference on population was just one instance of this. Again, because of the ingrained gentility of international diplomacy and because of the delicacy of dealing with a religious entity that immodestly calls itself "The Holy See," the United Nations was remarkably patient with the Vatican's bullying tactics at the Cairo conference. As a result the Vatican was able to take an idiosyncratic view on contraception and on abortion, a view that does not reflect the view of most Catholic theologians or Catholic people—or most religious people in the world—and foist it with real impact upon this crucial international assembly. This same rigorism is highly influential in the so-called "Catholic countries," such as those in Latin America where hierarchical power impedes progress in family planning policies.

Catholics and Contraception

If, as the great Jesuit Pierre Teilhard de Chardin said, nothing is intelligible outside its history, the history of the Christian resistance even to contraception reveals the origins of this strange taboo. (The subject of contraception is treated further in this volume by Thomas Shannon.) To illustrate my strategy of using history to achieve what Robert MacAffee Brown has called "caricature assassination," I will show how the roots of the anti-contraceptive tradition were an alien invasion of the Christian tradition. The early Christian church was not born with a detailed sexual ethic in hand. On matters sexual, it absorbed, almost unconsciously, the influential and widespread teaching of the Stoics.

The Stoics did not have a wholesomely integrated conception of the emotions. Cicero called them the *impedimenta*. They were impediments that got in the way of pure reason. The moral idea of the Stoics was *apatheia*, the absence of emotion in favor of a limpid and unperturbed rationality. What then of sex, with all of its commanding emotionality? Their answer was that sexuality was good when it served the rational end of reproduction. The Stoic Seneca, who was so influential with early Christian writers that Saint Jerome referred to him as "our Seneca," said that too much love of one's wife was shameful. (No word on a wife loving her husband "too much.") If one's wife is pregnant, said Seneca, there is no justification for copulation. Better, he said, to "imitate the beasts" who, he insisted, do not copulate during pregnancy. The Stoic Musonius Rufus said that intercourse for pleasure only was reprehensible.

Early Christian writers baptized this cold asceticism and eventually became unaware of its source. The Christian Clement of Alexandria depended substantially on Musonius in his treatment of the purposes of marriage. The Christian Origen follows the Stoic Ocellus Lucanus; the Christians Lactantius and Jerome adopt the severity of Seneca. Augustine urged, with what success we can imagine, that only intercourse for the sole purpose of generating was fully moral. Pope Gregory, for some reason called "the Great," said that couples must copulate without pleasure to avoid sin, even when their procreative intent is in full bloom. One need not wonder why the term "ecclesiogenic psychoneurosis" was coined.

This anti-sexual and anti-contraceptive doctrine worked its way into the warp and woof of Christian teaching. It was not until the Second Vatican Council in the 1960s that the other purposes of sex, such as the expression of love and mutual cherishing, were put on a par with procreation. The Vatican today still clings to this aberration of the Stoa by banning all contraception. (Inconsistently, it allows for contraception through the use of the rhythm method, defending the illogical position that temporal methods are conscionable but mechanical methods are not.) The Stoic view of sexuality leading to the ban on contraception is no more essential to Catholicism or Christianity than barnacles are to the hull of a ship.[34]

Recent polls show that Catholics generally have caught on to this and have abandoned the hierarchical taboos on abortion and contraception. In a 1995 survey Catholics were asked: "Do you think a woman who has an abortion for reasons other than her life being in danger can still be a good Catholic?" Sixty-nine percent said yes and 26 percent said no. When Catholics were asked if "using artificial birth control such as condoms or birth control pills is morally wrong," only 5 percent strongly approved and only 13 percent approved. Fifty-four percent disapproved and 28 percent disapproved strongly.[35] As a body repels a foreign substance, a newly literate laity have rejected the cruel and tainted absolutisms that found their way into the church.[36]

Though space permits no such comparable surveys of other religious histories, other religions do offer similar opportunities. None of them is a monolith on reproductive ethics or on any other subject. Indeed, it can be said accurately that there is not one Christianity, Judaism, Hinduism, Islam, etc., but many Christianities, Judaisms, etc. Efforts by hierarchs to portray one divinely revealed position on family planning and abortion are embarrassed by the facts of history. Though the methods of teaching and modes of hierarchy vary in all the world religions, openness to rational family planning including abortion can be found in the moral methods of the traditions.

In Islam, for example, Azizah Y. al-Hibri writes that "historically, the majority view among Muslim scholars on contraception has been that it is permissible with the wife's consent. . . . The wife's consent is required because Islam recognizes the wife's right to sexual enjoyment and procreation."[37] On abortion she writes: "Another major form of population control is abortion. The majority of Muslim scholars permit abortion, although they differ on the stage of fetal development beyond which it becomes prohibited."[38] Flexibility in moral teachings is countenanced in Islam. Changes in Islamic moral traditions will be guided by justice, the needs of the common good, benevolence, compassion, and the need to choose the lesser of two harms. These criteria obviously allow for movement on issues of reproductive rights. Other religions present similar bases for reforming natalist traditions. The Hindu stress on all persons as reflections of the divine and the primacy given to compassion in Chinese religions and Buddhism give grounds for a moral argument in favor of serving life and promoting harmony by achieving autonomy in fertility control. They also give a foundation for defending reproductive rights as human rights.

The classic religions survived, like all life forms, because they could adapt. Good scholarship is showing that the great religious traditions can be infused with new life and with good sense on reproductive issues. Strategy number one, then, is to show the solid traditional roots of reformist positions in reproductive ethics.

Conclusion

The supreme talent of *homo sapiens* is conversation, the ability to commune at the level of ideas, ideals, and valuations. To lose hope in that signal talent is the worst despair. The religions of the world will be players in reproductive policy, for good or for ill. They cannot be ignored; they must be engaged. Religions are the great symbol-makers and culture-shapers. Strange as they may appear to modern secularists, they are worthy and, indeed, essential partners in crucial conversations. Within their very variegated treasuries there are human achievements of heroic depth. Open minds will address them, do battle with them, and seek common ground where possible with them, even on heated issues such as abortion and contraception. Conservatives, while innocent of the progressive ingredients those religions contain, are more sophisticated in their understanding of the social power of religion than liberals and radicals. They can co-opt these social forces if liberals persist in their naive detachment. Engaging the world's religions is an indispensable part of any effort in social analysis and in any realistic discussion of sane reproductive policies. The human right to family planning, including contraception and abortion, can and must be seen as demanded by the sanctity of life. We dare not shy from the challenge that presents.

Notes

1. I used this imagery in my "The Feminization of God and Ethics," *Christianity and Crisis* 42, no. 4 (March 1982): 59–65.

2. Douglas Johnston and Cynthia Sampson, *Religion, the Missing Dimension of State-craft* (New York: Oxford University Press, 1994).

3. See Carol Bly, *Bad Government and Silly Literature* (Minneapolis: Milkweed Editions, 1986), 3.

4. Arnold Toynbee, *A Study of History*, abridgment by D. C. Somervell, vol. 2 (New York: Oxford University Press, 1957), 98–99.

5. Daniel C. Maguire and Larry L. Rasmussen, *Ethics for a Small Planet: New Horizons on Population, Consumption, and Ecology* (Albany: State University of New York Press, 1998).

6. David Loy "Religion and the Market," in *Vision of a New Earth: Religious Perspective on Population, Consumption and Ecology*, ed. Harold Coward and Daniel Maguire (New York: Suny, 1999).

7. 2 Cor. 3:17.

8. Luke 22:26.

9. Daniel L. Pals, *Seven Theories of Religion* (New York: Oxford University Press, 1996), 5.

10. Maguire and Rasmussen, *Ethics for a Small Planet*.

11. I make this statement on the basis of my participation in the Cairo conference as president of the Religious Consultation on Population, Reproductive Health and Ethics, a Non-Governmental Organization. The consultation is an international collegium of progressive feminist scholars from most of the world's religions who seek to mine the renewable moral energies of their traditions and apply them to issues of population, empowerment of women, health, and ecology.

12. The address of the Religious Consultation on Population, Reproductive Health and Ethics is 2717 E. Hampshire Avenue, Milwaukee, Wisc., 53211. Telephone: 414-962-166; facsimile: 414-962-9248.

13. Orville G. Brim, Jr., et al., *The Dying Patient* (New York: Russell Sage Foundation, 1970), 8.

14. See parts one and two of *Human Rights: A Compilation of International Instruments.* (New York: United Nations, 1994). See also John Kelsay and Sumner B. Twiss, *Religion and Human Rights* (New York: Project on Religion and Human Rights, 1994).

15. I treat this issue in Maguire and Rasmussen, *Ethics for a Small Planet*, 4–18.

16. See Kristin Luker, *Dubious Conceptions: The Politics of Teenage Pregnancy* (Cambridge: Harvard University Press, 1996).

17. *What Men Owe to Women: Positive Resources from the World's Religion*, ed. John Raines and Daniel Maguire (Albany: Suny Press, forthcoming Jan. 2001).

18. Another project of the Religious Consultation on Population, Reproductive Health and Ethics is tantalizingly entitled "Good Sex: Women's Religious Wisdom on Human Sexuality." Under the direction of Dr. Mary Hunt, Patricia Jung, and Radhika Balakrishnan, this project is headed by a group of women scholars from different world religions who are exploring the goodness of sexual pleasure too often slighted by male architects of the religious traditions.

19. Lloyd Steffen develops a "just abortion theory" in his *Life Choice: The Theory of Just Abortion* (Cleveland: Pilgrim Press, 1994).

20. Thomas Aquinas, *Summa Theologiae* I II q. 94, a.4, a.5. This insight does not preclude "negative absolutes," types of actions that are so destructive that choosing them could never be justified. Rape and nuclear war are two examples of this. See Daniel C. Maguire and A. Nicholas Fargnoli, "The Nature of Moral Principles," chap. 11 in *On Moral Grounds: The Art/Science of Ethics*. (New York: Crossroads, 1991), 109–120.

21. John Connery, *Abortion: The Development of the Roman Catholic Perspective*. (Chicago: Loyola University Press, 1977), 11. See also Daniel C. Maguire, "The Catholic Legacy and Abortion: A Debate," *Commonweal* 114, no. 20 (November 1987): 657–74.

22. Tertullian, *De Anima*, 25, 4, *Corpus Scriptorum Ecclesiasticorum Latinorum* 20: 341–42.

23. Augustine, *Enchiridion*, 85; *Patres Latini*, 40: 272.

24. Graciela Melo, ed., *Problematica Religiosa de la Mujer que Aborta* (Artes Publicationes: Colombia, 1996), 67. The Lastin American theologian who composed this part of the report had to do so anonymously due to pressure from the Catholic hierarchy. Theologian Graciela Melo's name as general editor is used. She died shortly before the publication date. With her death came her academic freedom.

25. Antoninus, *Summa Theologica*, Pars 2, t. 7, c.2, para. 2.

26. See Connery, *Abortion*, 125.

27. Thomas Sanchez, *De Matrimonio*, Lib. 7, c. 12, n. 6, d. 17, n. 15.

28. See Connery, *Abortion*, 226.

29. See Daniel C. Maguire, "Catholic Ethics in the Post-Infallible Church," chap. 15 in *The Moral Revolution* (San Francisco: Harper and Row, 1986), 181–220.

30. This relates to a Catholic moral theory called Probabilism. Probabilism states that where good people with sound reasons and/or reliable experts disagree on a moral issue, Catholics may in good conscience choose either view. The system is based on insight, not hierarchical authority, and it was in fact a bypass around an overly dictatorial teaching hierarchy.

31. See Daniel C. Maguire, "Catholic Options in the Abortion Debate: Probabilism in a Pluralistic Society," *Conscience* 17, no.2 (Summer 1996): 19–23. The tendency to give all teaching power to the hierarchy had many of its roots in the juridical reforms of the eleventh and twelfth centuries. Yves Congar finds in this period "the transition from an appreciation of the ever active presence of God to that of juridical powers put at the free disposal of, and perhaps, even handed over as its property to 'the Church,' i.e. the hierarchy." Congar, *Tradition and Traditions* (New York: Westminster, 1967), 135. This hierarchical grab of all teaching authority was not new with Vatican Council I, but it received a consolidation in that council and in the fearful encounter of the church with modernity. Only with Vatican Council II, 1962–1965, was some corrective action begun, but Pope John Paul II has attempted to stifle that gentle reform.

32. See Denise Shannon, "All Roads Led to Cairo," *Conscience* 15, no. 4 (Winter 1994–1995): 3–10, and, in the same volume, Christopher Gould, "Hellfire and Diplomacy: A Chronology of Vatican Opposition to the ICPD Program of Action," 14–19.

33. Lateran Agreement, Feb. 11, 1929 (Italy-Holy See, Art. XXVI), V.T.S. 161, Europe, TS No. 590019.

34. See Daniel C. Maguire, "Catholic Sexual and Reproductive Ethics: A Historical Perspective," *SIECUS Report* 15, no. 5 (1987): 1–4; John T. Noonan, Jr., *Contraception: A History of Its Treatment by the Catholic Theologians and Canonists* (Cambridge: Harvard University Press, 1986), 48.

35. These results are from a poll taken for *U.S. News*, designed by Celinda Lake and Ed Goeas and conducted by Market Facts Telenation.

36. See also *Catholics and Reproduction, a World View: Data from Studies of Attitudes and Practices* (Washington, D.C.: Catholics for a Free Choice, 1997).

37. Azizah Y. al-Hibri, "Family Planning and Islamic Jurisprudence," *Religious and Ethical Perspectives on Population Issues* (Washington, D.C.: Religious Consultation on Population, Reproductive Health and Ethics, 1993), 4.

38. Ibid., 6.

11

THOMAS A. SHANNON

Reproductive Technologies

Ethical and Religious Issues

This article will discuss several ethical dimensions of assisted reproduction. First, I will identify general ethical issues that have not been fully evaluated, primarily because of the way the field of assisted reproduction developed. Second, I will argue that while Roman Catholicism has a fairly developed and clear teaching about assisted reproduction and that while some of this teaching has a value beyond the boundaries of this religion, ultimately the teaching lacks credibility because of use of a problematic understanding of natural law. The teaching is overly physicalist or biological in its development of norms, and this narrowness of interpretation impedes Catholicism from responding constructively to historical changes in marriage and in the family. Finally, I will develop aspects of Roman Catholic social ethics that could contribute to a discussion of assisted reproduction, particularly within the discussion of health insurance. Here I will be moving beyond a traditional understanding of natural law but will remain within the general context of Roman Catholic social teaching. While criticizing many aspects of traditional Roman Catholic teaching, I want to argue that there are, nonetheless, resources within this tradition that are both constructive and useful in evaluating this important, developing branch of reproductive medicine.

Assisted Reproduction: An Overview

The birth of Louise Brown in England in 1978 was a reproductive revolution as profound as the introduction of artificial contraceptives in the 1950s. For several years,

Steptoe and Edwards had been doing animal experiments on *in vitro* fertilization with varying degrees of success. However, the main lines of the technique were established, and the outcome seemed to depend as much on luck as technique. Everything came together, though, in the birth of Louise Brown, and reproduction was never the same.

After this beginning, the use of this technology spread rapidly, first in England, Australia, and the United States and now around the world. Although it was far from established as successful, the technology moved immediately to the clinic. In the early decades of AR, few data were collected and few, if any, controlled studies were performed. Thus the details of AR were learned and gathered in a rather random fashion, remaining primarily within the particular clinic, since increased success gave the clinic a financial advantage. Fortunately, the technology itself and the various means of manipulating sperm, egg, and preimplantation embryo do not appear to be harmful to these entities. Nor does the technology appear to cause harm to the children born of the technology. The critical issue, though, is that we have learned this from clinical practice, not from carefully designed research protocols.

Because of the rapid move from experimental procedure to clinical practice, few, if any, regulatory standards were in place. There were no requirements for any type of board certification or for any particular training in human reproduction or obstetrics, with the possible exception of assisting at the birth itself. (Midwives, for example, need certification by the state, as well as those in the field of ob/gyn before they can assist at birth.) The same was true of the clinics themselves. These were essentially private enterprises and were not regulated either by the state or the medical establishment. Who was entitled to do what and based on what training and credentials was simply unclear. The alleged training standard of "see one, do one, teach one" appeared to be normative, not stereotypical.

As attention focused on the growing field and as the practice spread more widely, a core procedure of egg retrieval, fertilization, incubation, and implantation became established. This was helped by the publication of articles in professional journals, the establishment of several journals devoted to AR, new training programs at medical schools, and the development of guidelines by professional medical societies. More attention thus was paid to the biology of reproduction and the technologies used to assist in reproduction. Now, almost twenty years after Louise Brown's birth, AR is an accepted part of standard medical practice, some dimensions of which are now covered by many insurance plans.

But critical issues still remain. While AR is widely available in both hospitals and private clinics, access to it is still restricted, primarily by costs, with fees for a single IVF cycle ranging from $8,000 to $10,000. Although AR is covered by some insurance plans, what the plans cover varies widely. Some will pay for infertility workups; others will also pay for one or two cycles of in vitro fertilization. Still other plans will pay for some procedures and not others. Even if insurance pays for some parts of the procedure, there will be many out-of-pocket expenses, such as travel costs, hotel stays, and time off from work. And while costs are coming down, prices vary dramatically from clinic to clinic. Hardly anyone becomes pregnant on the first cycle, so cycles will be repeated and often new technologies used. One is quickly beyond one's insurance coverage. Thus accessibility to the technology is limited both by insurance limits and one's disposable income.

Some clinics pro-rate the costs of IVF, refunding many costs if no child is born. For example, Pacific Fertility Center, with branches in Los Angeles, San Francisco, and Sacramento, recently took out a half page ad in the *New York Times*.[1] For a set fee, the client receives a single cycle of IVF with either her eggs or a donor's eggs and, if she does not get pregnant on this try, will have all the remaining frozen embryos implanted. If the client does not carry a pregnancy for at least twelve weeks, she receives a 90% refund. Pacific Fertility Center also offers a variety of other financial options: a single cycle for customary fees, shared IVF egg donor programs so that two couples can split the fees, a plan for women forty-three years of age and younger that allows up to three IVF cycles for a single fee, and discounts of up to 35% for couples demonstrating financial need. There is also a *pro bono* grant program that provides free IVF services. [2]

A 1983 study, focusing on the first five years of IVF programs in Britain, Australia, and the United States, showed that while success rates of various AR technologies were increasing, they were still low. Steptoe and Edwards had reported an early success rate of 2% per embryo transfer; several years later this rate had risen to 9% per laparoscopy. Other groups in Australia and the United States report rates up to 20%.[3] Notice, though, two different measures of calculation of success rates: per embryo transfer and per laparoscopy. Such lack of standardization makes accuracy of results difficult. Also, the definition of success is not clear. One can be pregnant chemically in that a rise in hormones can be measured, or one can be pregnant clinically in that the embryo has actually implanted. Neither of these necessarily results in a live birth. Nor is a pregnancy of twelve weeks, which is the criterion for success, a necessary predictor of a live birth.

A recent story in the *New York Times* gave the success rate of various IVF clinics in that metropolitan area, defining success as a live birth. The rates for women under the age of thirty-nine ranged from a low of 9.3%, through about 20% at four clinics, to a high of 34% at one clinic.[4] In general, though, of the 267 clinics that report their data to the Society for Assisted Reproductive Technology, the professional association for individuals involved in IVF, the success rate is 21.2% per IVF cycle.[5]

General Ethical Issues

The costs associated with IVF raise several ethical issues. Rebate programs, at first flush, sound like a good idea. But some describe this as "at best an eye-catching marketing gimmick, and at worse a breach of medical ethics." An American Medical Association task force argued: "Such publicized guarantees manipulate and unfairly attract patients."[6] For example, Pacific Fertility Center charges $7,725 for its basic, single IVF cycle, while its rebate plan costs $12,500 and up. The plan looks good if one does not become pregnant on the first try, but there is a much more rigorous screening program for people to enter the rebate program, based on one's age and the nature of fertility problems. The desperation for a child may cause individuals to overlook costs or not to do a careful examination of costs or entrance criteria to various rebate plans. It is true that doctors in such programs may do more to enhance the odds of a pregnancy and that the plans can save a couple some money. But they can also lose money if they do not examine all of the fine print: for example, there is no rebate if there is a pregnancy loss after the twelfth week.

The discussion of success rates of IVF procedures also raises ethical issues. I have already noted the problems associated with the lack of common definitions of success as well as of pregnancy, and the choice of one standard over another can greatly increase one's success rate. And this leads to a second problem: the use of such success rates as the basis for advertising, which leads to an increase in clientele and, in turn, to greater income for clinics. IVF clinics appear to be the "only branch of medicine doing success-rate advertising on this scale." [7] Five clinics have had to change advertising claims because of Federal Trade Commission interventions. While most people know to be at least moderately suspicious of advertising claims, these appeals are being made to a rather large and also desperate and vulnerable audience. While such individuals should not be prevented from attempting to have a child, clinics can be held to a strict disclosure standard for both success rates and the basis of their calculations.

A third ethical problem is related to the so-called older woman seeking IVF. Success rates for women forty and older drop by a half to three-quarters of the average rate; these women therefore need very specific information on success rates. Moreover, an increase in the number of women over forty seeking IVF has given rise to a market in eggs from younger women. Some of these come from younger women who successfully underwent IVF and did not need all the eggs that were harvested. Others come from egg donor programs that pay women several thousand dollars to undergo egg retrieval. Such eggs are now part of the advertising campaign. For example, in the 13 January 1997 issue of the *New Yorker*, the Genetics and IVF Institute in Fairfax, Virginia, advertised the availability of almost 100 fully screened donors. While it is true that men have sold their sperm for decades for this purpose, the procedures for egg retrieval are dramatically different and expose the donor to the possibility of both short- and long-term health risks.

The Roman Catholic Ethical Perspective: *Donum Vitae*

In this section, I want to turn to a different, and perhaps unlikely, source for an evaluation of some ethical aspects of AR: the 1987 *Instruction* from the Congregation for the Doctrine of the Faith, *Donum Vitae* (DV). This source is unlikely because it prohibits almost every procedure in the area of AR. While I will eventually argue for the rejection of the core of *DV*'s natural law argument, there are perspectives in this document that are helpful in evaluating the cultural context in which AR occurs as well as the culture of the clinics themselves. I will identify *DV*'s opposition to AR and then turn to a discussion of its positive contributions.

The core argument is a reverse application of the traditional ethical argument used to prohibit artificial contraception. The argument is a classic natural law perspective which says, in the case of contraception, that to separate artificially the act of intercourse from its inherent biological reproductive teleology is to separate what

God intended to be united. To separate the unitive and procreative dimensions is to violate the natural integrity of the total act of intercourse. When applied to assisted reproduction, the identical argument is used, but only in reverse. That is, to attain egg and sperm and to unite them in a petri dish and then to implant the zygote is artificially to break apart the inherent unity of the act of intercourse. Or to use the words of *DV*:

> The Church's teaching on marriage and human procreation affirms the "insepara-ble connection, willed by God and unable to be broken by man on his own initia-tive, between the two meanings of the conjugal act: the unitive meaning and the procreative meaning."[8]

Citing *Humanae Vitae* the Congregation goes on to say that "it is never per-mitted to separate these different aspects to such a degree as positively to exclude either the procreative intention or the conjugal relation."[9] Finally, the Congre-gation identifies the key ethical flaw in both artificial contraception and artificial conception:

> Contraception deliberately deprives the conjugal act of its openness to procreation and in this way brings about a voluntary dissociation of the ends of marriage. Ho-mologous artificial fertilization, in seeking a procreation which is not the fruit of a specific act of conjugal union, objectively effects an analogous separation of the goods of marriage.[10]

Essentially the argument of *DV* met the same fate as that of its predecessor and source, *Humanae Vitae*. The majority of commentators, Catholic and non-Catholic alike, reject the primacy given to a biological structure over the personal dimension of the act of married intercourse. This overly biological reading of natu-ral law fits uneasily with the ethical standard suggested in the Vatican II document *Gaudium et Spes*, which suggests that the moral norm is to be "the nature of the human person and his acts."[11] Many would argue that the key to moral analysis is whether the marriage as a whole is open to procreation, not whether an individual act is. And even here, the tradition notes exceptions. Beginning with *Casti Connubi* and continuing through *Humanae Vitae*, valid reasons for avoiding conception (without the use of artificial contraception of course) included the health of the mother and the need to care for the welfare and education of one's current family. And much earlier Thomas Aquinas noted that reproduction was an obligation that fell on the species, not on any particular individual.

There is an irony in the moral analysis within *DV*: within the context of a mar-riage, two individuals *are* attempting to have a child. That is the object and intent of everything done within the context of AR. *DV* focuses only on the physical integrity of the act of sexual intercourse and ignores "the fact that husband and wife are seek-ing to become father and mother,"[12] which of course is what the tradition says is a goal of marriage. Why the physical integrity of the act should take moral priority over the intention of the husband and wife to become mother and father through the use of their own genetic material is both unexplained and unclear.

While the core argument of *DV* may be misplaced or wrong, the document does raise other features that can be helpful in thinking about the development and practice of AR. For example, *DV* recognizes that, thanks to scientific and medical progress, we have many more effective therapeutic resources available to us. But the document also notes that we "can acquire new powers, with unforeseeable consequences, over human life at its very beginning and in its first stages."[13] While *DV* uses this to argue for the prohibition of almost all reproductive technologies, that is not its only application. Research protocols do include the consideration of consequences, and therapeutic interventions are monitored for problems. But typically the focus is whether the intervention or procedure solves the problem. This occurs because our culture is results-oriented: we want to solve the problem and we want to solve it now—or yesterday. Only when unforeseen or unintended consequences occur does the focus shift. As I have noted, very little research was done on IVF in humans before various procedures were put into widespread clinical application. Fortunately, the outcomes did not prove to be problematic with respect to the well-being of the children born of these processes and, generally speaking, with respect to the well-being of the women utilizing the procedures. But that may be a matter of luck.

Nor should AR be used as a precedent for rapid clinical application of the next technology to be developed. We have a strong bias in this country to act and to refrain from critiques of people's actions. *DV* notes that we are faced with the "temptation to go beyond the limits of a reasonable dominion over nature."[14] The Congregation is not arguing that we should not intervene in nature or seek therapeutic relief. Rather it speaks to the dangers of overreach and of not thinking carefully before we act.

DV also notes that values cannot come exclusively from the science or technology itself:

> It would on the one hand be illusory to claim that scientific research and its application are morally neutral; on the other hand one cannot derive criteria for guidance from mere technical efficiency, from research's possible usefulness to some at the expense of other or, worse still, from prevailing ideologies.[15]

Science and scientific research are not neutral activities. They are engaged in to achieve certain ends, and these ends are based on particular values. We need to examine why this particular line of research, why this particular project, why this application. And in answering these questions we may learn that there are competing values—for example, service to the patient versus income stream. Certainly, individuals involved in IVF want to provide their patients with the best service possible. However, infertility is approximately a $350 million a year business. Competition for clients is keen. There is also competition between clinics to recruit successful physicians who must then achieve even higher success to justify their salaries. In this context, primacy is not necessarily given to a patient's best interest. We need to go beyond the science of IVF and the values it bears to provide an appropriate evaluation of the practice.

Additionally, the Congregation argues that "an intervention on the human body affects not only the tissues, the organs and their functions, but also involves the person himself on different levels."[16] Later, it approvingly quotes Pope John Paul II: "Thus, in and through the body, one touches the person himself in his concrete reality."[17] This points to several critical issues in contemporary medicine and particularly in assisted reproduction.

One is the tendency of modern medicine to objectify the body,[18] which began with the Cartesian perspective that the body was a machine. The Enlightenment tradition consolidated this perspective by focusing on the person as the essential self with the body as an external element, a machine-like addition. This reintroduced a Platonic dualism into philosophy that had been to a large extent overcome by Christianity's insistence on the unity of the person and the subjectivity of the body. For Christianity, it is only the living unity, a substantial union of body and soul, that is the person.

The important point here is that modern medicine has a philosophical perspective built into it. Ironically, that perspective has helped bring about enormous advances in modern medicine. Surgery, organ transplantation, the many visualization technologies, genetic engineering, and AR all rely, to some degree, on seeing the body as an object, as a composite of interchangeable parts or the sum of its parts. The problem occurs when we forget that this perspective has an embedded ideology that leads us to see ourselves in one dimension only: as object. Of course, one comes to the physician because of a problem and the desire to have it solved. But the problem exists within a person and may also raise a host of personal or psychosomatic issues. The particular problem can be solved technically, but the personal issues may remain.

For example, a man may discover that he has a low sperm count and that is the reason for the infertility. While a single sperm may be implanted in the egg and fertilization accomplished, he may feel inadequate, and such inadequacy may in fact be heightened by the continual presence of the child. Or the various tests and procedures for IVF may become routinized, and less attention paid to the woman who experiences these procedures and whose anxiety may be increasing as she gets deeper into the process. The procedures are not neutral somatic experiences. They are done in the context of biological abnormalities and a cultural context that disapproves of childlessness. If, additionally, they are done in isolation from the person's hopes, fears, and expectations, the person can be harmed even though the treatment was successful.

Particularly with IVF, there is the assumption that to cure the disease, repair the damage, or to circumvent the problem is to heal the person. The various technologies of AR, when successful, resolve childlessness but not infertility. Will the infertility that caused the childlessness still be a problem for the individual thus afflicted, as I noted above in the case of a man with low sperm count? Will the use of donor sperm or donor egg have an effect on the individuals or the couple? Or will the joy of the child remove any such difficulties? The fact that a pregnancy has been achieved does not necessarily resolve the totality of the problems associated with infertility: issues of identity, psychosocial integration, and, perhaps, feelings of inadequacy because of infertility.

An analogy is frequently made between individuals who achieve pregnancy through AR and those who have an ongoing condition such as diabetes, depression, or visual impairment. The symptoms of these chronic conditions may be resolved, but the underlying problem is not. Though insulin corrects the blood sugar and drugs may lift the depression, their very use and presence is a daily reminder of one's problem. A decline in the ability to focus one's eyes for reading is a normal consequence of aging and is easily correctable by a trip to the local drug store; nonetheless, the fact of our new and daily dependency on these glasses is a constant reminder of our aging. While some may take this in stride, for others it may be a major developmental crisis.

Thus the larger issue is the perception of the self and how that is related to the outcome of the treatment. For some, achieving a pregnancy and live birth may be enough. For others, the resulting child is a source of joy, but one's inability to do this without technical assistance may be a constant source of frustration. Infertility, even though resolvable, may be a severe blow to one's self-esteem. My point here is not to argue against the use of AR, but to remind us that we continuously need to think of the totality of the person, not just the biological functioning or the technical elements of a solution. If the main focus is on the techniques, if the biology becomes the center of attention, then IVF becomes much more production than reproduction. If the couple and their needs are kept to the foreground as much as possible, then the couple has a context in which to base and understand all the procedures that they will undergo. A great many of the procedures in which they will participate are very impersonal—and that is the way they must be. But if they can be made part of a larger process, grounded in the couples' relationship and their desire for a family, then some of the depersonalization can be softened and the impersonality of the procedures humanized. Even obtaining sperm, obviously not a high tech procedure in most cases, can be very depersonalizing and difficult if thought of as a procedure and not within a personal context. Even having one's partner present or involved in the process maintains the presence and reality of a relationship. This affirms the procreative dimension much more than being sent to a room to "obtain a sample."

The couple using IVF is essentially doing what another couple is doing without IVF: cooperating in the creation of a new being from their love and their bodies. From a moral perspective, there is no difference between IVF and physical intercourse. The psychological difference, which has moral overtones, is that given the conditions under which IVF occurs there is a danger of depersonalization, of stressing the means over the end. What is critical here is the context in which IVF is done and keeping one's attention on the couple, their relationship, and their desire for a family. While this will not ease all the tension, eliminate the pain, or resolve all the frustrations that come with IVF, the couple will at least have a critical moral center in which to understand what they are doing.

Finally, we need to consider the language of assisted reproduction. This term describes the procedure correctly. But there is a critical nuance between reproduction and procreation. Reproduction is a language of manufacture; it is a language of commodification. Procreation is the language of persons and personal engagement. Our language can shape our thinking, and if we use terms that connote objectification we may begin to think in terms of objectification. Of course, all the acts performed in AR are objectifications of the body or body parts. I am not arguing that such a process renders the acts unethical or invests them with a deep ethical flaw. But there is a tension between the technological procedures and language of IVF and its personal outcome. The former can make us forget the latter as well as serve to restructure our thinking because of the language we use to describe the process. The language and the techniques of IVF can help us forget that to touch the patient is to touch the person.

Mining the Resources

Let me conclude by reflecting on some broader issues related to Roman Catholicism, social ethics, and issues of public policy. I will not necessarily be arguing for a normative position on AR; Roman Catholicism has such a position, and I disagree with elements of it, as noted above. Rather, I will excavate the fundamental weaknesses of the official sexual ethic of Roman Catholicism and show why its social ethics are a better resource for responding to assisted reproduction. My aim is not to present a comprehensive or substantive position on AR, but to mine Catholic ethics for principles that are critical in this public policy debate.

Natural Law

The premise of *Donum Vitae*, as well as that of *Humanae Vitae*, is natural law traditionally understood. Priority is given to biological processes and procedures in understanding the morality of sexual acts. Such a priority is essentially rejected by a majority of contemporary Catholic theologians and ethicists. In *Humanae Vitae* the moral grounding of the argument against artificial contraception is the inseparable connection between intercourse and conception. So too with *Donum Vitae*. As previously noted, such an interpretation rejects or at least diminishes the moral significance of any intentionality on the part of the couple, e.g., to have a child as a part of their marriage, and posits the sufficiency of the physical integrity of the biological act as determinate for the moral evaluation of their actions. In this perspective the goal of a family—at least a traditional part of the understanding of marriage—is held hostage to biology.

The priority of the physical over the personal is deeply imbedded in the modern ecclesiastical tradition. In his book *Love and Responsibility*, written while John Paul II was still Cardinal Karol Wojtyla, we find an example of this framework for the moral evaluation of human acts. The order of nature has its origin in God, "since it rests directly on the essences (or natures) of existing creatures, from which arise all dependencies, relationships and connections between them."[19] Thus the order of nature grounds morality. Or, as John Paul again states it: "But before and above all else man's conscience, his immediate guide in all his doings, must be in harmony with the law of nature. When it is, man is just towards the Creator."[20]

The clear message here is that moral integrity consists in discovering the metaphysical order embedded in the biological order and then conforming ourselves to both. Thus not only does the natural law perspective as represented here call for caution and a sense of limits but also mandates a genuine non-intervention in the biological order. This overly biological view of natural law in turn shapes the Roman Catholic understanding of marriage. The primary focus is on the physical integrity of sexual relations between the couple, rather than how a couple, might achieve a family within the context of their marriage or how marriage might contribute to the social good.

In spite of the efforts of the current Pope to maintain this tradition, a slight, but significant, shift had already occurred. The Second Vatican Council took major strides forward in the theology of marriage by approving Paul VI's teaching that the procreative and unitive ends of intercourse were co-equal, though morally inseparable. This again spoke to the issue of natural law. The council proposed, for example, this as the norm of human activity: "That in accord with the divine plan and will, it should harmonize with the genuine good of the human race, and allow men as individuals and as members of society to pursue their total vocation and fulfill it."[21] This was further specified by the assertion that by the very fact of being created, "All things are endowed with their own stability, truth, goodness, proper laws, and order."[22] The council walked a fine line here, arguing for the integrity of the created order but not that created things are independent of God or that "man can use them without any reference to the Creator."[23] It vacillated between a less biological and a more personalistic understanding of natural law, suggesting that while physical reality is important, one also needs to look at the good of humanity and one's vocation in that context.

This tension was not resolved, as was shown clearly when *Gaudium et Spes* discussed human reproduction.

> Therefore when there is a question of harmonizing conjugal love with the responsible transmission of life, the moral aspect of any procedure does not depend solely on sincere intentions or on an evaluation of motives. It must be determined by objective standards. [24]

But the text goes on to say that these standards must be "based on the nature of the human person and his acts."[25] This part of the criterion, while rooted in the tradition, opened the way to a consideration of the person that incorporates more than the biology of his or her acts. But even this opening could not overcome the biologized understanding of natural law as the continuing standard for marital morality.

Given the tension that remained in the documents of Vatican II and the continued assertion of the definitive (some say infallible) character of *Humanae Vitae*, it is no wonder that the priority of the physical over the personal is almost unconsciously assumed as correct. Such an assumption, however, neglects to account for almost thirty years of continuous critique of this position by leading Catholic theologians and ethicists. These critiques focus on whether to define the object of morality as one's intentions or the physical object. Do impersonal structures take precedent over personal acts? Can the goal of a family, which is a major element in the theology of marriage, be frustrated because of malfunctioning biology? The critique continues to recognize the importance of the biological dimension of the person. What it does differently is to argue that the biological should not be understood as a physiological process that is morally normative, but rather as the person's mode of presence in the world, a dynamic and developing reality, a body-self. Through this incarnational presence we are both present to and bound to the world, society, community, and the dynamic of history.

Traditional Teachings on Marriage

The continued focus on the biological skews the official teaching on marriage by focusing mainly on the sexual—understood mainly but not exclusively as a biological reality—rather than the personal or social-ethical dimension. Traditionally, however, the goods of marriage are defined in terms of sacramentality, family, and personal fulfillment—a formulation going back to Augustine. The focus on sacramentality looks to the presence of grace, expressed and experienced through the mutual love of the partners and to the indissolubility of a valid marriage.

In the current code of canon law, marriage has been redefined as a covenant, not a contract. Covenant is the biblical term used to describe the love between God and Israel, which was extended to the relations between the people of the nation. This makes it possible to reconceptualize marriage within a more dynamic context, a more interpersonal framework, and to emphasize the graced dimension of all aspects of marriage, including the sexual. Thus while much attention is focused on the indissolubility of marriage as a feature of its sacramentality, there is also a critical opening to develop a much more dynamic theology of marriage based on the covenantal union of persons.

Because the concept of covenant extends to the relation between the members of the community, it also carries with it a social dimension. Marriage can model the virtues needed to keep the community together, it can show the service needed to ensure a harmonious community, it can present a constructive use of sexuality, and so on. The roles of marriage in community become constitutive elements of marriage, not just afterthoughts.

Family remains a key issue for Catholics, as indeed it does for growing numbers of individuals and groups within society. A hallmark of traditional Roman Catholic social teaching about the family was that it was the cornerstone and basis of social life. And so it was in pre–Industrial Revolution Western countries. However, after the Industrial Revolution, socialization as well as the production of goods, services, and foods were transferred outside the family. Thus the family changed from the cornerstone of society to one institution among many.

The response of the Catholic church was to try to hold on to its tradition as long as possible, losing many opportunities to construct a teaching that both respected the tradition and responded to changing times. Thus the tradition called for a living wage, but this was defined in terms of what the father of the family should be paid, assuming that the wife/mother would stay with the children. In something of a gesture to contemporary society, *Humanae Vitae* spoke of responsible parenthood—but only within the context of the traditional meaning of natural law.

The consequences of affirming the tradition in spite of a changing social world were twofold. First, the opportunity to address the positive dimension of the new social reality—as well as to critique its shortcomings—was missed. Calls for social reform, such as the emphasis on the living wage, were essentially strategies to restore the family to its status before the Industrial Revolution. Second, the changing role of women was not constructively addressed. Equality between men and women, even in current papal teaching, is defined metaphysically, not in terms of social roles and social conditions. The teaching that was developed was paternalistic; it sought to maintain the women's role as the heart of the family and to protect them from the dangers of the outside world. Teaching about the family, then, has focused on the ethics of reproduction, rather than on creatively developing a theology of the family in the modern world. Encyclicals on women have been written and theologies of marriage and the family have been developed, but these have been done within the traditional context and with the traditional concepts. The argument aims to restore the past rather than to construct the future.

Humanae Vitae did provide some seeds of renewal by officially recognizing that the unitive end of marriage is co-equal with the procreative end. Nonetheless, co-equality of the unitive and procreative still means *co*-equality, and this puts a burden on Catholic couples who discover they are infertile. These couples are told that a family is the fulfillment of marriage but are given few ways to achieve that. Thus, they may feel abandoned by the church at a time when they need the church most. Certainly adoption is an option, and many couples choose it. But the desire for a child of their own creation testifies to the embodied reality of marriage and to their relation with each other. While pregnancy through IVF may be one step removed from pregnancy through physical intercourse, adoption is yet another step removed. Thus for the infertile Catholic couple, the teaching on the co-equality of the procreative and unitive dimension of intercourse returns in a paradoxical way: given the depth of the unity in their marriage, a couple wishes to affirm the procreative dimension. But they are physically unable to do this and are told by the church that they are also morally unable to have children of their bodies through artificial means. Thus the very positive teaching on the place of children in marriage frustrates this couple because they are not morally able to avail themselves of alternative means to this end.

Finally, the church's emphasis on childbearing, intensified by the pronatalist assumptions of American society, inhibits the couple from considering infertility anything other than a loss. Again, a tie to Catholic social ethics might be useful here in helping to remind the couple, as well as the church, that there are other forms of generativity and fruitfulness within the community. While the pain of the loss from infertility will remain, the opportunity to consider these others forms of generativity through a life of service to others might help transform that pain.

Roman Catholic Social Ethics and Reproductive Issues

Over the past century, Roman Catholicism has amassed a rather comprehensive corpus of social teachings in areas such as wage justice, human dignity, human rights, economic justice, justice in the conduct of war, civil rights, and capital punishment. These teachings have had a major impact on American society in a way that the sexual ethic has not: recall the substantive discussions and indeed reactions of the federal government both to *The Challenge of Peace* and *Economic Justice for All*. To some extent, these teachings are built upon the edifice of natural law, particularly in the earlier encyclicals of Leo XIII and Pius XI. But human dignity and rights, based in the nature of the person rather than in biological nature, have played an increasingly critical role, particularly since John XXIII's *Pacem in Terris*. This trend continued, and in Vatican II the document *Gaudium et Spes* identified the person and his or her acts as a legitimate source of morality.

   The first and most critical difference between Catholicism's social and sexual ethic is that the sexual ethic, based on the inviolability of biological structure, *admits of no exceptions*. Thus, contraception is always wrong; IVF is always wrong. Social ethics are open to exceptions or compromise because they are based on obligations inherent in the relations of persons and institutions. Killing is wrong, *except* when in self-defense or when order by the state as in war or capital punishment. A living wage is mandatory *but* must be calculated with respect to a variety of social and economic circumstances. One way to explain this is to argue that in the field of social ethics, things are more complicated than with sexual ethics. The economic situation of a country is a complex phenomenon; foreign policy involves a host of difficult interactions. To consider these dimensions is not moral relativism, but an acknowledgement that complex situations require complex analysis.

   But I would also argue that with regard to sexual ethics, things are not as simple as the tradition would suggest. For example, the decision of whether or not to have a child is a complex one. One or both prospective parents may have a history of genetic disease in their family. The woman may have a medical condition that could compromise her own health during pregnancy. The couple may have debts from their education that they wish to deal with. Or a couple may identify social service as a priority for their marriage. Recognizing that consequences and circumstances have a role in sexual ethics (unfortunately a forgotten part of the Catholic tradition) would go a long way in helping individuals think through in a responsible manner critical decisions they need to make. It would also have the merit of keeping such individuals in contact with the church and its teachings. While there will surely be actions that Catholicism will always prohibit, this approach would provide a more open mode of analysis and a more nuanced argument in that it appeals to a broader normative framework. It would remain faithful to the best instincts of the tradition but would also appreciate the moral dimensions of the dynamic social situation in which we find ourselves.

   Roman Catholic social ethics can also make an enormous contribution to the question of health care in this country. Services for various reproductive technologies are but a subset of a much larger question of what services are covered by insurance and the even larger question of who is insured. Currently most people are insured through private payments, employment, or government programs such as Medicare or Medicaid. But there a large number of individuals who do not fit into these frameworks or who have inadequate coverage. A strong argument for universal coverage can be made from Roman Catholic sources: it is a basic matter of justice to citizens; it is in the best interests of the country as a whole; it is a long-term investment in a healthier population; it is an expression of care for the marginalized. Roman Catholic social ethics can argue strongly that the current system is unjust because so many are uninsured or underinsured, because benefits are distributed in favor of the wealthy or those fortunate enough to have employment, and because prevention is not adequately addressed.

   If coverage is a justice question for Catholic social ethics, so too is financing such coverage. Roman Catholic social ethics could make a strong argument for federal funding of such programs, and for a variety of other funding sources. One could argue, as did Pius XI, that the government should provide insurance only until individuals are able to do so for themselves. It could also be argued that insurance is no longer what it was at the time of Pius XI and now should be provided by the state. Wherever one wishes to enter the coverage and funding debate, there are many ethical issues that Roman Catholicism could constructively address.

The more engaging question, given some sort of universal care, is what to include in the basic benefits package. Few would have trouble with a basic package oriented to prevention, with provisions for routine physicals, vaccinations, prenatal care, well-baby care, dietary advice, etc. Such interventions are relatively inexpensive and have long-term benefits. The problem comes when we move beyond these interventions to others, such as expensive diagnostic and screening technologies, organ transplants, kidney dialysis—and assisted reproduction. Procedures like these are in fact provided for by many insurance programs obtained through employment.

How ought reproductive technologies to fare within a system of universal coverage? This question is made difficult because of several unarticulated assumptions on health care held by most Americans: the funding barrel has no bottom; since I have insurance, I'm entitled to everything; quality health care means as much as possible for as long as possible. Catholic social ethics would seriously challenge all of these assumptions. And such a challenge will not be warmly received, as we saw during the disastrous debate over health care in 1933.

Roman Catholic ethics could argue, on the basis of justice and the common good, that access to AR should not be part of a basic package of universal health coverage. First, the shift from the traditional understanding of natural law to a more historically grounded understanding of the person would argue that biological procreation need not have a place of privilege in a marriage. Also, if marriage is no longer a contract that gives partners access to the each other's bodies but a covenantal relationship, procreation becomes one among many goods of marriage, not necessarily the defining good. Marriage as a covenant has a more dynamic relation to society; in this context, we could recall the traditional teaching that reproduction is a species obligation, not an individual one. Thus, from a contemporary theology of natural law and of marriage, one can reasonably argue that reproduction is not essential to the integrity of a marriage. And if so, justice claims to including access to assisted reproduction in a basic health care package are weakened.

A second relevant principle is the traditional Catholic concept of the common good. Here one would focus on individual rights in relation to the good of society as well as to the good of the individual. At its best, the concept of the common good is a way to mediate what society and the individual owe each other. One of the strong implications is that, while everyone should be able to participate in social life and to achieve their potential, everyone is not entitled to everything. The concept of the common good would prioritize prevention over cure or, in the case of assisted reproduction, over compensation for a problematic biological condition. It could, in justice, also restrict access to expensive, low success, high risk, nonvalidated therapies. Artificial reproduction is certainly expensive and has a relatively low success rate. Having a family historically has been important for individuals and has been strongly encouraged by the Catholic church along with other religious organizations. Nonetheless, rethinking health insurance will force us to ask how central to individual fulfillment and desire, and how critical to the common good, is having a child of one's own body and partner. Is the provision of basic benefits to all not more important than ensuring that a small group have their reproductive desires fulfilled?

One solution, of course, would be to devise an insurance system so that individuals can, after receiving a basic package, buy other features such as coverage for artificial reproduction. Such a combination of private and public plans would certainly give the wealthy a major advantage. But if it were not totally inaccessible to the less wealthy, it would not be inherently unjust. From the perspective of Catholic social ethics, the key issue would be to ensure that the poor had access to services covered by the basic package. The question of access to other health care options, however, would continue to be welcomed in the context of much larger questions of economic justice within the society.

As I have shown, Roman Catholicism can engage in a very critical public policy debate over AR without making any reference to its sexual ethic, which prohibits AR as unnatural. The more critical Catholic arguments would focus on the relative importance of biological childbearing, funding for research into artificial reproduction, access to reproductive clinics, the place of artificial reproduction in relation to other health care services, and the status and role of children within our society. Catholicism has a vast treasury of social teachings that can be brought to bear on these and other questions, if it lets go of the traditional sexual ethic and develops a moral theology in dialogue with the past, but appreciative of contemporary issues and perspectives.[26]

Notes

1. *New York Times*, 18 October 1996, sec. B21.

2. Ibid.,

3. Clifford Grobstein, Michael Flower, and John Mendeloff, "External Human Fertilization: An Evaluation of Policy," *Science* 222 (14 October 1983): 127.

4. Trip Gabriel, "High-Tech Pregnancies Test Hope's Limit," *New York Times*, 7 January 1995, sec. A10.

5. Ibid., sec. A11.

6. Ann Wozencraft, "It's a Baby, or It's Your Money Back," *New York Times*, 25 August, 1996, 3:1.

7. Gabriel, "High-Tech Pregnancies," sec. A11.

8. *Donum Vitae*, II, B.4. The citation can also be found in Thomas A. Shannon and Lisa S. Cahill, *Religion and Artificial Reproduction* (New York: Crossroad, 1988), 161.

9. Ibid.

10. Ibid.

11. *Gaudium et Spes*, para. 51. The document can be found in David O'Brien and Thomas A. Shannon, *Catholic Social Thought: The Documentary History* (New York: Orbis Books, 1992), 200.

12. I am indebted to James Keenan, S.J., for this insight. See his "Moral Horizons in Health Care: Reproductive Technologies and Catholic Identity," in *Infertility: A Crossroad of Faith, Medicine and Technology*, ed. K. Wm. Wides (Netherlands: Kluwer Academic Publishers), 53–71, but especially see 61–62.

13. *Donum Vitae*, Introduction, 1. Also Shannon and Cahill, *Religion and Artificial Reproduction*, 1431.

14. Ibid. Also Shannon and Cahill, *Religion and Artificial Reproduction*, 141.

15. Ibid., 2. Also Shannon and Cahill, *Religion and Artificial Reproduction*, 143.

16. Ibid., 3. Also Shannon and Cahill, *Religion and Artificial Reproduction*, 144.

17. Ibid.

18. For an excellent overview of this perspective, see James F. Keenan, S.J., "Christian Perspectives on the Human Body," *Theological Studies* 55 (1994): 330–46. His work illuminated several of my perspectives on this topic.

19. Karol Wojtyla, *Love and Responsibility*, trans. H. T. Willetts (New York: Farrar, Straus, and Giroux, 1981), 246.

20. Ibid., 247. Italics in the original.

21. *Gaudium et Spes*, 209.

22. Ibid.

23. Ibid.

24. Ibid., 229.

25. Ibid.

26. I want to thank in a very particular way Kathleen Sands for twice reading this manuscript with a very critical and constructive eye. Her comments have been helpful not only with respect to the organization of the overall argument, but also in terms of pushing the thrust of the argument forward. I am extremely grateful for her editorial and collegial assistance.

12

JAMES MCBRIDE

"To Make Martyrs of Their Children"

*"Female Genital Mutilation,"
Religious Legitimation, and
the Constitution*

Sparked by Alice Walker's *Possessing the Secret of Joy* and *Warrior Marks* (with Pratibha Parmar), as well as her hour-long documentary of the same name, the controversy over what is dubbed "female genital mutilation" (FGM) has been propelled into the spotlight on network television and in North American newspapers and journals.[1] In 1994 Lydia Oluloro, an illegal immigrant from Nigeria, successfully fought deportation orders by the U.S. Immigration and Naturalization Service (INS), on the grounds that the return to her native country would subject her two American-born daughters, ages six and four, to this practice by her relatives.[2] More recently, Fauziya Kasinga, a member of the Tchamba-Kunsuntu tribe of northern Togo, initially lost her 1995 bid for asylum in the United States, claiming that FGM constituted persecution—a ruling later reversed by the Board of Immigration Appeals on June 13, 1996.[3] Protected by her father from this practice, the seventeen-year-old Kasinga fell under her aunt's authority upon her father's death. Arranging a polygynous union with a 45-year-old man, already with three wives, her aunt planned to subject Kasinga to FGM before the consummation of the marriage. Kasinga fled initially to Ghana and eventually arrived in the United States seeking asylum. Although the judge at the immigration hearing rejected her application (due to alleged inconsistencies in her testimony and questions about her credibility), the appeals court reversed the decision. In so doing, the court noted that post-*Oluloro* the INS had issued an FGM alert to its officers at U.S. ports of entry[4] and had established guidelines to handle asylum petitions arising from claims of FGM.[5] In its opinion, the court concluded that "FGM can be a basis for asylum"[6] under § 208 of the Immigration and Nationality Act (1994).[7] Among the opponents of FGM, the *Oluloro* and *Kasinga* cases represented hard-fought victories; however, the anti-FGM movement within the United States had more ambitious aims, including outlawing FGM here in the United States and employing American fiscal muscle to stop the practice abroad. These campaigns have raised serious political and ethical questions in the worldwide feminist community as well as significant domestic legal issues.

Within the broader context of the debate over FGM (particularly the charges of misogyny and countercharges of cultural imperialism), the purpose of this chapter is to address the constitutional questions raised by the "Federal Prohibition of Female Genital Mutilation Act," sponsored by Congresswomen Patricia Schroeder (D-Colo.), Barbara Rose Collins (D-Mich.), and Constance Morella (R-Md.) and added to Titles 1, 8, 18, and 22 of the U.S. Code. Stepping beyond the mandate of the United Nations and its agencies, which seek to stop FGM through the use of persuasion and education, this federal legislation invokes the force of law by criminalizing the practice in the United States when it is exercised on women under the age of eighteen and is not medically necessary.

Because FGM is most often associated with the religious ritual of *khitan*, authorized by the Islamic religion, and male circumcision is both widely practiced and legally sanctioned in the United States, these statutes generate significant First and Fourteenth Amendment concerns requiring judicial review. This chapter will elaborate those hermeneutical questions by framing this legislation within the context of free exercise and equal protection jurisprudence. Of particular concern is the controversy surrounding the "Religious Freedom Restoration Act" (RFRA; 1993),[8] which sought to reestablish the standard of "compelling state interest" in judicial review of free exercise cases—a standard previously struck down by the Supreme Court in *Employment Division, Department of Human Resources of Oregon v. Smith* (1990)[9] and most recently addressed by the High Court in *City of Boerne v. Flores* (1997).[10] Under the pre-*Smith* jurisprudential standard of the High Court, resurrected by RFRA, the state could abridge the free exercise of religion only if it showed a "compelling state interest."[11] The Court had recognized that one such compelling interest was the welfare of children. Under existing precedent, "parents may be free to become martyrs themselves. But it does not follow that they are free . . . to make martyrs of their children before they have reached the age of full and legal discretion when they can make a choice for themselves."[12]

Many feminist critics regard girls and young women subjected to FGM as just such "martyrs"—victims of a cruel, misogynist procedure—and those threatened with it need to be protected by law against the will of their parents and/or relatives. I join with these critics in condemning FGM. Although those of us who object to this practice hazard the risk of being charged with cultural imperialism, both humanitarian and feminist considerations make that risk worth taking. Federal and state legislation outlawing FGM is, in my opinion, an appropriate response to a custom that has been practiced not only abroad, but also increasingly here in the United States. The Centers for Disease Control and Prevention in Atlanta, surmise that up to 48,000 females under the age of eighteen in the United States either have already been subjected to or are being threatened with FGM.[13] This chapter addresses the constitutional grounds on which federal and state anti-FGM statutes may be challenged and argues that, in defending the physical integrity of girls and young women, the new laws violate neither the free exercise nor the equal protection rights of parents and the children they wish to "martyr."

In light of the U.S. Supreme Court's 1997 *Boerne* decision, which held RFRA unconstitutional and (for the second time) struck down the "compelling state interest" test, actions characterized by their practitioners as religiously inspired are no longer exempt from universally applicable, facially neutral laws, even where there exists no "compelling state interest." Hence, the practice of FGM cannot be defended by an appeal to the free exercise of religion, unless its proponents can show that an anti-FGM law was motivated by an antireligious prejudice directed toward a *specific* religious group. However, since FGM is a *cultural*, rather than an exclusively religious, custom, practiced by *many different* religious and national groups, it is unlikely that proponents of FGM could make a viable First Amendment claim that the anti-FGM law evinces a religiously based animus.

However, it is still open to question whether the courts could sanction a federal law that broadly bans all forms of FGM, including simple female circumcision, in a society that permits male circumcision without jeopardizing the equal protection rights of parents and their female children belonging to such religious and national groups. Because the statute is directed toward young females alone and necessarily differentiates between males and females, the Court is obliged to use "heightened" scrutiny in order to justify a gender-specific law based on biological sex. The article concludes by legitimating the divergent consequences of gender-based classification by appealing to an "ethics of sexual difference," hypothesized in Luce Irigaray's post-Lacanian feminist psychoanalytic work, and the pragmatism advocated by Stanley Fish in his work on interpretive communities.

Female Genital Mutilation

An expression coined by critics for the circumcision, excision, and infibulation of female genitals, FGM[14] has been practiced on 30 to 110 million women in some thirty countries, most of them in the dominantly Islamic nations of West, Central, and North Africa,[15] as well as in Indonesia, the largest Muslim country in the world. It is estimated that more than 2 million girls and young women undergo FGM each year in these countries where the percentage of the female population subjected to the procedure ranges from a mere 5% (Uganda, Tanzania) to more than 90% (Somalia, Sudan).[16]

FGM is a broad term that covers a multiplicity of practices. The Shandall system of classification suggests three types of procedures: (1) the removal of the hood or prepuce of the clitoris; (2) the excision of the clitoris itself along with the labia minora; and (3) the excision of the labia majora and the suturing closed of the vulva (with the exception of a small orifice for the flow of urine and menses).[17] In the *New England Journal of Medicine*, a prominent opponent of FGM, Dr. Nahid Toubia suggests that the Shandall typology is inaccurate, since in her extensive clinical experience in Africa she has never seen a case where merely the hood of the clitoris has been excised.[18] Even the most conservative procedure entails partial or full clitoridectomy, a practice commonly referred to as "*sunna* circumcision," that is, circumcision according to the religious tradition of the indigenous Islamic community. Although FGM is now performed in some countries by qualified medical personnel in hospitals and clinics (e.g., Somalia, Sudan, and Mali), it is most often undergone at the hands of medically unqualified persons—some of whom are traditionally revered older female practitioners, including midwives, and some of whom are men (for instance, barbers). The age of the female subject ranges from neonatal among the Ethiopian Falasha to adolescence in Nigeria; but most often the procedure is undertaken when the child is between three and eight years. Anesthesia is rarely, if ever, used, and, outside of hospitals, the Western medical practice of sterilization is rarely observed. Practitioners employ pieces of sharp glass, ritual knives, and razor blades to perform the procedure. Suturing is accomplished through the use of thorns and catgut. The subject's legs are wrapped tightly together, and then she is kept immobile for some five weeks in order for scar tissue to form over the genital area.

Not surprisingly, FGM has been associated with chronic medical problems. As the World Health Assembly noted in May 1993:

> Immediate risks include hemorrhage, tetanus, infection, and vesiculo-vaginal fistula. HIV infection can be contracted from the tools or instruments used. Long-term effects include problems of reproductive and general health such as urinary tract infections and coital difficulty, cysts and abscesses, keloid and severe scar formation, and difficulty when voiding and during menstruation. During childbirth, the risk of maternal death is doubled and the risk of a stillbirth increased several fold. Moreover, during childbirth, the risk of hemorrhage and infection is greatly increased, and long-term morbidity becomes cumulative and chronic.[19]

The report further notes that FGM "is now found in countries such as Australia, Europe and North America among migrant groups."[20]

Worldwide Campaign against Female Genital Mutilation

Despite the fact that FGM is embraced as a woman's rite of passage by women themselves in these cultures—indeed, in Kenya, where it is outlawed, a survey of 1,365 women indicated that it is supported by a 2–1 margin[21]—a wide range of feminist and womanist public figures have condemned FGM as misogyny. As Linda Weill-Curiel, the Parisian prosecutor who has indicted and convicted parents for child abuse in these cases, bluntly put it, "This is butchery invented to control women."[22] In her novel *Possessing the Secret of Joy*, a book that explores the effect of FGM on the protagonist Evelyn, Alice Walker curiously enough spoke her anguish through the words of a white male, a European psychiatrist, named Mzee, or "Old Man," by his African friends. She writes:

> They, in their indescribable suffering, are bringing me home to something in myself. I am finding myself in them. A self I have often felt was only halfway at home on the European continent. In my European skin. An ancient skin that thirsts for knowledge of the experiences of its ancient kin. Needs this knowledge, and the feel-

ings that come with it, to be whole. A self that is horrified at what was done to Evelyn, but recognizes it as something that is also done to me. A truly universal self.[23]

Echoing the same sentiments as those voiced by Alice Walker, the United Nations
and its agencies have taken the lead in condemning this practice (widely seen by
most member nations in terms of child abuse, gender-based *animus*, and outright
torture) as a violation of human rights.[24]

Appeals to respect the traditional culture of indigenous peoples to the contrary,
Alice Walker protested in her film *Warrior Marks* that "there is a distinction between torture and culture. And I maintain that culture is not child abuse. It is not
battering. These may well be customs. People customarily do these things, just as
they customarily enslaved people. But slavery is not really a culture."[25] Influenced
by the report of the London-based Minority Rights Group International in 1981, the
United Nations Working Group on Slavery in 1982 chose to broaden its definition
to include physical and sexual abuse in its most extreme forms (including FGM) as
tantamount to slavery itself—a comparison that deeply affronted representatives of
certain African nations, including Sudan and Senegal.[26] As Asha Samad, a medical
anthropologist from the City University of New York, noted, "Whenever outside
groups, as well meaning as they are, come in and try to develop media to attack
[FGM], then sometimes there's a backlash."[27] Indeed, Alice Walker herself has
been chided on the op-ed page of the *New York Times* by two Third World professional women in the article "The West Just Doesn't Get It" for her allegedly self-
anointed role as "heroine-savior" of African women. "Instead of being an issue
worthy of attention in itself," they wrote, "it has become a powerful emotive lens
through which to view personal pain—a gauge by which to measure distance between the West and the rest of humanity."[28] To these critics, Walker's campaign and
the vehement condemnation of FGM by Western feminists and other prominent
Americans smacked of cultural imperialism. "The fact that Alice Walker is black
doesn't mean anything," argued Nahid Toubia. "She's an American. [Her] film has
the subtle bigotry and cultural racism of the missionaries in Africa."[29]

Rather than criminalize these traditional, religiously legitimated acts and
anathematize the nations where they are practiced, most Third World anti-FGM
women's groups have endorsed a locally directed educative approach rather than
internationally mandated sanctions.[30] At the 1994 International Conference on
Population and Development held in Cairo, Egypt, participant nations recom-
mended that "steps to eliminate the practice should include strong community outreach programs involving village and religious leaders, education and counseling
about its impact on girls' and women's health, and appropriate treatment and reha-
bilitation for girls and women who have suffered mutilation."[31]

In the United States, however, prominent figures in both the public and private spheres suspected that these indigenous re-education campaigns would be inadequate. Again on the *New York Times* op-ed page, editor A. M. Rosenthal expressed frustration:

> Any attention to female mutilation arouses denunciation—angry arguments that it
> is a deeply embedded ritual that must be understood in local terms. It must be left
> to local people to handle, or try to diminish, without foreign interference.

The same "keep off" signs were posted when the issue was slavery or segregation in America, the burning alive of widows in India, the binding of the feet of
Chinese women. . . .

But nobody has the right to post "keep out" signs against fighting female genital mutilation. And no person, organization or government has the right in de-
cency to obey them.[32]

Accordingly, the success of re-education programs required none too subtle international pressure.[33] In the wake of the Cairo conference, the U.S. Congress was
urged by a number of its female members to engage in direct intervention by tying
foreign assistance for population control and reproductive health to the implementation of anti-FGM outreach programs. Introduced by Representative Morella, the
"International Population Stabilization and Reproductive Health Act" called on
the secretary of state to prepare for Congress "an annual country human rights report" on each recipient nation that would include "an assessment which makes reference to all significant forms of violence against women, including rape, domestic
violence and female genital mutilation." (§ 4[e][2][B]). Countries that failed to
make sincere efforts in curbing these human rights abuses would risk losing such
assistance altogether.[34] As the *New York Times* argued, the bill represented a welcome step by which First World women who do not "suffer the brutalities experienced by their third-world sisters" can speak for those women silenced by this
misogynous practice—even if many of the alleged victims welcome the ritual.[35]
Passed by Congress on September 30, 1996, and now in effect, this legislation authorized the secretary of the treasury to wield America's considerable financial
clout in order to influence Third World governments to end FGM.[36]

Domestic Legislation against Female Genital Mutilation

Although the controversy over FGM in international forums continued, the emergence of largely African migrant groups on U.S. soil opened a second front. Congresswomen Schroeder, Morella, and Collins sought to address the issue of FGM
in the United States by introducing H.R. 3247, the "Federal Prohibition of Female
Genital Mutilation Act of 1993." Amending Title 18 of the U.S. Code, the act reads
as follows: "Whoever knowingly circumcises, excises, or infibulates the whole or
any part of the labia majora or labia minora or clitoris of another person who has
not attained the age of 18 years shall be fined under this title or imprisoned not
more than 5 years, or both."[37] (Exceptions were to be made where such procedures
were medically necessary and performed by medically qualified personnel.[38]) To
temper the coercive threat of fines and imprisonment, the bill's authors also included a provision for a Health and Human Services outreach program among immigrant groups to instruct them, as well as medical students, about the physical and
emotional traumas associated with FGM.[39] Both the federal criminal ban on FGM
and the outreach program to immigrant groups have been paralleled by legislation
passed in a number of states, including California,[40] Delaware,[41] Minnesota,[42]
North Dakota,[43] Tennessee,[44] and Wisconsin.[45] Congresswoman Schroeder admitted that "some may argue that prohibiting the practice within our borders is cultur-

ally imperialistic"; however, she retorted, "I cannot agree. Imposing certain values on people living in this country is our prerogative."[46] Of course, Schroeder's claim is open to dispute: it is questionable whether a change of venue from international to domestic context renders charges of cultural imperialism moot. But before addressing the tensions between universalist and relativist claims, I would like to shift attention to the constitutional questions arising from the criminalization of the practice in the United States.

Legally speaking, FGM is controversial in two respects: (1) FGM is a religiously legitimated traditional ritual, and its criminalization raises free exercise claims under the religion clauses of the First Amendment[47]; and (2) since sex-based classification of its subjects is an "immutable characteristic" of these practices and male circumcision is a procedure widely accepted in the United States, the criminalization of FGM raises questions of "equal protection" under the Fourteenth Amendment.[48] Of course, these two issues assume (1) that FGM is truly a religious practice (which some Western critics and some prominent Muslims dispute); and (2) that male circumcision and FGM are *legally* (if not strictly speaking medically) analogous. If these assumptions hold true, state intervention to ban the practice in the United States would be subject to scrutiny by the federal courts under existing First Amendment free exercise jurisprudence and Fourteenth Amendment equal protection analysis.

Practitioners of FGM justify the procedure as a rite of passage from childhood into womanhood—a view shared by those of different religious backgrounds, including Islam, Christianity, and indigenous African faiths.[49] Most often among Muslims FGM is legitimated as a tradition mandated by Islam. Indeed, clitoridectomy is frequently called "*sunna* circumcision"—sunna being synonymous with the Islamic religion itself. *Sunna* circumcision is authorized by reference to the *Hadith*, the narratives surrounding the Prophet Mohammed collected by his followers.[50] According to the Shafi'i school of law (founded by al-Shafi'i, al Imam Abu 'Abd Allah Muhammad B. Idris, 767–820 C.E.), *khitan* is "equally obligatory for males and females. . . . As regards females, it is obligatory to cut off a small part of the skin in the highest part of the genitals."[51] To what extent the *Koran* and *Hadith* legitimate more radical procedures, including complete excision and infibulation, is open to theological interpretation.

Taha Ba'asher has observed that female circumcision is no longer practiced in Saudi Arabia, whose Wahabism is noteworthy for its affirmation of conservative, traditional Islamic values. Moreover, during the post–World War II era, the Mufti of Sudan no longer considered the procedure mandatory (although the practice continues unabated today).[52] However, in Egypt, where President Hosni Mubarak's opposition to the practice led to its ban by the government in 1996, an Egyptian court struck down the law against FGM on the grounds that it unduly restricted the freedom of Egyptian physicians to practice their profession as they saw fit. Conservative Muslim clerics regarded the ruling as a great victory for the faith. The *New York Times* reported that "Sheik Youssef al-Badri, who led the campaign against last year's ban, issued by Egypt's Health Ministry, celebrated the ruling. 'I will prostrate myself before Allah,' Sheik Badri said today. 'This is a return to Islam.'"[53]

Some American critics, however, argue that not only is FGM not truly Islamic, but it is also not even authentically religious:

Aside from the fact that the religious justification for female circumcision rests on an insufficient doctrinal foundation, the argument ultimately misuses religion as an instrument of fear, oppression and exploitation. A religion that is authentic in the principles it represents "aims at truth, equality, justice, love and a healthy wholesome life for all people, whether men or women." In contrast, the argument that circumcision is a religious requirement casts religion in the role of mandating mutilation, amputation, and infirmity of otherwise healthy female reproductive organs. The latter characterization is the complete antithesis of the ideals that religion should promote.[54]

Despite the sympathy one might have for the ideals expressed herein, the controversy over "true" Islam or "true" religion is, constitutionally speaking, irrelevant.

It is an established principle in First Amendment jurisprudence that the federal courts are incompetent to adjudicate these essentially theological disputes. Under the precedent of *U.S. v. Ballard* (1944),[55] the judiciary may only judge the sincerity of the belief, not whether the belief fits the jurist's conception of what religion in general is or a specific religion ought to be.[56] If the practitioners of FGM sincerely believe that these procedures are mandated by the Islamic religious tradition, they are religiously legitimated, even if other Muslims (let alone non-Muslims) dispute their authenticity. As even the Minority Rights Group International—one of the leading forces in the anti-FGM movement—admits, "The traditional operator says a short prayer: 'Allah is great and Mahomet is his Prophet. May Allah keep away all evils.'"[57] It seems that practitioners are sincerely motivated by their faith, although their religious practices may seem brutal and insensitive to some. But no matter how much the belief is disliked or abhorred, the courts are not free to consider these practices as other than religiously inspired. That does not mean that certain religiously legitimated practices cannot be outlawed by the state. Under the Supreme Court's June 1997 *Boerne* decision, legislation may restrict a religious practice, even if there is no "compelling governmental interest," as long as the law does not narrowly target a particular religion. Hence, federal statutes against FGM may pass constitutional muster if they do not violate the standard articulated by the Court in *Church of Lukumi Babalu Aye v. City of Hialeah*,[58] which proscribed legislation founded on religious animus.

In regard to the second assumption, some critics contend that male circumcision and FGM are not analogous, and therefore no "equal protection" claims are raised by permitting the former and criminalizing the latter. The proper analogy of FGM would not be circumcision, but rather castration.[59] "The equivalent to men," claimed Toubia on American television, "is the partial or total removal of the penis and even the worst type of infibulation would be the removal of everything outside, all the external genitals of the men—of course, without the testicles because the female ovaries are inside the body—and then stitching everything over and covering it, leaving just a hole for urine."[60]

Although it is true that male circumcision and "*sunna* circumcision" are not, physically speaking, analogous, it might be argued that they are religiously and functionally analogous. The same Arabic term *khitan* is employed to indicate male and female circumcision, and they are both read as signs of submission to Allah and of incorporation into the Islamic community of men and women. Moreover, neither gender-specific form of male and female circumcision negates the possibility of heterosexual congress. It does, however, raise the possibility that sexual pleasure of women may be diminished, particularly in cases of clitoral excision and infibulation. Some critics have suggested that FGM may lead in particular cases to psychosexual trauma, especially among immigrant women in Western countries,[61] although the anti-FGM Minority Rights Group admits that there is little or no evidence on this specific aspect of the issue.[62] Even Tobia agrees that "the assumption that all circumcised women have sexual problems or are unable to reach orgasm is not sustained by research or anecdotal evidence."[63] While the Freudian norm of vaginal orgasm may be largely discredited, the alternative ideal of clitoral orgasm, developed by Western sexologists, including Masters and Johnson, and Shere Hite and commended by Alice Walker,[64] is hardly preferred by Third World anti-FGM critics. To do so would invalidate the sexual experience of those women whom they want to help.

But perhaps most importantly, since American law criminalizes simple female-circumcision (the removal of the clitoral hood), *as well as* excision and infibulation, the statutory *ban* of FGM in part parallels what is the *permissible* circumcision of males. In this respect, the bill is tainted by language that seems simply too broad, and therefore its constitutionality may be jeopardized. The law's authors might have avoided this potentially fatal constitutional flaw by narrowly tailoring the language to enjoin excision and infibulation alone. However, there can be little doubt that even simple female circumcision is offensive to Western critics of FGM. It is deeply held that all three procedures—circumcision, excision, and infibulation—are parts of a single piece: a tradition deemed misogynous *in toto*, alien to Western ideals of human rights and American principles of sexual equality. Ironically, it is that very principle of sexual equality that works against the law. For the "equal protection" of citizens under the Fourteenth Amendment suggests that males and females not be treated differently. Hence, if male circumcision is permitted, then logically so too should female circumcision unless the "immutable characteristics" of biological difference necessitate an exception. But such an exception would require at least an "intermediate level of scrutiny" by the courts.

Free Exercise Considerations

Previous to *Employment Division, Department of Human Resources of Oregon v. Smith*, the Warren, Burger, and Rehnquist Courts had been bound by the "compelling state interest" standard in adjudicating free exercise cases established in *Sherbert v. Verner* (1963). Of course, statutes cannot hostilely target a particular religion or religion in general,[65] but where a generally applicable statute interfered with a religious practice, the regulation was subject to "heightened scrutiny" by the courts in order to ensure that free exercise rights were not wantonly violated. As Laurence Tribe argued, the state was obliged to show "first, that the regulation pursues a particularly important governmental goal, and second, that an exemption would substantially hinder the fulfillment of that goal."[66] Where such a goal could be accomplished without burdening a particular religious practice, such an exemption would be forthcoming. Justice Brennan noted that "only the gravest abuses, endangering paramount interests, give occasion for permissible limitation," of free exercise.[67]

This precedent that held sway in free exercise jurisprudence over nearly three decades was struck down by the High Court in 1990 by *Employment Division, Department of Human Resources of Oregon v. Smith.* In that case the respondents argued that the state's refusal to offer them unemployment benefits constituted religious discrimination, since their dismissal from state employment was based on their ingestion of peyote in a religious ritual of the Native American Church. Respondents urge us to hold, quite simply, that when otherwise prohibitable conduct is accompanied by religious convictions, not only the convictions but the conduct itself must be free from governmental regulation. "We have never held that," insisted Justice Scalia, "and decline to do so now."[68] Setting aside "compelling state interest" as a universal standard of free exercise jurisprudence, the Court held by a 5–4 majority that no exemptions for generally applicable, facially neutral criminal laws can be granted for religious practices unless the free exercise claim is coupled with another constitutional protection, for instance, freedom of speech or the press.[69]

The fear that such a precedent would jeopardize the well-being of religion in America, from the largest denomination to the smallest sect, led to a highly unusual coalition of religious figures and organizations, including ultraconservative televangelists and the highly liberal National Council of Churches. Through their efforts, Congress passed the "Religious Freedom Restoration Act of 1993" (RFRA) to redeem what had been lost in the *Smith* decision. The purposes of RFRA, as stated in the statute, were "(1) to restore the compelling interest test as set forth in *Sherbert v. Verner*, 374 U.S. 398 (1963) and *Wisconsin v. Yoder*, 406 U.S. 205 (1972) and to guarantee its application in all cases where free exercise of religion is substantially burdened; and (2) to provide a claim or defense to persons whose religious exercise is substantially burdened by government."[70] Although this legislation restored the standard of judicial review struck down by the 1990 *Smith* decision, it was highly questionable whether the High Court would feel obliged to follow it. In an academic conference, held in the spring of 1994 at the University of Montana School of Law, a straw poll of seven legal experts in First Amendment jurisprudence indicated that five of the seven found the statute, on its face, to be unconstitutional. The other two thought that the statute's constitutionality was at least problematic. From their point of view, the statute violated the separation of powers between the legislative and judicial branches of government.

Congress is deemed incompetent to judge the constitutionality of statutes, a role reserved exclusively for the judiciary. Moreover, it was questionable whether Congress had the right to dictate the standards by which the courts make such judgments—particularly when those standards had evolved according to the vicissitudes of case law. The High Court could simply choose to ignore the statute as irrelevant or strike it down as an unwarranted intrusion on its authority. However, RFRA did give those justices who wanted to reassess the jurisprudential consequences of the *Smith* decision moral, if not constitutional, leverage against the *Smith* majority. A number of justices expressed their willingness in *Smith* to reaffirm some form of the compelling state interest standard (including Justices O'Connor, Blackmun, Brennan, and Marshall[71]) or urged their colleagues in *Lukumi* to reconsider *Smith's* reversal of the compelling state interest doctrine (including Justices Souter, Blackmun, and O'Connor[72]). RFRA provided the impetus for a confrontation between the legislative and judicial branches as well as an opportunity to reverse the effects of *Smith*.

City of Boerne and the Demise of RFRA

The Supreme Court had the opportunity in 1997 to reconsider both the *Smith* decision and the constitutionality of RFRA in *City of Boerne v. Flores*. The Catholic archbishop of San Antonio brought suit to challenge San Antonio city authorities who had refused to issue a building permit to enlarge St. Peter's Catholic Church on the grounds that the plans violated the city's zoning restrictions. Invoking RFRA, the church's attorneys claimed that the city had not demonstrated any compelling state interest that would justify infringement upon the Catholic community's free exercise of religion. The city, in turn, challenged the constitutionality of RFRA and urged the Supreme Court to reaffirm the *Smith* decision, which validated universally applicable, facially neutral statutes, including San Antonio's local zoning ordinances.

The plaintiff argued that RFRA was a constitutional exercise of congressional authority under the Fourteenth Amendment. Since the free exercise of religion, guaranteed by the First Amendment, had been incorporated under the Fourteenth Amendment by *Cantwell v. Connecticut* (1940)[73] as a constitutionally protected liberty interest and had been made incumbent upon the states, Congress allegedly had the power to enforce the Fourteenth Amendment,[74] even against state and local authorities. In their ruling issued June 25, 1997, the majority opinion, authored by Justice Kennedy, chose to reject the plaintiff's arguments and to strike down RFRA.

The Court gave two reasons. First, in affirming the federalist notion of power-sharing between the national government and the states, the Court held that the congressional power to enforce the Fourteenth Amendment, including the right to the free exercise of religion, was not plenary, but rather remedial, i.e., limited to cases where governmental authorities have demonstrated some animus toward the rights of individual citizens. Hence, whereas Congress was within its power to pass the Voting Rights Bill to redeem the rights of black citizens, subject to state discriminatory practices, "RFRA's legislative record lacks examples of modern instances of generally applicable laws passed because of religious bigotry."[75] Since universally applicable, facially neutral laws do not specifically target particular religions, it is beyond the *remedial* power of Congress to proscribe their use by state and local authorities, even if some citizens are incidentally and adversely affected because of their religious beliefs. "RFRA is so out of proportion to a supposed remedial or preventive object that it cannot be understood as responsive to, or designed to prevent, unconstitutional behavior."[76] Second, the majority rejected RFRA as an unwarranted intrusion by the Congress on the High Court's domain. "The power to interpret the Constitution in a case or controversy remains in the Judiciary."[77] In a tone chastising its colleagues in the legislative branch, the majority reminded Congress that "it is this Court's precedent, not RFRA, which must control."[78] Absent a statute or ordinance specifically targeting a religious group, proscribed by the Court in *Lukumi*, *Smith's* affirmation of universally applicable, facially neutral statutes or ordinances, regardless of their incidental effect of religious believers, would remain the law of the land.

Justices O'Connor and Breyer dissented strongly, holding that "in light of both our precedent and our Nation's religious tradition, *Smith* is demonstrably wrong."[79] Justice Souter shared these doubts about the wisdom of the *Smith* ruling (which he had first articulated in his concurrence in *Church of Lukumi Babalu Aye*[80]) and joined O'Connor and Breyer in lamenting that the Court had not entertained the reargument of *Smith* with accompanying full briefs. Yet, the dissent in *Boerne* proved to be little more than a rear-guard action for justices whose position had been decisively defeated. The strength of the majority (6–3) indicated that *Smith* most likely will remain the standard in First Amendment free exercise jurisprudence for some time to come.

Had the Court affirmed RFRA and taken the opportunity to reverse the *Smith* decision, practitioners of FGM who are religiously motivated may have had a slim chance to challenge the ban on FGM, given its effect on the free exercise of religion. They may have argued that, absent a compelling governmental interest, parents should continue to have the right to subject their female children to this practice. The anti-FGM law directly intervenes in the home where the High Court has long recognized the sanctity of parental rights.

As the majority write in *Parham v. J. R.* (1979), "Our jurisprudence historically has reflected Western civilization concepts of the family as a unit with broad parental authority over minor children. Our cases have consistently followed that course: our constitutional system long ago rejected any notion that a child is 'the mere creature of the State.'"[81] Founded upon natural law theory and preserved in common law, parental custodial rights early on played a key role in adjudicating education cases before the Supreme Court.[82] The Court further recognized parental authority in areas beyond educational matters. "It is cardinal with us that the custody, care and nurture of the child first reside with the parents."[83]

These parental rights are founded on two sources of constitutional authority. "[F]reedom of personal choice in matters of . . . family life," wrote the Court in *Cleveland Board of Education v. LaFlair*, "is one of the liberties protected by the Fourteenth Amendment."[84] And although Justice William O. Douglas's statement in *Griswold v. Connecticut* (1965) that "the First Amendment has a penumbra where privacy is protected from governmental intrusion"[85] was associated with freedom of assembly, it is logical that this "penumbra" would extend to other First Amendment rights, including the free exercise of religion. Hence, the Court treads very carefully when it considers governmental intrusion into the private sphere of family life. In the celebrated 1972 *Wisconsin v. Yoder* decision,[86] the Supreme Court recognized the First Amendment right of Amish parents to withdraw their children from public schools and educate them at home. Does constitutional precedent then suggest that the state would have failed to demonstrate a "compelling state interest" in banning the religiously sanctioned practices of

FGM—indeed, in any parentally-sanctioned FGM procedures—if RFRA had been affirmed?

As commonly pointed out by constitutional scholars, in most cases since the establishment of the *Sherbert* standard in 1963, the state had been successful in demonstrating a compelling governmental interest. It was rare when the government failed to prove its case, which was the very reason for the attention given *Wisconsin v. Yoder*. It seemed to be the exception to the rule. It is more than likely that the state could sustain a compelling state interest in banishing FGM, unless *Yoder* could be shown to be authoritative in assessing the constitutionality of the statutory prohibition. In *Yoder*, great latitude was given parental authority, but the justices assumed that the interests of Amish parents and their children were not in conflict. They wrote, "Our holding in no way determines the proper resolution of possible competing interest of parents, children, and the State."[87] That conflict of interest between parent and child was manifest in instances where the welfare of the child was put at risk. "This case, of course, is not one in which any harm to the physical or mental health of the child or to the public safety, peace, order or welfare has been demonstrated or may be properly inferred."[88] As the Court noted in *Parham v. J.R.* (1979), "That some parents 'may at times be acting against the interests of their children' creates a basis for caution."[89] From the standpoint of its critics, FGM causes female children substantial physical and emotional trauma, and therefore the interests of parent and child diverge. "Unlike the Amish girl who can finish her education later in life if she chooses not to be Amish," wrote the bill's co-sponsor, Congresswoman Schroeder, "the girl who suffers genital mutilation is subject to a permanent, irreversible choice made by parents."[90] Hence, the circumstances of banning FGM are substantially different from those involved in the *Yoder* case. The criminalization of FGM with regard to children therefore would have been sustained not only under the *Smith* standard (facially neutral, generally applicable criminal law), but also most likely under the *Sherbert* standard (compelling state interest), if the Supreme Court had chosen to readopt it.

Indeed, the constitutionality of a statute that criminalized the use of FGM on an adult female would also be affirmed, even if she freely chose to undergo the procedure as an act of religious duty. Ever since *Roe v. Wade* (1973),[91] when the High Court first determined that a woman had a fundamental liberty interest to an abortion, the state retained the right to abridge her right to choose in order to protect maternal health during the second and third trimesters.[92] In the aftermath of *Planned Parenthood v. Casey* (1985),[93] which abandoned Justice Blackmun's trimester scheme and eroded a woman's fundamental liberty interest to an abortion, the state's right to intervene to protect a woman's health is, if anything, even stronger than twenty years ago.[94] It is unlikely that the U.S. Supreme Court, which has affirmed the constitutionality of most state abortion regulation (with the exception of spousal notification),[95] would hesitate to affirm a statute banning a practice so detrimental to women's health and maternal potential.

But in light of the *Boerne* decision, these arguments are moot. Advocates of FGM no longer have constitutional grounds under the First Amendment Free Exercise Clause to challenge the constitutionality of federal and state bans on FGM, *unless* they can demonstrate that the legislation was motivated by a religiously based animus. They might argue, as did the plaintiff's attorneys in *Church of Lukumi Babalu Aye v. City of Hialeah* (1993), that although the statute itself may *appear* to be facially neutral, it is not *in fact*, as evidenced by its legislative history. Reaffirming the *Smith* standard, the High Court struck down a series of municipal ordinances as unconstitutional since they were directed specifically toward the practice of the Santería religion. It was clear to the Court from reading the context of these ordinances that the city was openly hostile to the practice of Santería in Hialeah and sought to enlist the color of state law to suppress it.

Yet, based on the reading of the legislative history of the act, it is difficult to conclude that the sponsors evinced hostility to the Islamic faith itself. Critics of FGM frequently stated that FGM is at *variance* with the teachings of the Muslim religion; however, if the practitioners of FGM themselves regard these procedures as essentially religious rituals, is the act prohibiting FGM exclusively targeting the Islamic faith? If so, then it ought to be struck down according to *Lukumi*. In that instance, the city council knew that no other group practiced animal sacrifice in the city of Hialeah and that the target of the municipal ordinances would be exclusively the practitioners of a particular religion group. However, with regard to the statutory ban of FGM, it was recognized by the bill's co-sponsors and supporters that people of different faiths—Islamic, Christian, and indigenous African religions—followed this tradition. No particular religious tradition was targeted. Moreover, since FGM is a cultural practice embraced in its countries of origin by a wide range of people, both religious and nonreligious, it could not be the case that the legislation was covertly hostile to one religion in particular or even religion in general. Hence, the law genuinely meets the *Smith* standard of being facially neutral and generally applicable and avoids the flaws of legislation, fatal to a statute's constitutionality, so evident in the *Lukumi* decision.

In summation, whether or not the "compelling state interest" test survived, the anti-FGM ban could not be construed as a violation of its practitioners' free exercise of religion. Only one constitutional argument remains to defendants charged with the violation of the laws against FGM: the claim that the law abridges equal protection.

Equal Protection Considerations

Although the ban on FGM would survive a free exercise challenge, the question remains whether the statute violates the equal protection clause of the Fourteenth Amendment. In that the Federal Prohibition of Female Genital Mutilation Act outlaws *all* forms of FGM, including simple circumcision, the statute seeks to ban, at minimum, a procedure on females that is widely practiced on male children (nearly 60%) in the general population and that is religiously sanctioned in the Jewish community. Although the latter justifies the removal of part or all of the foreskin covering the glans of the penis of the male infant (traditionally on the eighth day) by reference to Genesis 17:11–12, male circumcision among the populace as a whole is legitimated in terms of health reasons, including the reduction in risk of penile and cervical cancer and sexually transmitted diseases like HIV. Popularized during the late nineteenth century as a means to discourage masturbation, male circumcision has been opposed in more recent times by those who hold that the practice jeopardizes the lives of infants, exposes them to unwarranted pain and health risks, diminishes sexual pleasure in adulthood, and consequently is medically unnecessary and a form of "child abuse."[96] Campaigns organized by such groups as the Intact Baby Movement and the National Organization of Circumcision Information Center have met with little success in generating public opposition to male circumcision. In *London v. Glasser* (1987), the California Supreme Court denied review of a case, previously dismissed by trial and lower appeals courts, in which it was alleged that a boy's constitutional rights were violated by circumcision (battery and false imprisonment).[97] Personal injury lawyers have been notably unsuccessful in suing hospitals and physicians for "depriving" males of their foreskins.[98] The legislative history of the FGM act, however, suggests that, whereas male circumcision is not regarded as "child abuse," FGM is, at least in the minds of the bill's sponsors. The distinction triggers equal protection concerns and places a burden on the government to show why such unequal treatment of males and females might be necessary.

Prior to 1971, the Supreme Court held that gender-based classifications did not require any special scrutiny, most often since they were regarded as "benign," i.e., designed to protect women in their traditional roles. However, *Reed v. Reed* (1971)[99] heralded a new era for the Court in terms of the equal protection of women. Although the Court claimed to use only "mere rationality" in declaring unconstitutional a statute preferring men to women as estate administrators, *Reed* signaled to legal scholars that equal protection claims would be examined with closer scrutiny than before. The four-justice plurality opinion, authored by Justice Brennan in *Frontiero v. Richardson* (1973),[100] explicitly disavowed the "mere rationality" standard, substituting "strict judicial scrutiny" by including gender classification with such other "suspect categories" as race, alienage, and national origin. The Court, however, was one vote short of establishing "strict-scrutiny" as the requisite standard in gender-based equal protection actions and three years later retreated in *Craig v. Boren* (1976)[101] by adopting an "intermediate level" of scrutiny. The justices held that "classifications by gender must serve important governmental objectives and must be substantially related to achievements of those objectives."[102] Whereas statutes examined under the lens of strict scrutiny almost always failed to pass constitutional muster, an intermediate level of review provided considerably more breathing space for the longevity of a statute governing gender relations.

Recently in *Fishbeck v. North Dakota*,[103] the U.S. Court of Appeals for the Eighth Circuit considered a suit filed by the mother of a baby son, who, contrary to the mother's wishes, was subjected to circumcision at the behest of the father. The plaintiff argued that, under the Equal Protection Clause of the Fourteenth Amendment, the North Dakota statute that banned FGM[104] should make it incumbent upon the Court to prohibit the practice of male circumcision. The Court declined to grant the mother standing to litigate on the grounds that, since the boy had already been circumcised, the case was moot.[105] Despite the Eighth Circuit's ruling, neither the federal nor state courts have yet to consider a claim that will surely ensue in a criminal prosecution of parents who violate federal or state statutes against FGM—a claim that is the reverse of *Fishbeck* and would not suffer from mootness. Such a criminal defendant may claim that, if male circumcision is legal, the Equal Protection Clause of the Fourteenth Amendment should equally protect female circumcision.

Defenders of the law may argue that, if the prevention of child abuse and protection of women's health are legitimate state interests and if FGM is demonstrated to endanger both women and children, then it stands to reason that banning FGM satisfies the "intermediate level of scrutiny" demanded by Fourteenth Amendment jurisprudence: it easily reaches the level of "important governmental objectives" and is "substantially related to achievements of those objectives." However, such a conclusion still does not explain why male circumcision is not considered child abuse, whereas FGM is. Both the American College of Obstetricians and Gynecologists and the American Pediatric Association have concluded that male circumcision is not an absolute medical necessity. Therefore, male circumcision should not be routine. These conclusions suggest that male circumcision is tolerated simply because it is customary, whereas FGM is not simply because it is foreign to American culture. In the eyes of some, the justification for gender-based classification and consequent unequal treatment therefore stands squarely on an uninterrogated cultural imperialism.

An Irigarayan Strategy

I want to suggest an alternative resolution to the equal protection question. Whereas legislation has been scrutinized by the Court to determine if biological factors encoded in statutes impermissibly have a disparate effect on men and women, the Court needs to recognize and embrace an "ethics of sexual difference"[106]: that the effects of male circumcision and FGM are different because male and female sexuality *in toto* are different. And it is not only that FGM endangers the physical health of its victims (so too does male circumcision, according to its opponents), it also removes the possibility for women to experience themselves as other than appendages to an androcentric culture and a masculinist psychic economy. In her work as a post-Lacanian feminist psychoanalyst, Luce Irigaray has argued that woman has been traditionally inscribed as the "other of the same" in patriarchal cultures—as the deviant, the marginalized, and the silenced—whose body and psyche are construed androcentrically. "He contains or envelops her with walls while enveloping himself and his things with her flesh."[107] Her very being is constructed as a mirror reflecting male political and sexual dominance.[108] In contrast to the androcentric construction of women in a patriarchal society, Irigaray sees in women's physiology an elaborate metaphor for the difference between men and women, between phallogocentric speech and gynocentric human relations that transcend and/or antedate speech. In contrast to androcentric language based on the logic of binary opposition, women's experience is founded on the morphology of her genitals. The woman's relational view of the world flows from a precognitive physical sensation. "As for woman, she touches herself in and of herself without any need for mediation, and before there is any way to distinguish activity from passivity. Woman 'touches herself' all the time, and moreover no one can forbid her to do so, for her genitals are formed of two lips in continuous contact."[109] This experience, which Irigaray calls "retouching,"[110] is metaphorized into the foundation of woman's difference from man, from the ethics of human relations to "women's ways of knowing." Clitoridectomy, excision of the labia minora and majora, and infibulation therefore are androcentric practices that efface this primal experience. By transforming girls into an androcentric image of women, these practices *eliminate* the fundamental difference of women from men—a difference that, for Irigaray, is woman, both anatomically and psychically.

Since the 1970s the Supreme Court has taken steps to rectify in law what has been notably unjust in an androcentric society. Whereas in the past women have been subjected to male hegemony in America through cultural and physical coercion, for instance, discrimination in schooling and employment and domestic violence, the judiciary has increasingly sought to legally recognize and protect the autonomy of women as free moral agents with equal rights. Except in cases of psychiatric treatment, women in America have been largely free from the horrors of FGM; however, FGM now threatens to reverse the gains that women have made in affirming these rights within the public and private spheres. Arguments about it as a ritual initiation into womanhood notwithstanding, the purpose of FGM seemingly is to construct woman and her sexuality phallomorphically for the sake of male pleasure and authority, even though it may cause her great physical and emotional pain and endanger her life and that of her child. Whereas Irigaray reads female genitals metaphorically as an affirmation of female *jouissance* and an opening to a new era of feminine spirituality, circumcision, excision, and infibulation close and cut off women from that future. An ethics of sexual difference recognizes that there is more than one sex and that unequal treatment—treating men and women differently—may be required for equal protection of men and women. For equality should not be confused with sameness. "The strategy of equality." Irigaray argues, "should always aim to get differences recognized."[111] Sameness in patriarchal culture is law that silences women. Sameness in patriarchal law is culture rendered male.

From an Irigarayan perspective, the ban on FGM coupled with the legality of male circumcision ensures that the movement toward equality between men and women will advance by treating men and women differently. Under U.S. constitutional precedent, the Equal Protection Clause has been judicially applied in cases where individuals of different races, ethnic groups, alienage, or sexes are similarly situated. In other words, similarly situated individuals cannot be treated differently. If individual male and female children are similarly situated, e.g., subject to male circumcision and female circumcision (rather than excision or infibulation), respectively, then to permit one practice and ban the other would violate Equal Protection and the very existence of anti-FGM statutes would be jeopardized. However, if the relation of female sexual organs to female sexuality and the female psyche is *in toto* different from that of the relation of male sexual organs to male sexuality and the male psyche, as Irigaray suggests, then male and female children are not similarly situated. In that case, banning FGM and permitting male circumcision would not violate the Equal Protection Clause.

Unfortunately, this legal argument, which ensures the protection of women and female children as well as the continued practice of male circumcision (particularly important to the Jewish community), is ironically undermined by several notable feminist critiques of the Irigarayan position. Since the first appearance of the "new French feminism" and *l'écriture feminine* in the 1970s as a force with which to be reckoned, numerous feminist critics have assailed Irigaray's position as "essentialist," i.e., women's position in society is predestined by her anatomy. Monique Plaza has argued that Irigarayan philosophy is no more than the return of the "Eternal Feminine."[112] Although Irigaray uses post-Lacanian psychoanalytic theory to deconstruct the patriarchal social order, some feminist critics, like Toril Moi,[113] suspect that Irigaray's attempt to articulate the "other of the same" in a gynocentric language is futile and simply reinscribes stereotypes of patriarchal rule. In any case, as Carolyn Burke argues, "We cannot 'apply' Irigaray's writing in any direct fashion."[114] If, contrary to Irigaray, women and men are not different, if their sexuality is a social construct, then they are similarly situated. Progressive feminism that seeks equality between the sexes, even if it means the abandonment of protections extended to women in an androcentric society, therefore strengthens the Equal Protection Clause arguments of those who would practice FGM. For if men and women are treated as if they are similarly situated, then how could the criminalization of FGM, but not that of male circumcision, be justified?

A Fishian Way Out?

The apparent contradiction between permitting male circumcision and prohibiting FGM suggests that there is something fundamentally unfair and intolerant about the latter's criminalization. It has become something of a crisis of conscience, particularly for those American feminist academics who pride themselves on their sensitivity and tolerance. Charges of cultural imperialism, particularly by Third World women who themselves have worked through educational means to end FGM, burn in their ears, and they are torn between their zealous defense of innocent young girls, subjected to a seemingly horrendous fate, and their belief in the right of self-determination, garnered from their experience as women oppressed by a male-dominated society. To choose between the two alternatives—to support or oppose the ban on FGM—is a "can't win" situation. One either tolerates a misogynous practice or becomes, in the eyes of many Third World Women, the latter-day incarnation of the 1950s "ugly American"—bigoted, opinionated, and condescending. There is seemingly no way out of the dilemma, as long as one holds to the values of a liberal society.

However, it is in this context that the observations of Stanley Fish, the renowned literary critic and legal scholar, may prove helpful. For Fish, liberalism is one of our most cherished illusions. In the tension between the two poles of liberalism illustrated above—humanitarianism and self-determination—the individual apparently must sacrifice one liberal value at the altar of the other. But the game played by those of us who live and believe in a liberal society is a collective hallucination. "Liberalism," contends Fish, "doesn't exist."[115] Liberalism reached its ascendancy in the Enlightenment and ensuing revolutions by overthrowing religious worldviews; yet, that did not mean that liberalism itself was not an ideology with well-defined boundaries. "Liberalism is tolerant only *within* the space demarcated by the operations of reason; anyone who steps outside that space will not be tolerated."[116] It may be true that liberalism was able to "grab the high moral ground"[117] by being notably more tolerant than its predecessors; however, that did not mean it was not intolerant.

What is "beyond the pale" always exists, although, in our myopia, we infrequently look up to see what lies at the liminal bounds of our society. Sequestered comfortably in the midst of everyday life, we can afford to be tolerant. In what he himself has entitled "Fish's first law of tolerance-dynamics," Fish argues that "toleration is exercised in inverse proportion to there being anything at stake."[118] The less significant the issue, the more tolerant we are. But for feminist scholars, lawyers, and activists, there is a great deal at stake over the issue of female genital mutilation, not only for those women who have been or will be victimized, but also for those who resist what may be considered a vestige of patriarchal barbarism. Scanning the horizon of the liberal society, critics of FGM see the "other" who lives "beyond the pale" staring back. The moment of engagement for both sides is mutually uncomprehending. The issue exposes not only the limits of tolerance, but also the problematic of liberalism's belief in its own "rational" discourse. Practitioners of FGM, whether motivated by religion or custom, seem impervious to liberalism's "reason." "It follows, then, that when observations made within different paradigms conflict, there is no principled (i.e., nonrhetorical) way to adjudicate the dispute."[119] Being "fair" in such a situation is an impossibility. There is no position that stands outside the dispute that can reconcile the irreconcilable. Intellectuals may harbor the illusion that understanding the illusion of "fairness" in a liberal society privileges their viewpoint, but their very insight itself is a political position. They are no more outside of the fray than any other political actor. What Fish calls the "antifoundationalist theory hope,"[120] which transcends the conflict of partisan politics, no more provides a way out of political dilemmas than do party platforms.

The dilemma faced by feminists therefore unmasks not just the "unfairness" inherent in the particular circumstances, but rather the "unfairness" that is and always was the very condition of a liberal society. The impossibility of "pure justice" in the liberal political order offers two alternatives: either resignation and reticence or political engagement and rhetoric. Political apathy, however, is an impossible choice for most individuals who reach an impasse through political engagement. The only alternative is to enter the fray, even though "fairness" is precluded from the very outset. For it is only through rhetorical strategies that political actors can convert their opponents or impose their political viewpoint. These strategies are certainly the ones adopted by Representative Schroeder, Alice Walker, and others—female politicians, womanist writers, and feminist academics—in order to either educate and transform those who embrace FGM or to compel their compliance with its ban. In America, as in all human societies, relations among individuals in a community are mediated by law, and law, Fish reminds us, is force. The use of coercion, whether it is a penal code or the leverage gained from tying strings to foreign assistance, is a rhetorical strategy that, although distasteful to those of us accustomed to liberal illusions of "fairness," is inevitable. Neither Pat Schroeder nor Alice Walker have a guilty conscience. The Fishian approach suggests that, for those of us opposed to FGM, neither should we.

Notes

1. Alice Walker, *Possessing the Secret of Joy* (New York: Simon & Schuster, 1993), and Alice Walker and Pratibha Parmar, *Warrior Marks: Female Genital Mutilation and the Sexual Blinding of Women* (New York: Harcourt Brace, 1993).

2. See Timothy Egan, "Ancient Ritual and a Mother's Asylum Plea," *New York Times*, 4 March 1994, sec. A23. Also Stuart Wasserman and Maria Puente, "Mutilation Fear Wins Halt to Deportation," *USA Today*, 24 March 1994, p. 1.

3. 1996 WL 379826 (B.I.A.).

4. INS Resource Information Center, *Alert Series-Women-Female Genital Mutilation*, Ref. No. AL/NGA/94.001 (July 1994).

5. Phyllis Coven, Office of International Affairs, INS, *Considerations for Asylum Officers Adjudicating Claims from Women* (1995).

6. 1996 WL 379826 (B.I.A.) at 2.

7. " (a) Authority to apply for asylum
"(1) In general
"Any alien who is physically present in the United States or who arrives in the United States (whether or not at a designated port of arrival and including an alien who is brought to the United States after having been interdicted in international or United States waters), irrespective of such alien's status, may apply for asylum in accordance with this section or, where applicable, section (b) of this title.
8 U.S.C. § 1158.
"(b) Asylum interviews . . .
"(ii) Referral of certain aliens
"If the officer determines at the time of the interview that an alien has a credible fear of persecution (within the meaning of the clause (v)), the alien shall be detained for further consideration of the application for asylum. . . .
"(v) Credible fear of persecution defined
"For the purposes of this paragraph, the term 'credible fear of persecution' means that there is a significant possibility, taking into account the credibility of the statements made by the alien in support of the alien's claim and such other facts as are known to the officer, that this alien could establish eligibility for asylum under section 1158 of this title."
8 U.S.C. § 1225.

8. 42 U.S.C. § 2000bb.

9. 494 U.S. 872 (1990).

10. 1997 WL 345322 (1997).

11. *Sherbert v. Verner*, 374 U.S. 398, 406 (1963).

12. *Prince v. Massachusetts*, 321 U.S. 158, 170 (1944).

13. Sharon Lerner, "Rite or Wrong," *Village Voice*, 1 April 1997, 45.

14. Although advocates of female circumcision, excision of the clitoris, and infibulation of the vaginal opening regard "female genital mutilation" as a culturally biased, pejorative label, I believe that, given the pain, emotional trauma, and devastating gynecological and obstetric consequences of these procedures, the term "FGM" is fully warranted.

15. Among these countries are Benin, Burkina Faso, Chad, Djibouti, Egypt, Ethiopia, Gambia, Guinea, Ivory Coast, Kenya, Mauritania, Niger, Nigeria, Oman, Senegal, Sierra

Leone, Somalia, Sudan, Tanzania, Togo, Uganda, United Arab Emirates, Upper Volta, and Yemen.

16. See Joan Beck, "We Must Not Ignore the Cultural Abuse of Women and Girls," *Chicago Tribune*, 6 February 1994, p. 3; see also Nahid Toubia, "Female Circumcision as a Health Issue," *New England Journal of Medicine* 331, no. 11 (15 September 1994): 712–16

17. Ahmed Abu-el-Futuh Shandall, "Circumcision and Infibulation of Females," *Sudanese Medical Journal* 5, no. 4 (1967). Cited in J. A. Verzin, "Sequelae of Female Circumcision," *Tropical Doctor* 5 (1975): 163–69.

18. Toubia, "Female Circumcision," 712. Cf. Minority Rights Group International, *Female Genital Mutilation: Proposals for Change* (1992), n.p.: "This [circumcision], the mildest type, affects only a small proportion of the millions of women concerned."

19. *Female Genital Mutilation: World Health Assembly Calls for the Elimination of Harmful Traditional Practices*, World Health Organization, Press Release, 12 May 1993.

20. Ibid.

21. William Raspberry, "Barbaric 'Tradition' Is Really Torture Aimed at Females," *Chicago Tribune*, 29 November 1993, p. 19.

22. Marlise Simons, "Mutilation of Girls' Genitals: Ethnic Gulf in French Court," *New York Times*, 23 November 1993, sec. A13.

23. Walker *Possessing the Secret of Joy*, 86.

24. See *Declaration of the Rights of the Child* (1959): "The child shall enjoy special protection . . . to enable him [*sic*] to develop physically, mentally, morally, spiritually and socially in a healthy and normal manner and in conditions of freedom and dignity"; *Declaration on the Elimination of Discrimination Against Women* (1967), Article 3: "All appropriate measures shall be taken to educate public opinion and to direct national aspirations towards the eradication of prejudice and the abolition of customary and all other practices which are based on the idea of the inferiority of women"; *Declaration on the Protection of All Human Persons from Being Subjected to Torture and Other Cruel Inhuman or Degrading Treatment or Punishment* (1975), Article 2: "Any act of torture or other cruel, inhuman or degrading treatment or punishment is an offense to human dignity and shall be condemned as a denial of the purposes of the Charter of the United Nations and as a violation of the human rights and fundamental freedoms proclaimed in the Universal Declaration of Human Rights." Also, *Female Circumcision: Statement of WHO Position and Activities*, World Health Organization, Press Release, June 1982: "WHO supports the recommendations of the Khartoum Seminar of 1979 on Traditional Practices Affecting the Health of Women. These were that governments should adopt clear national policies to abolish female circumcision, and to intensify educational programs to inform the public about the harmfulness of female circumcision. . . .

"WHO has consistently and unequivocally advised that female circumcision should not be practiced by any health professionals in any setting—including hospitals or other health establishments."

25. Cf. Note, "What's Culture Got to Do with It? Excising the Harmful Tradition of Female Circumcision," *Harvard Law Review* 106 (1993): 1944.

26. See Katherine Brennan, "The Influence of Cultural Relativism on International Human Rights Law: Female Circumcision as a Case Study," *Law and Equality* 7 (1989), 383.

27. *Nightline*, ABC News (10 February 1994).

28. Seble Dawit and Salem Mekuria, "The West Just Doesn't Get It," *New York Times*, 7 December 1993, sec. A27.

29. Jo Carol Becker, "Alice Walker's Cause in the Post-Bobbit Era" *New York Observer*, 29 November 1993.

30. See, e.g., Association of African Women for Research and Development (AAWORD); Women's Action Group on Female Excision and Infibulation (WAGFEI);

Inter-African Committee on Traditional Practices Affecting the Health of Women and Children; FORWARD International; Commission Internationale Pour L'Abolition des Mutilations Sexuelles; National Council of Women in Kenya; and Les Femmes Voltaique.

31. *Draft of Conference Recommendations,* A/Conf.171/L.1, 49 (English).

32. A. M. Rosenthal, "Female Genital Mutilation," *New York Times,* 23 December 1993.

33. See Minority Rights Group International, *Female Genital Mutilation,* n.p.: "Donor governments and international agencies should request aid recipients to incorporate in the projects they are funding, measures *to abolish practices sustaining the perpetuation of female genital mutilation.*"

34. "The bill is needed," argued A. M. Rosenthal of the *New York Times.* "The goal could be to use international clout: give special help to governments fighting mutilation on their soil, cut grants and loans to governments that refuse or stall." Rosenthal, "Female Genital Torture," *New York Times,* 12 November 1993, sec. A33. Cf. Maynard H. Merwine, "How Africa Understands Female Circumcision" (letter to the editor), *New York Times,* 24 November 1993: "To demand, as Mr. Rosenthal does, that economic aid be used to force a change in a tradition central to many Africans and Arabs is the height of ethnocentrism. A better approach would be for Western peoples to try to understand the importance of these traditions to those who practice them. The West should encourage Africans to have the surgical part of the ceremony performed by competent medical practitioners."

35. "Born Female and Fettered," *New York Times,* 19 February 1994, p. 18.

36. "Beginning 1 year after September 30, 1996, the Secretary of the Treasury shall instruct the United States Executive Director of each international financial institution to use the voice and vote of the United States to oppose any loan or other utilization of the funds of their respective institution, other than to address basic human needs, for the government of any country which the Secretary of the Treasury determines—

"(1) has, as a cultural custom, a known history of the practice of female genital mutilation; and

"(2) has not taken steps to implement educational programs designed to prevent the practice of female genital mutilation."
22 U.S.C. § 262k–2(a).

37. 18 U.S.C. § 116 (a).

38. "(b) A surgical operation is not a violation of this section if the operation is—

"(1) necessary to the health of the person on whom it is performed, and is performed by a person licensed in the place of its performance as a medical practitioner; or

"(2) performed on a person in labor or who has just given birth and is performed for medical purposes connected with that labor or birth by a person licensed in the place it is performed as a medical practitioner, midwife, or person in training to become such a practitioner or midwife."
18 U.S.C. § 116 (b)(1) & (2).

39. "(b) The Secretary of Health and Human Services shall do the following:

"(1) Compile data on the number of females living in the United States who have been subjected to female genital mutilation (whether in the United States or in their countries of origin), including a specification of the number of girls under the age of 18 who have been subjected to such mutilation.

"(2) Identify communities in the United States that practice female genital mutilation, and design and carry out research activities on the physical and psychological health effects of such practice. Such outreach activities shall be designed and implemented in collaboration with ethnic groups practicing such mutilation and with representatives of organizations with expertise in preventing such practice.

"(3) Develop recommendations for the education of students of schools of medicine and osteopathic medicine regarding female genital mutilation and complications arising from such mutilation. Such recommendations shall be disseminated to such schools." 1 U.S.C. §1(b).

40. Ca. Penal § 273.4; Ca. Health & Safety § 124170.

41. 11 Del. [Penal] C. § 780.

42. M.S.A. § 609.2245 [Penal]; M.S.A. § 144.872 [Health].

43. NDCC, 12.1–36–01 [Penal].

44. T.C.A. § 39–13–110 [Penal].

45. W.S.A. 146.35 [Penal & Health].

46. Patricia Schroeder, "Female Genital Mutilation—A Form of Child Abuse," *New England Journal of Medicine* 331, no. 11 (15 September 1994): 739.

47. U.S. Constitution, First Amendment: "Congress shall make no law respecting an establishment of religion or prohibiting the free exercise thereof."

48. U.S. Constitution, Fourteenth Amendment: "No State shall make or enforce any law which shall abridge the privileges or immunities of citizens of the United States; nor shall any State deprive any person of life, liberty, or property, without due process of law; nor deny to any person within its jurisdiction the equal protection of the laws."

49. Other common explanations used to justify FGM include: to augment male sexual pleasure, to inhibit women's sexual desire, to protect women from rape, to guarantee her chastity, to enhance her marriageability, to improve the aesthetic appearance of female genitals, and to enhance her cleanliness.

50. See, e.g., Ibrahim Bukhari, *Anbiya', bab 8*, and Muslim, Fada'il, *Trad. 151*.

51. *Muhyi al-Din Abu Zakariya' Yahya B. Sharaf B. Muri, Commentary on Muslim, Tahara, trad.* 50 (ed. Cairo, 1283, i, 328). See "Circumcision," *The Encyclopedia of Islam*, new ed., ed. C. E. Bosworth et al., vol. 5 (Leiden: Brill, 1986), 20–22.

52. Taha Ba'asher, "Psychosocial Aspects of Female Circumcision" (paper presented before the Symposium on the Changing Status of Sudanese Women, 23 February–1 March 1979), cited in Minority Rights Group International, "Female Genital Mutilation," n.p. Cf. Nahid Toubia, "Testimony on Female Genital Mutilation," Subcommittee on International Security, International Organizations, and Human Rights, Committee on Foreign Affairs, House of Representatives, Congress of the United States, 28 September 1993, 4: "To justify this gross social injustice we have been told for years that it is part of being a good woman and that it is a sacred requirement of religion. We now know that it is not sacred and has nothing to do with religion."

53. *New York Times*, 26 June 1997, sec. A12. The Egyptian court, however, maintained the ban against FGM by medically-*unqualified* persons, e.g., midwives, barbers, etc., who traditionally used razors or sharp stones to perform the procedure.

54. "What's Culture Got to Do with It?" 1944, 1952. There is no indication that the author's opinion in this "student note" was informed by any academic expertise in world religions in general or Islam in particular.

55. *U.S. v. Ballard*, 322 U.S. 78 (1944).

56. "If one could be sent to jail because a jury in a hostile environment found those teachings false, little would be left of religious freedom." Ibid, 87.

57. Minority Rights Group, *Female Genital Mutilation*, n.p.

58. *Church of Lukumi Babalu Aye v. City of Hialeah*, 508 U.S. 520 (1993).

59. Rosenthal, "Female Genital Mutilation": "Representative Schroeder's fact list says the male equivalent would be amputation or cutting of the penis and its surrounding tissues—a description that should get any Congressman's attention."

60. *Nightline*, ABC News (10 February 1994).

61. Toubia, "Female Circumcision," 714.

62. Minority Rights Group, *Female Genital Mutilation*, n.p.: "To those from other cultures unfamiliar with the force of this particular community identity, the very concept of amputation of the genitals carries a shock value which does not exist for most women in the areas concerned. For them, not to amputate would be shocking. . . . But the fact is that in psychiatric or psychoanalytic terms, we simply do not know."

63. Toubia, "Female Circumcision," 714.

64. See, e.g., Alice Walker's citation of the Hite Report in the appendix "Female Genitalia" of her *Warrior Marks*, 365.

65. In *Lukumi Babalu Aye*, the city of Hialeah had passed city ordinances against animal sacrifice within city limits, excepting kosher slaughter. The court found that an ostensibly neutral ordinance was actually motivated by animus toward practitioners of the Santería religion.

"Although a law targeting religious beliefs as such is never permissible, if the object of a law is to infringe upon or restrict practices because of their religious motivation, the law is not neutral.

"We reject the contention advanced by the city that our inquiry must end with the text of the laws at issue. Facial neutrality is not determinative. The Free Exercise Clause, like the Establishment Clause, extends beyond facial discrimination. The Clause 'forbids subtle departures from neutrality' and 'covert suppression of religious beliefs.' Official action that targets religious conduct for distinctive treatment cannot be shielded by mere compliance with the requirement of facial neutrality. The Free Exercise Clause protects against government hostility which is masked, as well as overt." *Lukumi*, 508 U.S. at 533 (citations omitted).

66. Laurence Tribe, *American Constitutional Law* (Mineola, N.Y.: Foundation Press, 1977), 1251.

67. *Sherbert v. Verner*, 374 U.S. 398, 406 (1963), citing *Thomas v. Collins*, 323 U.S. 516, 530 (1945).

68. *Smith*, 494 U.S. at 882. The dissent argued that precedent permitted religious exemption from universally applicable, facially neutral laws except in cases where the government showed a "compelling state interest" by citing the following cases: *Hernandez v. Commissioner*, 490 U.S. 680 (1989), *Hobbie v. Unemployment Appeals Commission of Fla.*, 480 U.S. 136 (1987), *Bowen v. Roy*, 476 U.S. 693 (1986), *United States v. Lee*, 455 U.S. 252 (1982), *Thomas v. Review Bd. of Indiana Employment Security*, 450 U.S. 707 (1981), *Wisconsin v. Yoder*, 406 U.S. 205 (1972), and *Sherbert v. Verner*, 374 U.S. 398 (1963). See *Smith*, 494 U.S. at 907.

69. *Smith*, 494 U.S. at 881.

70. 42 U.S.C. § 2000bb(b).

71. *Smith*, 494 U.S. at 903 (O'Connor, J. concurring in judgment) ("The Court's ruling today not only misreads settled First Amendment precedent; it appears to be unnecessary to this case. I would reach the same result applying our established free exercise jurisprudence") and *Smith*, 494 U.S. at 907 (Blackmun, J., Brennan, J., and Marshall, J., dissenting) ("[The majority] effectuates a wholesale overturning of settled law concerning the Religion Clauses of our Constitution. One hopes that the court is aware of the consequences. This distorted view of our precedents leads the majority to conclude that strict scrutiny of a state law burdening the free exercise of religion is a 'luxury' that a well-ordered society cannot afford, and that the repression of minority religions is an 'unavoidable consequence of democratic government.' I do not believe the Founders thought their dearly bought freedom from religious persecution a 'luxury,' but an essential element of liberty—and they could not have thought religious intolerance 'unavoidable,' for they drafted the Religion Clauses precisely in order to avoid that intolerance" [citations omitted]).

72. *Lukumi*, 508 U.S. at 571 (Souter, J., concurring in judgment) ("The *Smith* rule may be

reexamined consistently with principles of *stare decisis*") and *Lukumi*, 508 U.S. at 577 (Blackmun, J., and O'Connor, J., concurring in judgment) ("I continue to believe that *Smith* was wrongly decided, because it ignored the value of religious freedom as an affirmative individual liberty and treated the Free Exercise Clause as no more than an antidiscrimination principle").

73. "The First Amendment declares that Congress shall make no law respecting an establishment of religion or prohibiting the free exercise thereof. The Fourteenth Amendment has rendered the legislatures of the states as incompetent as the Congress to enact such laws." *Cantwell v. Connecticut*, 310 U.S. 296, 303 (1940).

74. §5 of the Fourteenth Amendment: "The Congress shall have the power to enforce, by appropriate legislation, the provisions of this article."

75. *Boerne*, 1997 WL 345322 at 13.

76. Ibid. at 13.

77. Ibid. at 10.

78. Ibid. at 16.

79. Ibid. at 22.

80. *Lukumi*, 508 U.S. at 571–72.

81. *Parham v. J.R.*, 442 U.S. 584, 602 (1979).

82. See *Meyer v. Nebraska*, 262 U.S. 390 (1923), and *Pierce v. Society of Sisters*, 268 U.S. 510 (1925).

83. *Prince*, 321 U.S. at 166. Cf. *May v. Anderson*, 345 U.S. 528, 533 (1953), where the Court held that parents exercise an "immediate right to the care, custody, management and companionship of . . . minor children."

84. *Cleveland Board of Education v. La Fleur*, 414 U.S. 632, 639–40 (1974).

85. *Griswold v. Connecticut*, 381 U.S. 479, 483 (1965).

86. *Wisconsin v. Yoder*, 406 U.S. 205 (1972).

87. Ibid. at 231.

88. Ibid.

89. *Parham*, 442 U.S. at 602 (citation omitted).

90. Schroeder, "Female Genital Mutilation," 740.

91. *Roe v. Wade*, 410 U.S. 113 (1973).

92. "With respect to the State's important and legitimate interest in the health of the mother, the 'compelling point,' in the light of present medical knowledge, is at approximately the end of the first trimester. This is so because of the now-established medical fact . . . that until the end of the first trimester mortality in abortion may be less than mortality in normal childbirth. It follows that, from and after this point, a State may regulate the abortion procedure to the extent that the regulation reasonably relates to the preservation and protection of maternal health." Ibid. at 163 (citations omitted).

93. *Planned Parenthood v. Casey*, 505 U.S. 833 (1985).

94. "The State has legitimate interests from the outset of the pregnancy in protecting the health of the woman and the life of the fetus that may become a child." Ibid. at 846.

95. *Casey* itself overruled previous Supreme Court rulings that had struck down such state restrictions on abortion as the physician must inform the patient of the risks of abortion, alternatives to abortion, and the gestational age of the fetus; the physician must inform the patient of state-printed materials describing alternatives to abortion; requiring parental consent to perform an abortion on a minor; and a 24-hour waiting period.

96. See, e.g., William E. Brigman, "Circumcision as Child Abuse: The Legal and Constitutional Issues," *Journal of Family Law* 23, no. 3, (1984–1985): 337.

97. London v. Glasser, S001009, *cert. denied* (29 July 1987).

98. Rorie Sherman, "Circumcision Suits Risky to Pursue," *National Law Journal*, 10, no. 4 (22 February 1988): 9.

99. 404 U.S. 71 (1971).

100. 411 U.S. 677 (1973).

101. 429 U.S. 190 (1976).

102. Ibid.

103. 115 F.3d 580 (1997).

104. "12.1–36–01 Surgical alteration of the genitals of female minor—
"Penalty—Exception.

"1. Except as provided in subsection 2, any person who knowingly separates or surgically alters normal, healthy, functioning genital tissue of a female minor is guilty of a Class C felony.

"2. A surgical operation is not a violation of this section if a licensed medical practitioner performs the operation to correct an anatomical abnormality or to remove diseased tissue that is an immediate threat to the health of the female minor. In applying this subsection, any belief that the operation is required as a matter of custom, ritual, or standard of practice may not be taken into consideration." NDCC, 12.1–36-01

105. "She believes that circumcision of males is just as wrong as that of females, and that the State is at fault for not treating the two procedures equally. Still, we do not see that the plaintiff Fishbeck has standing to invoke the federal judicial process. The injury that her son received, if it is an injury, is in the past. Nothing that happens in this lawsuit can change it. Similarly, there is no measurable likelihood that the situation will recur in the future." *Fishbeck*, 115 F.3d at 581.

106. Luce Irigaray, "Sexual Difference," in *An Ethics of Sexual Difference*, trans. Carolyn Burke and Gillian C. Gill (Ithaca, N.Y.: Cornell University Press, 1993), 5–19.

107. Ibid., 11.

108. Luce Irigaray, "The Blind Spot of an Old Dream of Symmetry," *Speculum of the Other Woman*, trans. Gillian C. Gill (Ithaca, N.Y.: Cornell University Press, 1985), 54.

109. Luce Irigaray, *This Sex Which Is Not One*, trans, Catherine Porter with Carolyn Burke (Ithaca, N.Y.: Cornell University Press, 1985), 24.

110. Luce Irigaray, "The limits of transference," in *The Irigaray Reader*, trans. David Macey with Margaret Whitford, ed. Margaret Whitford (London: Basil Blackwell, 1991), 110.

111. Luce Irigaray, "Why define sexed rights?" in *je, tous, nous. Toward a Culture of Difference*, trans. Alison Martin (New York: Routledge, 1993), 84.

112. Monique Plaza, "'Phallomorphic Power' and the 'Psychology of Woman': A Patriarchal Chain," trans. M. David and J. Hodges, in *Human Sexual Relations: A Reader*, ed. Mike Brake (New York: Penguin, 1982), 352. See Ann Rosalind Jones, "Writing the Body: Toward an understanding of *l'écriture feminine*," *Feminist Studies* 7, no. 2 (Summer 1981) 247–63.

113. "Irigaray's attempt to establish a theory of femininity that escapes patriarchal specul(ariz)ation necessarily lapses into a form of essentialism. Her efforts to provide woman with 'a gallant representation of her own sex' are likewise doomed to become another enactment of the inexorable logic of the Same." Toril Moi, *Sexual/Textual Politics: Feminist Literary Theory* (London: Routledge, 1985), 143.

114. Carolyn Burke, "Irigaray through the Looking Glass," *Feminist Studies* 7, no. 2, (Summer 1983): 303.

115. Stanley Fish, *There's No Such Thing as Free Speech . . . and It's a Good Thing Too* (New York: Oxford University Press, 1994), 138.

116. Ibid., 137.

117. Ibid., 138.

118. Ibid., 217.

119. Stanley Fish, *Doing What Comes Naturally: Change, Rhetoric and the Practice of Theory* (Durham: Duke University, 1989), 487.

120. Ibid., 322–24.

13

RITA NAKASHIMA BROCK

Politicians, Pastors, and Pimps

Christianity and Prostitution Policies

When Fortress Press published *Casting Stones: Prostitution and Liberation in Asia and the United States*,[1] Marshall Johnson, director of the Lutheran Press, received several phone calls from pastors protesting a book on prostitution published by a religious press. Johnson's reply: "One of the few things of which we can be fairly certain about Jesus is that he had a remarkably positive attitude toward prostitutes." The editors at Fortress and those indignant clergy demonstrate the range of traditional Christian perspectives on prostitution, from sympathetic to righteously indignant.

Throughout our history, sympathetic Christians, both laity and clergy, have often evidenced a skepticism toward any structures of power that judge people based on conventional forms of morality. Jesus, who drew on the Hebrew prophetic tradition, is described as refusing to scapegoat prostituted women or judge women by double standards; he seems to have respected many kinds of marginalized people, who were active and important in his movement.[2] This compassionate attitude toward the most outcast in conventional society has fueled many movements for justice, civil rights, and liberation. That Christian commitment to justice also lies behind this analysis of secular and sacred attitudes and policies on prostitution.

In contrast to a compassionate perspective, those most powerful in the official, clerical church have often used their power to persecute, ostracize, or execute those deemed outside their definition of orthodox theology and behavior. Of special note in the material below is how far many church theologians strayed from the gospels in their judgments about prostituted women and how much state policy follows from official church attitudes, rather than from movements for justice. This essay explores that problematic history and its impact on public policy, suggests solutions for better policy, and explores the possibilities of a liberating Christian theology.

The Church Theologians

During the 1996 U.S. elections, Dick Morris, the presidential advisor and architect of traditional family values, was discovered consorting with a prostitute. If we think his behavior violates traditional family values, we would be wrong for much of Christian history. In fact, many of the church's major formative theologians assumed that prostitutes were necessary to preserve the patriarchal family, and they advocated social policies on that basis. The history of official church theology and policy gives us a picture not only of Christianity's sex policies, but also of secular state laws concerning prostitution, which are still influenced by the patriarchal values of the official church, despite the constitutional separation of church and state.

Most major theologians in the first millennium and a half of Christian history wrote about the body and sex from the experience of celibacy, and they problematized sexuality altogether, as well as most forms of human physical intimacy.[3] We must keep in mind, however, that sexuality was ambiguous and politically charged, especially in the early history of the church under Roman persecution, and modern attitudes about human sexuality as personal fulfillment were unknown.[4]

Prostitutes were a necessary evil, according to Thomas Aquinas, as they were permitted by God in order to prevent male lust from escalating out of control. "Sewers," he notes, "are necessary to guarantee the wholesomeness of palaces." Otherwise, he worried, "sodomy" and other worse crimes might result. While the money paid to prostitutes is paid for an unlawful purpose, according to Aquinas, the giving itself is not unlawful and the woman could retain what she received.[5] In other words, prostitutes protect the "good" women of the family from the demands of male sin.

This dichotomy of female sewers and saints is one of the origins of the madonna/whore phenomenon in the West, where women are regarded as either pure and "good" or sexually active and "bad." Simone de Beauvoir noted that:

> it has often been remarked that the necessity exists of sacrificing one part of the female sex in order to save the other and prevent worse troubles . . . . a caste of 'shameless women' allows the 'honest woman' to be treated with the most chivalrous respect.[6]

Legislation about prostituted women follows this division of females into good, chaste women (the "virgin" Mary) and bad, sexual women (the "prostitute" Mary Magdalene—who was in fact a resurrection witness and is never said to be a prostitute in the Christian Scriptures). Medieval canon lawyers developed the legislation that came to dominate in Europe. Modesty in behavior was women's protection, and any woman who did not act modestly, who, for example, was sexually ardent, was deemed at heart a prostitute, though she need not be classified as one as long as she remained faithful to her husband. During periods in history when women who were wives were severely restricted in movement, clothing, residence, etc., prostitutes were tolerated and allowed to move with few restrictions. In the early Middle Ages, prostitutes in Europe had guilds and even marched with guild status in religious processions.[7]

Medieval canon lawyers regarded women as having no self control, particularly in regard to sexual matters.[8] In this sense, any woman was assumed to be at heart a prostitute unless she could prove herself otherwise. Hence, the rigidity of dress, conduct, and movement of women testified to their status as "good" or "bad." This meant, however, that medieval church lawyers did not especially condemn the prostitute for her activities, as she was merely acting out the sexuality that good women repressed; they felt that the more severe punishment should fall on those who made a profit from her—i.e., pimps, procurers, brothel keepers, and even customers. While they recognized that many women turned to prostitution out of economic necessity, this was not a mitigating circumstance (despite the fact that poverty *was* taken to be a mitigating circumstance in stealing or murder). The canon lawyers did, however, count a woman or girl sold into prostitution not culpable for her actions.[9]

The sex industry flourished in medieval Europe as it has throughout human history when women are economically dependent on men and when traditional patterns of economic support are disrupted by wars, poverty, rapid urbanization, or natural disasters. Prostituted slaves followed various European armies and were regarded as essential not only for sexual services, but also for medical care, cooking, laundry, and cleaning camp. In addition, the church provided a steady supply of customers. For example, when the Council of Constance was held in Switzerland between 1414 and 1418 in order to end the great Schism and to reform the medieval church, nearly 700 prostitutes also came to town to provide sexual services for the ecclesiastics.[10]

The church had great influence on the development of secular prostitution law, an influence that was quite ambiguous. In the later Middle Ages prostitution was regulated by forcing prostitutes to live in certain parts of the city, to wear certain types of dress, and to refrain from public soliciting. Attempts to prohibit it were found impossible to maintain, and most city governments quickly went back to regulating prostitutes.[11]

The Protestant reformers of the sixteenth century are widely regarded as having a more positive view of sexuality because they repudiated celibacy and abolished monasticism. However, it is more accurate to say that they held a more negative view of celibacy as a possible means of grace.[12] The reformers generally did not affirm the sexuality of women as part of their "reform." Rather, marriage became the sole locus of sexual activity for both men and women.[13] In a posted warning to Wittenburg students about consorting with prostitutes, Luther prefigured the several changes that would come about in both ecclesiastical and civil attitudes toward prostitution as the result of "reform":

> Through special enemies of our faith the devil has sent some whores here to ruin our poor young men. As an old and faithful preacher I ask you in fatherly fashion, dear children, that you believe assuredly that the evil spirit sent these whores here and that they are dreadful, shabby, stinking, loathsome, and syphilitic, as daily experience unfortunately demonstrates.[14]

Luther shifted the locus of immoral agency from male lust to the prostitute who has been sent by the devil to corrupt "poor young men." One wonders whose daily experience he meant and who is included as a child of God. The deep misogyny in this statement has its echoes in the attitude of those pastors who believed a Christian press should not discuss prostitution. Protestant reformers, who blamed the "sinful" prostitute rather than the pimp, the procurer, the brothel owner, or the customer, contributed further to confusing the root causes and agents of culpability with the victims of immoral behavior.

The Realities

In reality, Western prostitution historically involved coercion of those prostituted. Factors such as the disruption of economic support systems for women and children, as well as gender systems that subordinate women and others who are young and vulnerable, feed systems that serve the needs and whims of those with power. Prostitution has involved the use of slave brothels by armies and temples. Prostituted children have often been sold, kidnapped or entrapped into prostitution, as they are today. Rape and violence are used to socialize girls for being prostituted, and the use of drugs and alcohol entraps those exploited. The attempt to capture such phenomena under the labels of "choice" or "sin" simply masks exploitation, both historically and currently.

The dominant American culture is shaped by the legacy of Christian religious dualism, which projects blame for prostitution on females. In the popular culture and in social policy, Christian values about sex and sensuality continue to predominate, either in prudishness about the body or in counterreactions that overemphasize sex and use it to shock or sell products.[15] That which passes for a progressive libertarian, nonjudgmental attitude toward sexuality often relies on its opposite for its power to lure or to be iconoclastic. Libertarian ideologies that depict prostitution as an example of sexual freedom mask its exploitative dimensions, which are enormous. Christian condemnations of prostitution, libertarian arguments for legalization, and laws about prostitution focus on the regulation of human sexual activity, rather than on the misuse of power.

Today, the *average* age of entry into prostitution in the United States is fourteen and *at least* 85% are victims of sexual abuse. Most adult women began being prostituted as children. Young women are sometimes lured into what is marketed to them as "easy" money and exciting glamour, illusions promoted by much of mainstream advertising, which commercializes sex. Pimps wait in bus stations, roam city streets, visit adolescent beauty pageants, and wander shopping malls recruiting girls and boys. Pimps provide the commodity purchased by the politicians, manual laborers, diplomats, doctors, celebrities, judges, police officers, and pastors who cruise the poor neighborhoods of cities and towns looking for children and young women to perform for them. To survive being raped, having strangers violate one's body, enduring repeated physical violence, working 365 days a year, and living under the constant shadow of murder or arrest requires the psychological resources used by those enduring torture and war. Many do not survive, and those that do are not unscathed. The close proximity or overlap of prostitution with the drug trade in most countries enmeshes addiction and high-stakes violence with sexual exploitation. The primary goal of those prostituted is survival, which usually means tolerating brutality from a pimp or brothel manager—in addition to avoiding arrest, or being cheated, humiliated, beaten, mutilated, or murdered. There is nothing particularly glamorous about the reality of the experience. As one survivor reports:

> A fifty dollar bill. . . . When I stepped into your car you violated my body, asking me to call you "daddy." . . . You not only fucked with my body, you fucked with my mind. Afterwards, I held the fifty-dollar bill to my stomach as I threw up, sickened by what had just happened. And that feeling is still the same, even after four years have passed me by. I've been violated by every type of man—rich, poor, ugly, good looking, every race. I have no respect for you.[16]

This contempt for customers, usually called johns or tricks, expressed by this survivor, is typical and is usually hidden behind whatever performance is required to please the customer for pay.

The Historical Legacy

Christian official theology has had an enormous impact on how the laws about prostitution throughout the world, and especially in the United States and Asia, have been developed. Though U.S. constitutional law forbids an explicit link between the church and the state, in fact many of the laws surrounding prostitution are deeply rooted in the Christian history of the West. Official Christianity, as men in power have understood and used it, has had a direct role in social attitudes toward the body and sex, and those social attitudes carry over into legislation.

The Supreme Court of the United States in 1908 succinctly gave the moral and paternalistic arguments for the prohibition of prostitution:

> [Prostitution] refers to women (*sic*) who for hire or without hire offer their bodies to indiscriminate intercourse with men. The lives and example of such persons are in hostility to the idea of the family, as consisting in and springing from the union for life of one man and one woman in the holy estate of matrimony; the sure foundation of all that is stable and noble in our civilization, the best guaranty of that reverent morality which is the source of all beneficent progress in social and political improvement.[17]

Defining prostitution as *female* promiscuity, the Court echoed a history of Christian attitudes. The Supreme Court describes it as violating "holy" matrimony, the bedrock of civilization and guarantor of morals. This mentality about heterosexual marriage echoes still in the conservative rhetoric surrounding gay marriage, out-of-wedlock pregnancy, and feminism. The implicit assumptions lie with regulating sexual activity, not misused power, since marriage itself has both dimensions of power and the regulation of sexual activity.

The impact of Christianity on international law has influenced the most recent development of legal statutes in Asia. Where once prostitution was regarded with attitudes much like those in medieval Europe, as necessary though perhaps not desirable, the historical impact of both Protestant moralism and the Catholic counter-Reformation on current international law was to strengthen the view that prostitution is a religious and civil offense and should be criminalized.[18]

As with all social institutions, sex industries and sexual exploitation exist within particular societies because political, economic, and other forces of dominance and control enable, undergird, and reinforce their presence, even when those forces are at odds with other forces, such as laws or religious values, that prohibit them. Human beings tend to engage in behavior that is sanctioned or ignored, and to refrain from behavior that is unthinkable or that receives strong social, emotional, economic, and juridical discouragement. Without considering these *many* factors, religious tendencies to moralize and pass judgments remain impotent, and the American tendency to focus on individual behavior and legislate it remains woefully inadequate. In addition, human behavior in any culture tends to be far more complex and contradictory that any examination of ideas and policies would reveal, and there are those in power in every culture who would never consider participating in exploitation despite the social forces sanctioning it. That prostitution is, however, such a pervasive, profitable, and powerful industry of global proportions should give us pause and prompt us to ask why—especially given its negative social consequences. Attempts to reformulate discussions of prostitution outside religious discourse have had little success in addressing any of the problems surrounding prostitution because the religious dimension forms a substructure that needs examination.

Societies that prohibit prostitution tolerate it in some form. Arguments for both prohibiting and legalizing prostitution in the West use rhetoric that, at the United Nations, has shifted from immorality and paternalism to the language of human rights. The practice of prostitution itself is judged harmful to the person soliciting prostitution and the customer. Whether this harm is deemed disease, vulnerability to exploitation, or sexual dysfunction, the argument is that people must be protected against this "self-inflicted" harm. Because people are deemed to possess certain inalienable human rights and prostitution is now defined as harm, people must be prohibited from engaging in sex work in order to protect their human rights.

That shift is the foundation of the United Nations Convention for the Suppression of the Traffic in Persons and of the Exploitation of the Prostitution of Others. The Universal Declaration of Human Rights, prepared by the commission on Human Rights set up by the UN Economic and Social Council, was adopted by the General Assembly in 1948. It concentrates heavily on "Western civil and political rights" and tends to ignore or downplay economic or social rights. The two main premises of the document are the autonomy or capacity for self-governance of each individual and the equality of each person under the law—which we know for most of U.S. history and much of the world means the male, propertied individual.[19] For example, the document states:

> Sexual autonomy appears to be a central aspect of moral personality through which we define our ideas of a free person who has taken responsibility for his or her life.[20]

The rhetoric presupposes the rational, individual moral agent described in enlightenment philosophy (the rational, male individual), which itself has roots in an earlier religious understanding of the autonomous soul.[21] The UN Convention defines prostitutes as "victims," shifting the human rights language somewhat. The Convention asserts that traffic in persons is "incompatible with the dignity and worth of the human person and endangers the welfare of the individual, the family and the community."[22] While this document targets the procurer, the pimp and the brothel owner, and moves toward including misused power in its definition of prostitution, the net effect of the document has been devastating for prostituted girls and women. When it was ratified in Asian countries, it eliminated the legal status of prostitution and contributed to exploitation because the new laws against prostitution were used only against those prostituted and not against the exploiters.[23] Even if arrested, most johns, pimps, and brothel owners have the resources to hire legal help. They may themselves be public officials or have financial connections to those prosecuting arrests. Few are convicted and even fewer serve time. However, unless their pimps help them, prostitutes usually have few resources if arrested. Their police records are often quite extensive.

Keeping the focus on the prostitute as a criminal resonates with old ideas of the sinful, wanton woman and virtually assures that sex workers will be trapped in a cycle of exploitation that requires them to seek protection from prosecution for doing work that they are often forced, either literally by physical means, or by poverty, family violence, sexual abuse, or abandonment, to perform. While not all law enforcement authorities exploit prostitutes, there is a high percentage of corruption among police and government officials (including the military) in countries where prostitution is illegal. Personal testimonies from prostitutes describe johns from all branches of politics, law enforcement, and religions, as well as repeated abuse by arresting officers.

The law and the criminal justice system have historically (and still today) often served to trap women in the sex industry by giving them a criminal record that effectively prevents them from easily obtaining other kinds of employment. This parallels an earlier era that labeled them "fallen." Legal systems that prohibit prostitution tacitly support sexual exploitation by profiting from the collection of fines, by allowing men to traffic in women with impunity, and by paying the forces of law to arrest and prosecute those prostituted—in other words, by focusing on regulating the sexual activity of the least powerful.[24] The prohibition of prostitution, justified in the modern context as protecting women's "human rights," actually makes them subject to blackmail, rape, and battering without recourse to legal protection because it does not nuance the limits of adult "choice" and the complex factors that create powerlessness and desperation. The "licenses" required of women who work in the so-called "hospitality" industry, a euphemism for prostitution, regulate prostitution without legalizing or decriminalizing it because they both disguise and allow control of the sexual services expected of the women. These "licenses" help monitor women's employment in these industries and are designed to require regular physical checkups, primarily for venereal disease and AIDS, *without making prostitution legal*.

Policies concerning prostitution should be directed at root causes of exploitation and toward protecting victims—children, victims of rape and assault, homeless women and children—regardless of their economic state, occupation, or status.

The prohibition of prostitution works to funnel juveniles into prostitution instead of protecting them. Many studies of juveniles in prostitution have shown that those exploited have run away from home. A high percentage are sexual abuse survivors or are supporting a drug habit. They flee to a big city where they are picked up by pimps, often at the bus stations as they exit the bus. Police use loitering and prostitution laws to pick up these young people, and if they have been arrested for a status offense, they are sent back to their parents, only to run again.[25]

The prohibition of prostitution ensures that juveniles will be treated like criminals and not as sexual abuse victims or addicts. Once understood as criminals, they become labeled unworthy of our compassion and help. The moral stigma attached to having been prostituted is misplaced. The customers of prostituted juveniles are the morally culpable criminals but are not usually prosecuted as child sexual abuse offenders, which is what they are, regardless of whether or not they paid to conduct the abuse. A minor cannot consent to abuse—the responsible party is the adult. In a Minneapolis-based study of young people in prostitution, the authors found that many customers specifically looked for juvenile prostitutes the same age as their own children.[26]

Other forms of oppression compound the penalties of prohibition. For example, U.S. women of color serve proportionately longer sentences and receive higher fines. "Racism makes Black women and girls especially vulnerable to sexual exploitation and keeps them trapped in prostitution."[27] Even though only approximately 40% of street prostitutes are women of color in the United States, they are 55% of those arrested and 85% of those who do jail time.[28]

Poor neighborhoods of African Americans, Native Americans, Hispanics, Asian Americans, and whites are areas that attract purveyors of the flesh market in its many forms. Rents are lower, and city officials are much more likely to look the other way when the sleaze does not impact their families or property values. Johns prefer the anonymity of not being in their own neighborhoods when they visit porn shops and prostitutes. Public officials may also be encouraged to look the other way by kickbacks and bribes. All of this works to undermine the safety, sense of well-being, and community pride of those in poorer neighborhoods who suffer the indignities visited on their women and children.

Laws against prostitution isolate our sons and daughters, sisters, brothers, and mothers, giving them a permanent record as offenders of moral and civil statutes that separates them from the rest of society, keeps them from escaping, and increases the danger of the work—creating a perpetual underclass, deemed criminal, for sexual exploitation. There is a direct correlation between the amount of violence perpetrated against sex workers and the degree of illegality of the work.[29]

Given the above problems with prohibition, legalization might seem a better choice. It, too, however, has drawbacks. The arguments for legalization presuppose the same Western human rights rhetoric as the arguments for prohibitions. This rhetoric can be adapted to a market mentality that assumes that persons "own" their own bodies and therefore can legitimately profit from the sale of their bodies. Prostitution, it has been said, is a "victimless crime," and prosecution only wastes police time and money. Again, the focus is on regulating or not regulating sexual behavior. In the centuries before "reform," prostitution was often legalized and regulated.

Kathleen Barry refers to this system as "The State as Pimp."[30] Regulation by the state allows commercialized sexual activity to be taxed, monitored, licensed, zoned, publicized, and given health coverage.

No argument for legalization acknowledges the numbers of children who are prostituted or the dangerous and violent nature of much of the work. The rhetoric of legalization mirrors the libertarian-style speeches used by pimps to convince those they exploit that they are simply engaging in a "glamorous" business. Legalization rhetoric also presupposes a form of individualism irrelevant for children and many ethnic subcultures based in traditional societies.

The various pronouncements, social attitudes, and legal policies that surround prostitution have little to do with reality or with reducing sex industry activity. The acts of those exploited do not involve lust, sexual desire, personal choice, or self-inflicted harm; they are more accurately placed in the category of survival strategies used by abused minors, those economically exploited, and survivors of sexual and other violence. The ambiguities and perplexities surrounding prostitution policy reflect religious conflicts between defending the status and power of institutional authority (and those who hold it) and advocacy and compassion for the downtrodden. American law carries the same tensions, as the ideal of individual liberty and fairness for all is, in actual fact, limited to those with property, money, and power. Every excluded group—enslaved Africans, women, Asian and Native Americans—have needed to gain power and influence in their struggle to protect themselves from exploitation. Hence, religious and legal ideals rarely serve the weak and vulnerable.

Better Policies: Decriminalization, NOT Legalization

The history of theology, canon law, and social and legal policy has done little to confront the damaging aspects of prostitution as a system of exploitation. Instead, blame and punishment have moved in the wrong direction by being inflicted on the least powerful in systems of exploitation. The racist and economic elements behind enforcement of policy demonstrate vividly how such mystification harms the most vulnerable.

Given the need for more pragmatic, non-judgmental approaches to prostitution that can protect the most vulnerable, many grassroots women's organizations advocate decriminalization, which means the repeal of all existing laws governing voluntary sexual exchanges in adult (over age eighteen), *nonviolent*, consensual relationships, whether or not money changes hands. Where countries have decriminalized prostitution but left the laws against pimping and pandering, "Prostitutes . . . feel the prohibition reinforces their dependence on abusive men, and they are working to change those laws." This is because when prostitutes report being beaten or raped by pimps, the police ignore the battery or rape and concentrate on the pimping as a crime:

> Decriminalization allows for the possibility that the lives of prostitutes can become
> less dangerous. For one thing, under a comprehensive decriminalization scheme,

it would be possible for prostitutes to join unions and engage in collective bargaining in order to improve their working conditions.[31]

But decriminalization should be done with great care, so that those victimized by pimps, brothels, and bars have legal recourse against violence and exploitation, not merely personal freedom to organize. Decriminalization that focuses on exploitation should be accompanied by stronger prohibitions and enforcement of laws against the sexual exploitation of children and all forms of coercion, including threats of violence, assault, battery, and rape. Like crimes such as rape, the prostitution of women and children involves the use of sexuality as an instrument of power and violence and is not about human sexuality per se, except as a tool of dominance.

Genesis House, My Sister's Place, EMPOWER, GABRIELLA, and many other grassroots organizations[32] in both Asia and the United States favor decriminalization of prostitution to help women who wish to leave prostitution get jobs without the barrier of a criminal record, to be free of blackmail threats by police and pimps alike, and to find some self-esteem for the work they have done as a means of survival. Decriminalization will help women who remain in the sex industry by enabling them to prosecute offenders for violence perpetrated against them and to retain their earnings because they will not need to give their income to pimps or to pay for protection. When given safe space to recover and examine their lives, those who have been prostituted must also come to terms with their own choices and behaviors, both good and ill, and understand themselves as moral agents of their lives.

Nelia Sancho, regional coordinator of the Asian Women Human Rights Council and the president of its Philippine section, is also a founding member and former secretary general of GABRIELLA. She argues:

> Decriminalizing prostitution is an important agenda for women in the prostitution trade, to provide them the space to exert some form of control in their lives as prostitutes. In illegalizing prostitution, women are always made the victims by the male-dominator in the society.[33]

None of these grassroots organizations favored legalization, which they are careful to distinguish from decriminalization. Legalization allows the state to coerce behavior from those who are already controlled by the power of others. Legalization usually involves the licensing of those who prefer to use assumed names and remain anonymous. It also allows the state to designate sex industry areas, which most often are found in poor and ethnic neighborhoods,[34] where the citizens do not have the clout of rich suburbs and have less access to "check and state government" (cash and politics). Legalization also raises questions about how prohibiting the trafficking in women across borders for forced prostitution could be enforced, a problem at issue in post–Cold War Europe as poor women from Eastern Europe are being trafficked to prostitution centers in areas such as Amsterdam and Tel Aviv.

In the United States, prostitution laws are enacted state by state, and in fact, ordinances vary by city. The brothels in the state of Nevada are licensed; independent prostitution, including street-walking, massage parlor work, call girls, or escort services, is illegal. Women who work in Nevada's licensed brothels are extremely limited in their movements outside the brothel. They are often required to work fourteen-hour shifts, seven days a week for three weeks straight. The brothel enforces its own rules of condom use, either prohibiting or requiring them. The prostitutes have almost no right to refuse a customer. and the exhausting schedule of ten to fifteen customers per day means that many of them use drugs and alcohol to cope. A doctor provides regular health checks.[35] By almost any definition this is legalized exploitation, and it is the pattern most favored by those who seek to "reform" prostitution, reform often disguised under libertarian rhetoric about nonpuritanical sexual attitudes, as if coerced sex were not about power and exploitation. Even in Western Europe, where prostitution is often legal, the importation of Eastern European women trafficked to legal areas has not alleviated the exploitative and abusive nature of what happens to many of them.

One mildly hopeful sign in the midst of so much legal inequality regarding prostitution is a law enacted first in Florida and then in Minnesota in the mid-1990s. This law makes it legal for anyone "coerced" into prostitution to sue the one who has coerced her for damages. "Coerce," in this statute:

> means to use or threaten to use any form of domination, restraint or control for the purpose of causing an individual to engage in or remain in prostitution or to relinquish earnings derived from prostitution. Coercion exists if the totality of the circumstances establish the existence of domination, restraint or control that would have the reasonably foreseeable effect of causing an individual to engage in or remain in prostitution or to relinquish earnings from prostitution[36].

The statute then defines twenty-three specific forms of coercion. If one deems her or himself coerced into prostitution, she/he may sue johns, pimps, or madams for "economic loss, including damage, destruction, or loss of use of personal property, loss of past or future income or earning capacity and income, profits or money owed to the plaintiff from contracts with the person."[37] Ignorance of the age of a minor does not constitute a legitimate defense under this new statute, because a minor cannot consent to abuse. While this law has possibilities of putting more power in the hands of victims, it is not a solution to the problem and can only be used by those willing to relive their past trauma in court and to use their real names on court records.

A similar law being considered in Ontario, Canada, may present practical ways to redirect legal activity in regard to sex work. It clearly defines the prostituted person as potentially the victim of abuse and coercion. Those blameworthy are not just her procurer or her pimp, but also her customer.

In June 1995 the first john ever convicted of engaging in child prostitution in a foreign country was convicted of the crime in his homeland. Under the active lobbying of ECPAT (End Child Prostitution in Asian Tourism), the international anti–child prostitution organization begun in Bangkok over a decade ago, a number of Asian countries have passed laws prohibiting child prostitution, a response to its massive escalation. Since the campaign began, 160 have been arrested in Thailand, Sri Lanka, and the Philippines. Unfortunately, it was possible for the men arrested simply to flee home and escape conviction. In the past few years, a number of Western countries have made it illegal to engage in child prostitution, even outside the country. Countries with such a law include Australia, New Zealand, Germany, the United States, and Sweden, which is where this first conviction happened. While such legislation may appear to be an attempt to empty the ocean with a teaspoon, rigorous use of the law may encourage those toying with the idea of child prostitution to think again if the number of convictions begins to rise. Unfortunately for the U.S. effort, the New York office of ECPAT has closed for lack of funds, eliminating a source of information for the U.S. Justice Department.[38]

The attitude of society toward prostitution expressed through the system of laws is punitive, where those who suffer most from the abuses of the sex industry are punished by law and those who perpetrate the sex industry are, by and large, never penalized. They are not penalized because they, in their attitudes, values, and behaviors, differ little from the men who write, enforce, and administer the laws—or who write theology from the male gaze. The behavior of those prostituted is defined as deviant, but the behavior of men who exploit them is ignored or implicitly regarded as normative for masculine behavior.

Spiritual Resources for Change

Attitudes toward the body, women, and sexuality form and are formed by the structures of a culture, its laws, economic practices, familial relationships, religions, gender structures, and political processes. The history of a culture reveals how these dimensions interact with attitudes, values, and behavior. To understand sex industries more completely, therefore, we must attend closely to the historically contingent constructions of the body, women, and sexuality that they mirror. And in the United States, transforming our understanding means noting the long pathological Christian legacy around sexuality, power, and women. Prostitution, because it constitutes a major aspect of legal and social policy, provides a window on the pathology of sexuality in a society.

This Christian theological legacy begins with the assumption that sexuality embodies sin. Far from illuminating the reality of the sex industry as a system of exploitation of the vulnerable, young, and poor, the Christian pathologizing of sex has obscured its dynamics. The ideology of sin has often entrapped women, because once having been labeled as "fallen," they had little hope of ever getting free from prostitution, except under the paternalistic benevolence of the church, many of whose clerics were customers.

This oversimplification of sin and its narrow identification with sex leads to the avoidance of discussions of the moral complexities of human life. The oversimplification continues to place responsibility for sexual exploitation on the victims of the system, who are regarded as giving evidence of their sinful natures. Their plight is rarely seen as caused by the misuse of power by exploitative systems. Women who escape are supposed to feel grateful that they are forgiven and regarded as redeemed despite their "fallen" natures, which reinforces the idea of their powerlessness, even as they are held responsible for what happened to them.

Exploitation is wrong because the misuse of power, even by good people for a good cause, dehumanizes all involved. Whether victims of misused power are innocent or not is irrelevant. Prostituted girls have had their innocence stolen and survive only if they learn to use what power they have to function. Hence, we need to focus not on forgiveness of the "fallen" girl, but on what is wrong with exploitative systems and behavior—on misuses of power.

The spirit/flesh split; the association of sexuality and profound embodiment with sin; the subordination and exploitation of women and children; the protection of power; and the political/economic nature of marriage become clearer when we look carefully at how Christianity and American culture have handled prostitution or, perhaps more accurately, tried not to see it. Because of long historical roots in Christianity, the problems surrounding prostitution in the dominant American culture are deeper than the answers that science, law, medicine, morality, or psychology can provide. They are spiritual.

The dominant American culture is deeply rooted in a worldview uncomfortable with its own flesh, with the limitations of that flesh, and with its refusal to be controlled under the ideologies of mechanical, financial, scientific, and moral systems. Thus we do not live in a healthy harmony and attunement with our flesh, but in pieces, trying to control its energies and demands with drugs, caffeine, alcohol, diet, diversionary entertainments, medications, therapy, surgery, and sheer willpower. We have a tendency to relate to our bodies as instruments for efficiency and success—tools of our minds. Transforming our understanding of prostitution and our flesh means attending to the resources Christianity, in its liberative forms, offers us for reconceiving sin, healing, liberation, and grace.

Christian theology must speak a liberating word in the face of a phenomenon so exploitative and destructive of human life that most of us find its horrors unimaginable. In that speaking we must struggle to articulate the grace of our flesh, of the value of loving and being attuned to our body-self. While the understandings of sin, healing, and grace presented below have continuities with traditional theology, that theology is also challenged by the reality of prostitution to be truer to the Christian call for justice, mercy, and compassion—and to the fundamental New Testament insight that the spirit is known in the flesh, which is the doctrine of the incarnation.

In turning a liberative perspective on those prostituted, two principles are crucial: (1) listen carefully to those who live with the consequences of being exploited and do not hurt or further victimize those already exploited by systems of injustice; and (2) whenever possible, involve those exploited in creating their own solutions and strategies for survival. This acute attunement to concrete context and human experience is a hallmark of feminist and liberation theologies. This attunement challenges conventional theologies that protect power and privilege.

Instead of seeing sin in sexual behavior, which has created veils of shame and guilt even around healthy sexual feelings, we must see it in the abuse of power. A major tragedy of male dominance has been to confuse sex with power and with violence. This confusion is evident in the theological identification of sin with sexuality, which masks sin as the abuse of power. Liberation theologians have suggested that sin, in its social dimensions, is organized in human systems of power. These systems magnify the abuse of power, especially in its economic and political forms, a view consistent with many biblical approaches to sin as collective. Hence, sin is a social phenomenon with a structured, social, historical character.[39]

But sin comes also in individual acts, which cause harm, whether or not they are magnified by social systems. Feminist theologian Mary Potter Engel suggests Christians should also measure sin by what destroys right relationship. She proposes that we identify sin as the distortion of feeling, as the betrayal of trust, as lack of care, and as lack of consent to vulnerability.[40] Her definition of personal sin parallels Nel Noddings's articulation of evil as that which causes intractable, irredeemable, or deliberately inflicted pain, such as torture and rape; that which makes anyone helpless to act on his or her own or others' behalf; and that which separates us from relationships of love and care.[41] A sensitive reading of biblical ideas of sin also leads toward an understanding of sin as that which destroys right (or just) relationships. By these criteria, the theologians who mystify prostitution, as well as the pimp, procurer, police, and customer participate in creating evil through their misuse of power and their exploitation and use of the young and vulnerable.

The response to such sin and evil, a response that opens doors for justice and healing, involves, in the perpetrator, repentance and the willingness to change, to develop a healthy, responsible self. For the vulnerable who are exploited, we must make safe spaces for holy outrage to erupt; support for grief, regret, and sometimes repentance for their own misuses of power to surface; and places for social networks for change to organize.

Healing and grace come from many quarters. In the midst of exploitation and despair, grassroots workers dispense condoms, good advice, and health care; anger fuels resistance to pain; caring acts make change possible; and hope shimmers quietly in the midst of gloom—moments when doors to healing are opened. The healing process is difficult because healing from pain means revisiting it, and turning to things that numb pain may seem easier than the reliving of horror. The levels of trauma and abuse that must be healed are deep both in the psyche and in the abused body. The body stores our spiritual and material legacy. The longer our life expectancy, the more the accumulation of such legacies becomes evident. They leave their telltale marks on our flesh and return as time bombs that explode years later when we least expect it. The body's refusal to let us forget forever is its spiritual gift, its demand that we awaken from denial and learn to breathe, to be present, to heal.

Moments of grace come in unexpected places.

A small cluster of women stood in a circle on the sidewalk at the edge of Waikiki beach. They held each other in the dark around a large trash barrel over which was laid a circular plank covered with an altar cloth, candles, a Bible, and gold stars. One of the women wore a clerical robe and stole. The other half dozen, their heavy make-up caught in the soft glow of candlelight, were dressed for street-walking, one in spiked heels, gold mini-skirt and halter top; another in white, silver-studded cowboy boots, fringed jeans, bolero jacket, and dangling earrings; a third in a tight black spandex, strapless mini-dress and red mules. As the service began, the clergywoman invited each young woman to say her own, real name out loud, as an act of claiming herself outside her prostitute persona. In a quiet, tentative voice, each woman spoke her name in turn. It was midnight, and they celebrated Christmas Eve together as fashionably dressed men and women hurried past on their way to mass at the Episcopal church around the corner.[42]

Grace is a continual process of uncovering the indisputable fact that we are human, and because we are human we are not destined for slavery but for love and freedom, for the grace of God. Grace is neither the product of a religious conversion separate from the ordinary, prosaic dimensions of human history nor only the breaching of walls that separate human beings from each other and God. Our attention to social movements reminds us that the very structures of society and religion that conspire to mystify oppression and to separate God from humanity and us from each other must be called into account.

The most neglected dimension of grace is the social process by which we are freed from sin into new dimensions of human life in which it is possible to behave decently and responsibly. As Leonardo Boff has said, "It is not just the individual being who must be liberated and justified. The same must happen to the whole network of their active relationships that keep them bound to socioeconomic and political realities and their structured sinfulness."[43]

The grace of social movements is not in "triumphing over evil," although thoroughgoing engagement of all forms of oppressive power, both private and public, is a necessity. Nor is it the establishment of a one-religion state; it is rather the infusion of religious conscience and consciousness in our political work. Grace belongs to our participation in social action with others who know the sex industry is so harmful that it cannot be tolerated in a decent society. The mutual sustenance derived from such participation counteracts many forms of resistance to change and backlash. Repression and denial, both within and among ourselves and in and with the wider society, will inevitably result in misrepresentation, infighting, loss, fear, and pain. The larger struggle continues and is part of how Christians can incarnate grace in a democratic society that struggles to be just. It is political holiness. As Archbishop Oscar Romero once said:

> Living as we do in a world in such evident need of social transformation, how shall we not ask Christians to incarnate the justice of Christianity, to live it in their homes and in their lives, to strive to be agents of change, to strive to be new human beings?[44]

The scope of the problem we are confronting in our attempts to stop the sexual exploitation of women, men, and children by commercialized sex is increasingly global. To stem the tide of its growth will require all our efforts.

Notes

1. A book I coauthored with Susan Thistlethwaite, from which much of this essay is drawn, *Casting Stones: Prostitution and Liberation in Asia and the United States.* (Minneapolis: Fortress Press, 1996).

2. For studies of the activity and role of women, see Elizabeth Schüssler Fiorenza's *In Memory of Her: Feminist Theological Reconstruction of Christian Origins* (New York: Crossroad, 1983), and Elaine Pagels, *The Gnostic Gospels: A New Account of the Origins of Christianity.* (New York: Random House, 1979).

3. See John Boswell's *The Kindness of Strangers: Child Abandonment in Western Europe from Late Antiquity to the Renaissance* (New York: Pantheon, 1988), for a discussion of

the fate of oblates promised to the church at a young age. The monastic code was severe with regard to children and what we now understand as needs for nurturance.

4. See Peter Brown, *The Body and Society: Men, Women, and Sexual Renunciation in Early Christianity* (New York: Columbia University Press, 1988).

5. Thomas Aquinas, *Summa Theologica*–II, Q. X, Art. II and II-II Q.lx, 2, and 5, II-II, LXXXVII, 2, ad 2, and II-II, CXVIII, 8, ad. 4, in the edition translated by the English Dominicans, 22 vols. (London: Burns, Oates & Washburne, 1922).

6. Simone de Beauvoir, *The Second Sex*, (New York: Vintage, 1974), 618.

7. See Vern Bullough and Bonnie Bullough, *Women and Prostitution: A Social History* (Buffalo, N.Y.: Prometheus, 1987).

8. See James Brundage, "Prostitution in the Medieval Canon Law" (paper presented at the Medieval Conference, Western Michigan University, Kalamazoo, Mich., 1972), cited in Bullough and Bullough, *Women and Prostitution*, 119.

9. *The Summa Parisiensis on the Cecretum Gratiani*, c. 32, q. 5, c. 1 ad. v. Tolerabilius, ed. Terence P. McLaughlin (Toronto: Pontifical Institution of Medieval Studies, 1952).

10. See Bullough and Bullough, *Women and Prostitution*, 129.

11. *Monumenta Germaniae historica Legum*, sec. 4, const. 1, 240.

12. Martin Luther, *Works*, ed. Jaroslav Pelikan et al. (Philadelphia: Muhlenberg ad Concordia, 1955ff), LXVIII, 278.

13. Luther, *Works*, XLIV, 1–8.

14. Martin Luther, *Letters of Spiritual Counsel*, ed. And trans. Theodore G. Tappert (Philadelphia: Westminster Press, 1955), 293.

15. One reason such values persist, however, is that they share patriarchal values about women and sexuality with many other so-called "higher" religions. See chapters one and two of Brock and Thistlethwaite, *Casting Stones*.

16. "Dear Mr. Trick," WHISPER 8, no. 2 (Winter 1993): 6–7, letters written by juvenile survivors of prostitution to the men who bought and sexually abused them.

17. David A. J. Richards, "Commercial Sex and the Rights of the Person: A Moral Argument for the Decriminalization of Prostitution," in *Women and the Law*, ed. Mary Joe Frug (Westbury, N.Y.: Foundation Press, 1992), 647.

18. See especially chapter four of Brock and Thistlethwaite, *Casting Stones*.

19. Natalie Kaufman Hevener, ed., *International Law and the Status of Women* (Boulder, Colo.: Westview Press, 1983).

20. Richards, "Commercial Sex," 649.

21. For discussions of concepts of self in Western and cross-cultural perspectives, see Catherine Keller's *From a Broken Web: Sexism, Separation, and Self* (Boston: Beacon, 1986) and Alasdair MacIntyre, "Individual and Social Morality in Japan and the United States: Rival Conceptions of the Self," *Philosophy East and West* 40, no. 4 (October 1990): 489–97.

22. Hevener, *International Law*, 79.

23. Thanh-Dam Truong, *Sex, Money and Morality: Prostitution and Tourism in South-East Asia* (London: Zed Books, 1990), 155.

24. Evelina Giobbe, "An Analysis of Individual, Institutional, and Cultural Pimping," *Michigan Journal of Gender and Law* I (1993): 33–59.

25. Susan Thistlethwaite, interview with Larkin Street social workers, Larkin Street Youth Center, 1044 Larkin Street, San Francisco, Calif. 94109, June 1992. Larkin Street's mission is to locate homeless and runaway youth, help them find alternatives to street life, and help them stay off the streets.

26. Michael Baizerman et al., "Adolescent Prostitution," *Children Today* 8 (September–October 1979): 20–24.

27. Vednita Nelson, "Prostitution: Where White Racism and Sexism Intersect," *Michigan Journal of Gender and Law* I (1993), 83.

28. Bernard Cohen, *Deviant Street Networks: Prostitution in New York City* (New York: Crown, 1980).

29. "The countries with the most restrictive legal systems, including the United States and many countries in Southeast Asia, have the most problems with violence against prostitutes (and women perceived to be *like* prostitutes), thefts associated with prostitution, pimping (especially brutal pimping), and the involvement of juveniles. Conversely, the countries with the least restrictive measures, including the Netherlands, West Germany, Sweden, and Denmark, have the least problems." From *Sex Work: Writings by Women in the Sex Industry*, ed. Frederique Delacoste and Priscilla Alexander (Pittsburgh: Cleis Press, 1987), 195–96.

30. See Kathleen Barry, *Female Sexual Slavery* (Englewood Cliffs, N.J.: Prentice-Hall), 1979.

31. Delacoste and Alexander, *Sex Work*, 210.

32. Genesis House (Chicago), My Sister's Place (Seoul), EMPOWER (Bangkok), and GABRIELLA (Manilla) are some of the oldest and most stable of such grassroots organizations. Others include the Rainbow Project (Taipei), Home for the Rebirth of Women (Honolulu), Pride (Minneapolis), and HELP (Tokyo). In researching our book, Sue Thistlethwaite discovered that many organizations that work to help those prostituted are poorly funded and have a high turnover in staff. WHISPER, one of the oldest and most active organizations in Minneapolis and a valuable source of information and activism, closed in September 1996. Organizations close because of loss of funds, high staff burnout levels, and internal tensions. Because many are started and/or staffed by survivors of prostitution, which often involves serious abuse and addictions, the slippage back into self-destructive behavior is always a danger. However, social workers and others who lead such organizations are often not adequately grounded in the gritty realities of life on the street and may resort to ineffective or bureaucratic solutions.

33. Nelia Sancho, "Should Prostitution be Legalized?" *Laya: Feminist Quarterly* 2, no. 3 (March 1993): 37.

34. Most pornography stores, strip shows, and nude or topless bars are found in low-income neighborhoods. See the discussion in Van F. White's "Pornography and Pride," in *Making Violence Sexy*, ed. Diana Russell (New York: Teachers College Press, 1993).

35. Delacoste and Alexander, *Sex Work*, 210.

36. *Laws of Minnesota for 1994* chap. 624, H. F. No. 2519.

37. Ibid.

38. Lynn Thiesmeyer, a professor at Keio University, Fujisawa, Japan, in researching sex tourism, interviewed an official at the U.S. justice department who noted that ECPAT had been a source of information on child prostitution arrests in Asia. Her comments were contained in an e-mail message in September 1996.

39. See Gustavo Gutierrez, *A Theology of Liberation* (Maryknoll, N.Y.: Orbis Books, 1973); Elsa Tamez, *The Amnesty of Grace* (Nashville: Abingdon Press, 1995).

40. Mary Potter Engel, "Evil, Sin, and the Violation of the Vulnerable," *Lift Every Voice: Constructing Christian Theologies from the Underside.*, ed. Susan Thistlethwaite and Mary Potter Engel (San Francisco: Harper and Row, 1990), 156–63.

41. Nel Noddings, In *Women and Evil* (Berkeley: University of California Press, 1989).

42. Reverend Pam Vessels, who runs a shelter for girls and women seeking to leave prostitution, reported this story in a personal interview in January 1993 in Honolulu, Hawaii.

43. Leonardo Boff, *Liberating Grace* (Maryknoll, N.Y.: Orbis Press, 1979), 153.

44. From Jon Sobrino, *The Spirituality of Liberation: Toward Political Holiness* (Maryknoll, N.Y.: Orbis Press, 1988), 44.

Index

Abortion, 3, 7, 94, 164–65, 189–200, 231
Aid to Dependent Families with Children
    (AFDC), 76–77, 80–81
Al-Hibri, Azizah, 199
Allison, Dorothy, 109
Amendment Two, Colorado, 72
American Baptist Churches USA, 74n.47
American Civil Liberties Union, 7, 10
Anderson, Benedict, 114
Aquinas, Thomas, 51, 195, 207, 246
Assisted Reproduction, 158, 203–11, 216–17
Augustine, 195, 198, 213

Ba'asher, Taha, 225
Baird, Robert, 105
Baptist Joint Committee, 10
Beattie Jung, Patricia, 171
Bellah, Robert, 12–13
Bennett, William, 114, 140, 141, 143, 148, 150
Bernardin, Cardinal Joseph, 193
Berrigan, Daniel, 193
Bible, 37, 49, 54, 167, 169–80, 257
    on abortion, 194
    on adultery, 24
    on the family, 79

on homosexuality, 25–26, 174–80
on marriage, 93, 173
on prostitution, 245, 246
Birth control, 94. See also contraception
    movement, 149
Bisexuality, 158, 160, 171
Boff, Leonardo, 259
Bounds, Elizabeth, 77
Brown, Robert MacAffee, 198
Buddhism, 16, 20n.10, 125, 186, 199
Burke, Carolyn, 230
Butler, Judith, 110, 112, 115

Call to Renewal Conference, 74
Campaign for Human Development
    (Catholic Charities), 74
Capitalism, free market, 11–12, 13, 80, 81,
    167, 187
    transnationalization of, 114, 117, 156
Carby, Hazel, 33
Carter, Stephen, 9
Celibacy, 55, 94, 178, 246, 247
    priestly, 48, 63n.14
Charitable Choice Provision, 8, 61, 73–74
Child care, 81, 151

Children, 28, 53, 117, 248, 252
    and prostitution, 25–52, 253, 254, 255, 257,
        259
Christian Coalition, 9, 116, 118, 119. *See also*
    "Contract with the American Family"
Christian Right, 105, 106, 114–19, 155, 171.
    See also Religious Right
Christian sexual ethics, 44–45, 49–54, 198
Church of the Brethren, 62
Church of the Latter Day Saints, 62
Church-state separation, 165, 167, 169, 249.
    See also First Amendment
Circumcision, female , 221, 227. *See also*
    Female genital mutilation
Circumcision, male, 221, 225, 226, 227,
    232–36
    in Judaism, 232, 236
Civil religion, 12–13
Clinton, President Bill, 3, 77, 101, 138, 139,
    142–44, 150
Collins, Representative Barbara Rose, 220,
    224
Common good, the, 45, 51, 160, 166, 191,
    216–17
Connery, John, S.J., 194
Conservatism, 105, 116–19
Contraception, 188, 190–94, 197, 198–200,
    203, 206–7, 211, 215. *See also* Birth
    control
"Contract with America," 105, 116–17, 120
"Contract with the American Family," 105,
    116, 120
Culture religion, 167–79. *See also* Civil
    religion
Culturism. *See* Culture religion

Dannemeyer, William, 114
Davis, Madeline, 109
De Beauvoir, Simone, 246
De Chardin, Pierre Teilhard, 198
Decriminalization
    of prostitution, 253–54
    of sodomy, 62
Defense of Marriage Act, 3, 16, 127, 119,
    131
Delay, Representative Tom, 143, 144, 145,
    147
D'Emilio, John, 109
Democracy, 18, 167
Democratic deliberation, 82–83

DIGNITY, 63
Dobson, James, 79
Dole, Bob, 104, 105, 119, 149
Double-standard, 7, 36, 43, 193, 245
Duggan, Lisa, 72

Echols, Alice, 108
Eck , Diana, 13, 157, 164
Engel, Mary Potter, 258
Episcopal Church, 63, 125, 74n.47, 157,
    172–73
Essentialism
    defined, 45
    in feminism, 236
    in sexual ethics, 45–46, 158, 211
Evangelical Lutheran Church in America,
    62, 77, 74n.47

Family
    in constitutional law, 230
    contemporary patterns, 42–43, 76, 78–79,
        104–5
    history, 93–102
    as public concern, 3, 5, 7, 61, 106, 113, 110
Family planning, 189, 191–93, 197, 199, 200
Family Research Council, 118
"Family values," 5, 11–13, 60, 104–20, 246
Farrell, Janet, 139
Federal Prohibition of Female Genital
    Mutilation Act, 220, 224, 232
Female genital mutilation/FGM, 219–38 *See
    also* Female circumcision
Female-headed families, 138. *See also* Single
    motherhood
Feminism 12, 18, 31. *See also* Religious
    feminism
    and the family, 98–102,
    as family, 108–10
    and the FGM debate, 220, 222, 223, 234,
        236, 237
    and the "sex wars," 107
First Amendment, 5, 9, 186, 226. *See also*
    Church-state separation
    Free Exercise Clause, 9, 126, 220, 221, 225,
        227–32
    No Establishment Clause, 129– 130
Fish, Stanley, 236–38
Fordice, Governor Kirk, 141
Foucault, Michel, 110–12, 113, 114, 115
Fourteenth Amendment, 229

Equal Protection Clause, 220, 221, 225, 226–27, 232–36

Fraiman, Susan, 113

Fraser, Nancy, 82

Frazier, E. Franklin, 148

Freedom of speech, 72, 228

Freeman, Estelle, 109

Freidan, Betty, 99n.16, 104

Gay rights, 3, 5, 65–69, 119, 157–58, 170, 188. *See also* Sexual dissent
  and free speech, 72–73
  groups, 63 (*see also* Human Rights Campaign)
  religious opposition, 65, 69–70
  religious support, 62–64
  as "special rights," 66

Gays, 25, 29, 124–25, 127, 129, 160. *See also* Lesbians

Gays, ordination of, 63, 157, 172–73

"The Gay Agenda" (video), 160

"Gay Rights, Special Rights" (video), 114

Gender, 14, 185
  distinct from sexuality, 110
  sexualized, 33–36, 108, 112

Girls
  African American, 143–44
  and FGM, 220, 221, 222, 231, 236
  and prostitution, 257

Globalization, 11, 13, 80, 155, 156–57, 163
  defined, 156

Gomes, Peter, 170

Government, 106, 138, 156, 169, 185
  diminishment of, 8, 105
  privatization of, 5, 7
  and social provision, 75, 81

Guy-Sheftall, Beverly, 147

Hall, Jacqueline Dowd, 33

Halley, Janet, 66, 72

Hamer, Dean, 66

Health care, 74, 81, 151
  insurance, 204–5, 215, 217

Herman, Didi, 114

Heteronormativity, 9. *See also* Heterosexism
  defined, 70
  as state religion, 72

Heterosexism, 170–73, 174, 176, 177, 179
  defined, 171

Heterosexuality, compulsory, 28, 112

Hinduism, 11, 199

HIV/AIDS, 156, 159, 164

Hoagland, Sarah, 107

Hollibaugh, Amber, 109

Homosexuality. *See also* Sexual preference
  in the Bible, 126, 170–79
  fixity of, 64–66
  genetic studies, 48–49
  in Judaism, 25, 126
  in public discourse, 66–69, 114, 115, 118, 120, 158, 165

Horsburgh, Beverly, 145, 151

Howard, Penelope, 139

Human rights, 190–91, 199–200, 214
  and FGM, 223, 224, 227
  and prostitution, 250, 251

Human Rights Campaign, 10, 66, 119–20

"Illegitimacy." *See also* Single motherhood
  in public discourse 75–76, 135
  as racialized discourse, 140–41, 147–48
  in welfare legislation 73, 136,

Institute for Religion and Democracy, 162

In Vitro Fertilization, 204, 206, 208–11, 214. *See also* Assisted Reproduction

Irigaray, Luce, 234–36

Islam, 188, 189
  and female circumcision, 220, 221, 222, 225, 226, 232
  sexual ethics, 199

JanMohamed, Abdul R., 113

Jewish sexual ethics, 23–31
  feminist transformations of, 37–38
  on homoeroticism, 25, 126
  on marriage, 127–29
  pro-natalism, 128

Jones, Monica, 139

Judaism, 188, 189
  Central Conference of American Rabbis (Reform), 63, 74n.47
  Conservative, 126
  National Council of Jewish Women, 74n.47
  Orthodox, 126
  Reconstructionist, 62–63, 127–9
  Reform, 127
  Union of American Hebrew Congregations, 10, 62, 74n.47

Kinsey, Alfred, 48

Lapovsky, Elizabeth, 109
Lesbians 25, 29, 64–65, 127, 129, 155, 159, 162
   in feminism, 109
Lévi-Strauss, Claude, 110
Lewinsky affair, 3–4
Liberalism, 236–37
Litman, Rabbi Jane, 131
Lorde, Audre, 108
Loury, Glenn, 141, 148, 150
Loy, David, 187
Luker, Kristin, 34, 77–78
Luther, Martin, 247–48
Lutheran Church, 125

Marriage, 55, 136
   in bible, 93, 173, 176
   in Christian history, 93–98
   as civil and religious rite, 124
   heterosexual and same-sex, compared, 128
   and procreation, 128–29, 207, 211–13, 216
Mead, Margaret, 47
Metropolitan Community Church, 62, 63
Missouri Lutheran Synod, 62
Moi, Toril, 236
Monogamy, 55, 68, 173, 176
Moraga, Cherríe, 109
Moral Majority, 3, 43
Morella, Representative Constance, 220,
   224
Morris, Dick, 246
Moynihan, Daniel Patrick, "Report on the
   American Negro Family," 76, 140, 141,
   148, 150
Mubarak, President Hosni, 225
Murray, Charles, 137
Muslim Americans, 13, 118, 157, 163, 164

National Council of Churches, 74n.47
National Progressive Baptists, 142, 144
Native American Church, 10, 228
Native Americans, 170
Natural law
   and parental rights, 230
   in Roman Catholic teachings, 203, 206–7,
      211–12, 214, 216
   in sexual ethics, 46, 51
Nestle, Joan, 109
Noddings, Nel, 258

Omolade, Barbara, 149

Packwood, Senator Robert, 150
Pals, Daniel, 188
Papal teachings
   Casti Connubi, 207
   Donum Vitae, 206–8, 211, 214
   Gaudium et Spes, 207, 212, 214
   Humanae Vitae, 207, 211–12, 213, 214
   Pacem in Terris, 214
Parental rights, 117, 230–31
Patriarchy/patriachalism, 107, 159, 235
   and the family, 93, 101, 112, 149
   in religion, 12, 79
Pellauer, Mary, 31–32
People for the American Way, 10
Personal Responsibility and Work Opportu-
   nity Reconciliation Act, 3, 7, 119,
   73–74. *See also* Charitable Choice
   Provision
   and the father-headed family, 76
   and "illegitimacy," 136, 139, 140
   and the right to work, 80–81
Plaza, Monique, 230
Popes
   John XXIII, 214
   John Paul II, 193, 208, 211
   Leo XIII, 214
   Paul VI, 212
   Pius XI, 214, 215, 216
Postmodernity, 11
Poverty, 73, 191
   causes, 77, 78, 80, 81
   and religious ethics, 74, 79–81
   and social provision, 135, 136, 138, 142,
      146, 151
   as a women's issue, 75–79, 100
Pregnancy, 193, 195, 198. *See also* Teen
   pregnancy
   unwanted, 190, 191–2, 194
Presbyterian Church, USA, 62, 63, 74n.47,
   157, 162
Private/public, dichotomy of, 8–11, 60–61,
   69–71
   historical origins, 96–97
Privatization
   of government, 5, 7–8
   in public discourse 167, 168, 169
   of religion, 97
Pro-choice position, 194–97

Pro-life movement, 190, 192
Pronatalism, 53, 129, 129, 214
  right to natality, 151
Pro-sex movements, 107. *See also* Sex
  radicalism
Prostitution, 6, 144, 186, 245–59
  Christianity and, 246–49, 256–59
  and women of color, 252, 254, 255, 259
Protestant Christianity, 118, 167–174, 179–80
Protestant sexual ethics, 44–45, 51, 95–96,
  176
Public discourse, 60, 68–69, 155, 159–63
  bible in, 167, 170, 173–74, 180
  and "family values," 60, 118, 120
  on FGM, 237
  on prostitution, 250, 252, 253
  religion in, 4, 9, 17, 64, 70, 81–83, 101–2,
  167
  on welfare 136–38, 141–42, 145, 146, 148
  (*see also* "Welfare mothers")
Public ethics, 60–61, 68–70, 72–73, 82–83
Public rhetoric. *See* Public discourse
Race
  and "illegitimacy," 139–42, 146–51
  as sexualized, 33–35, 108, 109, 112–13
  and social provision, 76–77
Rape, 28, 53, 186, 192, 224
  and abortion, 193
  in Gen. 19, 174–75
  and prostitution, 248, 251, 253, 258
Reed, Ralph, 76
Reformed Church in America, 62
Re-Imagining Conference, 6, 155, 161–63
Religion, 70–71, 81–83, 186–90, 193,
  199–200. *See also* Culture Religion
  academic study and teaching of, 10, 17,
  158, 164–65
  de-privatization of, 5, 7
  dis-establishment of, 106 (*see also* First
  Amendment)
  privatization of, 60–61, 97
  and social provision, 8, 74–77, 79–81,
  141–42
Religious Coalition for Reproductive
  Rights, 10
Religious Consultation on Population,
  Reproductive Health and Ethics, 190,
  192
Religious ethics
  of poverty and work, 79–81

and public ethics, 6, 18–19, 131
  of reproduction, 188–90
Religious feminism, 12, 18, 161
  Jewish, 24
Religious Freedom, 14, 16, 156, 163. *See also*
  First Amendment
  and sexual dissidence, 69–71
Religious Freedom Restoration Act, 9–10,
  220, 221, 228, 229, 231
Religious pluralism, 13, 16, 125, 155, 157, 163
Religious progressivism, 5–7, 16–18, 60–64,
  69–71, 158
  and same-sex marriage, 126, 129
Religious Right, the, 3,5, 79, 156, 158–59.
  See also Christian Right
Reproductive ethics, 187, 190, 199, 196
Reproductive rights, 188–90, 199
Reproductive technologies. *See* Assisted
  Reproduction
Rivers, Caryl, 143
Roman Catholic sexual ethics, 45–47, 49, 51,
  203, 204–8, 211–14
  on abortion, 157, 194–96
  on contraception, 198–99
  on homosexuality, 6, 10, 62, 63, 65, 69
  on marriage and family, 210–14
Roman Catholic social ethics, 6, 203, 21,
  214–17
  compared with sexual ethics, 193, 215, 217
Romero, Archbishop Oscar, 259
Rosenthal, A.M., 223
Rubin, Gayle, 28–29, 110, 112, 115

Sachet, Carol, 32
Safer sex, 159
Same-sex marriage, 62–63, 124–31, 158, 163, 249
Sancho, Nelia, 254
Sanger, Margaret, 149
Sanday, Peggy Reeves, 47
Santería, 232
Schroeder, Representative Patricia, 224, 225,
  237
Schüssler Fiorenza, Elisabeth, 27
Secularism, 8–11, 71, 97, 106, 167, 187
Sedgwick, Eve, 70
Sex, 185–86
  moral significance of, 4, 23, 30–33, 67–68,
  110, 211
  political significance of, 5, 110–15
  potentialities of, 53–54, 67

Sex education, 3, 188
Sex radicalism, 68, 10, 112. *See also* Pro-sex
    movements
Sex workers, 251–52
    organizations, 254
Sexism, 191–92
    defined, 185
Sexual desire. *See* Sexual pleasure
Sexual dissent, 67–68, 71–73
    defined, 62n.1
Sexual ethics, 26, 31–32, 36–40, 51–53,
    66–69, 186
Sexual exploitation, 248–57, 259
Sexual mores, 23–24, 42, 157–59
Sexual norms. *See* Sexual regulation
Sexual orientation. *See* Sexual preference
Sexual pleasure, 18, 54, 198
    and Christianity, 51, 94
    and FGM, 227, 233
    and Islam, 199
    and Judaism, 28
Sexual practices, 31, 107–10, 119
Sexual preference, 48–49, 64–67, 114, 158,
    171, 172, 173
Sexual privacy, 4, 9, 60–61, 68, 129
Sexual regulation, 18, 110–15, 150–51
    and Christian social movements, 106
    and feminism, 107–10
    in Judaism, 24–25
    through law, 53
    and prostitution, 247, 249–52
Sexual violence, 28, 107, 108, 248, 253
Sexuality, 55, 185, 191–92
    and economic class, 108, 109, 112
    history of idea, 64
    social construction of, 24, 36, 45, 47
Silk, Mark, 6
Single motherhood, 3, 77–78, 135–51. *See
    also* "Illegitimacy"
Sirico, Father Robert, 143
Smith, Ralph, 171
Smith, Ruth, 79
Social constructivism, 14, 24, 45, 47, 158
Social provision. *See* Welfare
Society of Friends, 125
    American Friends' Service Committee,
    74n.47
    North Pacific Yearly Meeting, 62
Southern Baptist Convention, 62, 65, 69
Spillers, Hortense, 110

Talent, Representative James, 144
Teen pregnancy, 3, 34, 76–78, 138
Temporary Aid to Needy Families (TANF),
    73, 145
Thomas, Justice Clarence, 34
    Thomas-Hill hearings, 35
Toubia, Dr. Nahid, 221, 223, 226, 227
Transgenderism, 158, 171
    and civil rights, 160
Tribe, Lawrence, 227

Unification Church, 161
Unitarian Universalist Association, 62–63,
    125, 74n.47
United Church of Christ, 62, 63, 74n.47, 125
United Methodist Church, 63, 74n.47, 162
United Nations, 190, 197
    Commission on Human Rights, 190, 250
    Conference on Population and Develop-
    ment, 189, 223
    Covenant on Civil and Political Rights, 190
    Covenant on Economic, Social and Civil
    Rights, 190
    Covenant for the Suppression of the Traf-
    fic in Persons and of the Exploitation
    of the Prostitution of Others, 250–51
    Universal Declaration of Human Rights,
    190, 250
United States Supreme Court, 235, 249
    Boerne v. Flores, 9, 72, 220, 221, 226, 229
    Bowers v. Hardwick, 3, 9, 63,
    Cantwell v. Connecticut, 229
    *Church of Lukumi Babalu Aye v. City of
    Hialeah*, 226, 230, 232
    Cleveland Board of Education v. La Flair,
    230
    Craig v. Boren, 233
    *Employment Division, Department of
    Human Resources of Oregon v. Smith*,
    130, 220, 227–32
    Frontiero v. Richardson, 233
    Griswold v. Connecticut, 9, 230
    Parham v. J.R., 230, 231
    Planned Parenthood v. Casey, 231
    Reed v. Reed, 233
    Roe v. Wade, 9, 231
    Sherbert v. Verner, 227, 228, 231
    United States v. Ballard, 226
    United States v. Carolene Products, 66
    Wisconsin v. Yoder, 228, 230, 231

U.S. Catholic Conference, 10, 77
   The Challenge of Peace, 214
   Economic Justice for All, 214

Vatican, the, 189, 195–98

Wages, 100, 151, 156, 165
   Catholic teachings on, 213, 214, 215
   minimum wage, 73, 80, 81
Walker, Alice, 219, 222–23, 237, 238
Wealth, distribution of, 100. *See also* Poverty
Webster, Paula, 109
Welfare, public, 73–74, 76, 105, 119, 136. *See also* Aid to Families with Dependent Children
"Welfare mothers," public images of, 34, 142–46, 152
White House Working Group on the Family, 144
Whiteness, as privilege, 150
Whitman, Governor Christine, 139

Williams, Delores, 161
Wilson, James Q., 145
Wilson, William Julius, 78
Women
   access to public life, 75–77
   African American, 35, 76–77, 113, 135–52
   in Christian history, 93–98
   racial/ethnic and class differences, 97–99
   Roman Catholic, 164, 213–14
Women's rights
   in constitutional law, 233
   and FGM, 220–27, 234–36
   as human rights, 251, 253
   reproductive, 191–93, 196
WomenChurch Convergence, 6, 164
Work, 73–75, 80–82, 96–99, 101
   childrearing as, 75, 96, 101
   as responsibility, 73–74
   as right, 80–82
   women's unpaid, 96–97, 99, 101
Wuthnow, Robert, 69–70